Vauxhall Chevette Owners Workshop Manual

by J H Haynes
Member of the Guild of Motoring Writers

and Peter Strasman

Models covered

All versions of the Chevette Hatchback, Saloon
& Estate, and Bedford Chevanne with 1256 cc
engine

Does not cover Chevette Hatchback 2300 HS model

ISBN 1 85010 008 X

© Haynes Publishing Group 1976,1978,1979,1982,1983

ABCDE
FGH·

Printed in England *(285 - 9J4)*

HAYNES PUBLISHING GROUP
SPARKFORD YEOVIL SOMERSET BA22 7JJ ENGLAND
distributed in the USA by
HAYNES PUBLICATIONS INC
861 LAWRENCE DRIVE
NEWBURY PARK
CALIFORNIA 91320
USA

Acknowledgements

Thanks are due to Vauxhall Motors Limited for the provision of technical information and certain illustrations. Castrol Limited provided lubrication data, and the Champion Sparking Plug Company supplied the illustrations showing the various spark plug conditions.

The Vauxhall Chevette used in our workshops as the project car was supplied by Crocketts garages Limited of Midsomer Norton. John Kuzenka of that establishment was particularly helpful.

About this manual

Its aims

The aim of this Manual is to help you get the best value from your car. It can do so in several ways. It can help you decide what work must be done (even should you choose to get it done by a garage), provide information on routine maintenance and servicing, and give a logical course of action and diagnosis when random faults occur. However, it is hoped that you will use the Manual by tackling the work yourself. On simpler jobs it may even be quicker than booking the car into a garage, and going there twice to leave and collect it. Perhaps most important, a lot of money can be saved by avoiding the costs the garage must charge to cover its labour and overheads.

The Manual has drawings and descriptions to show the function of the various components so that their layout can be understood. Then the tasks are described and photographed in a step-by-step sequence so that even a novice can do the work.

Its arrangement

The manual is divided into thirteen Chapters, each covering a logical sub-division of the vehicle. The Chapters are each divided into Sections, numbered with single figures, eg 5; and the Sections into paragraphs (or sub-sections), with decimal numbers following on from the Section they are in, eg 5.1, 5.2, 5.3 etc.

It is freely illustrated, especially in those parts where there is a detailed sequence of operations to be carried out. There are two forms of illustration: figures and photographs. The figures are numbered in sequence with decimal numbers, according to their position in the Chapter: eg Fig. 6.4 is the 4th drawing/illustration in Chapter 6. Photographs are numbered (either individually or in related groups) the same as the Section or sub-section of the text where the operation they show is described.

There is an alphabetical index at the back of the manual as well as a contents list at the front.

References to the 'left' or 'right' of the vehicle are in the sense of a person in the driver's seat facing forwards.

Vehicle manufacturers continually make changes to specifications and recommendations, and these, when notified, are incorporated into our manuals at the earliest opportunity.

Whilst every care is taken to ensure that the information in this manual is correct, no liability can be accepted by the authors or publishers for loss, damage or injury caused by any errors in, or omissions from, the information given.

Introduction to the Vauxhall Chevette

The Chevette was originally introduced in 1975 as a three-door 'Hatchback', sharing many components with the Opel Kadett and the other GM 'T' cars. The engine is the same as that used in the smaller capacity Vivas and the general mechanical layout is conventional.

In 1976 two- and four-door Saloon versions were launched followed by an Estate version later in the same year. Automatic transmission was introduced on L and GL models in 1979.

The Chevette is available in a number of models ranging from economy E and ES to GL versions, and additionally the Chevanne panel van version is available.

Contents

1975 Vauxhall Chevette L Hatchback

1980 Vauxhall Chevette L 4-door Saloon

General dimensions, weights and capacities

Overall length
Hatchback models ... ... 155.3 in (3944.0 mm)
Saloon models ... ... 164.4 in (4178.0 mm)
Estate models ... ... 164.9 in (4191.0 mm)
Van models ... ... 165.3 in (4200.0 mm)

Overall width
All models ... ... 61.8 in (1570 mm)

Overall height
Hatchback models ... ... 51.5 in (1308.5 mm)
2-door Saloon models ... ... 51.5 in (1308.5 mm)
4-door Saloon models ... ... 51.3 in (1303.0 mm)
Estate models ... ... 52.1 in (1324.0 mm)
Van models ... ... 52.4 in (1330.0 mm)

Wheelbase
All models ... ... 94.3 in (2395.0 mm)

Track (front and rear)
All models ... ... 51.2 in (1300.0 mm)

Turning circle (wall to wall) ... ... 32.8 ft (10 m)

Kerb weights (nominal)
2-door ES and E models ... ... 1821 lb (826 kg)
4-door E model ... ... 1885 lb (855 kg)
2-door L model ... ... 1841 lb (835 kg)
4-door L model ... ... 1903 lb (863 kg)
4-door GL model ... ... 1918 lb (870 kg)
4-door GLS model ... ... 1929 lb (875 kg)
3-door Estate E model ... ... 1930 lb (875 kg)
3-door Estate L model ... ... 1951 lb (885 kg)
3-door Hatchback ES and E models ... ... 1865 lb (846 kg)
3-door Hatchback L model ... ... 1885 lb (855 kg)
3-door Hatchback GL model ... ... 1918 lb (870 kg)
3-door Hatchback GLS model ... ... 1960 lb (889 kg)
Chevanne model ... ... 1874 lb (850 kg)
Note: On models with automatic transmission add 55 lb (25 kg)

Maximum gross vehicle weight
Hatchback and Saloon models ... ... 2897 lb (1314 kg)
Estate models ... ... 2943 lb (1335 kg)
Van models ... ... 2976 lb (1350 kg)

Maximum towing capacity (trailer with brakes) ... ... 2240 lb (1016 kg)

Maximum roof rack load ... ... 132 lb (60 kg)

Engine (oil capacity) ... ... 5.5 Imp pints (3.13 litres)

Gearbox (oil capacity)
Up to chassis number FY 127596 ... ... 0.9 Imp pints (0.51 litres)
Chassis number FY 127596 on ... ... 1.09 Imp pints (0.62 litres)

Automatic transmission (fluid service refill) ... ... 4.5 Imp pints (2.6 litres)

Rear axle (oil capacity) ... ... 1.2 Imp pints (0.68 litres)

Cooling system (coolant capacity with heater)
Manual transmission models ... ... 10.2 Imp pints (5.8 litres)
Automatic transmission models ... ... 10.7 Imp pints (6.1 litres)

Fuel tank (capacity)
Hatchback models ... ... 8.0 Imp galls (38 litres)
Saloon, Estate and Van models ... ... 10.0 Imp galls (45 litres)

Buying spare parts & vehicle identification numbers

Buying spare parts

Spare parts are available from many sources, for example: Vauxhall garages, other garages and accessory shops, and motor factors. Our advice regarding spare parts is as follows:

Officially appointed Vauxhall garages - This is the best source of parts which are peculiar to your car and otherwise not generally available (eg; complete cylinder heads, internal gearbox components, badges, interior trim etc). It is also the only place at which you should buy parts if your car is still under warranty: non-Vauxhall components may invalidate the warranty. To be sure of obtaining the correct parts it will always be necessary to give the storeman your car's engine and chassis number, and if possible, to take the old part along for positive identification. Remember that many parts are available on a factory exchange scheme - any parts returned should always be clean! It obviously makes good sense to go straight to the specialists on your car for this type of part for they are best equipped to supply you.

Other garages and accessory shops - These are often very good places to buy material and components needed for the maintenance of your car (eg; oil filters, spark plugs, bulbs, fan belts, oils and grease, touch-up paint, filler paste etc). They also sell general accessories, usually have convenient opening hours, charge lower prices and can often be found not far from home.

Motor factors - Good factors will stock all of the more important components which wear out relatively quickly (eg; clutch components, pistons, valves, exhaust systems, brake cylinders/pipes/hoses/seals/shoes and pads etc). Motor factors will often provide new or reconditioned components on a part exchange basis - this can save a considerable amount of money.

Vehicle identification numbers

Modifications are a continuing and unpublished process in vehicle manufacture quite apart from major model changes. Spare parts manuals and lists are compiled upon a numerical basis, the individual vehicle numbers being essential to correct identification of the component required.

When ordering spare parts, always give as much information as possible. Quote the car model, year of manufacture, body and engine numbers, as appropriate.

The car *identification plate* on early models is fitted on the upper surface of the instrument panel and is legible through the windscreen.

The service parts *identification plate* is affixed to the side of the engine compartment and bears the following information:

Model
Market
Job no.
Paint code
Trim code
Option code

Car identification plate located on instrument panel

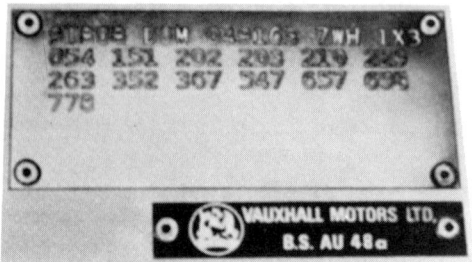

Under bonnet identification plate

Location of engine number adjacent to alternator bracket

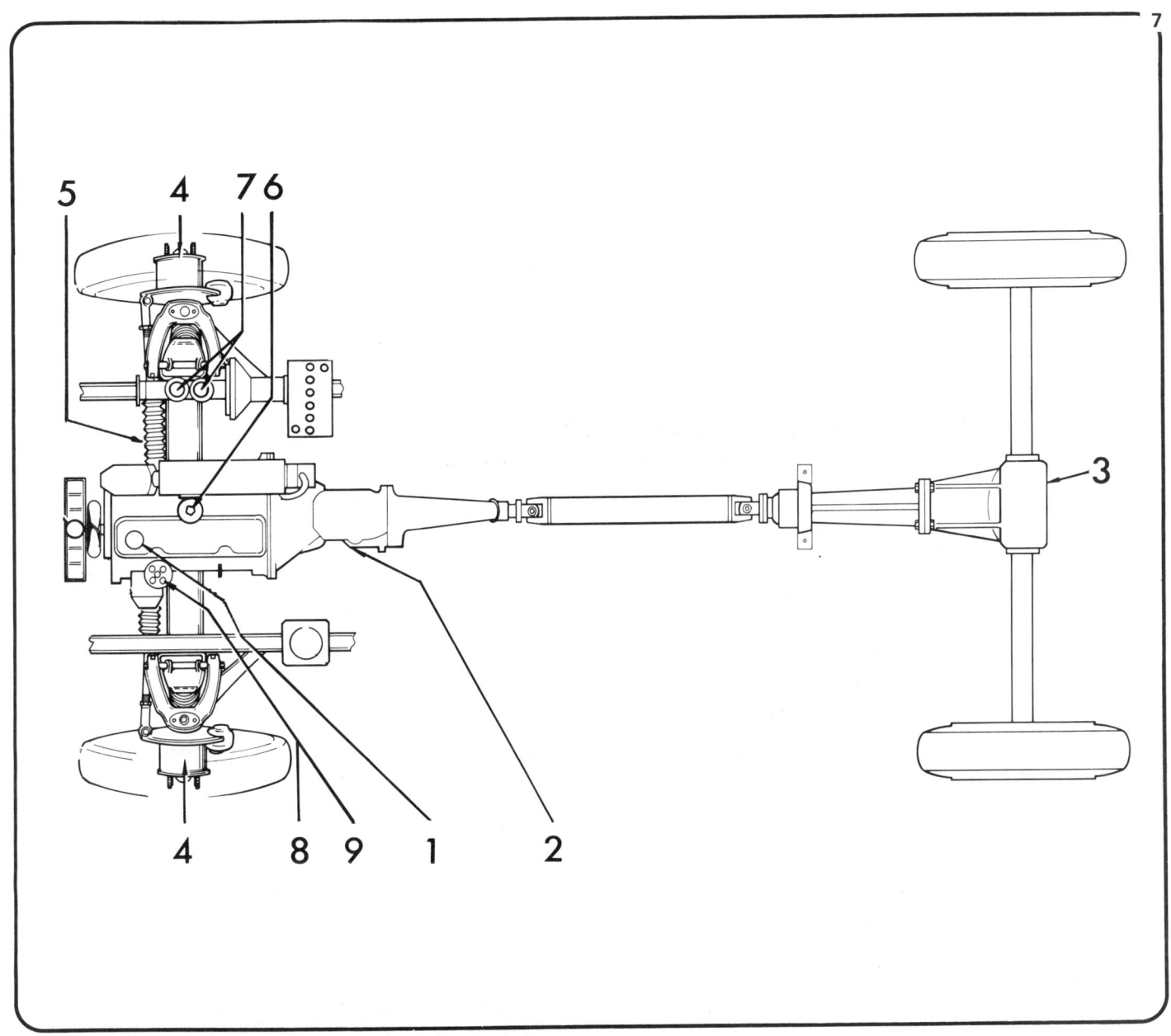

Recommended lubricants and fluids

Component or system	Lubricant type or specification	Castrol product
1 Engine	SAE 20W/50 multigrade engine oil ...	... Castrol GTX
2 Gearbox	SAE 80EP gear oil	... Castrol Hypoy Light
Automatic transmission	Dexron ® automatic transmission fluid ...	... Castrol TQ Dexron RII
3 Rear axle*	SAE 90EP gear oil	... Castrol Hypoy BEP90
4 Front wheel bearings	Multi-purpose lithium based grease ...	... Castrol LM grease
5 Steering gear	Multi-purpose lithium based grease ...	... Castrol LM grease
6 Carburettor damper	SAE 10W/40 multigrade oil	... Castrolite
7 Brake master cylinder	Hydraulic fluid to SAE J1703/DOT 3 ...	... Castrol Universal Brake & Clutch fluid
8 Distributor spindle and advance mechanism	SAE 20W/50 multigrade engine oil ...	... Castrol GTX
9 Distributor cam	Multi-purpose lithium based grease ...	... Castrol LM grease
Chassis (general)	Multi-purpose lithium based grease ...	... Castrol LM grease
Hinges, locks, pivots, etc	Light lubricating oil	... Castrol Everyman oil
Battery terminals	Petroleum jelly	... —

Note: *The above are general recommendations. Lubrication requirements vary from territory-to-territory and also depend on vehicle usage. Consult the operators handbook supplied with your car.*
* Where an axle has to be topped-up or drained and refilled before completing 10 000 miles (16 000 km), or when new hypoid gears are fitted, use only the special lubricant supplied by your Vauxhall dealer.

Routine maintenance

Maintenance is essential for ensuring safety and desirable for the purpose of getting the best in terms of performance and economy from the car. Over the years the need for periodic lubrication - oiling, greasing and so on - has been drastically reduced if not totally eliminated. This has unfortunately tended to lead some owners to think that because no such action is required the items either no longer exist or will last for ever. This is a serious delusion. It follows therefore that the largest initial element of maintenance is visual examination. This may lead to repairs or renewals.

In the summary given here the 'essential for safety' items are shown in **bold type**. These **must** be attended to at the regular frequencies shown in order to avoid the possibility of accidents and loss of life. Other neglect, results in unreliability, increased running costs, more rapid wear and more rapid depreciation of the vehicle in general.

Every 250 miles (400 km) travelled or weekly

Steering

Check the tyre pressures, including the spare wheel.
Examine tyres for wear or damage.
Is steering smooth and accurate?

Location of spare wheel

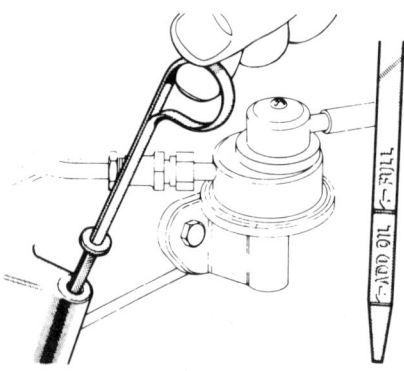

Location and marking of engine oil dipstick

Brakes

Check reservoir fluid level.
Is there any fall off in braking efficiency?
Try an emergency stop. Is adjustment necessary?

Lights, wipers and horns

Do all bulbs work at the front and rear?
Are the headlamp beams aligned properly?
Do the wipers and horns work?
Check windscreen tailgate window washer fluid level.

Engine

Check the sump oil level and top-up if required.
Check the radiator coolant level and top-up if required.
Check the battery electrolyte level and top-up to the level of the plates with distilled water as needed.

Every 6000 miles (9600 km) or at six monthly intervals

Check front hub bearing adjustment.
Check disc pads and brake shoes for friction material wear.
Adjust clutch free-travel
Change engine oil and renew oil filter element.

Topping up the engine oil

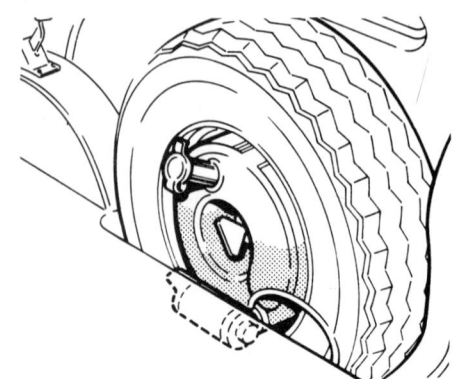

Tailgate window washer reservoir location on Estate models

Check and if necessary, top-up gearbox oil level.
Check and if necessary, top-up rear axle oil level.
Check brake hydraulic system for leaks, damaged pipes etc.
Examine thickness of tyre treads.
Check and adjust, if necessary, front wheel alignment.
Examine exhaust system for corrosion and leakage.
Lubricate all controls and linkages.
Check for wear in steering gear and balljoints and condition of rubber bellows, dust excluders and flexible coupling.
Clean and adjust spark plugs.
Clean and adjust contact breaker points and lubricate.
Top-up carburettor damper.
Lubricate door locks and hinges.
Check and if necessary, top-up automatic transmission fluid level.

Every 12000 miles (19300 km) or annually

Inspect condition of wiper blades and renew if necessary.
Inspect security of seat belts and anchorages.
Check antifreeze strength and top-up if necessary.
Clean corrosion from battery terminals and apply petroleum jelly.
Check fanbelt tension and adjust if necessary.
Renew spark plugs.
Renew contact breaker points and check ignition timing.
Clean fuel pump filter.
Clean crankcase breather valve hose.
Adjust valve clearances.
Renew air cleaner element.

Every 24000 miles (38600 km) or at two yearly intervals

Dismantle, clean and relubricate front hub bearings.
Check and adjust if necessary the headlamp alignment.

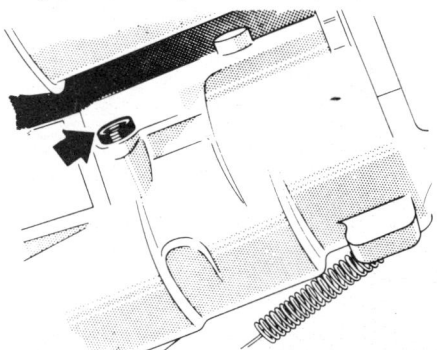

Gearbox filler/level plug. Use a 3/8 in AF hexagon key

Inspect and if necessary, renew any suspension bushes which have deteriorated or worn.
Check torque of all suspension bolts and nuts
Drain, flush and refill cooling system with antifreeze mixture.
Change automatic transmission fluid and adjust low band servo.

Every 48000 miles (77000 km)

Bleed brake hydraulic system of old fluid, renew all rubber seals, check and if necessary, renew any damaged pipes and refill system with clean fluid.
Check propeller shaft joints for wear and renew shaft if evident.
Check underbody for rust or corrosion and clean and apply new protective sealant where necessary.

Rear axle filler/level plug. Use an 8 mm hexagon key.

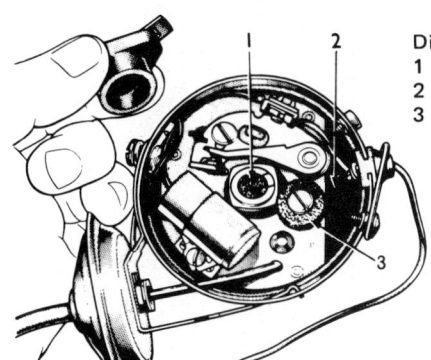

Distributor lubrication points
1 Felt pad
2 Baseplate hole
3 Cam lubricator (grease only)

Jacking and towing

Jacking

When changing a roadwheel, the jack supplied with the car may be used, inserting it into the jacking points which are located below the bodysills. Where maintenance or repairs are being carried out, use a jack located either under the front crossmember or the rear axle casing tubes. Before getting under the car, always supplement the jack with axle stands or blocks positioned under the bodyframe members.

Towing

Towing eyes are provided at the front and rear of the car for being towed and towing another vehicle. When being towed make sure that the steering column lock is unlocked by inserting the ignition key and turning it to the accessory position. Remember that the brake servo unit will not be operative with the engine stopped, and that more effort will be required on the brake pedal.

On automatic transmission models the car may be towed with the selector lever in 'N' (neutral) for distances up to 35 miles (50 km) at speeds not in excess of 35 mph (50 km/h). Where it is necessary to exceed these limits, the propeller shaft must be disconnected or the driving wheels raised from the ground.

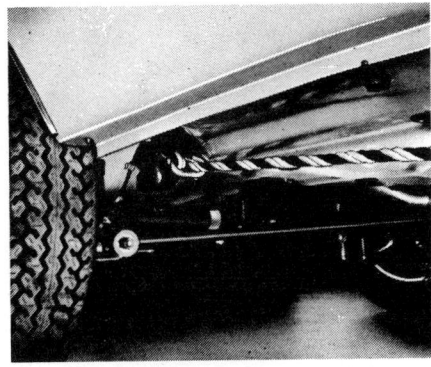

Rear towing eye location

Chapter 1 Engine

For modifications, and information applicable to later models, see Supplement at end of manual

Contents

Specifications

Engine general

Type	Four in-line, overhead valve
Displacement	76.6 cu. in (1256 cc)
Bore	3.188 in (80.98 mm)
Stroke	2.40 in (60.96 mm)
Firing order	1 - 3 - 4 - 2
Compression ratio:	
Standard	9.2 : 1
Low	7.3 : 1
Power (all at 5600 rev/min)	
Bhp:	
DIN (70 020)	58.5
SAE (J245)	56.5
CV or PS (DIN 70 020)	59.4
KW (DIN 70 020)	45.5

Cylinder head

Material	Cast iron
Minimum cylinder head depth after refacing:	
Standard compression	3.185 in (80.90 mm)
Low compression	3.235 in (82.17 mm)
Valve seat angle	45°

Valves

Seat angle	44°
Seat width:	
Inlet	0.05 to 0.06 in (1.3 to 1.5 mm)
Exhaust	0.06 to 0.08 in (1.5 to 2.0 mm)
Stem diameter:	
Inlet	0.2748 to 0.2755 in (6.980 to 6.998 mm)
Exhaust	0.2745 to 0.2752 in (6.972 to 6.990 mm)
Stem clearance in guide:	
Inlet	0.0005 to 0.002 in (0.013 to 0.051 mm)
Exhaust	0.0013 to 0.0028 in (0.033 to 0.071 mm)

Minimum valve head thickness:

Inlet	0.03 in (0.8 mm)
Exhaust	0.04 in (1.0 mm)
Valve spring free-length	1.5 in (38.0 mm)
Tappet diameter	0.4712 to 0.4718 in (11.968 to 11.984 mm)
Tappet clearance in block	0.0006 to 0.0019 in (0.015 to 0.048 mm)
Valve clearance (hot)	0.008 in (0.2 mm)
Valve timing (inlet valve point of maximum opening)	107° after TDC

Camshaft

Journal diameter:	
Front	1.6127 to 1.6132 in (40.963 to 40.975 mm)
Centre	1.5930 to 1.5935 in (40.462 to 40.475 mm)
Rear	1.5733 to 1.5738 in (39.962 to 39.975 mm)
Clearance in bearings	0.0010 to 0.0025 in (0.025 to 0.064 mm)
Camshaft endfloat	0.002 to 0.009 in (0.05 to 0.23 mm)
Thrust plate thickness	0.123 to 0.126 in (3.12 to 3.20 mm)

Cylinder block

Material	Cast iron
Cylinder bore diameter (standard)	3.188 in (80.98 mm)
Minimum depth after refacing (top face to main bearing cap face) ...	7.508 in (190.7 mm)
Piston clearance in bore	0.0009 to 0.0014 in (0.023 to 0.036 mm)
Piston rings:	
Depth (top and centre ring)	0.077 to 0.078 in (1.96 to 1.98 mm)
End gap	0.009 to 0.020 in (0.23 to 0.51 mm)
Groove clearance:	
Top ring	0.0019 to 0.0039 in (0.048 to 0.099 mm)
Centre ring	0.0016 to 0.0036 in (0.041 to 0.091 mm)
Gudgeon pin clearance in bore at 68°F (20°C)	0.00025 to 0.00045 in (0.006 to 0.011 mm)

Connecting rods

Big-end bearing clearance	0.0010 to 0.0029 in (0.025 to 0.074 mm)
Endfloat	0.004 to 0.010 in (0.10 to 0.25 mm)

Crankshaft

Crankpin diameter	1.8302 to 1.8310 in (46.487 to 46.505 mm)
Main journal diameter	2.1255 to 2.1260 in (53.988 to 54.000 mm)
Endfloat	0.002 to 0.008 in (0.05 to 0.20 mm)

Lubrication

Oil pump drive spindle:	
Endfloat	0.007 to 0.010 in (0.18 to 0.25 mm)
Clearance in pump body	0.0006 to 0.0017 in (0.015 to 0.043 mm)
Impellers:	
Endfloat	0.002 to 0.005 in (0.05 to 0.13 mm)
Radial clearance in body	0.002 to 0.005 in (0.05 to 0.13 mm)
Backlash between teeth	0.004 to 0.008 in (0.10 to 0.20 mm)
Oil pressure relief valve spring free-length	1.96 in (49.8 mm)
Oil pressure (hot) at 3000 rev/min	55 to 65 lb/in^2 (3.87 to 4.57 kg/cm^2)
Oil capacity (including filter)	5.5 Imp. pints (3.13 litres)

Torque wrench settings

	lb ft	Nm
Cylinder head bolts	55	74
Flywheel bolts	30	41
Main bearing bolts	82	113
Connecting rod bolts	25	35
Oil filter centre bolt	14	19
Engine front mounting bolts	29	40
Engine rear mounting to gearbox	32	44
Rear mounting to crossmember bolts	28	39
Clutch to flywheel	14	19
Bellhousing to crankcase	25	35
Crankshaft pulley bolt	40	55
Camshaft sprocket bolt	35	48
Starter motor bolts	30	41
Timing cover bolts	24	33
Manifold bolts	30	41
Oil pump to crankcase	20	28
Camshaft thrust plate bolts	20	28
Spark plugs	25	34

1 General description

1   The engine is of 4 cylinder, in-line overhead valve type (photos).

2   A low compression option is available in certain territories.

3   The crankshaft is of three bearing type, the centre main bearing incorporates flanges which act as thrust washers to control crankshaft endfloat.

4   The camshaft is chain driven from the crankshaft and is supported in three bearings. A hydraulic type timing chain tensioner is fitted.

5   The inclined valves operate directly in the cylinder head and are operated by rockers mounted on individual hollow studs, no rocker shaft being used in the arrangement.

6   A semi-closed crankcase ventilation system is used, the hose connecting between the rocker cover and the air cleaner with a branch to a restricted union on the intake manifold.

7   Positive lubrication is provided by an internally mounted, crankcase oil pump, driven from the camshaft. Engine oil is fed through an externally mounted full-flow filter to the engine oil galleries and nozzles as necessary, to ensure complete lubrication.

8   The oil pump lower cover incorporates a pressure relief valve.

9   The engine front mountings are of shear type to afford a measure of safety against rearward movement of the engine in the event of a front end collision (photo).

1.1A View of engine compartment from above

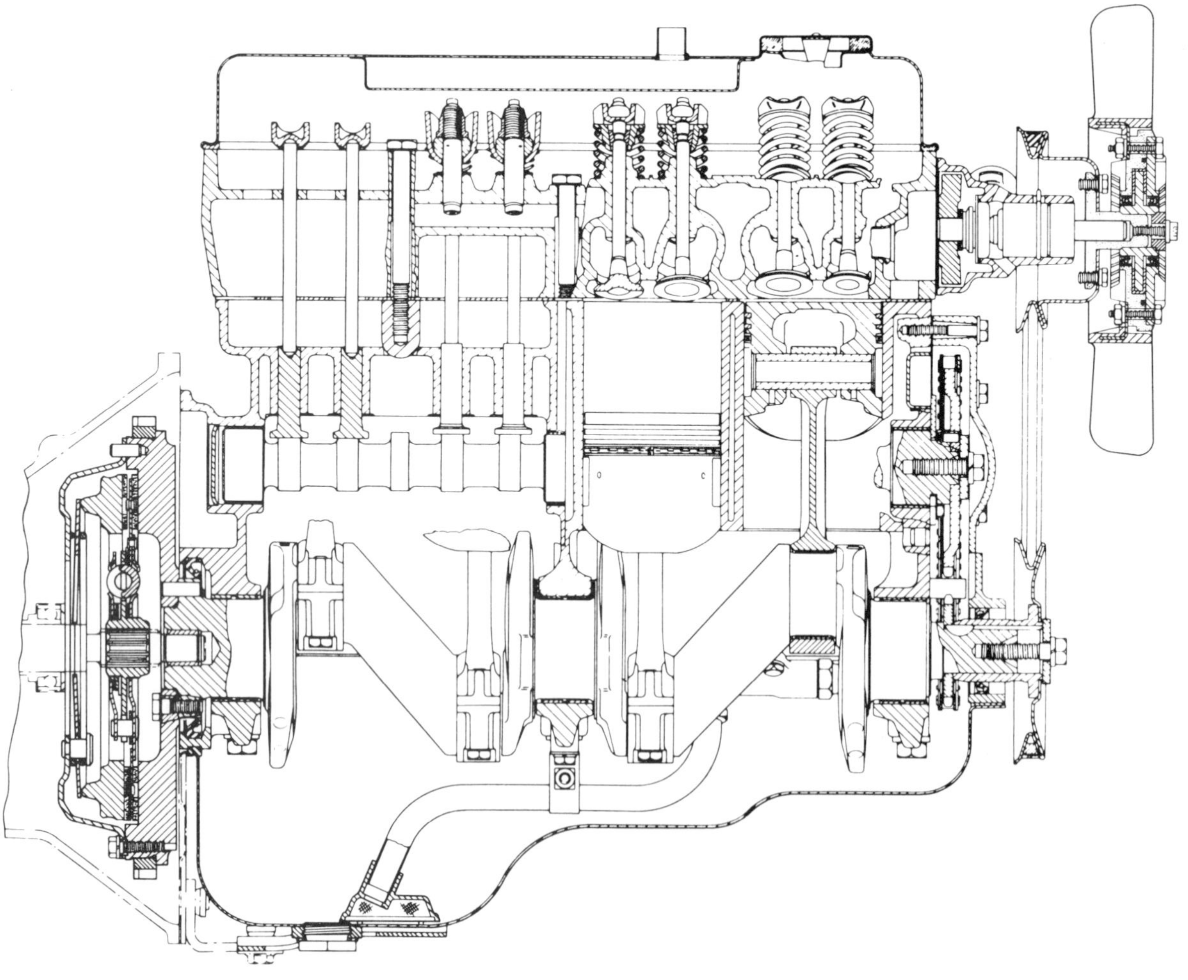

Fig. 1.1. Sectional view of the engine

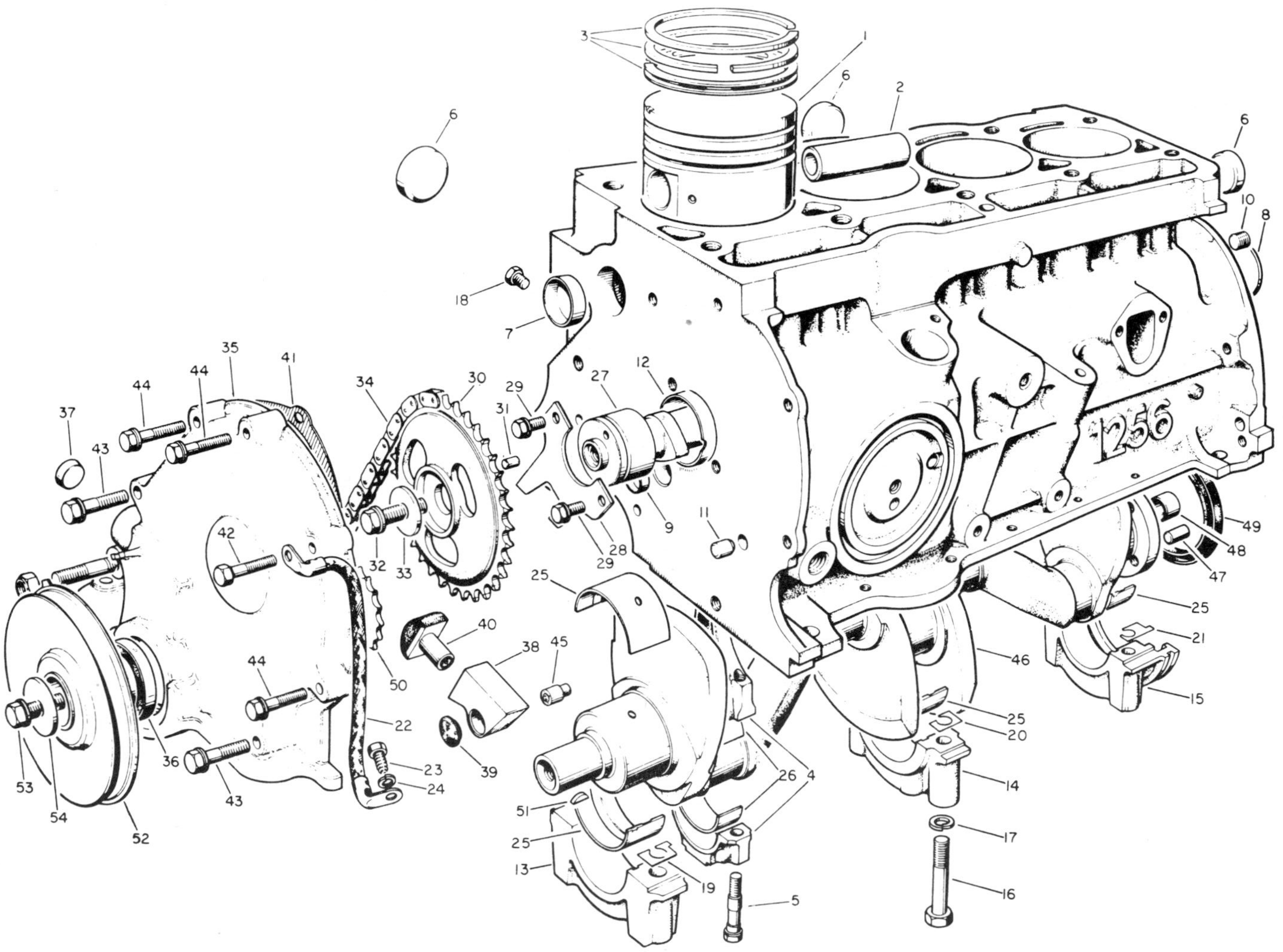

Fig. 1.2. Cylinder block components

1   Piston
2   Gudgeon pin
3   Piston rings
4   Connecting rod and big-end cap
5   Big-end bolt
6   Core plugs
7   Core plug
8   Camshaft rear plug
9   Oil gallery
10 Oil gallery

11 Oil hole plug
12 Camshaft front bearing
13 Front main bearing cap
14 Centre main bearing cap
15 Rear main bearing cap
16 Main bearing cap bolt
17 Lockwasher
18 Cylinder block drain plug
19 Shim
20 Shim
21 Shim

22 Engine earth strap
23 Bolt
24 Lockwasher
25 Main bearing shells
26 Big-end bearing shells
27 Camshaft
28 Camshaft thrust plate
29 Bolt
30 Camshaft sprocket
31 Dowel
32 Camshaft sprocket bolt

33 Washer
34 Timing chain
35 Timing cover
36 Timing cover oil seal
37 Timing cover plug
38 Tensioner body
39 Button
40 Tensioner pad assembly
41 Gasket
42 Bolt
43 Bolt

44 Bolt
45 Oil nozzle
46 Crankshaft
47 Flywheel dowel
48 Input shaft spigot bush
49 Crankshaft rear oil seal
50 Crankshaft sprocket
51 Woodruff key
52 Crankshaft pulley
53 Bolt
54 Washer

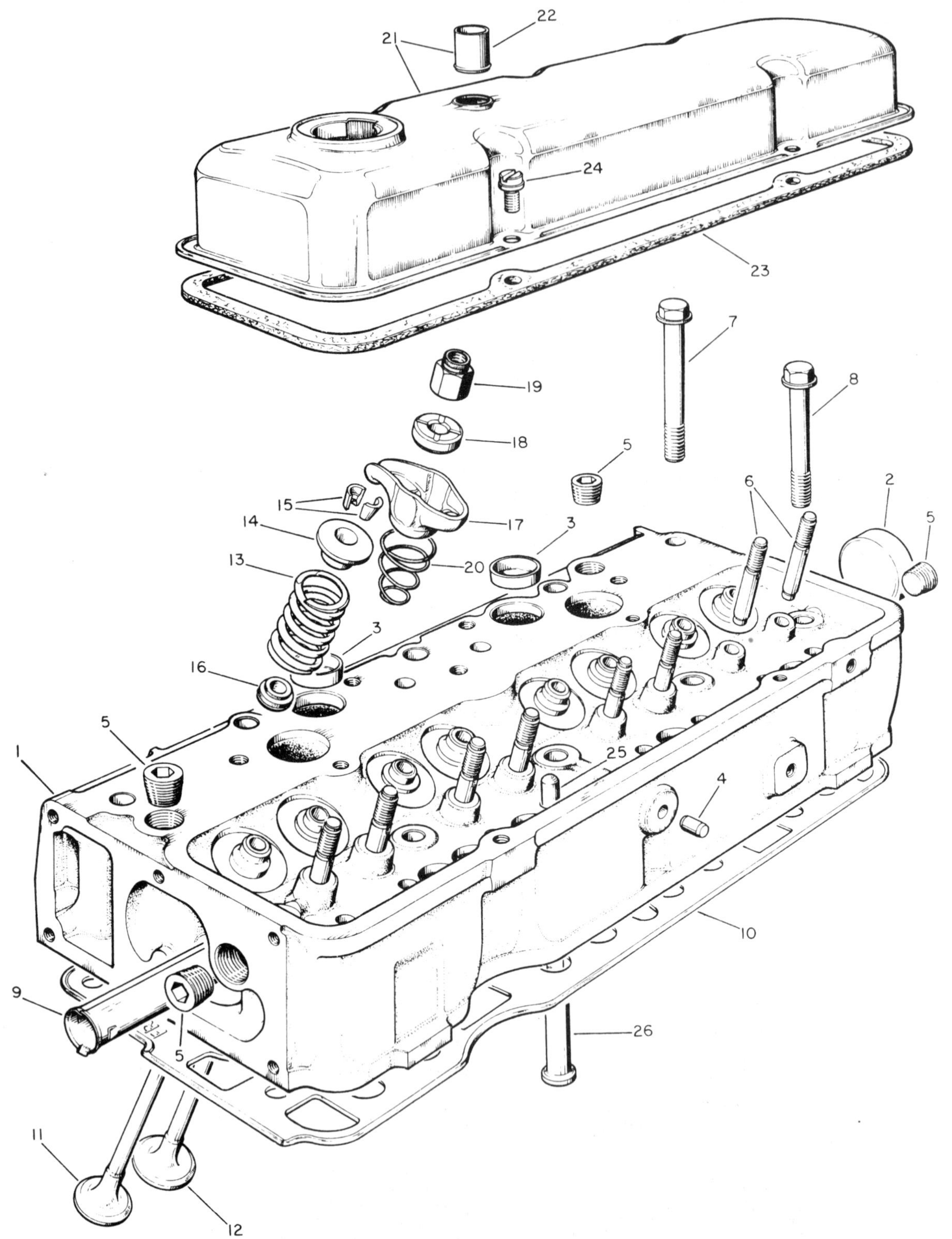

Fig. 1.3. Cylinder head components

1 Cylinder head	8 Cylinder head bolt (short)	15 Split collets	21 Rocker cover
2 Core plug	9 Water distribution tube	16 Valve stem oil seal (inlet only)	22 Breather pipe connection
3 Core plugs	10 Cylinder head gasket	17 Rocker	23 Gasket
4 Oil hole plug	11 Exhaust valve	18 Rocker ball	24 Cover screw
5 Water plug	12 Inlet valve	19 Rocker nut	25 Push-rod
6 Rocker studs	13 Valve spring	20 Rocker spring	26 Tappet (cam follower)
7 Cylinder head bolt (long)	14 Retainer		

2 Major operations possible with engine in car

The following operations can be carried out without having to remove the engine from the car:
1 *Removal and servicing of the cylinder head.*
2 *Removal of sump. This will first necessitate disconnection of the radiator hoses and steering shaft flexible coupling, also removal of the steering gear to crossmember bolts and the engine front mounting nuts.*
3 *Removal of piston/connecting rod assemblies (through top of block) after first withdrawing the sump.*
4 *Removal of the timing cover, chain and gears after first withdrawing the radiator.*
5 *Removal of the oil pump (after first withdrawing the sump), see paragraph 2.*
6 *Renewal of the engine mountings.*

3 Major operations only possible after removal of engine from car

The following operations can only be carried out after removal of the engine from the car:
1 *Removal of the camshaft.*
2 *Removal of the tappets (cam followers).*
3 *Renewal of the crankshaft main bearings.*
4 *Renewal of the crankshaft rear oil seal.*
5 *Removal of the flywheel (can also be achieved by leaving engine in position and withdrawing gearbox - see Chapter 6).*

4 Methods of engine removal

The engine can be removed complete with gearbox or independently, leaving the gearbox in position in the car.

5 Engine/gearbox - removal

1 Open the bonnet to its fullest extent, mark the position of the hinge plates on the underside of the bonnet and then remove the securing bolts (photo).
2 With the help of an assistant, lift the bonnet from the car and store it somewhere where it will not get scratched.

1.1B View of right-hand side of engine compartment

1.1C View of left-hand side of engine compartment

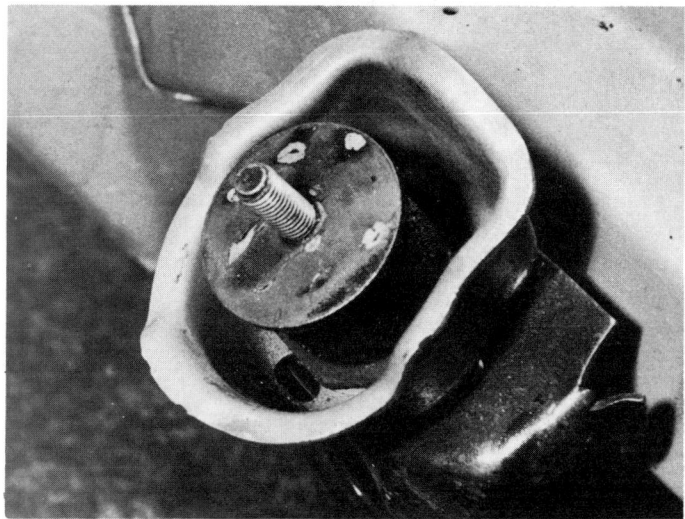

1.9 Shear type engine mounting

5.1 Bonnet hinge detail

3 Disconnect the lead from the battery negative terminal.

4 Protect the tops of the front wings with thick cloth to prevent scratching during removal of the engine.

5 Drain the cooling system (see Chapter 3).

6 Disconnect the radiator hoses and remove the radiator from the engine compartment (photo).

7 Drain the engine oil.

8 Disconnect the coil to distributor HT lead.

9 Disconnect the leads from the oil pressure switch and the water temperature sender unit (photo).

10 Disconnect the LT lead from the distributor.

11 Disconnect the cables from the starter motor.

12 Disconnect the fuel inlet pipe from the fuel pump and plug the pipe to prevent loss of fuel.

13 Disconnect the leads from the alternator.

14 Disconnect the heater flow and return water hoses.

15 Remove the air cleaner and then disconnect the accelerator and choke controls from the carburettor.

16 Disconnect the clutch operating cable from the release fork and then remove the cable assembly from the bellhousing.

17 Disconnect (six bolts) the twin exhaust downpipes from the manifold.

18 Unbolt and remove the starter motor.

19 Working inside the car, release the flexible boots from the gearshift lever retaining cap and twist it in a clockwise direction. Withdraw the lever.

20 Working underneath the car, disconnect the speedometer cable from the gearbox and the leads from the reverse lamp heads (photo).

21 Mark the edges of the propeller shaft rear flange and the pinion drive flange (to ensure that they are reconnected in their original positions) and then unbolt the flanges and withdraw the propeller shaft. Some loss of oil may occur from the rear of the gearbox as the propeller shaft is withdrawn. To prevent this happening, cover the end of the extension housing with a plastic bag and retain it with a strong rubber band.

22 Fit chains or slings securely to the engine and using a suitable hoist, lift the engine just enough to take its weight and then disconnect the engine front mountings from the crankcase brackets (photo).

23 Place a jack under the gearbox and then unbolt the rear mounting.

24 Make a last check to ensure that all wires, cables and hoses have been disconnected and then start to hoist the combined engine/gearbox from the engine compartment, simultaneously, lowering the gearbox jack. Once the clutch bellhousing has cleared the lower edge of the engine compartment rear bulkhead, the engine/gearbox can be lifted out at a steeply inclined angle (photo).

6 Engine - separation from gearbox

1 With the engine and gearbox now removed from the vehicle, unscrew and remove the bolts which connect the clutch bellhousing to the engine block.

2 Pull the gearbox from the engine in a straight line and support the gearbox so that its weight does not hang upon the gearbox primary shaft, even momentarily, whilst it is still engaged with the clutch mechanism.

7 Engine - removal without gearbox

1 Carry out the operations 1 to 15, in Section 5.

2 Disconnect (six bolts) the twin exhaust downpipes from the manifold.

3 Unbolt and remove the starter motor.

4 Unbolt and remove the bolts which secure the clutch bellhousing to the engine crankcase.

5 Place a supporting jack under the gearbox.

6 Fit chains or slings securely to the engine and using a suitable hoist, lift the engine just enough to take its weight and then disconnect the engine front mountings from the crankcase brackets.

7 Taking care that the gearbox jack is secure, pull the engine forward (with the hoist fully supporting its weight) until the input shaft of the gearbox clears the clutch mechanism on the flywheel and then hoist the engine up and out of the engine compartment at a steeply inclined angle.

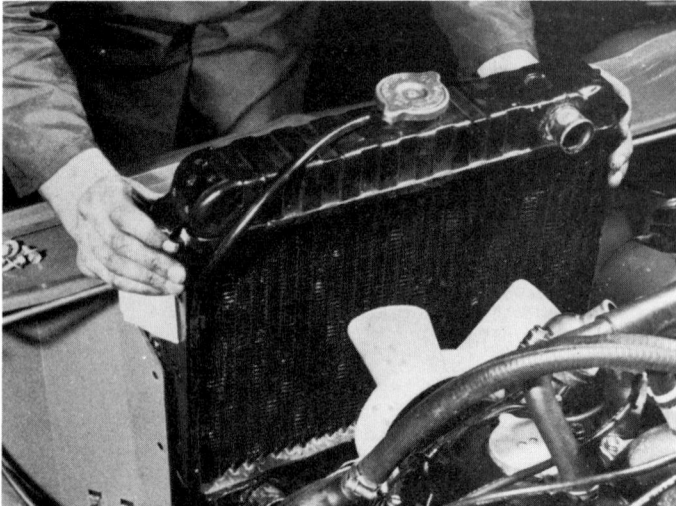
5.5 Removing radiator

5.9 Location of the oil pressure switch

5.20 Speedometer cable attachment to gearbox

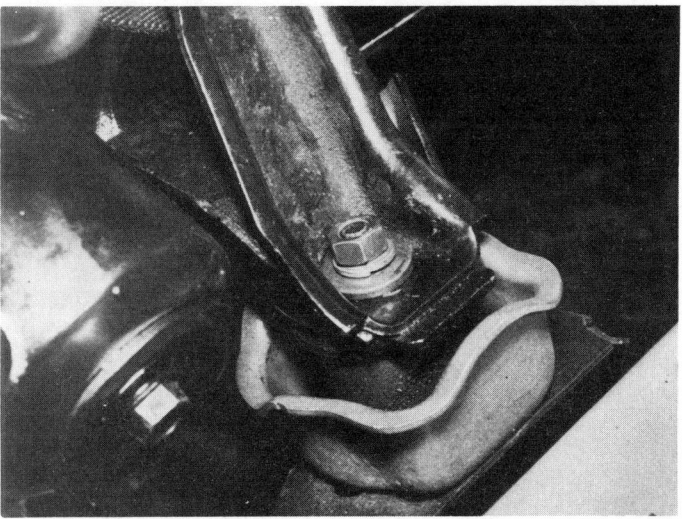

5.22 Left-hand engine mounting

5.24 Hoisting engine

8 Engine - dismantling general

1 It is best to mount the engine on a dismantling stand but if one is not available, then stand the engine on a strong bench so as to be at a comfortable working height. Failing this, the engine can be stripped down on the floor.

2 During the dismantling process the greatest care should be taken to keep the exposed parts free from dirt. As an aid to achieving this, it is a sound scheme to thoroughly clean down the outside of the engine, removing all traces of oil and congealed dirt.

3 Use paraffin or a good grease solvent. The latter will make the job much easier, as, after the solvent has been applied and allowed to stand for a time, a vigorous jet of water will wash off the solvent and all the grease and filth. If the dirt is thick and deeply embedded, work the solvent into it with a wire brush.

4 Finally wipe down the exterior of the engine with a rag and only then, when it is quite clean should the dismantling process begin. As the engine is stripped, clean each part in a bath of paraffin or petrol.

5 Never immerse parts with oilways in paraffin, ie; the crankshaft, but to clean, wipe down carefully with a petrol dampened rag. Oilways can be cleaned out with wire. If an air line is present all parts can be blown dry and the oilways blown through as an added precaution.

6 Re-use of old engine gaskets is false economy and can give rise to oil and water leaks, if nothing worse. To avoid the possibility of trouble after the engine has been reassembled **always** use new gaskets throughout.

7 Do not throw the old gaskets away as it sometimes happens that an immediate replacement cannot be found and the old gasket is then very useful as a template. Hang up the old gaskets as they are removed on a suitable hook or nail.

8 To strip the engine it is best to work from the top down. The sump provides a firm base on which the engine can be supported in an upright position. When this stage where the sump must be removed is reached, the engine can be turned on its side and all other work carried out with it in this position.

9 Wherever possible, replace nuts, bolts and washers fingertight from wherever they were removed. This helps avoid later loss and muddle. If they cannot be replaced then lay them out in such a fashion that it is clear from where they came.

9 Ancillary components - removal

1 With the engine removed from the car and separated from the gearbox, the externally mounted ancillary components should now be removed before dismantling begins.

2 The following is a suggested sequence of removal, detailed descriptions are to be found in the relevant Chapters of this manual:

Alternator (Chapter 10).
Clutch assembly (Chapter 5).
Manifolds and carburettor (Chapter 3).
Flywheel (four bolts).
Engine mounting brackets.
Oil filter (Section 13, this Chapter).
Distributor and spark plugs (Chapter 4).
Fuel pump (Chapter 3).
Fan assembly (Chapter 2).
Water pump/thermostat assembly (Chapter 2).

10 Cylinder head - removal

If the head is to be removed with the engine still in the car, first carry out the following operations:

Drain the cooling system.
Remove the manifolds, complete with carburettor.
Remove the water pump.
Disconnect the lead from the battery negative terminal.

1 Remove the four rocker cover securing screws and lift the rocker cover away. If it is stuck, insert a blunt blade between the cork gasket and the cylinder head and ease it all round.

2 If preferred, the pushrods may be withdrawn at this stage by swivelling each rocker after releasing the self-locking nuts. Keep them in order for exact replacement in their original positions.

3 Unscrew each of the cylinder head bolts a half turn at a time in the reverse order to that shown in Fig. 1.21.

4 With all the bolts removed, lift the cylinder head from the block. If it is stuck, tap it upwards using a block of wood and a hammer. On no account, insert any lever into the gasket joint.

5 Remove the cylinder head gasket.

11 Cylinder head - dismantling

1 From the centre of each rocker, unscrew and remove the self-locking nut. Extract the rocker ball, the rocker and spring. Keep all components in their original fitted sequence.

2 The valves can be removed from the cylinder head by the following method. Compress each spring in turn with a valve spring compressor until the two halves of the collets can be removed. Release the compressor and remove the spring and spring retainer.

3 If, when the valve spring compressor is screwed down, the valve spring retaining cap refuses to free to expose the split collet, do not continue to screw down on the compressor as there is a likelihood of damaging it.

4 Gently tap the top of the tool directly over the cap with a light hammer. This will free the cap. To avoid the compressor jumping off the

valve spring retaining cap when it is tapped, hold the compressor firmly in position with one hand.

5 Slide the rubber oil control seal off the top of each inlet valve stem and then drop out each valve through the combustion chamber.

6 It is essential that the valves are kept in their correct sequence unless they are so badly worn that they are to be renewed. Numbering from the front of the engine, exhaust valves are 1-4-5-8 and inlet valves 2-3-6-7.

12 Sump - removal

The sump can be removed with the engine in position in the car, but first carry out the following operations:
Drain the engine oil.
Drain the cooling system.
Disconnect both radiator hoses.
Disconnect the steering shaft flexible coupling.
Disconnect steering gear to front crossmember bolts and also disconnect the front engine mounting bolts from the crankcase brackets.
Raise the engine as necessary by lifting it with a hoist.

1 Unscrew and remove all the sump bolts, releasing them only one half turn at a time in diagonal sequence to avoid distortion.

2 If the sump is stuck tight, run a blunt knife round the gasket to release it.

13 Oil pump and oil filter - removal

If the oil pump is to be removed with the engine still in the car, first withdraw the sump as described at the beginning of Section 12.

1 Disconnect the oil intake pipe support from the main bearing cap.

2 Unscrew and remove the oil pump securing bolts and withdraw the pump from its engagement with the camshaft drive gear.

3 The oil filter is simply removed by unscrewing the centre bolt. As the oil filter body is withdrawn, the loss of oil trapped within it will occur.

4 Discard the internal filter element. The new element will be supplied complete with new sealing rings.

14 Timing cover, gears and chain - removal

If the timing cover, gear and chain are being removed with the engine in the car, then the following operations must first be carried out:
Drain the cooling system.
Remove the radiator and fanbelt.
Remove the sump.

1 Unscrew and remove the crankshaft pulley bolt. If the sump has been removed, place a block of wood between a crankshaft web and the internal wall of the crankcase to prevent the crankshaft rotating as the bolt is unscrewed. If the engine is in the car or the sump has not yet been removed, withdraw the starter motor and jam the flywheel starter ring gear with a large screwdriver or cold chisel. The crankshaft pulley bolt can then be unscrewed.

2 Withdraw the crankshaft pulley. If this is tight, use two levers placed behind the pulley at opposite points to extract it.

3 Unscrew and remove the timing cover securing bolts and withdraw the cover and its gasket.

4 Hold the chain tensioner pad in the fully depressed state and withdraw the chain tensioner assembly from its location.

5 Unscrew the camshaft sprocket bolt and then withdraw the sprocket complete with chain, at the same time unlooping the chain from the crankshaft sprocket.

15 Camshaft and tappets - removal

1 With the engine inverted, unbolt and remove the two camshaft thrust plate bolts and withdraw the thrust plate.

2 Withdraw the camshaft from the front of the crankcase, taking care not to damage the three camshaft bearings as the lobes of the cams pass through them.

3 Extract the tappets (cam followers), keeping them in strict sequence

Fig. 1.4. Oil pump intake pipe attachment (1) and pump mounting bolts (2) (Sec. 13)

for refitting in their original positions. A suction type valve grinding tool is useful in extracting the tappets.

16 Piston/connecting rod - removal

If the engine is still in the car, carry out the following operations:
Remove the cylinder head.
Remove the sump.

1 Turn the crankshaft so that no. 1 crankpin is at the lowest point of its travel.

2 Examine the adjacent surfaces of the big-end cap and the rod for matching numbers. If these are not evident, dot punch the cap and rod of each connecting rod assembly so that not only is its respective cylinder bore identified but also which side of the engine the punch marks face.

3 Unscrew and remove the big-end bearing cap bolts and withdraw the cap complete with bearing shells.

4 Push the connecting rod/piston assembly out of the top of the cylinder block.

5 Repeat the foregoing operations on the three remaining piston/ connecting rod assemblies.

6 If the original bearing shells are to be refitted (unwise unless they are virtually new), mark their original locations also, whether fitted to cap or rod, using pieces of masking tape.

17 Crankshaft and main bearings - removal

1 Check the main bearing caps for location marks. If these are not evident, dot punch the caps and crankcase so that there is no doubt which cap is front, centre or rear and also which way round it is fitted.

2 Unscrew and remove the main bearing cap bolts and withdraw the caps complete with bearing shells. Retain and identify any shims which are found under the main bearing caps as they must be returned to their original locations.

3 Lift the crankshaft carefully from the crankcase.

4 Extract the bearing shells from the crankcase recesses. If the original shells are to be refitted, mark their locations using pieces of masking tape.

18 Examination and renovation - general

With the engine now completely stripped, clean all components and examine everything for wear. Each part should be checked and where necessary renewed or renovated as described in the following Sections.

19 Oil pump - examination and renovation

1 The strainer is a push fit on the oil intake pipe and can be pulled off for cleaning.

2 Remove the oil pump cover (two bolts) and check the impellers for (i) endfloat in the pump body, (ii) radial clearance, (iii) backlash

between the teeth. The permitted tolerances are given in Specifications.

3 If wear is evident in the components, it is better to purchase a new pump complete. but if individual spare parts are available, make sure that the drive spindle impeller is pressed onto the spindle so that the clearance 'A' (Fig. 1.6) is between 0.007 and 0.010 in. (0.18 and 0.25 mm) when the face of the impeller is in contact with the pump body.

4 The oil pressure relief valve is non-adjustable but it is possible after high mileages for the coil spring to weaken (check free-length in Specifications Section).

20 Crankcase ventilation system

1 This comprises a hose connected between the rocker cover and the air cleaner with a branch pipe running to a restrictor screwed into the intake manifold.

2 Occasionally examine the condition and security of the hoses and periodically disconnect them and clean them out, removing any sludge or congealed oil.

21 Crankshaft and main bearings - examination and renovation

1 Remove the crankshaft rear oil seal and discard it.

2 Examine the bearing surfaces of the crankshaft for scratches or scoring and using a micrometer, check each journal and crankpin for out of round. Where this is found to be in excess of 0.001 in. (0.0254 mm) the crankshaft will have to be reground and undersize bearings fitted.

3 The crankshaft can be reground to a maximum of 0.040 in. (1.016 mm) undersize, but your Vauxhall dealer will decide how much is required and supply the matching undersize main and big-end shell bearings.

4 When installed, the main bearings should have a running clearance of between 0.0010 and 0.0025 in. (0.025 and 0.064 mm) and the big-end bearings 0.0010 and 0.0029 in. (0.025 and 0.074 mm). These tolerances can only be checked using a proprietary product such as 'Plastigage' and it is usually assumed that where the reconditioning has been carried out by a reliable company that the running clearances will be correct.

5 Crankshaft endfloat, with main bearing caps fully tightened, should be between 0.002 and 0.008 in. (0.05 and 0.20 mm). The endfloat is controlled by the thrust flanges on the centre main bearing shells.

6 If the gearbox input shaft spigot bush needs renewal, extract it by tapping a thread in it. The new bush requires no lubrication.

22 Cylinder block and crankcase - examination and renovation

1 The cylinder bores must be examined for taper, ovality, scoring and scratches. Start by carefully examining the top of the cylinder bores. If they are at all worn a very slight ridge will be found on the thrust side. This marks the top of the piston ring travel. The owner will have a good indication of the bore wear prior to dismantling the engine, or removing the cylinder head. Excessive oil consumption accompanied by blue smoke from the exhaust is a sure sign of worn cylinder bores and piston rings.

2 Measure the bore diameter just under the ridge with a mircometer and compare it with the diameter at the bottom of the bore, which is not subject to wear. If the difference between the two measurements is more than 0.008 in. (0.2032 mm), then it will be necessary to fit special pistons and rings or have the cylinders rebored and fit oversize pistons.

3 If the bores are slightly worn but not so badly worn as to justify reboring them, then special oil control rings and pistons can be fitted which will restore compression and stop the engine burning oil. Several different types are available and the manufacturer's instructions concerning their fitting must be followed closely.

4 If new pistons are being fitted and the bores have not been reground, it is essential to slightly roughen the hard glaze on the sides of the bores with fine glass paper so the new piston rings will have a chance to bed in properly.

5 Examine the crankcase for cracks and leaking core plugs. To renew a core plug, drill a hole in its centre and tap a thread in it. Screw in a bolt and using a distance piece, tighten the bolt and extract the core plug. When installing the new plug, smear its outer edge with gasket cement.

6 Probe oil galleries and waterways with a piece of wire to make sure that they are quite clear.

23 Piston/connecting rod assemblies - examination and renovation

1 The big-end shell bearings will have been supplied to match the reground crankshaft.

2 If the pistons are to be renewed to suit a rebored cylinder block, then this is a job best left to your Vauxhall dealer as the gudgeon pin is an interference fit in the small end and precise heating of the connecting rod and the use of a press and installation tool are required to carry out the operation successfully.

3 When correctly assembled, the notch on the piston crown should be in alignment with the numbering on the connecting rod.

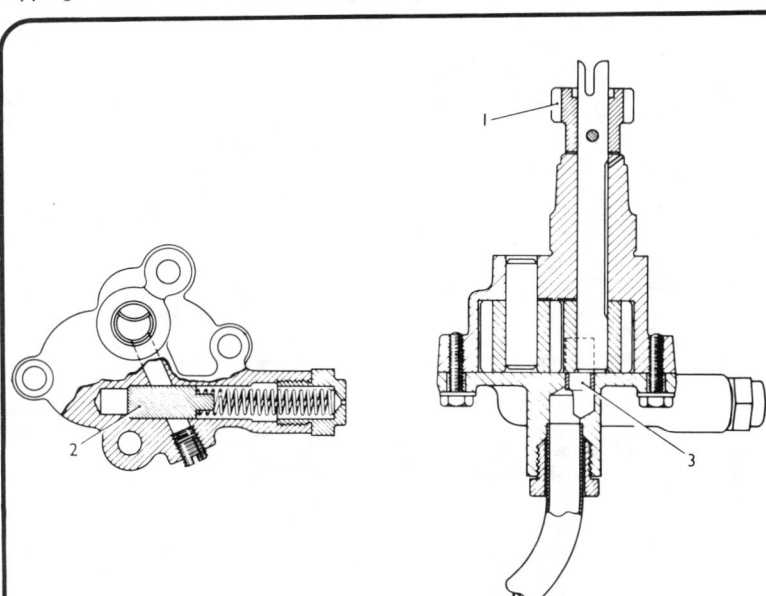

Fig. 1.5. Sectional views of oil pump (Sec. 19)

1 Drive gear   2 Pressure relief valve   3 Anti-drainage pipe

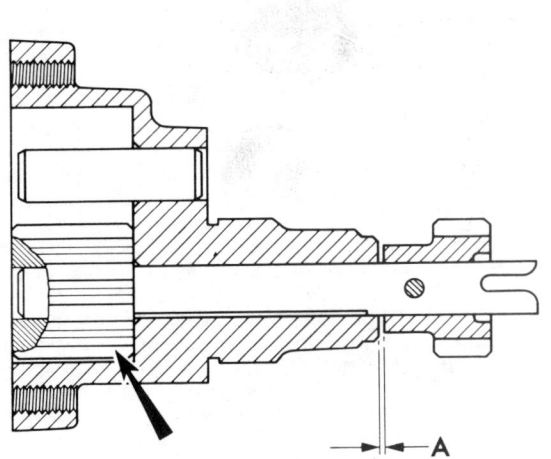

Fig. 1.6. Oil pump/drive gear impeller end-float diagram (Sec. 19)

A = Drive gear to body clearance 0.007 to 0.010 in. (0.18 to 0.25 mm). Impeller arrowed

4 If new piston rings are to be fitted to the original pistons, remove the old rings by expanding them and withdrawing them with a twisting motion. The use of two or three old feeler blades placed at equidistant points between the piston and ring will prevent a ring dropping into an empty groove during removal.

5 Install the new rings by reversing the removal process, but make sure that the following conditions are complied with:

(i)   The top compression ring is stepped to avoid the wear ridge which will have formed at the top of the cylinder bore.

(ii)   Top and centre ring end gaps and groove clearances are as given in Specifications Section.

(iii)   Install centre ring with stepped face downwards (top ring can be fitted either way up).

(iv)   Space piston ring gaps at equidistant points so that the gaps are not in alignment.

(v)   Make sure that the ends 'A' and 'B' (Fig. 1.7) of the bottom oil control ring spacer, do not overlap but are engaged with each other as shown. Ensure that the rail ends 'C' do not align with the gap of the spacer.

24 Camshaft and tappets - examination and renovation

1 Examine the camshaft bearing surfaces, cam lobes and gearteeth for wear or scoring. Renew the shaft if evident.

2 The camshaft bearings can be renewed, if worn, in the following way.

3 Obtain a piece of tubing, slightly smaller in diameter than the bearing outer diameter. Drive out the bearings towards the rear, noting in the case of the rear one that the expansion plug seal will be ejected.

4 Install the new bearings so that their oil holes coincide with the oilways in the cylinder block. The notch in each bearing must face the front of the engine.

5 Install a new expansion plug at the back of the rear bearing, having first coated its outside edge with jointing compound.

6 The bearings are finished to size and require no reaming.

25 Timing gears and chain - examination and renovation

1 Examine the teeth on the camshaft and crankshaft sprockets. If these are at all hooked in appearance renew the sprockets.

2 Examine the chain tensioner. If either the rubber positioning plug or the rubber pad are worn or have perished or hardened, renew them.

3 Examine the timing chain. If it has been in operation for a considerable time or if when held horizontally (link plates facing downwards) it takes on a deeply bowed appearance, renew it.

4 The timing chain oil nozzle acts as a mounting for the chain tensioner. If there is any excessive movement of the tensioner on the nozzle, remove the nozzle and install a new one (interference fit) in the cylinder block. The position of the oil discharge hole in the nozzle is not important.

26 Cylinder head - decarbonising, valve grinding, renovation

1 This operation will normally only be required at comparatively high mileages due to the improvements in fuel and oil quality and to the better design of engine breathing systems. However, when persistent 'pinking' occurs and engine performance has badly deteriorated, but it is perfect tune, then decarbonising and valve grinding will be required.

2 With the cylinder head removed, use a blunt scraper to remove all trace of carbon and deposits from the combustion spaces and ports. Scrape the cylinder head free from scale or old pieces of gasket or jointing compound. Clean the cylinder head by washing it in paraffin and take particular care to pull a piece of rag through the ports and cylinder head bolt holes. Any grit remaining in these recesses may well drop onto the gasket or cylinder block mating surface as the cylinder head is lowered into position and could lead to a gasket leak after reassembly is complete.

3 With the cylinder head clean, test for distortion if a history of coolant leakage has been apparent. Carry out this test using a straight edge and feeler gauges or a piece of plate glass. If the surface shows any warping in excess of 0.004 in. (0.1016 mm), then the cylinder head will have to be resurfaced which is a job for a specialist engineering company.

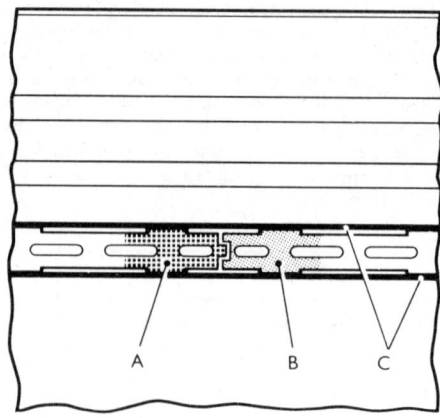

Fig. 1.7. Oil control ring installation diagram. For key see text (Sec. 23)

4 If the engine is in the car, clean the tops of the pistons and the upper edges of the cylinder bores. It is essential that great care is taken to ensure that no carbon gets into the cylinder bores as this could scratch the cylinder walls or cause damage to the piston and rings. To ensure this does not happen, first turn the crankshaft so that two of the pistons are at the top of their bores. Stuff rag into the other two bores or seal them off with paper and masking tape. The waterways should also be covered with small pieces of masking tape to prevent particles of carbon entering the cooling system and damaging the water pump.

5 Press a little grease into the gap between the cylinder walls and the two pistons which are to be worked on. With a blunt scraper carefully scrape away the carbon from the piston crown, taking great care not to scratch the aluminium. Also scrape away the carbon from the surrounding lip of the cylinder wall. When all carbon has been removed, scrape away the grease which will now be contaminated with carbon particles, taking care not to press any into the bores. To assist prevention of carbon build-up the piston crown can be polished with a metal polish. Remove the rags or masking tape from the other two cylinders and turn the crankshaft so that the two pistons which were at the bottom are now at the top. Place rag or masking tape in the cylinders which have been decarbonised and proceed as just described.

6 Examine the heads of the valves for pitting and burning, especially the heads of the exhaust valves. The valve seatings should be examined at the same time. If the pitting on valve and seat is very slight the marks can be removed by grinding the seats and valves together with coarse, and then fine, valve grinding paste.

7 Where bad pitting has occurred to the valve seats it will be necessary to recut them and fit new valves.

8 Valve grinding is carried out as follows: Smear a trace of coarse carborundum paste on the seat face and apply a suction grinder tool to the valve head. With a semi-rotary motion, grind the valve head to its seat, lifting the valve occasionally to redistribute the grinding paste. When a dull matt even surface finish is produced on both the valve seat and the valve, wipe off the paste and repeat the process with fine carborundum paste, lifting and turning the valve to redistribute the paste as before. A light spring placed under the valve head will greatly ease this operation. When a smooth unbroken ring of light grey matt finish is produced, on both valve and valve seat faces, the grinding operation is completed.

9 Clean away every trace of grinding paste and if available, use an air-line to blow out the ports and valve guides.

10 If the valve guides are worn (indicated by a side-to-side rocking motion of the valve), oversize valves are available in steps from 0.003 in. (0.0762 mm) to 0.012 in. (2.591 mm) but the valve guides will have to be reamed out to accommodate them and to provide the specified stem to guide clearance (see Specifications Section).

11 If the original valve springs have been in use for 20,000 miles (32,000 km) or more, renew them, also the valve stem oil seals. The latter are fitted to inlet valves only.

12 Extract the water distribution tube from the cylinder head and clean it free from any corrosion (photo).

13 Probe the oil discharge holes in the rocker studs and check that the rocker and rocker ball are not worn. Test the rocker stud self-locking nuts on the stud threads. The torque required to turn them must not be less than 3 lb ft (4 Nm) otherwise renew them.

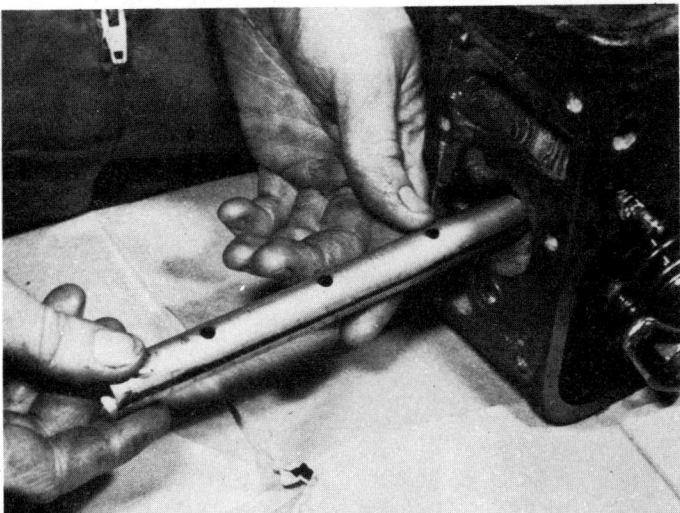

26.12 Cylinder head water distribution tube

Fig. 1.8. Rocker stud oil discharge hole (Sec. 26)

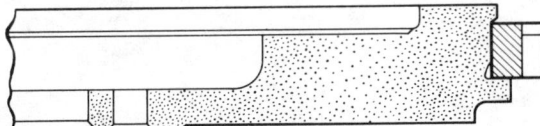

Fig. 1.9. Method of mounting flywheel ring gear (Sec. 27)

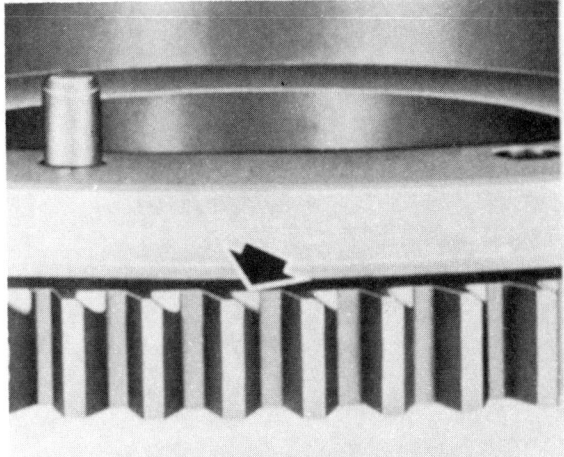

Fig. 1.10. Location of starter ring gear tooth chamfers (Sec. 27)

27 Flywheel - examination and renovation

1   Examine the clutch driven plate mating surface of the flywheel. If this is scored or shows signs of many small cracks, then it should either be renewed or refaced.
2   Examine the teeth of the flywheel starter ring gear. If they are chipped or worn, the ring must be renewed. To do this, split the ring with a cold chisel. Note that the ring is located in a shallow groove and cannot be removed by trying to knock it from the flywheel.
3   Heat the new ring to 608°F (320°C) in an electric oven and then quickly fit it to the flywheel so that the chamfered side of the teeth is towards the clutch side of the flywheel.
4   Allow the ring to cool naturally without quenching.

28 Engine reassembly - general

1   To ensure maximum life with minimum trouble from a rebuilt engine, not only must everything be correctly assembled, but everything must be spotlessly clean, all the oilways must be clear, locking washers and spring washers must always be fitted where indicated and all bearing and other working surfaces must be thoroughly lubricated during assembly.
2   Before assembly begins renew any bolts or studs, the threads of which are in any way damaged, and whenever possible use new spring washers.
3   Gather together a torque wrench, oil can and clean rag, also a set of engine gaskets, crankshaft front and rear oil seals and a new oil filter element.

29 Crankshaft and main bearings - installation

1   Clean the backs of the bearing shells and the bearing recesses in both the crankcase and the caps.
2   Make sure that the centre flanged bearing shell is located in the crankcase and then fit the remaining shells (photo).
3   Oil the bearings liberally.
4   Fit a new oil seal to the rear end of the crankshaft, so that its lip is towards the crankshaft web (photo).
5   Apply a trace of jointing compound to the seal groove in the crankcase and then lower the crankshaft into position. Keep the crankshaft level during this operation to prevent distortion of the seal lip (photo).
6   Apply a wide bead of sealant to the rear bearing cap register (2) (Fig. 1.11) but not to the surface (1).
7   Smear the outside edge of the crankshaft rear oil seal with jointing

29.2 Centre main bearing showing thrust flanges of shell

29.4 Crankshaft rear oil seal

29.5 Crankshaft installed in crankcase

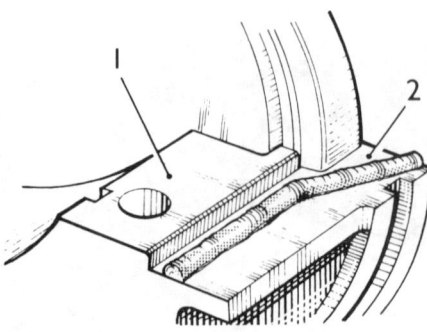

Fig. 1.11. Rear main bearing cap register surfaces (1 and 2) (Sec. 29)

29.7 Installing crankshaft rear bearing cap

29.8 Tightening a main bearing cap bolt

30.3 Piston/connecting rod installation using piston ring compressor

30.7 Installing a big-end cap

31.1 Using a valve grinding suction tool to install a tappet

31.2 Installing the camshaft

31.3 Correct installation of camshaft thrust plate

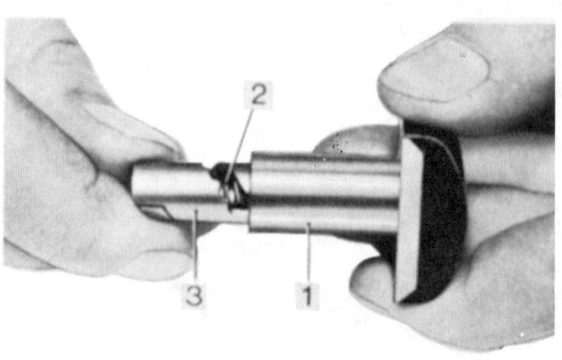

Fig. 1.12. Reassembling timing chain tensioner (Sec. 32)

1 Sleeve   2 Spring   3 Piston

compound and then install the rear bearing cap, the correct way round (photo). Ensure that any shims are refitted in their original positions under the main bearing caps. Note the bolt on the centre main bearing cap to which the oil pump pick-up pipe is attached.

8 Fit the front and centre main bearing caps (the correct way round) complete with their shells and then insert and tighten all main bearing cap bolts to the specified torque (photo).

9 Check the crankshaft endfloat using a dial gauge or feeler blades. This should be as specified in Specifications, provided the centre flanged shell bearings are to manufacturer's specified tolerance.

10 Turn the crankshaft and check that it rotates smoothly during a complete revolution.

30 Piston/connecting rod - refitting

1 The assemblies will have been prepared as described in Sections 22 and 23.

2 Apply engine oil liberally to the cylinder bores and to the piston rings.

3 Fit a piston ring compressor to no. 1 piston and then insert the connecting rod into the cylinder bore nearest the front of the block. Check that the notch in the piston crown faces the front of the engine (photo).

4 With the piston skirt having entered the cylinder bore and the compressor resting squarely on the block, place the wooden handle of a hammer on the centre of the piston crown and then tap the head of the handle sharply to drive the piston assembly into the bore.

5 With the crankpin at its lowest point, carefully pull the connecting rod downward and connect it to the crankshaft. Make sure that the big-end bearing shell has not become displaced.

6 Install the big-end bearing cap (complete with bearing shell, making sure that the matching marks on the rod and cap are in alignment and are on the correct side of the engine. This will be automatic, provided the piston and connecting rod have been correctly assembled and the notch on the piston crown is correctly positioned.

7 Screw in the big-end bolts and tighten to the specified torque (photo).

8 Repeat the foregoing operations on the remaining three piston assemblies.

31 Camshaft and tappets - installation

1 With the engine inverted, oil the tappet blocks and install them in their original sequence (photo).

2 Oil the camshaft bearings and carefully insert the camshaft from the front of the cylinder block (photo).

3 Install the thrust plate and securing bolts, making sure that the plate is exactly positioned as shown (longer fork nearest chain tensioner slipper) (photo), in order to permit correct fitting of the timing chain tensioner.

4 The camshaft endfloat should be between 0.002 and 0.009 in. (0.05 and 0.23 mm) which can be tested with feeler blades or a dial gauge. If the endfloat exceeds that specified, renew the thrust plate.

32 Timing components - refitting

1 Rotate the crankshaft and the camshaft (with sprocket temporarily fitted) until the timing marks are adjacent to each other and a line drawn between the centres of the crankshaft and camshaft will pass through them.

2 If the chain tensioner has been dismantled, first install the spring '2' (Fig. 1.12) and piston '3' in the sleeve '1' of the pad assembly. Engage the pip inside the sleeve with the groove in the piston. Now compress the components until the pip engages in the recess at the end of the piston groove. The piston will now remain retracted.

3 Install the retracted pad assembly in the tensioner body.

4 Install the tensioner assembly to the oil nozzle mounting on the front face of the block.

5 Engage the timing chain with the crankshaft sprocket and then engage the camshaft sprocket within the upper loop of the chain. Now install the camshaft sprocket complete with chain so that the timing marks are as described in paragraph 1. A certain amount of repositioning of the chain and camshaft sprocket will be required to

achieve this (photo).

6 Install the camshaft sprocket bolt and tighten to the specified torque.

7 Depress and then release the pad of the chain tensioner. This will disengage the internal pip and enable the tensioner to take up its operational tension.

8 Remove the timing cover oil seal and drive in a new one, using a piece of tubing as a drift. Apply engine oil to the seal lips and then install the timing cover, using a new gasket. Tighten the bolts only finger-tight at this stage.

9 Install the crankshaft pulley and tighten its securing bolt to the specified torque (photo).

10 Finally tighten the timing cover bolts to the specified torque.

33 Oil pump and sump - refitting

1 Rotate the crankshaft by means of the pulley bolt until the pointer on the crankshaft pulley is opposite the TDC mark on the timing cover, with no. 1 piston on the compression stroke. This can be established by checking that nos. 1 and 2 tappets (counting from the front of the engine) are resting on the lowest profile of the camshaft lobes.

2 Turn the oil pump drive gear until the drive spindle slot takes up the position shown in the illustration (Fig. 1.15).

3 Install the oil pump to the crankcase, using a new flange gasket. Make sure that with the oil pump bolts inserted finger-tight, engagement of the camshaft drive-gear has caused the large and small segments of the drive spindle (when viewed from above) to take up the position shown. (Fig. 1.16) If not, withdraw the pump and by trial-and-error, adjust the oil pump gears until the correct setting is achieved (photo).

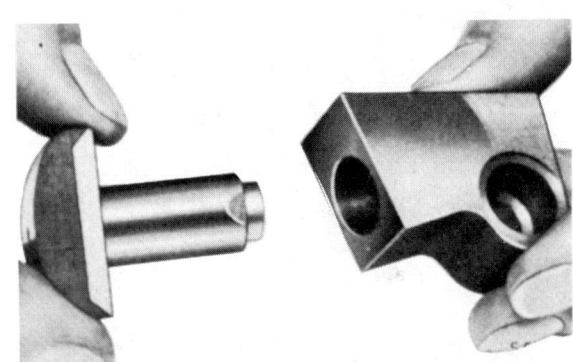

Fig. 1.13. Installing chain tensioner pad assembly to body (Sec. 32)

32.5 Timing chain components showing alignment of sprocket marks

32.9 Installing crankshaft pulley

Fig. 1.14. Engine timing marks (Sec. 33)

1   Crankshaft pulley pointer   2   Timing cover TDC mark

Fig. 1.15. Oil pump drive spindle set ready for installation (Sec. 33)

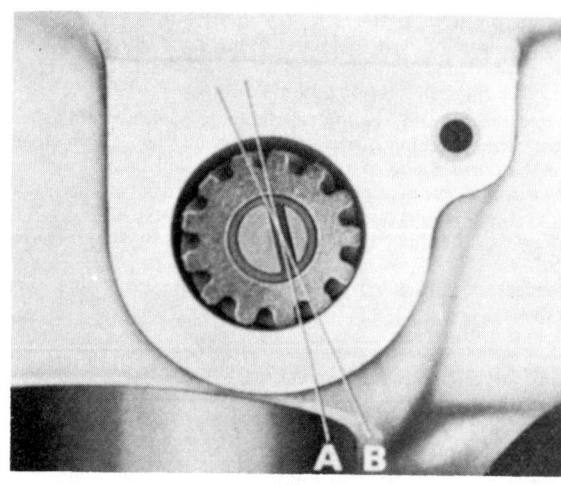

Fig. 1.16. Alignment of oil pump drive spindle (viewed from above) after correct installation. A to B is permitted tolerance (Sec. 33)

33.3 Installing oil pump

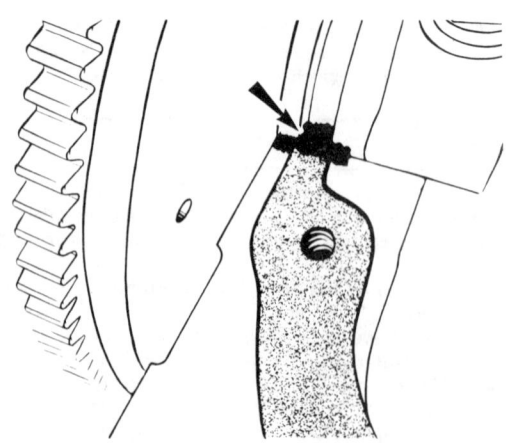

Fig. 1.17. Sealing sump gasket at rear bearing cap (Sec. 33)

4   Tighten the oil pump bolts to the specified torque.
5   Reconnect the pick-up tube support to the securing bolt located on the centre main bearing cap.
6   The sump gaskets should now be installed. To do this, first clean the mating faces of sump and crankcase, also the rear bearing cap seal groove.
7   Apply suitable jointing compound to the corners formed by the rear main bearing cap seal groove and the crankcase. Install the sump gasket so that the ends of the gasket are located in the cap groove and then apply more jointing compound to seal the ends of the gasket within the

groove (photo).
8   Warm the rear seal and shape it to fit the groove in the bearing cap.
9   Install the seal so that the chamfers 'A' (Fig. 1.18) face inwards. Apply jointing compound to the junctions of the seal and gasket and then install the sump, tightening the bolts in diagonally opposite sequence. Do not overtighten them.
10 Note the gearbox to sump bracket brace. The inclusion of the lockwasher '3' is essential (Fig. 1.19).

34 Cylinder head - reassembly and installation

1   Install the valves in their original sequence or if new ones have been purchased, to the seats to which they have been ground.
2   Fit new valve stem oil seals and circlips to the four inlet valve guides.
3   Insert the first valve into its guide, first having applied engine oil liberally to its stem (photo).
4   Fit the valve spring, the retaining cap and then compress the valve spring and locate the split collets in the cut-out of the valve stem. Release the compressor. Repeat these operations on the remaining seven valves (photo).
5   When all the valves have been installed, place the cylinder head flat on the bench and using a hammer and a block of wood as an insulator, tap the end of each valve stem to settle the components.
6   Install the rocker balls (photo).
7   Install the rocker springs so that the smaller coil is nearer the cylinder head.
8   Install the rockers and the self-locking nuts, only screwing on the nuts a few turns.

33.7 Fitting sump gasket

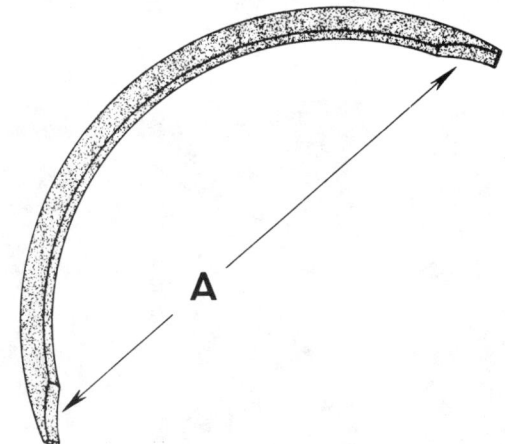

Fig. 1.18. Rear main bearing cap oil seal chamfers (A) (Sec. 33)

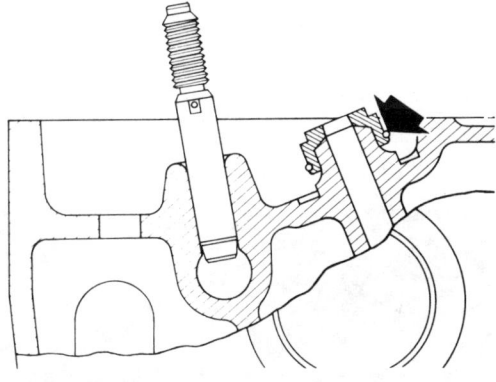

Fig. 1.20. Location of an inlet valve oil seal (arrowed) (Sec. 34)

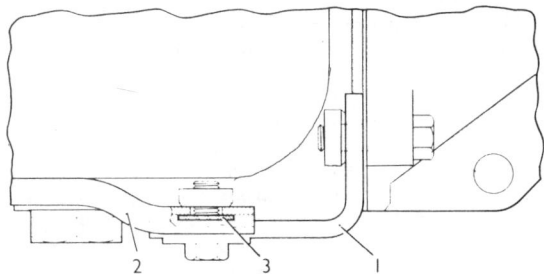

Fig. 1.19. Components of the gearbox to sump brace (Sec. 33)

1   Gearbox brace
2   Sump bracket
3   Lockwasher

34.3 Installing a valve

34.4 Fitting valve split collets

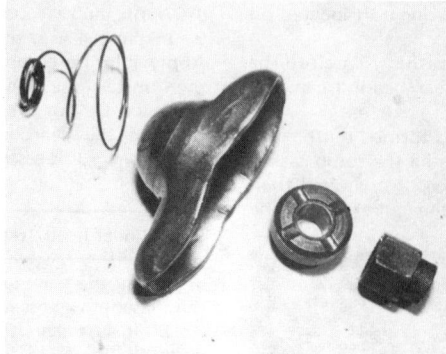
34.6 Rocker components

34.9 Installing cylinder head gasket

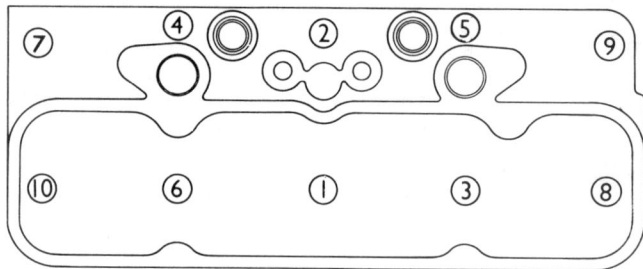
Fig. 1.21. Cylinder head bolt tightening sequence diagram (Sec. 34)

34.11 Installing a pushrod

34.12 Checking and adjusting a valve clearance

35.3 Installing the oil filter

35.4 Installing the flywheel

9   Make sure that the faces of the cylinder head and the cylinder block are perfectly clean and then lay a new gasket on the cylinder block so that the word 'Front' is visible from above and correctly located. Do not use any kind of jointing compound (photo).

10 Lower the cylinder head into position, insert the cylinder head bolts and tighten them to the specified torque and in the sequence shown, in Fig. 1.21.

11 Each rocker can now be swivelled aside and the respective pushrod installed. Apply engine oil to all the rocker components (photo).

12 The valve clearances should be set with the engine running and hot, as described in Section 38, but at this stage they should be adjusted to approximate clearances so that the engine can be started and run. To do this, apply a ring spanner to the crankshaft pulley bolt and turn the crankshaft until no. 1 piston is at TDC (top-dead-centre). This can be established by placing a finger over no. 1 plug hole and when compression can be felt, continue turning until the crankshaft pulley pointer is opposite the TDC mark on the timing cover. Insert an 0.008 in. (0.20 mm) feeler blade between the end of no. 1 valve stem and the rocker and adjust the rocker self-locking nut until the feeler blade is a

stiff sliding fit. Repeat the operation (without moving the crankshaft) on no. 2 valve. The clearances for both inlet and exhaust valves are the same (photo).

13 Turn the crankshaft until no. 3 piston is at TDC and repeat the adjustment procedure on valves 5 and 6 (counting from the front of the engine).

14 Turn the crankshaft until no. 4 piston is at TDC and repeat the adjustment procedure on valves 7 and 8.

15 Turn the crankshaft until no. 2 piston is at TDC and repeat the adjustment procedure on valves 3 and 4. If the foregoing sequence of adjustment is followed, it will prevent the crankshaft from being rotated unnecessarily as the engine firing order is 1-3-4-2.

35 Ancillary components - installation

1   This is a reversal of the removal sequence given in Section 9, of this Chapter.

2   Full details of component installation are given in the relevant

Chapters of this manual, but the following points should be noted.
3   Always install a new oil filter sealing ring in the cylinder block groove. Tighten the centre-bolt only to specified torque (photo).
4   When installing the flywheel bolts, smear their threads sparingly with a suitable sealer. Excessive amounts of sealer may damage the crankshaft oil seal. Tighten the flywheel bolts to the specified torque (photo).
5   Adjust the fanbelt as described in Chapter 2, Section 12.

36 Engine - installation without gearbox

1   This is a reversal of the removal operations described in Section 7, of this Chapter, but check the following points:
   (i)   *That the clutch driven plate has been centralised, as described in Chapter 5.*
   (ii) *That the engine front mountings are correctly assembled as shown in Fig. 1.23. Never use longer bolts in the engine mounting bolts than those used originally, or they may foul the crankshaft (photo).*

37 Engine - installation complete with gearbox

1   Connect the engine and gearbox. This is quite straightforward provided the clutch driven plate has been centralised, as described in

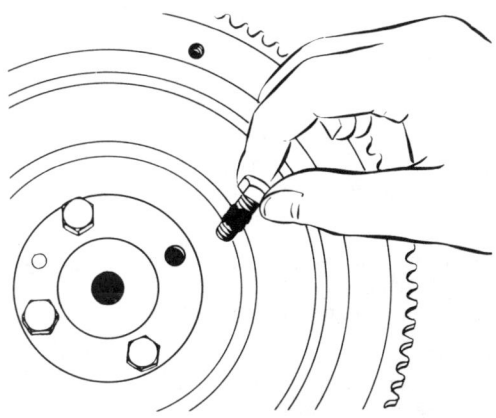

Fig. 1.22. Inserting a flywheel retaining bolt with sealer applied to the threads to prevent oil seepage from the crankcase (Sec. 35)

36.1 Right-hand (cast type) engine mounting

Chapter 5.
2   Tighten the clutch bellhousing bolts to the specified torque.
3   Reverse all the operations described in Section 5 of this Chapter, making quite sure that the assembly of the engine front and rear mountings is as illustrated in Figs. 1.23 and 1.24.

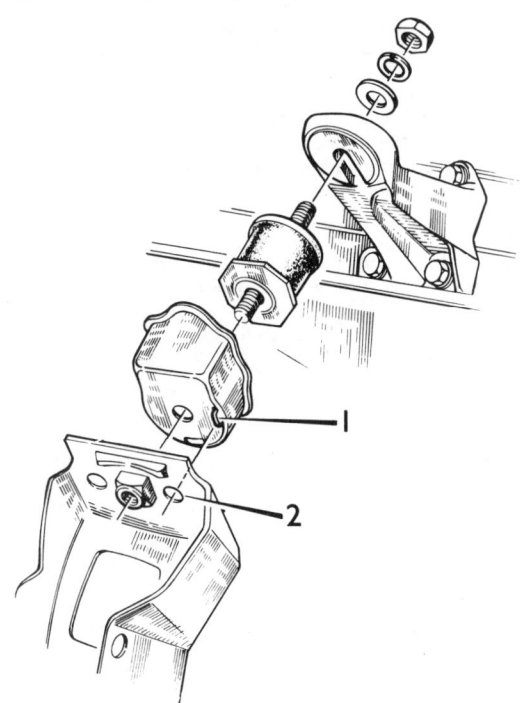

Fig. 1.23. Exploded view of an engine front mounting (Secs. 36 and 37)

1   *Tang for location in hole (2)*

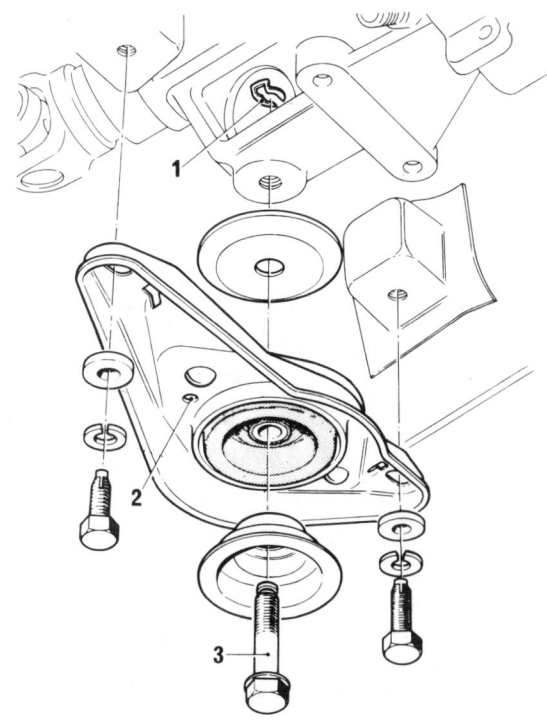

Fig. 1.24. Exploded view of the engine/gearbox rear mounting (Sec. 37)

1   *Retaining clip*
2   *Hole (to be positioned on right-hand side, some components have arrow to indicate front of crossmember)*
3   *Bolt*

4 Refill the cooling system with antifreeze mixture, to the proportions given in Chapter 2.
5 Refill the engine with oil.
6 Check and top-up the gearbox oil level.

38 Engine - adjustment after major overhaul

1 With the engine refitted to the vehicle, give a final visual check to see that everything has been reconnected and that no loose rags or tools have been left within the engine compartment.
2 Turn the engine slow running screw in about ½ turn (to increase slow running once the engine is started) (Chapter 3). This faster slow-running will be needed due to the tightness of the new engine components.
3 Pull the choke fully out and start the engine. This may take a little longer than usual as the fuel pump and carburettor bowl will be empty and need initial priming.
4 As soon as the engine starts, push the choke in until the engine runs at a fast tickover and examine the engine for leaks. Check particularly the water hoses and oil filter and fuel hose unions.
5 Run the vehicle on the road until normal operating temperature is reached.
6 Check and re-adjust the valve clearances by the following method: switch off the engine, disconnect the breather hose from the rocker cover, the coil cover, plug leads, distributor cap and slacken the bolt which holds numbers 3 and 4 spark plug leads to the support bracket. Unscrew the rocker cover screws and lift off the cover.
7 Reconnect the ignition components and start the engine. Unscrew the throttle stop screw until the engine runs as slowly as possible.
8 Insert a feeler blade (0.008 in/0.20 mm) between each valve stem and its rocker in turn and adjust the rocker nut until the feeler can be withdrawn with a stiff pull.
9 Adjust the throttle speed screw to give normal idling speed and then switch off the ignition and refit the rocker cover.
10 Where new internal components have been installed, the engine speed should be restricted for the first 500 miles (800 km) and at this mileage, the engine oil should be renewed, the cylinder head bolts checked for correct torque (unscrew each bolt one ¼ turn and then tighten to specified torque and in recommended sequence). Finally, check and adjust the valve clearances.

39 Fault diagnosis - engine

Symptom	Reason
Engine fails to start	Discharged battery
	Loose battery connection
	Disconnected or broken ignition leads
	Moisture on spark plugs, distributor or leads
	Incorrect contact points gap, cracked distributor cap or rotor
	Incorrect spark plug gap
	Dirt or water in carburettor jets
	Empty fuel tank
	Faulty fuel pump
	Faulty starter motor
	Faulty carburettor choke mechanism
Engine idles erratically	Air leak at intake manifold
	Leaking cylinder head gasket
	Worn timing sprockets
	Worn camshaft lobes
	Overheating
	Faulty fuel pump
Engine 'misses' at idling speed	Incorrect spark plug gap
	Uneven compression between cylinders
	Faulty coil or condenser
	Faulty contact points
	Poor connections or condition of ignition leads
	Dirt in carburettor jets
	Incorrectly adjusted carburettor
	Worn distributor cam
	Air leak at carburettor flange gasket
	Faulty ignition advance mechanism
	Sticking valves
	Incorrect valve clearance
	Low cylinder compression
Engine 'misses' throughout speed range	Dirt or water in carburettor or fuel lines
	Incorrect ignition timing
	Contact points incorrectly gapped
	Worn distributor
	Faulty coil or condenser
	Spark plug gaps incorrect
	Weak valve spring
	Overheating

Symptom	Reason
Engine stalls	Incorrectly adjusted carburettor
	Dirt or water in fuel
	Ignition system incorrectly adjusted
	Sticking choke mechanism
	Faulty spark plugs or incorrectly gapped
	Faulty coil or condenser
	Incorrect contact points gap
	Exhaust system clogged
	Distributor advance inoperative
	Air leak at intake manifold
	Air leak at carburettor mounting flange
	Incorrect valve clearance
	Sticking valve
	Overheating
	Low compression
	Poor electrical connections on ignition system
Engine lacks power	Incorrect ignition timing
	Faulty coil or condenser
	Worn distributor
	Dirt in carburettor
	Spark plugs incorrectly gapped
	Incorrectly adjusted carburettor
	Faulty fuel pump
	Weak valve springs
	Sticking valve
	Incorrect valve timing
	Incorrect valve adjustment
	Blown cylinder head gasket
	Low compression
	Brakes dragging
	Clutch slipping
	Overheating

Chapter 2 Cooling system

For modifications, and information applicable to later models, see Supplement at end of manual

Contents

Specifications

System type	Thermo syphon belt driven pump, pressurized
Radiator cap pressure	13.5 to 17.5 lbf/in^2
Thermostat opens	190°F (88°C)
System capacity	10.2 pints (5.80 litres)

Torque wrench settings

	lb ft	Nm
Fan securing screw	14	19
Water pump bolts	18	24

1 Cooling system - general description

The cooling system is of pressurized type and includes a front mounted radiator, a belt-driven water pump and a viscous-coupling type fan.

A thermostat is located in the outlet side of the water pump.

The radiator is not provided with a drain plug but one is installed on the right-hand side of the cylinder block.

The principle of the system is that cold water in the bottom of the radiator circulates upwards through the lower radiator hose to the water pump, where the pump impeller pushes the water round the cylinder block and head through the various cast-in passages to cool the cylinder bores, combustion surfaces and valve seats. When sufficient heat has been absorbed by the cooling water, and the engine has reached an efficient working temperature, the water moves from the cylinder head past the now open thermostat into the top radiator hose and into the radiator header tank.

The water then travels down the radiator tubes when it is rapidly cooled by the in-rush of air when the vehicle is in forward motion. A five-bladed fan, mounted on the water pump pulley, assists this cooling action. The water, now cooled, reaches the bottom of the radiator and the cycle is repeated.

When the engine is cold the thermostat remains closed until the coolant reaches a pre-determined temperature (see Specifications). This assists rapid warming-up.

Water temperature is measured, by an electro-sensitive capsule located immediately below the thermostat housing. Water from the engine cooling system is used to provide warmth to the car interior through the medium of a heater assembly (see Chapter 12).

2 Cooling system - draining

1 It is preferable to drain the cooling system when the engine has cooled. If this is not possible, then place a cloth over the radiator cap and turn it slowly in an anticlockwise direction until the first stop is reached. Wait a minute or two with the cap in this position to allow the pressure in the system to escape. Continue turning the cap fully anticlockwise and remove it.

2 If the coolant is to be retained for further use, place a suitable container under the radiator and then disconnect the bottom hose.

3 Place a second container under the engine and remove the drain plug from the right-hand side of the cylinder block.

3 Cooling system - flushing

1 The radiator and waterways in the engine after some time may become restricted or even blocked with scale or sediment which reduce the efficiency of the cooling system. When this condition occurs or the coolant appears rusty or dark in colour the system should be flushed. In severe cases reverse flushing may be required as described later.

2 With the bottom radiator hose still disconnected and the cylinder block drain plug removed, move the heater control lever to the red position.

3 Insert a hose in the radiator filler neck and allow water to run through the system until it flows from both outlets quite clear in colour. Do not flush a hot engine with cold water.

4 In severe cases of contamination of the coolant, reverse flush the system. To do this, remove the radiator, as described in Section 6, invert it and insert a hose in the bottom water outlet. Continue flushing until clear water comes freely from the top tank.

5 The use of chemical cleaners should only be used as a last resort and the regular renewal of the antifreeze mixture should obviate the need for flushing or other cleaning treatment.

4 Cooling system - filling

1 Reconnect the radiator bottom hose.

2 Tighten the cylinder block drain plug.

3 Place the heater control lever to the red position.

4 Pour coolant (of the specified antifreeze mixture - see next Section)

into the radiator filler neck. Pour slowly and stop when the level reaches 1 in. (25.0 mm) below the base of the filler neck.

5 If after operating the car, the heater fails to warm up, then there is probably an airlock in the system and it must be cleared in the following way.

6 Disconnect the upper end of the hose which runs between the cylinder head and the heater control valve. Make sure that the radiator cap is in position, the heater control set to 'HOT' and the engine off.

7 Hold the hose upright and using a funnel, pour coolant into the hose until it flows from the control valve.

8 Reconnect the hose to the control valve, run the engine and then check and top-up the coolant level in the radiator.

5 Antifreeze mixture

1 The coolant should be renewed every two years not only to maintain the antifreeze properties, but also to prevent corrosion in the system which would otherwise occur as the strength of the inhibitors in the coolant becomes progressively less effective.

2 Before adding antifreeze to the system, check all hose connections and check the tightness of the cylinder head bolts as such solutions are searching. The cooling system should be drained and partly refilled with clean water as previously explained, before adding antifreeze.

3 The quantity of antifreeze which should be used for various levels of protection is given in the table below, expressed as a percentage of the system capacity.

Antifreeze volume	Protection to	Safe pump circulation
25%	$-26^{\circ}C$ $(-15^{\circ}F)$	$-12^{\circ}C$ $(\ 10^{\circ}F)$
30%	$-33^{\circ}C$ $(-28^{\circ}F)$	$-16^{\circ}C$ $(\ \ 3^{\circ}F)$
35%	$-39^{\circ}C$ $(-38^{\circ}F)$	$-20^{\circ}C$ $(-\ 4^{\circ}F)$

4 Where the cooling system contains an antifreeze solution any topping-up should be done with a solution made up in similar proportions to the original in order to avoid dilution.

6 Radiator - removal, inspection, cleaning and refitting

1 Drain the cooling system, as described in Section 2.

2 Disconnect the top hose from the radiator header tank pipe and the overflow tube from the reservoir (if fitted).

3 Disconnect the bottom hose from the radiator outlet pipe.

4 Unscrew and remove the six retaining bolts which secure the radiator to the front engine compartment mounting panel (photo).

5 Lift out the radiator, taking care not to damage the cooling fins. Do not allow antifreeze solution to drop onto the bodywork during removal as damage may result.

6 Radiator repair is best left to a specialist but minor leaks may be tackled with a proprietary product.

7 The radiator matrix may be cleared of flies by brushing with a soft brush or by hosing.

8 Flush the radiator as described in Section 3 according to its degree of contamination. Examine and renew any hoses or clips which have

deteriorated.

9 Installation is a reversal of removal.

7 Radiator pressure cap

1 If escaping pressure can be heard from the top of the radiator or if the coolant level requires constant topping-up, it can be assumed that the pressure cap is at fault, provided of course that there are no other leaks in the system.

2 The radiator cap can be tested at most garages and if it is found to be faulty, replaced with one of similar rating (13.5 to 17.5 lbf/in²).

8 Thermostat - removal, testing and refitting

1 A faulty thermostat can cause overheating or slow engine warm up. It will also affect the performance of the heater.

2 Drain off enough coolant through the radiator drain tap so that the coolant level is below the thermostat housing joint face. A good indication that the correct level has been reached is when the cooling tubes are exposed when viewed through the radiator filler cap.

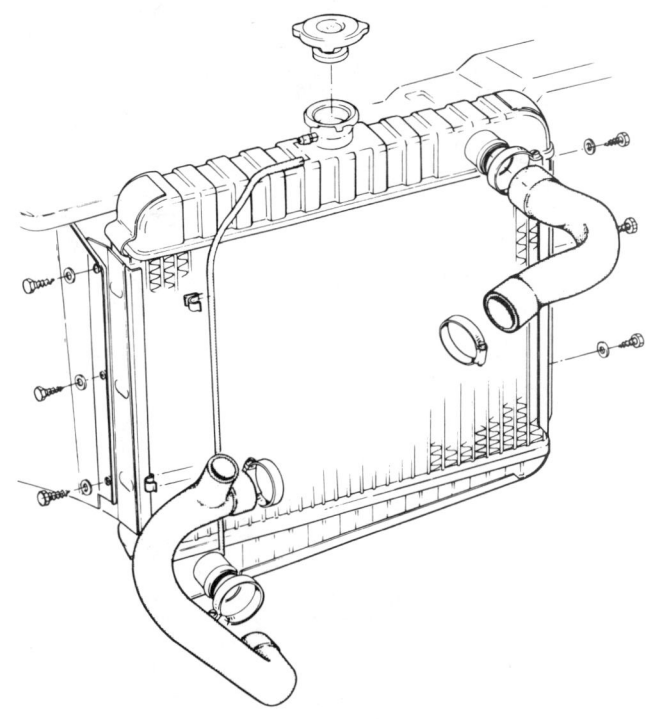

Fig. 2.2. Radiator components (Sec. 6)

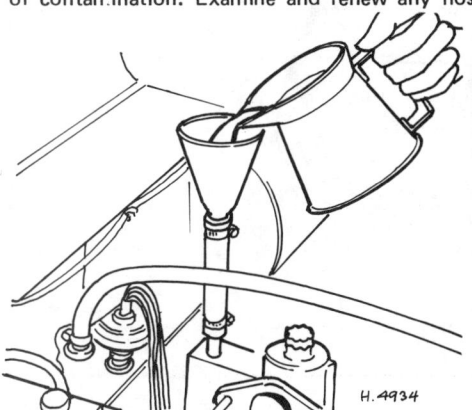

H. 4934

Fig. 2.1. Removing air lock from cooling system (Sec. 4)

6.4 Location of radiator securing bolts (one side)

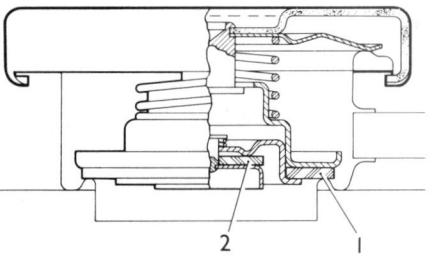

Fig. 2.3. Sectional view of the radiator cap (Sec. 7)

1 *Pressure valve*
2 *Vacuum valve*

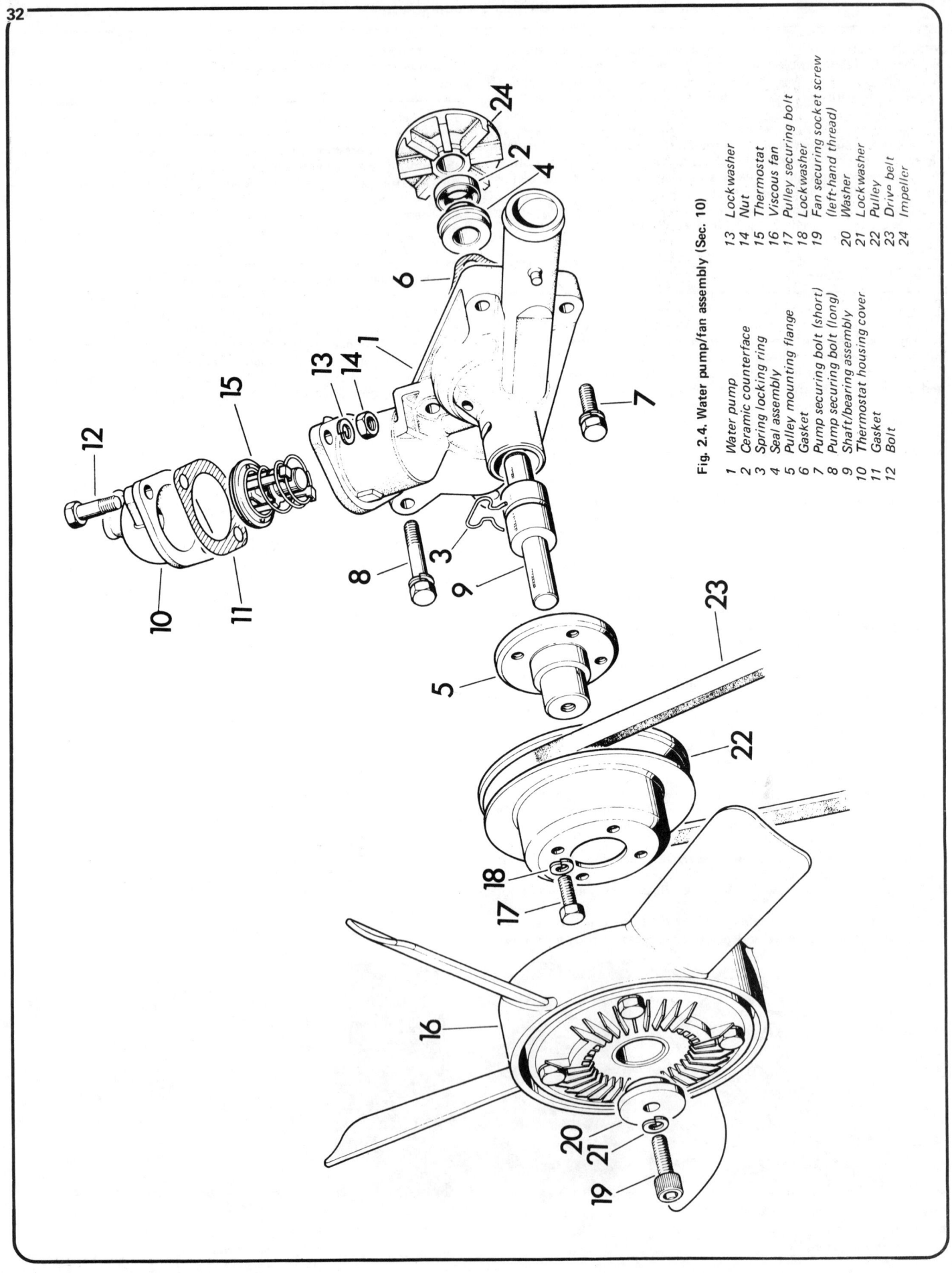

Fig. 2.4. Water pump/fan assembly (Sec. 10)

1 Water pump
2 Ceramic counterface
3 Spring locking ring
4 Seal assembly
5 Pulley mounting flange
6 Gasket
7 Pump securing bolt (short)
8 Pump securing bolt (long)
9 Shaft/bearing assembly
10 Thermostat housing cover
11 Gasket
12 Bolt
13 Lockwasher
14 Nut
15 Thermostat
16 Viscous fan
17 Pulley securing bolt
18 Lockwasher
19 Fan securing socket screw
   (left-hand thread)
20 Washer
21 Lockwasher
22 Pulley
23 Drive belt
24 Impeller

3 Unscrew and remove the two retaining bolts and withdraw the thermostat cover sufficiently to permit the thermostat to be removed from its seat in the cylinder head.

4 To test whether the unit is serviceable, suspend the thermostat by a piece of string in a pan of water being heated. When the water boils, the thermostat valve should open ½ in. (12.5 mm). When the valve has cooled, make sure that it is completely closed.

5 Refitting is a reversal of removal but use a new flange gasket and check that the thermostat jiggle pin is at the highest point once the thermostat is seated in the housing.

9 Water pump - removal and installation

1 Drain the cooling system and disconnect the fanbelt.

2 Disconnect the hoses from the water pump and unbolt and remove the pump/fan assembly as a unit. There is no need to remove the radiator for this operation provided care is taken not to damage the fins (photo).

3 Installation is a reversal of removal but make sure that the mating faces are clean, use a new joint gasket and tighten the securing bolts to the correct torque. Refit and adjust the fanbelt, as described in Section 12.

10 Water pump - overhaul

1 It is recommended that when the pump becomes faulty that it is renewed either with a new component or a reconditioned unit. For those who wish to repair the original assembly, carry out the following operations.

2 Unbolt and remove the viscous fan and drive pulley from the water pump flange. Note that the fan securing screw has a left-hand thread.

3 Using a two-legged puller, withdraw the impeller from the shaft.

4 Extract the seal and ceramic counterface from the pump body.

5 Release the spring locking ring by squeezing it and then press the shaft/bearing assembly, complete with pulley flange, from the pump body.

6 The shaft/bearing assembly is renewed as an assembly. Press it into the pump body so that the shorter end of the shaft enters first and the second groove from the front aligns with the locking groove in the body. Install the spring locking ring.

7 Assemble the seal so that the pips engage with the grooves and install it to the pump body. A little grease may be applied to the outside edge of the seal to facilitate fitting.

8 Install the ceramic counterface so that the rubber face is towards the impeller.

9 The impeller and the pulley flange must be pressed onto the shaft, so that the dimensions shown in Fig. 2.8 are attained.

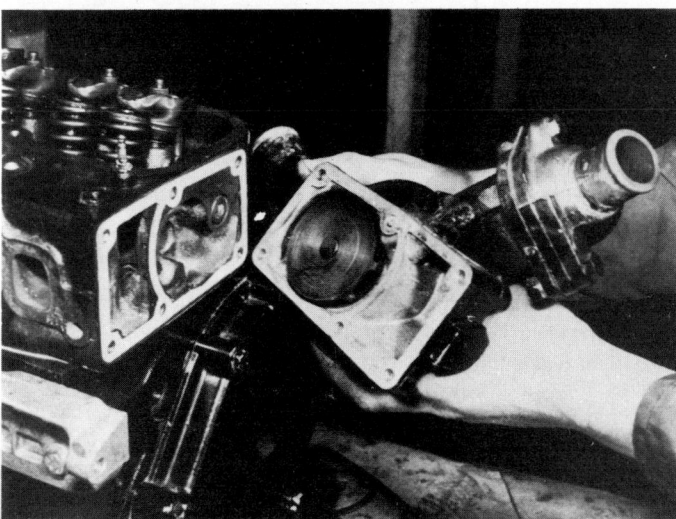

9.2 Removing water pump assembly

11 Fan assembly - testing, removal and refitting

1 This is of viscous type and is a sealed unit. At certain upper engine speeds, the fan 'free-wheels' so saving engine power when the ram effect of cooling air due to the forward motion of the car, is adequate.

2 In the event of overheating, first check the drivebelt tension (see next Section).

3 Any fault which could include excessively cool running or visible oil leaks, will necessitate renewal of the complete fan unit.

4 Removal of the fan unit is best accomplished by first removing the radiator, although by using a short Allen key to loosen the retaining screw it may be possible to remove the fan unit with the radiator in place. Extra care will be needed to avoid damaging the radiator matrix.

Fig. 2.5. Releasing water pump spring locking ring (Sec. 10)

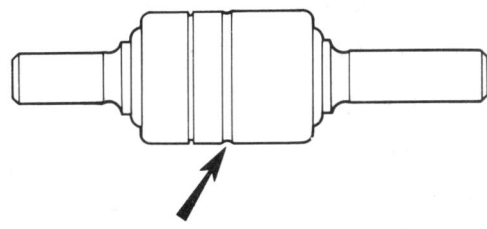

Fig. 2.6. Water pump shaft/bearing locking ring groove (arrowed) (Sec. 10)

Fig. 2.7. The two sections of the water pump seal (Sec. 10)

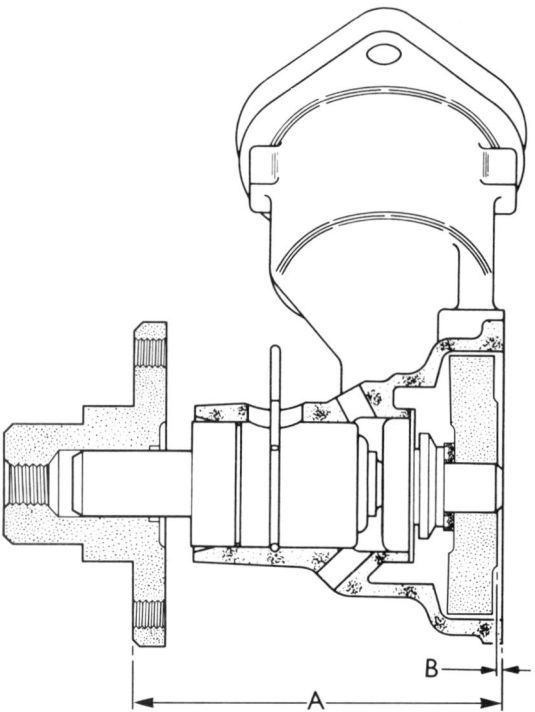

Fig. 2.8. Sectional view of the water pump showing setting of pulley mounting flange and impeller (Sec. 10)

A = 3.46 in. (88.0 mm)   *B = 0.044 to 0.046 in. (1.12 to 1.17 mm)*

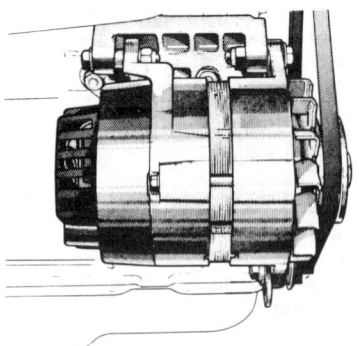

Fig. 2.9. Alternator mounting and adjustment bolts (Sec. 12)

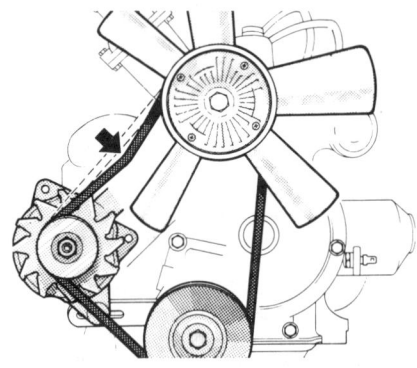

Fig. 2.10. Point at which to test drivebelt deflection (Sec. 12)

12 Fanbelt - renewal and adjustment

1   To renew the drivebelt, slacken the alternator mounting bolts and the adjustment strap bolts.
2   Push the alternator in towards the engine and then slip the belt from the alternator pulley, finally withdrawing it from the crankshaft and fan pulleys.
3   Installation is a reversal of removal.
4   Whenever a belt is fitted or at regular intervals (see Routine Maintenance Section), adjust the belt in the following way. Pull the alternator away from the engine until the slack is taken out of the belt. Tighten (but do not fully tighten) the bolts in the following sequence: (i) front mounting, (ii) adjustment strap bolt, (iii) rear mounting.
5   Test the belt deflection (0.28 in/7.0 mm) with the thumb as shown (Fig. 2.10). If necessary adjust the position of the alternator on its mountings until the tension is correct and then fully tighten the alternator bolts in the sequence previously described and finally tighten the bolt which secures the adjustment strap to the engine.
6   If a lever is being used to move the alternator away from the engine, always make sure that the bolts are released first and that the lever is **applied only to the alternator drive end shield.**

13 Fault diagnosis - cooling system

Symptom	Reason
Overheating	Low coolant level
	Faulty radiator pressure cap
	Thermostat stuck shut
	Drive belt slipping or incorrectly tensioned
	Clogged radiator matrix
	Incorrect engine timing
	Corroded system
Cool running	Incorrect type thermostat
	Faulty fan viscous coupling
Slow warm up	Thermostat stuck open
Coolant loss	Faulty radiator pressure cap
	Split hose
	Leaking water pump to block joint
	Leaking core plug
	Blown cylinder head gasket

Chapter 3 Fuel system

For modifications, and information applicable to later models, see Supplement at end of manual

Contents

Specifications

Fuel pump ... ... Mechanical

Pressure ... ... 2½ to 3½ lb/sq. in

Carburettor
Type	Stromberg 150CD—SEV
Identification:	
Standard compression engine	3696B
Low compression engine	3698
Metering needle	BIDV
Jet orifice	2.54 mm
Fast idle cam	M2
Inlet needle valve	1.5 mm
Inlet valve washer (thickness)	1.6 mm
Idling speed	800 to 850 rev/min

Fuel tank
Capacity	8.4 Imp gal (38 litres)
Fuel octane rating:	
Standard compression engine	97
Low compression engine	90

Torque wrench settings
	lb ft	Nm
Fuel pump bolts	20	28
Inlet manifold bolts	25	35
Exhaust manifold bolts	28	39
Carburettor flange bolts	24	33

1 General description

The fuel system comprises a rear mounted fuel tank (located below the load carrying compartment right-hand floor panel), a camshaft-operated fuel pump and a Stromberg carburettor.

The air cleaner is of temperature-controlled type and incorporates a disposable paper element.

2 Air cleaner - description and testing

1 The air cleaner comprises three major components: (i) a temperature sensing unit, (ii) a vacuum capsule, (iii) an exhaust manifold shroud.

2 Cold air is drawn into the air cleaner at engine compartment temperature while hot air is drawn through a flexible hose from the exhaust manifold shroud, which is secured by four bolts.

3 The vacuum capsule is connected to a control damper assembly

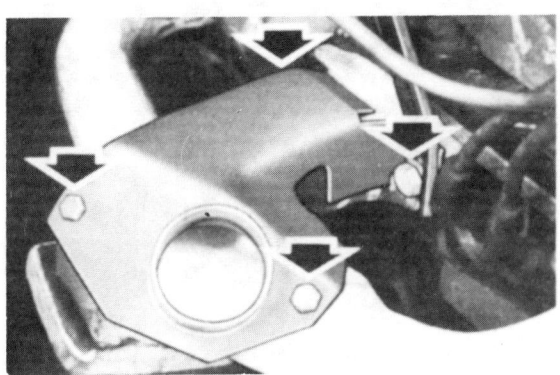

Fig. 3.1. Exhaust manifold shroud securing bolts (Sec. 2)

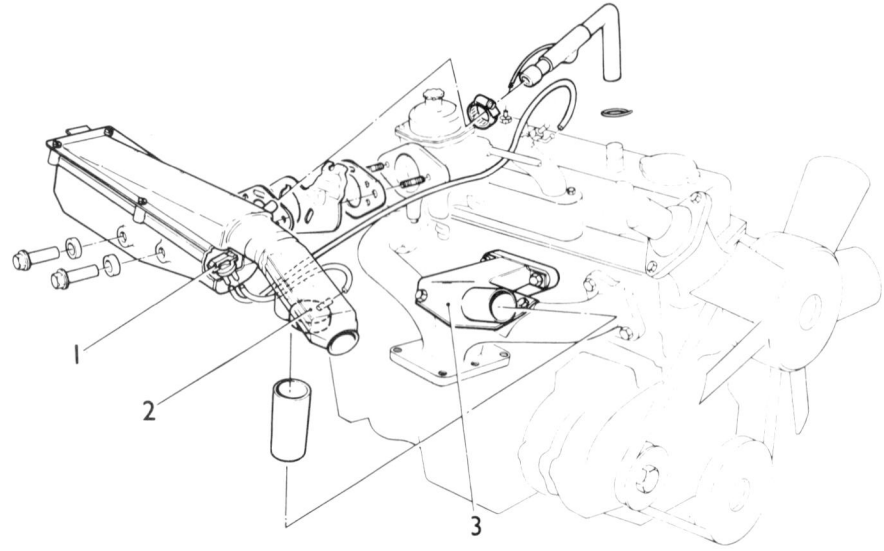

Fig. 3.2. Air cleaner assembly (Sec. 2)

1   Temperature sensor   2   Vacuum capsule   3   Exhaust manifold shroud

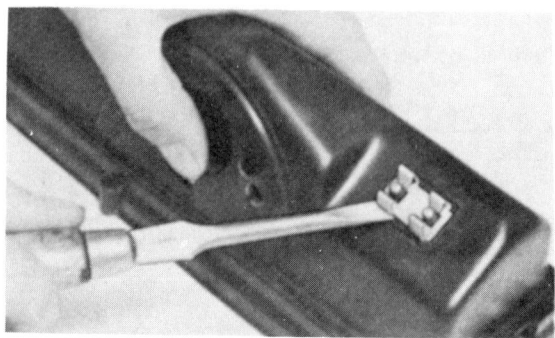

Fig. 3.3. Levering off the air cleaner sensor unit (Sec. 2)

Fig. 3.5. Fuel pump components (Sec. 4)

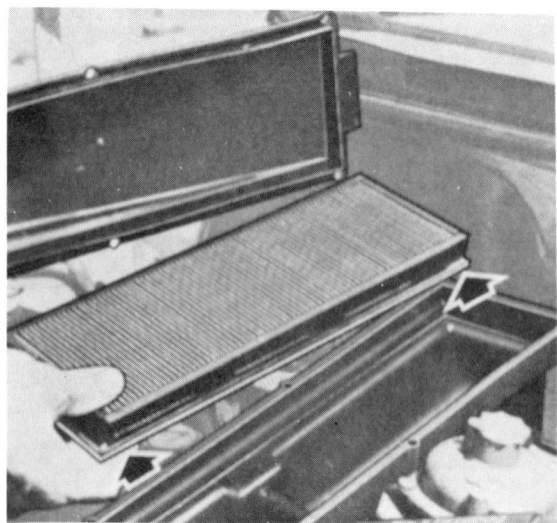

Fig. 3.4. Installing the air filter element (Sec. 3)

5.3 Removing the fuel pump

which regulates the intake of hot and cold air to provide air of even and optimum temperature for the carburettor.

4   When the engine is running, the degree of vacuum in the capsule is dependent upon the temperature sensor unit. This is of bi-metal spring construction and opens to bleed air into the vacuum line (which runs from the intake manifold to the vacuum capsule) whenever the temperature within the air cleaner rises above 104°F (40°C).

5   When starting a cold engine, the cold air port will be closed until air drawn from the exhaust shroud is warm enough to actuate the sensor unit.

6   A fault in the operation of one or more of the components of the air cleaner may not be apparent in warm weather, but in colder conditions, surging, flat spots or stalling and a general tendency to weakness may be noticed.

7   To check the operation of the air cleaner, use a mirror to view the attitude of the damper through the air cleaner intake spout. If the engine is cold (below 90°F/33°C) the cold air intake port will be seen to be closed. If the engine and air cleaner temperatures are above this level, the cold air port will be open. If there is any deviation from the correct damper positions, check the linkage for binding and the connecting hoses for security and then test the operation of the sensor unit. To do this, have the engine cold, remove the air cleaner cover and install a thermometer adjacent to the sensor unit using a piece of adhesive tape. Replace the cover. Start the engine and as soon as the damper is seen to open the cold air port, remove the air cleaner cover and read the thermometer. This should indicate between 90 and 115°F (33 and 47°C). If the damper does not open within this range, renew the sensor unit by levering off its retaining clip.

3   Air cleaner element - renewal

1   Every 12000 miles (19000 km) the air cleaner element should be renewed. Earlier renewal may be required if the car is operated in very dusty conditions.

2   Disconnect the crankcase breather hose from the air cleaner.

3   Disconnect the flexible hot air intake pipe from the air cleaner.

4   Disconnect the hose from the vacuum capsule which is located on the underside of the air cleaner.

5   Remove the top cover after unscrewing the six securing screws.

6   Lift out the element and discard it. Clean the interior of the air cleaner body.

7   Installation of the new element is a reversal of removal, but make sure that the rubber sealing ring of the element is at the bottom.

4   Fuel pump - description, testing and cleaning

1   The fuel pump is located on the left-hand side of the crankcase and it is operated by a rocker arm which is in contact with an eccentric on the camshaft.

2   The pump is of sealed construction and apart from cleaning the filter screen at recommended intervals, no dismantling is possible and in the event of a fault developing, the pump must be renewed complete.

3   To test the operation of the pump, disconnect the fuel pipe from the carburettor. Spin the engine on the starter (having first disconnected the LT lead from the coil to prevent the engine firing) and observe whether well defined spurts of fuel are ejected from the open end of the pipe. If they are, then the pump is operating correctly.

4   To clean the filter, first disconnect the fuel inlet pipe from the pump and plug the pipe to prevent loss of fuel. It is recommended that the level of fuel in the tank is kept as low as possible, before commencing this servicing operation.

5   Unscrew the pump cover centre screw and lift away the cover, sealing ring and gauze filter.

6   Brush any dirt from the gauze and pump interior and reassemble. On some pumps, the filter gauze incorporates four pegs. These must face towards the top cover. **Do not overtighten the cover centre screw.**

5   Fuel pump - removal and installation

1   Disconnect the fuel inlet pipe and plug it to prevent loss of fuel.

2   Disconnect the fuel outlet pipe from the pump.

3   Unscrew and remove the two pump securing bolts and lift the pump from the crankcase (photo).

4   Installation is a reversal of removal, but use new sealing gaskets on the flange and replace any insulator which was originally fitted. Make sure that the rocker arm goes above the camshaft eccentric before installing the securing bolts and tightening to the specified torque.

6   Fuel tank - removal, servicing and installation

1   Remove the left-hand side panel from the load carrying area. This is secured by five press studs and a lever will have to be inserted between the trim and body panels to release them.

2   Remove the right-hand trim panel in a similar manner and then extract the upper securing screw from the fuel tank filler pipe protective shroud.

3   Remove the floor panels, noting that the filler pipe shroud is integral with the right-hand panel.

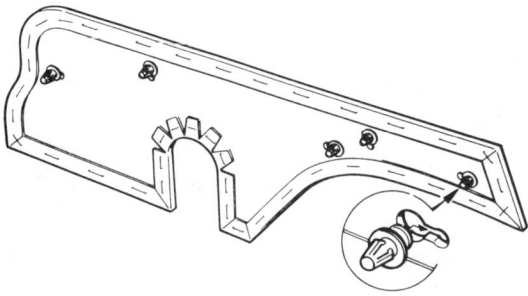

Fig. 3.6. Body interior trim panel clips (Sec. 6)

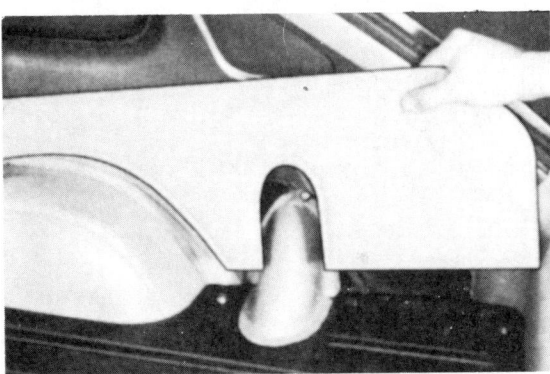

Fig. 3.7. Removing right-hand interior trim panel (Sec. 6)

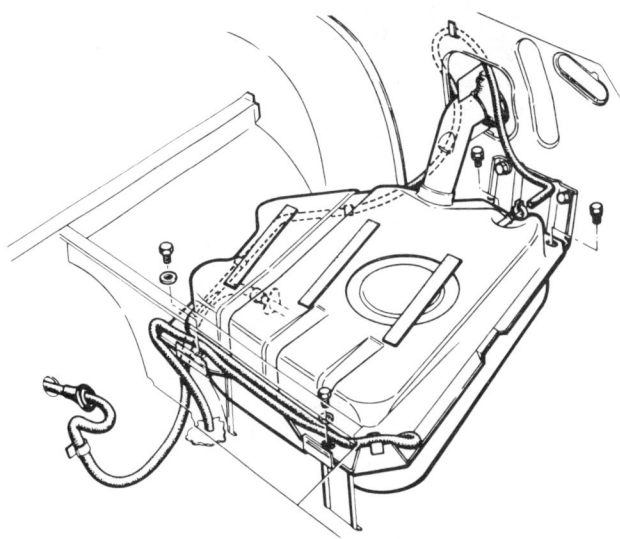

Fig. 3.8. The fuel tank and connections (Sec. 6)

4 Disconnect the fuel outlet pipe (no drain plug is fitted) and let the fuel in the tank drain into a suitable container.
5 Disconnect the fuel tank vent pipe.
6 Disconnect the lead from the fuel level transmitter unit.
7 Unscrew and remove the four tank securing bolts and lift the tank from its location, at the same time manipulating the filler pipe through its body sealing grommet.

8 A leak in a fuel tank should be repaired by specialists or a new tank fitted. **Never be tempted to solder or weld a leaking fuel tank.**
9 If the tank is contaminated with sediment or water, it can be swilled out using several changes of fuel, but if any vigorous shaking is required to dislodge accumulations of dirt, then the tank transmitter unit should first be removed, as described in the next Section.
10 Installation of the fuel tank is a reversal of removal.

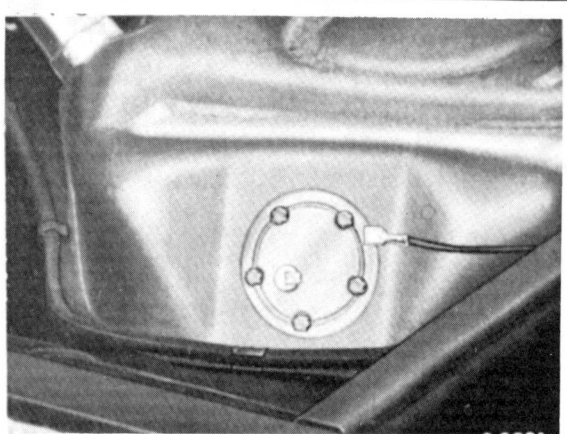

Fig. 3.9. Fuel tank transmitter unit correctly installed (Sec. 7)

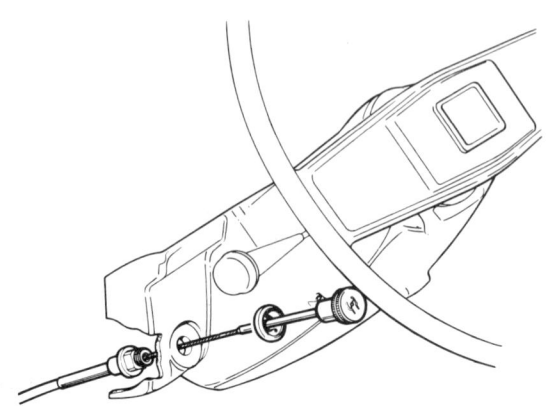

Fig. 3.10. Choke control attachment to steering column shroud (Sec. 8)

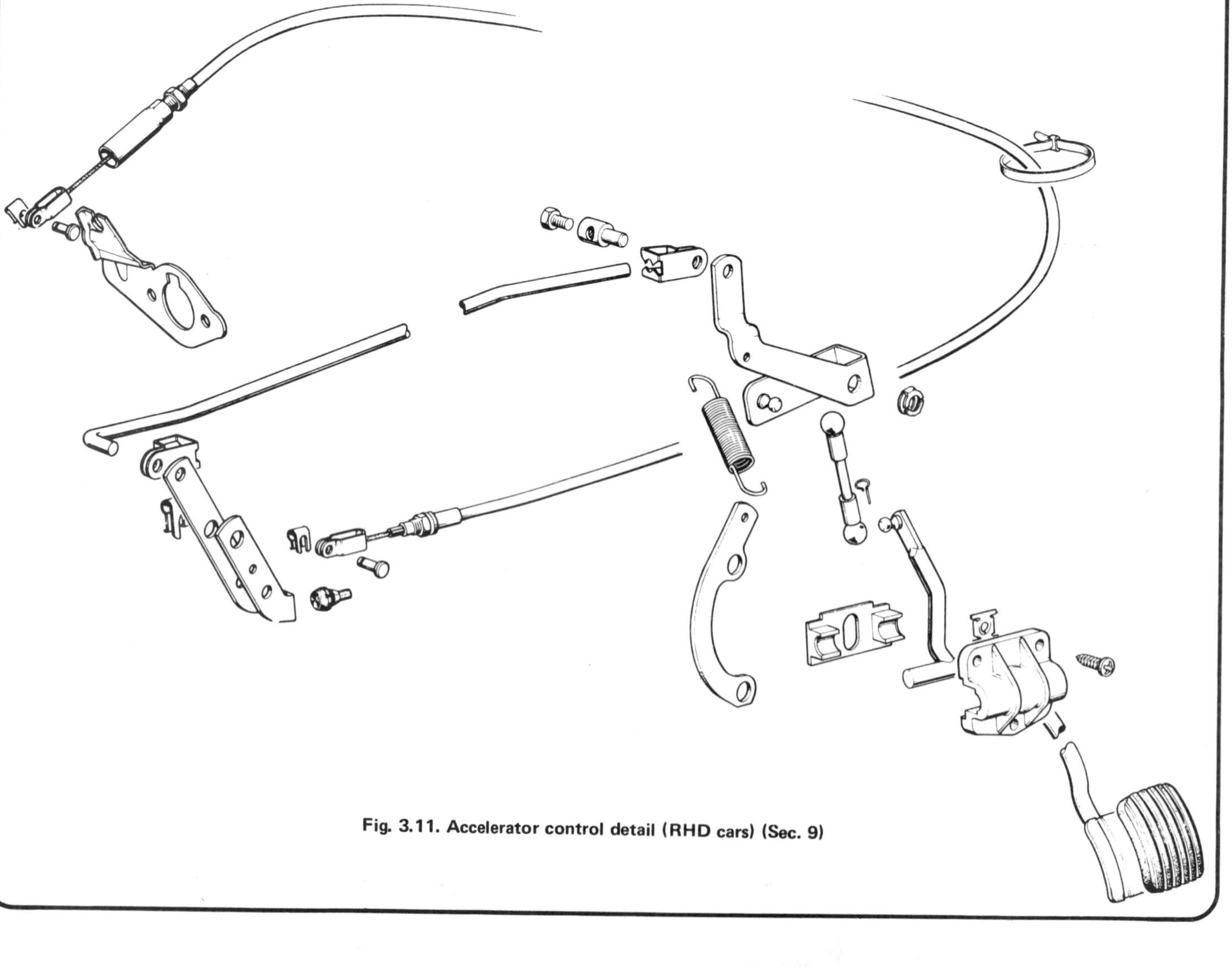

Fig. 3.11. Accelerator control detail (RHD cars) (Sec. 9)

7 Fuel tank transmitter unit - removal and installation

1 Carry out the operations given in paragraphs 1 to 6 of the preceding Section.

2 Unscrew and remove the five securing bolts and withdraw the unit carefully, so that the float mechanism is not damaged.

3 Installation is a reversal of removal, but always use a new flange gasket which has been smeared on both sides with jointing compound. Also apply jointing compound to the threads of the securing bolts. It is essential that when installed, the terminal on the transmitter is horizontal and pointing towards the left-hand side of the car.

8 Choke control cable - removal and refitting

1 The choke control inner cable and knob can be withdrawn completely after disconnecting the cable from the carburettor choke operating lever.

2 Should the outer cable have to be removed, the locking ring which secures it to the lower half of the steering column shroud will have to be unscrewed. For this, a pair of thin round-nosed pliers can be used to engage in the two holes in the locking ring.

3 Refitting is a reversal of removal but before connecting the inner cable to the carburettor, check that the choke valve plate is fully open and then depress the choke knob fully and then withdraw it about 1/8 in. (3.2 mm). This will provide just enough slack to ensure that the choke remains fully off even under extreme engine movement on its flexible mountings.

9 Accelerator control - dismantling and adjustment

1 The pendant type accelerator pedal is secured to the fascia panel by three screws. After removal of these screws, the composite rod and cable assembly can be dismantled for renewal of any worn component.

2 After reassembly, or if the cable has stretched and pedal free-movement has become excessive, carry out the following adjustment procedure.

3 Disconnect one end of the linkage rod which runs between the pedal and the cable relay levers.

4 Position the lever '1' against the rubber stop '2' (Fig. 3.13). With the carburettor throttle lever in the fully closed position, rotate the cable locknuts until all slack is removed from the cable and then back off the upper nut 1½ turns and lock it in this position to the support bracket with the lower nut.

5 *On right-hand drive cars:* Jam the throttle lever on the carburettor in the fully open position. Slacken the clamp bolt '1' (Fig. 3.15) and with the accelerator pedal held 0.40 in. (10.0 mm) from the toe board, retighten the clamp bolt.

6 *On left-hand drive cars:* Jam the throttle lever on the carburettor in the fully open position. Detach the clip '1' from the swivel '3' and then remove the swivel from the pedal lever '2' (Fig. 3.17). Hold the pedal 0.20 in. (5.0 mm) from the toe board and then screw the swivel up or down the threaded rod until the swivel is in perfect alignment with the hole in the pedal lever. Refit the clip.

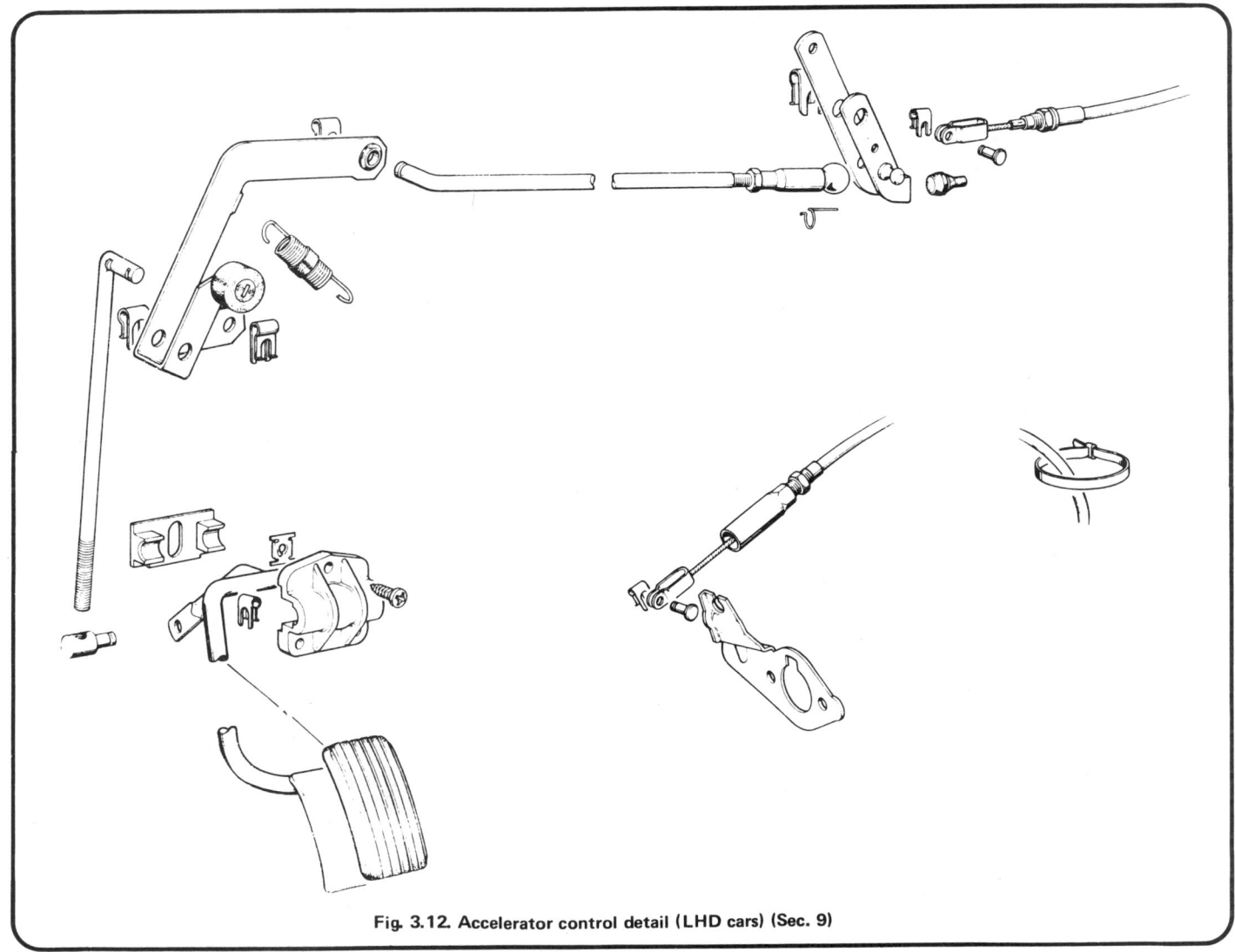

Fig. 3.12. Accelerator control detail (LHD cars) (Sec. 9)

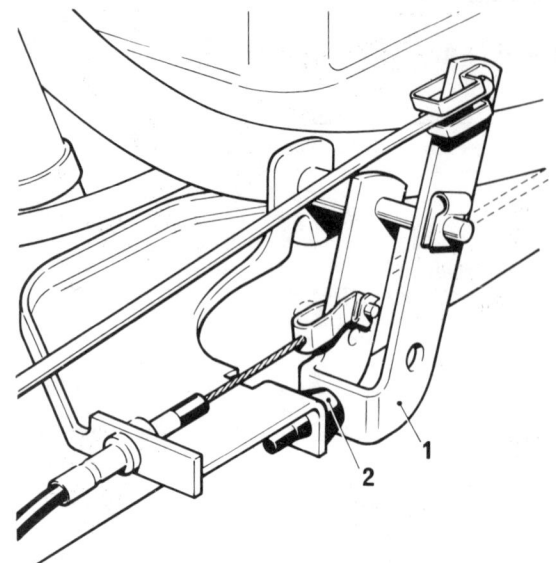

Fig. 3.13. Throttle cable detail (1) cable relay lever (2) rubber stop (Sec. 9)

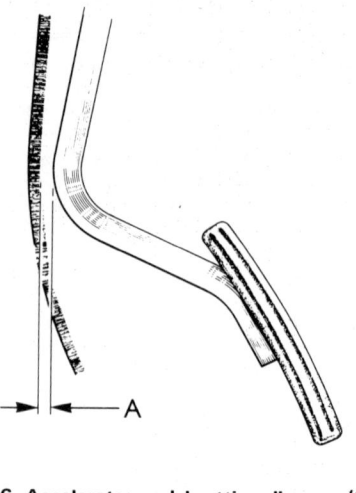

Fig. 3.16. Accelerator pedal setting diagram (Sec. 9)

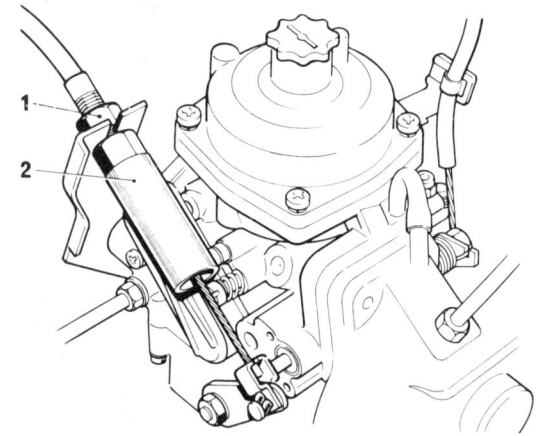

Fig. 3.14. Throttle cable adjuster and locknuts (1 and 2) (Sec. 9)

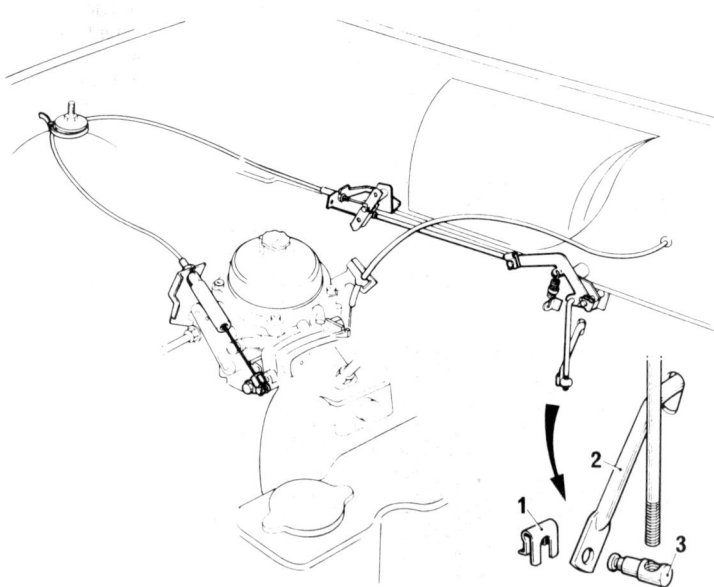

Fig. 3.17. Accelerator clip (1) pedal lever (2) and swivel (3) (LHD cars) (Sec. 9)

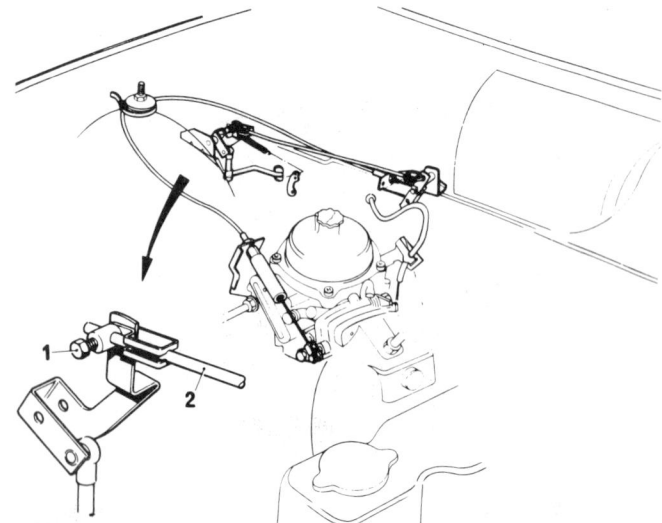

Fig. 3.15. Accelerator rod clamp bolt (1) and position rod (2) (RHD cars) (Sec. 9)

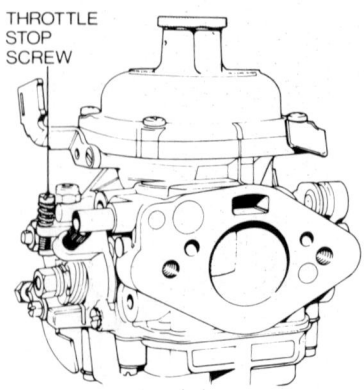

Fig. 3.18. Location of throttle stop screw (Sec. 11)

10 Carburettor - general description

1 The carburettor is a Stromberg 150CD-SEV, constant vacuum type and incorporates a variable jet which is controlled by an air valve piston and metering needle. The latter is spring-loaded against one side of the jet, to ensure a consistent fuel flow.

2 The carburettor has a manually-operated disc type cold starting device.

3 A temperature compensator is incorporated to offset variations in mixture strength caused by heat transfer from the engine to the carburettor body.

4 The carburettor is pre-set and any adjustment should be restricted to the idle bleed trimming screw (see Section 11). Only if the carburettor has been dismantled and reassembled, will re-setting of the jet adjuster be required, as described in Section 16.

11 Carburettor - idling speed adjustment

1 The throttle stop screw should be adjusted until the engine idling speed is between 800 and 850 rpm. Obviously, this can only be accurately set by connecting a tachometer to the engine, but normally this can be judged fairly well. Do not permit too low an idling speed.

2 On new cars, the idle trim screw is unscrewed slightly to provide a slightly weak mixture. Should the idling become uneven, turn the trim screw gently clockwise. **On no account screw it hard into its seat.**

3 The foregoing is the limit of adjustment operations. Where it is not possible to achieve smooth idling, look for air leaks in the inlet manifold gasket, the vacuum pipes and crankcase breather hose.

12 Carburettor - fast idle and cold start setting

1 When the choke control knob is fully withdrawn, the fast idle cam on the carburettor will rotate and open the throttle lever to a faster than normal setting.

2 In order that the fast idle speed is as specified, the stop screw should be adjusted (with the choke fully off) so that dimension 'A' is 0.10 in. (2.5 mm) as shown in Fig. 3.20.

3 A spring-loaded pin is provided to ensure that the cold start mixture is correct for various climatic conditions. Where the temperature is above 0°F (−18°C) the pin should be set at right-angles to the groove '3' (Fig. 3.21). Where the temperature is below this level, set the pin in its groove. To turn the pin, first depress it against the pressure of its spring.

13 Carburettor damper - maintaining oil level

1 Every 6000 miles (9600 km), unscrew and remove the hydraulic damper from the top of the carburettor.

2 Remove the air cleaner element (Section 3) and raise the carburettor air valve piston by inserting a finger into the air intake.

3 Check the level of the oil in the hollow guide rod and top-up if necessary with 10W/30 engine oil until the level is 0.30 in. (8.0 mm) below the top of the guide rod.

4 Reassemble by reversing the order of removal but make sure that the small collar on the damper rod enters the hollow guide rod before screwing the damper cap down.

14 Carburettor vent valve - adjustment

1 Fumes from the carburettor float chamber are vented internally to the air cleaner at engine speeds above fast idle. At lower speeds, the extraction of fumes direct to atmosphere is controlled by a ventilator valve.

2 To check the correct setting of the valve, adjust the stop screw '1' (Fig. 3.23) until a 2 mm twist drill can be inserted between the valve lever and the stop screw post. Note that the stop screw is an interference fit in the carburettor body, and extreme care should be taken when making an adjustment to avoid breaking it.

3 If this adjustment is necessary, the throttle stop screw will also need re-adjustment to maintain the specified idling speed.

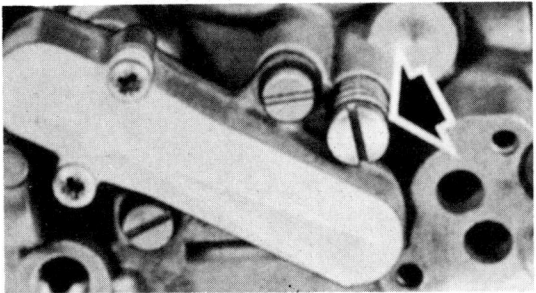

Fig. 3.19. Carburettor idle trim screw (arrowed) (Sec. 11)

This screw is not fitted to later models

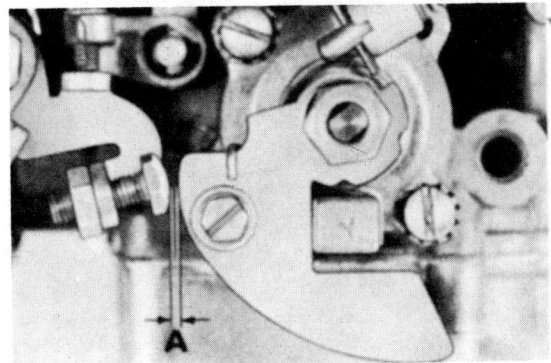

Fig. 3.20. Fast idle setting diagram (Sec. 12)

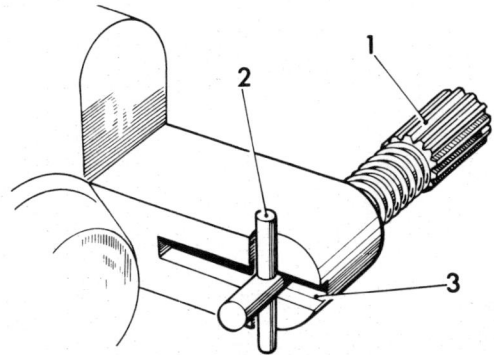

Fig. 3.21. Cold start device (Sec. 12)

1   Spring-loaded stop   2   Pin   3   Groove

Fig. 3.22. Refitting damper to carburettor (Sec. 13)

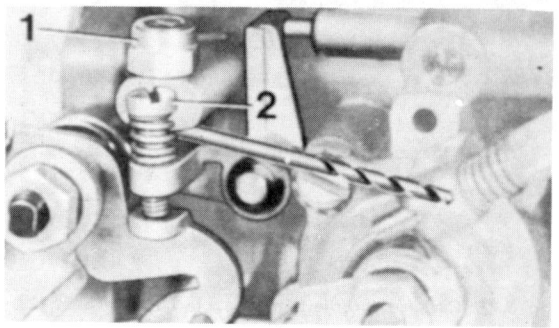

Fig. 3.23. Float chamber vent valve setting (Sec. 14)

1   Stop screw   *2   Throttle stop screw*

15 Carburettor - removal and installation

1   Remove the air cleaner cover and element, as described in Section 3.
2   Unbolt and remove the air cleaner body from the carburettor air intake flange.
3   Disconnect the fuel inlet pipe from the carburettor.
4   Disconnect the distributor vacuum pipe from the carburettor.
5   Disconnect the choke and accelerator controls from the carburettor.
6   Unbolt the carburettor from the inlet manifold and withdraw it.
7   Installation is a reversal of removal, but always use new flange gaskets.

16 Carburettor - dismantling and reassembly

1   Clean the exterior of the carburettor before dismantling.

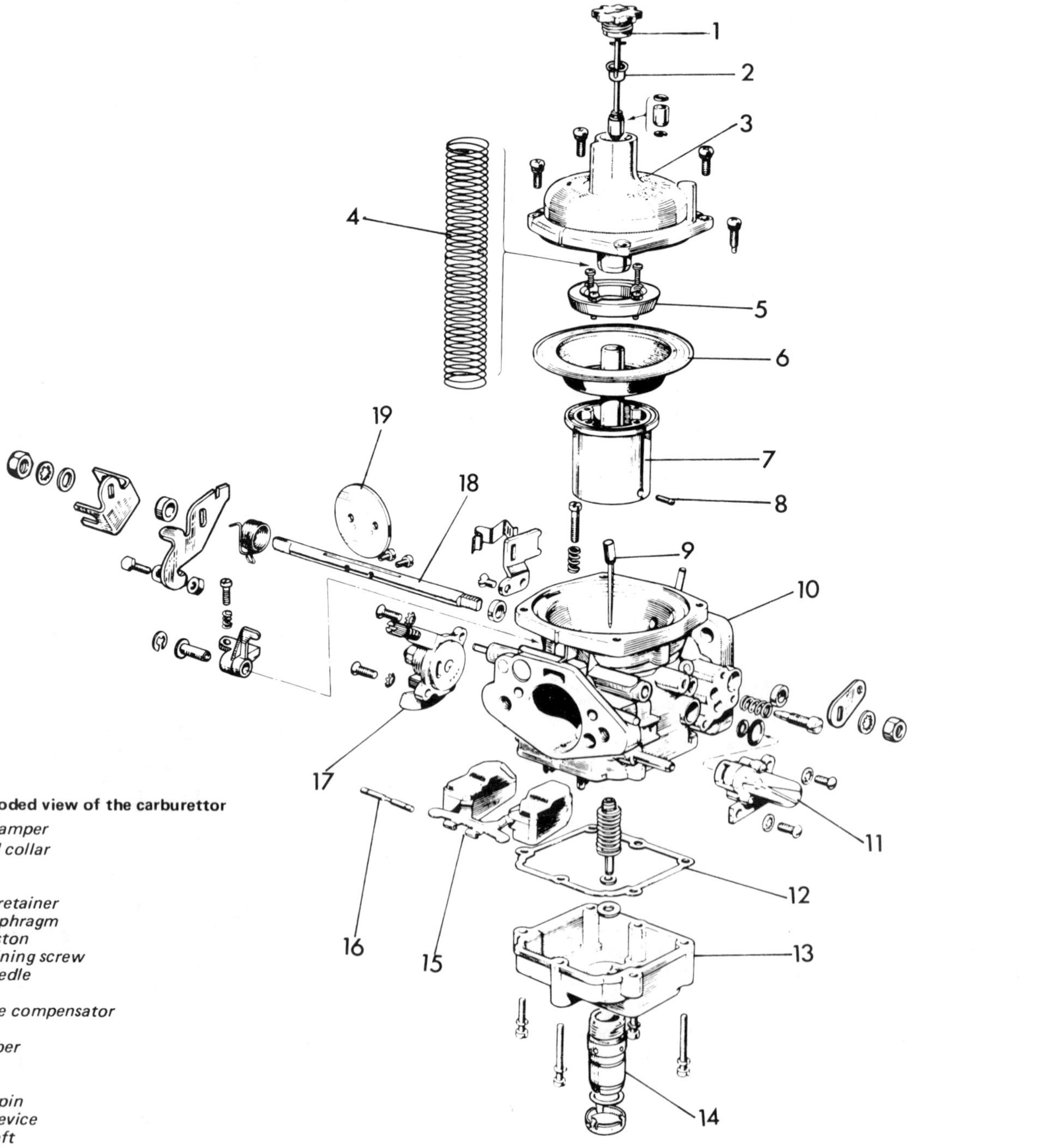

Fig. 3.24. Exploded view of the carburettor

1   Hydraulic damper
2   Damper rod collar
3   Cover
4   Spring
5   Diaphragm retainer
6   Flexible diaphragm
7   Air valve piston
8   Needle retaining screw
9   Metering needle
10 Body
11 Temperature compensator
12 Gasket
13 Float chamber
14 Jet adjuster
15 Floats
16 Float pivot pin
17 Cold start device
18 Throttle shaft
19 Throttle valve plate

2   The carburettor will normally only require dismantling to renew a split diaphragm or to check and adjust the float level. Dismantling the throttle valve plate or shaft or the choke mechanism is not recommended and if these components are worn it will be preferable to purchase a new or rebuilt unit.

3   Withdraw the hydraulic damper.

4   Unscrew the four cover securing screws and remove the cover.

5   Extract the spring, the air valve piston/diaphragm assembly, complete with metering needle.

6   If the diaphragm is to be renewed, unscrew and remove the retaining ring.

7   To remove the float chamber, pull off the jet cap and unscrew and remove the six securing screws. Pull the float chamber from the carburettor body. If it is stuck tight, rotate the jet adjuster slightly, having first made sure that the relative positions of float chamber and jet adjuster have been marked in manufacture, otherwise do so now. On no account attempt to remove the nylon plug from the centre of the jet adjuster.

8   Extract the float pivot, remove the twin floats and then unscrew the inlet needle valve, noting the integral filter.

9   If essential, the metering needle can be detached from the air valve piston after releasing the grub screw.

10 Clean all components and renew any that are worn. Obtain new gaskets, seals etc. as necessary or in the form of a repair kit.

11 Screw in the needle valve ensuring that the original washer is fitted or one of equivalent thickness.

12 Refit the float and then check the float level. To do this, invert the carburettor and with the weight of the floats on the needle valve, measure the dimension 'A' (Fig. 3.28) which is between the highest point of the float and the flange (gasket removed) of the carburettor body. If this dimension (0.63 to 0.67 in./16.0 to 17.0 mm) varies, bend the tag which contacts the end of the needle valve.

13 If the jet assembly has been removed and dismantled, reassemble it and screw it into position making sure that the washers and 'O' rings are correctly located.

14 Screw the jet adjuster fully into the carburettor body, install a new float chamber gasket and the float chamber itself.

15 If the metering needle has been removed from the air valve piston, reassemble it so that the nylon washer is flush with the face of the air valve piston.

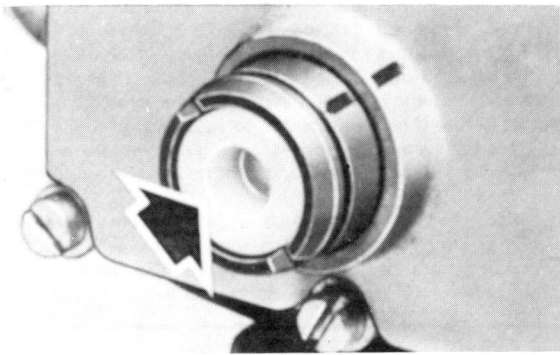

Fig. 3.25. Jet adjuster (cap removed) (Sec. 16

Fig. 3.26. Fuel inlet needle valve (Sec. 16)

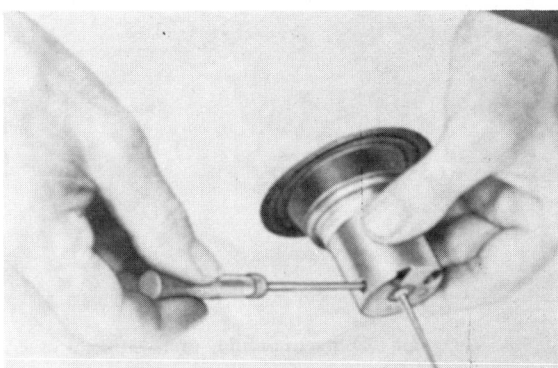

Fig. 3.27. Releasing metering needle retaining screw (Sec. 16)

Fig. 3.28. Float setting diagram (Sec. 16)

Fig. 3.29. Components of the jet assembly. Nylon washer (arrowed) (Sec. 16)

Fig. 3.30. Setting metering needle in air valve piston (Sec. 16)

16 Make sure that the grub screw is not overtightened and that it impinges on the flat that is ground on the side of the needle casing, otherwise the needle will not be biased away from the depression holes in the face of the air valve piston. The metering needle calibration number is visible if the needle is pulled gently from its casing.

17 To install the new diaphragm, engage the tongue on the diaphragm lower face with the slot in the air valve piston rim. Fit the diaphragm retaining ring.

18 Insert the air valve/diaphragm assembly, taking great care not to damage the metering needle as it enters the jet. Engage the tongue on the upper edge of the diaphragm in the slot in the carburettor body.

19 Install the cover so that the projection on the hydraulic damper housing is towards the air cleaner mounting flange.

20 Install the carburettor to the engine and top-up the damper, as described in Section 13.

21 It will be remembered that the jet adjuster has been screwed fully in to facilitate installation of the float chamber. Before the engine is started, it must be unscrewed two complete turns using a 'C' spanner or other suitable tool (some early models may be fitted with a serrated adjusting nut).

22 Start the engine (this will take a little longer than usual as the float chamber is empty) and run until normal operating temperature is reached.

23 Check all the adjustments given in Sections 11, 12 and 14 and then check the mixture quality by lifting the air valve piston 0.04 in. (1.0 mm) using a thin screwdriver inserted into the carburettor air intake. With the engine idling, the action of lifting the air valve piston will produce one of the following reactions:

(i)   Engine speed rises momentarily and then resumes normal idling - mixture correct.
(ii)   Engine speed rises and remains at this higher level before returning to idling - mixture rich.
(iii)   Engine speed drops or engine speed stalls - mixture weak.

With condition (ii), to weaken the mixture turn the adjuster jet anti-clockwise when viewed from above (ie upwards into the carburettor). Then repeat the test.

With condition (iii), to enrich the mixture turn the adjuster jet clockwise when viewed from above (ie downwards out from the carburettor). Then repeat the test. Do not turn the adjuster jet more than ¼ turn at a time between tests.

24 It is emphasised that the foregoing procedure is not precise and a CO meter should be employed to accurately set the position of the jet adjuster. If necessary, the idle trim screw can be unscrewed (not more than four complete turns) to attain the necessary exhaust emission levels (2.5 to 3.5%).

17 Manifolds and exhaust system - general

1 The intake manifold is bolted to the top face of the cylinder head. Always use new gaskets when installing and tighten the securing bolts to the specified torque (photo).

2 The exhaust manifold is mounted on the right-hand side face of the cylinder head (photo).

3 To facilitate connection of the twin exhaust downpipes to the manifold, insert the bolts '1' and '2' (Fig. 3.35) through the gasket and screw them two or three turns into the flange. Now hook the slotted side of the exhaust pipe flange over these bolts. The downpipes will now be supported while the remaining bolts are screwed in. Tighten the centre bolts before the outer ones, all to specified torque.

4 The exhaust system comprises a twin downpipe, a resonator, a silencer section and a tailpipe and second resonator. The system is supported on rubber rings.

5 Examination of the exhaust pipe and silencers at regular intervals is worthwhile as small defects may be repairable when, if left they will almost certainly require renewal of one of the sections of the system. Also, any leaks, apart from the noise factor, may cause poisonous

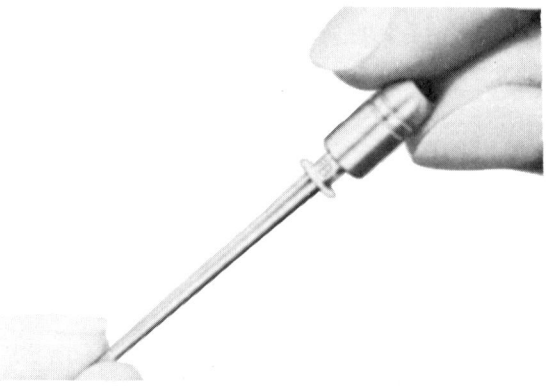

Fig. 3.31. Metering needle identification mark (Sec. 16)

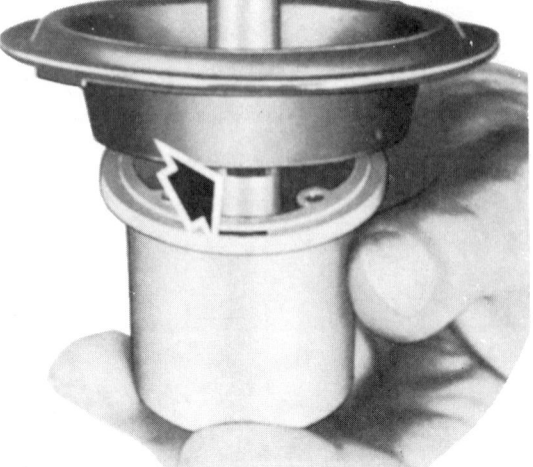

Fig. 3.32. Installing diaphragm to air valve piston (Sec. 16)

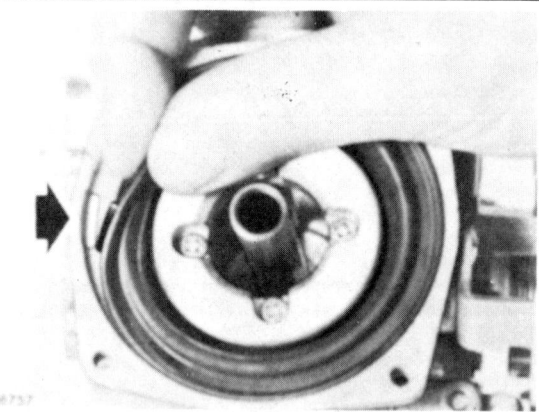

Fig. 3.33. Installing diaphragm to body of carburettor (Sec. 16)

Fig. 3.34. Tool engagement holes for rotating jet adjuster (Sec. 16)

17.1 Installing intake manifolds complete with carburettor

17.2 The exhaust manifold

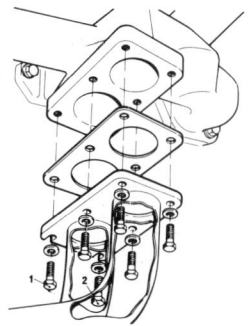

Fig. 3.35. Exhaust manifold to downpipe attachment (1 and 2) bolts for flange slots (Sec. 17)

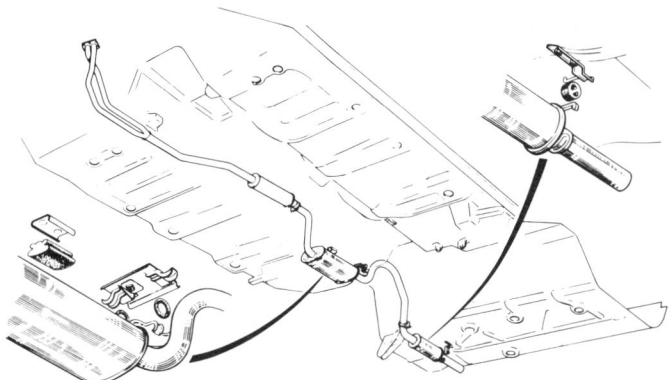

Fig. 3.36. The exhaust system (Sec. 17)

exhaust gases to get inside the car which can be unpleasant, to say the least, even in mild concentrations. Prolonged inhalation could cause sickness and giddiness.

6   As the sleeve connections and clamps are usually very difficult to separate, it is quicker and easier in the long run to remove the complete system from the car when renewing a section. It can be expensive if another section is damaged when trying to separate a bad section from it.

7   Refitting should be carried out after connecting the two sections together. De-burr and grease the connecting socket and make sure that

the clamp is in good condition and slipped over the front pipe but do not tighten it at this stage.

8   Connect the system to the manifold and connect the rear support strap. Now adjust the attitude of the silencer so that the tension on the two rubber support rings will be equalized when fitted.

9   Tighten all pipe clamps and check that there is a minimum clearance of 0.7 in. (18.0 mm) between the exhaust system and the floor panel to prevent overheating of the panel. If the clearance is less than specified, bend the ring support hooks on the underside of the floor panels.

18 Fault diagnosis - fuel system and carburation

Symptom	Reason
Excessive fuel consumption*	Air filter choked
	Leaks in fuel tank, carburettor or fuel lines
	Fuel level in float chamber too high
	Mixture too rich
	Incorrect valve clearances
	Dragging brakes
	Tyres underinflated

May also be caused by a faulty condenser or counterweights in the ignition distributor

Insufficient fuel delivery or weak mixture	Stuck carburettor inlet needle valve
	Faulty fuel pump
	Leaking fuel pipe unions
	Leaking inlet manifold gasket
	Leaking carburettor mounting flange gasket
	Incorrect carburettor adjustment

Chapter 4 Ignition system

For modifications, and information applicable to later models, see Supplement at end of manual

Contents

Specifications

System type	12v battery with ballast resistance wire and coil

Distributor

Contact breaker gap	0.020 in (0.50 mm)
Dwell angle	35 to 37° (up to engine No. 1639762)
Mainshaft endfloat	0.002 to 0.005 in (0.05 to 0.13 mm)
Static timing	9° BTDC
Rotational direction	Anticlockwise
Firing order	1 - 3 - 4 - 2
Centrifugal advance	

Engine speed	Degrees advance
760 to 1000 rpm	No advance
1200 rpm	1½ to 3½
1800 rpm	6½ to 8½
2500 rpm	7½ to 9½
4000 rpm	9¼ to 11¼
5000 rpm	10½ to 12½
6000 rpm	12½ (max.)

Spark plugs

Type	AC 42 XLS
Gap	0.040 in (1.0 mm)

Torque wrench settings

	lb ft	Nm
Spark plugs	25	35

1 General description

The ignition system is conventional and comprises a 12V battery, coil, distributor and spark plugs. The distributor is driven by a skew gear on the camshaft in tandem with the oil pump.

In order that the engine can run correctly it is necessary for an electrical spark to ignite the fuel/air mixture in the combustion chamber at exactly the right moment in relation to engine speed and load. The ignition system is based on feeding low tension (LT) voltage from the battery to the coil where it is converted to high tension (HT) voltage. The high tension voltage is powerful enough to jump the spark plug gap in the cylinders many times a second under high compression pressures, providing that the system is in good condition and that all adjustments are correct.

The ignition system is divided into two circuits: the low tension circuit and the high tension circuit.

The low tension (sometimes known as the primary) circuit consists of the battery, lead to the ignition switch, lead from the ignition switch to the low tension or primary coil windings (terminal +), and the lead from the low tension coil windings (coil terminal —) to the contact breaker points and condenser in the distributor.

The high tension circuit consists of the high tension or secondary coil windings, the heavy ignition lead from the centre of the coil to the centre of the distributor cap, the rotor arm, and the spark plug leads and spark plugs.

The system functions in the following manner. Low tension voltage is changed in the coil into high tension voltage by the opening and closing of the contact breaker points in the low tension circuit. High tension voltage is then fed via the carbon brush in the centre of the distributor cap to the rotor arm of the distributor cap, and each time it comes in line with one of the four metal segments in the cap, which are connected to the spark plug leads, the opening and closing of the contact breaker points causes the high tension voltage to build up, jump the gap from the rotor arm to the appropriate metal segment and so via the spark plug lead to the spark plug, where it finally jumps the spark plug gap before going to earth.

The ignition advance is controlled both mechanically and by a vacuum operated system. The mechanical governor mechanism comprises two lead weights, which move out from the distributor shaft as the engine speed rises due to centrifugal force. As they move outwards they rotate the cam relative to the distributor shaft, and so advance the spark. The weights are held in position by two light springs and it is the tension of the springs which is largely responsible for correct spark advancement.

The vacuum control consists of a diaphragm, one side of which is connected via a small bore tube to the carburettor, and the other side to the contact breaker plate. Depression in the inlet manifold and carburettor, which varies with engine speed and throttle opening, causes the diaphragm to move, so moving the contact breaker plate, and advancing or retarding the spark. A fine degree of control is achieved by a spring in the vacuum assembly.

2 Contact breaker points - adjustment and lubrication

1 To check the contact breaker gap (which will tend to decrease as the plastic heel is worn away by the distributor cam), remove the distributor cap and the rotor.
2 Turn the crankshaft by applying a spanner to the crankshaft securing bolt, until the heel of the movable contact breaker is on a high point of the cam. Alternatively, engage top gear and push the car.
3 Insert a feeler blade and check the gap between the two contact breaker points which should be 0.020 in. (0.50 mm). If the gap is incorrect, slacken the fixed contact screw '1' (Fig. 4.1) and insert a screwdriver into the adjustment slot. Move the contact breaker plate until the feeler blade is a sliding fit between the points. Re-tighten the securing screw.
4 Periodically, inject two or three drops of oil through the hole in the distributor baseplate to distribute the mechanical advance counterweights.
5 Using a pair of long-nosed pliers, squeeze the legs of the lubricator clip together and remove it. Work a little lithium based grease into the foam plastic lubricator and then refit it.
6 Refit the rotor and the distributor cap.
7 Where a dwell meter is available, this should be used to set the contact points gap.

Fig. 4.1. Contact breaker securing screw (1) and adjustment slot (2) (Sec. 2)

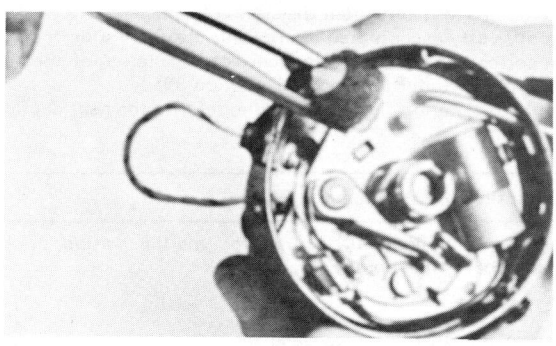

Fig. 4.2. Removing distributor cam lubricator (Sec. 2)

3 Contact breaker points - renovation or renewal

1 Open the contact breaker points and examine the condition of their faces. If they are blackened or pitted, remove the contact breaker points assembly in the following way.
2 Press the spring movable contact arm so that it clears the retaining stubs of its anchor insulator.
3 Lift the movable arm from the pivot.
4 Withdraw the two lead tags from the insulator, remove the fixed contact plate securing screw and lift the fixed contact from the distributor baseplate.
5 Dress each contact smooth and square on an oilstone, removing any 'pips' or 'craters'. If the faces are eroded or grinding would make them very thin, then a new set of points should be obtained. Reassemble the arms and check that when the points are closed, their faces make full contact with each other.
6 Apply a drop of oil to the moving arm pivot and having cleaned the baseplate and the contact faces with a fuel or methylated spirit moistened cloth, refit the assembly to the distributor baseplate but do not fully tighten the fixed breaker arm screw.
7 Make sure that the spring arm of the movable contact and the two lead tags are assembled in the correct sequence.
8 Adjust the points gap, as described in Section 2.
9 Check the setting of the rotor arm spring as shown in Fig. 4.4.

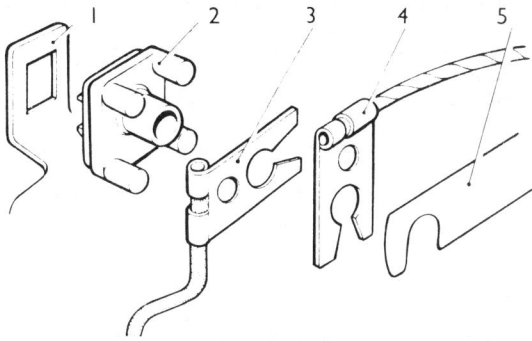

Fig. 4.3. Assembly sequence of LT insulator block on distributor body (Sec. 3)

1 Contact breaker baseplate
2 Insulator
3 Lead from condenser
4 LT lead
5 Spring arm of movable contact

4 Condenser - testing, removal and refitting

1 The condenser ensures that with the contact breaker points open, the sparking between them is not excessive to cause severe pitting. The condenser is fitted in parallel and its failure will automatically cause failure of the ignition system as the points will be prevented from interrupting the low tension circuit.
2 Testing for an unserviceable condenser may be effected by switching on the ignition and separating the contact points by hand. If this action is accompanied by a blue flash then condenser failure is indicated. Difficult starting, missing of engine after several miles running or badly pitted points are other indications of a faulty condenser.
3 The surest test is by substitution of a new unit.
4 To renew the condenser, release the distributor cap.
5 Remove the rotor.
6 Disconnect the condenser lead from the insulator on the side of the distributor body and then remove the screw which secures the condenser to the baseplate.
7 Refitting is a reversal of removal. Note the earth lead which is secured beneath the head of the condenser securing screw.

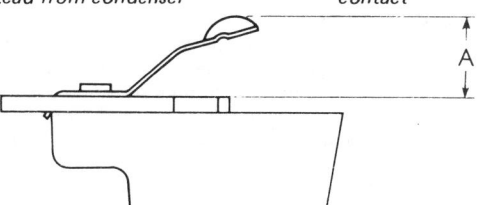

Fig. 4.4. Correct rotor arm spring setting (Sec. 3)

A = 0.30 to 0.34 in. (7.5 to 8.5 mm)

5 Distributor - removal and installation

1 Disconnect the HT leads from the spark plugs and from the centre terminal of the coil.
2 Disconnect the LT wire which runs between the (−) terminal of the coil and the distributor.
3 Unscrew and remove the bolt which secures the distributor clamp

plate to the cylinder block. On no account unscrew the pinch bolt or the ignition will have to be retimed as described later in this Section (photo).

4 The distributor can now be withdrawn from its recess (photo).

5 Installation is simply a matter of turning the distributor shaft until the large and small segments will mate with those visible at the top of the drive spindle from the oil pump. Push the distributor into its recess and insert and tighten the clamp plate bolt. The timing which was set before removal will now automatically be restored.

6 If during removal or subsequent dismantling, the clamp plate pinch bolt was disturbed, or if a new or reconditioned distributor is being installed, installation must be carried out in the following way.

7 Turn the crankshaft until no. 1 piston is on its compression stroke with the crankshaft pulley pointer opposite the 9° BTDC mark.

8 With the clamp plate pinch bolt only finger-tight, install the distributor into its recess so that the segments of the drive spindle mate and the vacuum capsule on the distributor body is towards the front of the engine. Screw in and tighten the clamp plate to cylinder block screw.

9 Now turn the distributor body until the contact points are just about to open and then tighten the clamp plate pinch bolt.

10 Any difficulty encountered in installing the distributor or timing the ignition correctly may be due to incorrect installation of the oil pump and drive spindle (refer to Chapter 1, Section 33).

11 For precise ignition timing procedure, refer to the next Section.

5.3 Location of distributor clamp plate securing bolt and pinch bolt

6 Ignition timing - adjustment

One of two methods may be used to time the ignition, the use of a stroboscope being the more accurate.

Test bulb

1 Remove the distributor cap and then connect a 12 volt test bulb between a good earth and the LT lead from the coil negative terminal.

2 Rotate the crankshaft by applying a spanner to the crankshaft pulley bolt until, with no. 1 piston on its compression stroke (ascertained by removing no. 1 spark plug and feeling the compression being generated with the finger), the crankshaft pulley pointer is opposite the 9° BTDC mark on the timing cover.

3 Release the distributor clamp plate pinch bolt.

4 Switch on the ignition and turn the distributor body until the test lamp just lights up.

5 Tighten the pinch bolt, switch off the ignition and remove the test lamp.

6 Refit the distributor cap.

Stroboscope (timing lamp)

7 Disconnect the vacuum pipe which runs between the distributor and the carburettor. Disconnect the pipe at the distributor end and plug the pipe.

8 Apply chalk or white paint to the crankshaft pulley pointer and the 9° BTDC mark on the timing cover.

9 Connect the stroboscope in accordance with the manufacturer's instructions (usually interposed between the end of no. 1 spark plug HT lead and no. 1 spark plug terminal).

10 Start the engine and reduce its idling speed to about 400 rpm, to ensure that the centrifugal advance mechanism does not operate.

11 Point the stroboscope at the timing marks and they will appear to be stationary. If they are in alignment, then the ignition timing is correct. If not, slacken the distributor clamp plate pinch bolt and turn the distributor body one way or the other, as necessary, to produce alignment. Retighten the pinch bolt.

12 A check on the operation of the mechanical advance mechanism can also be carried out with the aid of the stroboscope. With the engine still running and the stroboscope pointing at the timing marks, speed up the engine momentarily by moving the throttle lever. The pulley pointer should appear to move away in an anticlockwise direction from the mark on the timing cover.

13 A check on the operation of the vacuum advance unit can be made by switching off the engine and removing the distributor cap. Unplug the vacuum pipe, and attach one end to the distributor vacuum unit. Suck the other end and observe whether the movable baseplate in the distributor rotates. If it does, then it can be assumed that the unit is serviceable.

5.4 Withdrawing distributor

Fig. 4.5. Ignition timing marks (Sec. 5)

1 Crankshaft pulley pointer   2 9° BTDC mark

14 Remove the stroboscope, remake the spark plug and vacuum pipe connections.

7 Distributor - dismantling and reassembly

1 The distributor is designed for operation over very high mileages and when wear does eventually take place, it is recommended that a new or rebuilt unit is obtained rather than overhaul the original. However, for those who wish to dismantle and repair a faulty or worn distributor, the following points are given as a guide.
2 Check that spare parts are available, especially the mainshaft assembly which has an identification number on its underside.
3 The vacuum unit can be withdrawn after removal of three screws.
4 Do not attempt to separate the movable and fixed baseplates. These are only available as a complete unit.
5 The mainshaft assembly can be withdrawn after driving out the retaining pin (Fig. 4.9).
6 If a new mainshaft assembly is installed, the retaining pin hole will have to be drilled using a number 30 drill, so that when assembled, the shaft endfloat is within the specified limits (Fig. 4.10). This is not really a job for the home mechanic.

8 Coil - description and polarity

1 The coil is bolted to the cylinder head and a cover is fitted over the terminal end (photo).
2 High tension current should be negative at the spark plug terminals.

To ensure this, check the LT connections to the coil are correctly made.
3 The LT wire from the distributor must connect with the negative (—) terminal on the coil.
4 The coil positive (+) terminal is connected to the ignition/starter switch.
5 An incorrect connection can cause as much as a 60% loss of spark efficiency and can cause rough idling and misfiring at speed.
6 A resistance is incorporated in the wiring harness and this is in circuit all the time that the engine is running. When the starter is actuated however, the resistance is bypassed to provide increased voltage at the spark plugs.
7 Testing the coil needs special equipment and the best way is by substitution of a new unit.

9 Spark plugs and HT leads - general

1 Correct functioning of the spark plugs is vital for the highest performance and engine efficiency. The spark plugs installed as standard equipment cannot be improved upon.
2 At intervals of 5,000 miles (8000 km) remove the spark plugs, clean and regap them to 0.040 in. (1.0 mm). Cleaning can be carried out using a wire brush but taking the plugs to a service station to be sand blasted is to be preferred.
3 The spark plug gap is of considerable importance, as, if it is too large or too small the size of the spark and its efficiency will be seriously impaired.
   To set it, measure the gap with a feeler gauge, and then bend open, or close, the outer plug electrode until the correct gap is achieved. The

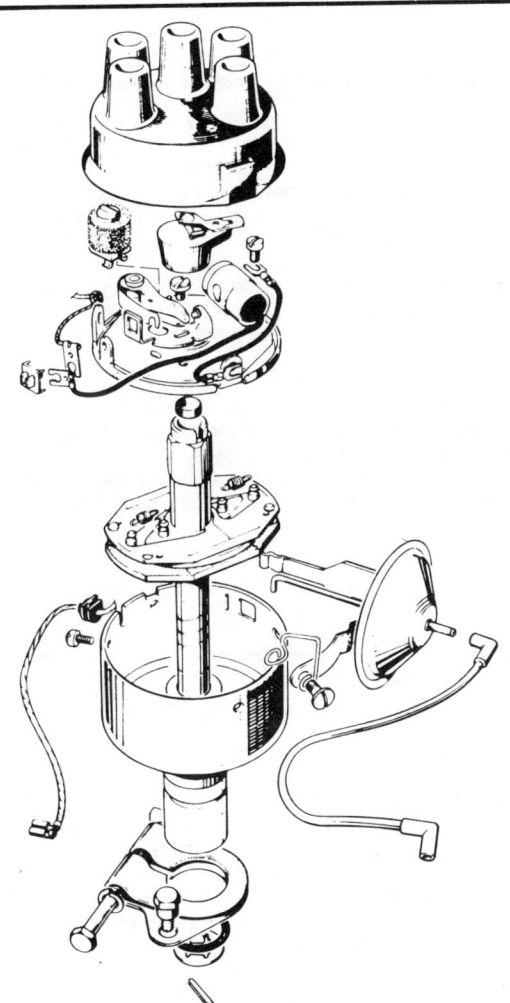

Fig. 4.6. Exploded view of the distributor (Sec. 7)

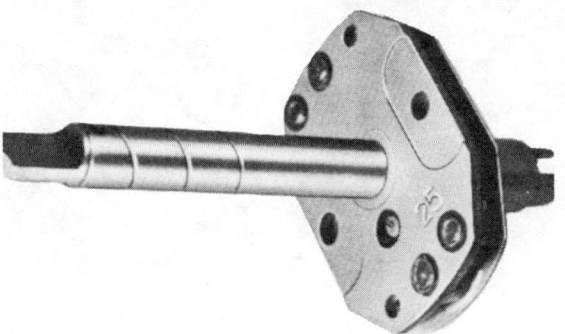

Fig. 4.7. Location of distributor shaft identification number (Sec. 7)

Fig. 4.8. Removing vacuum unit from distributor body (Sec. 7)

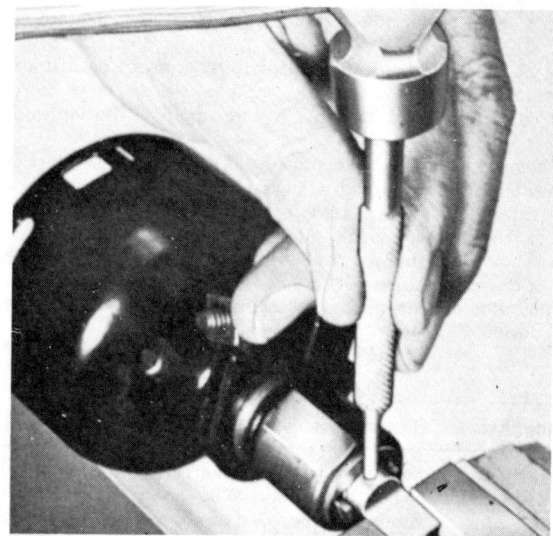

Fig. 4.9. Removing distributor shaft retaining pin (Sec. 7)

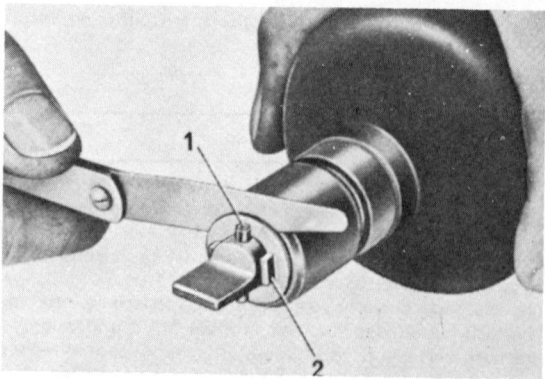

Fig. 4.10. Checking distributor shaft endfloat (Sec. 7)
1   Retaining pin   2   Tabbed thrust washer

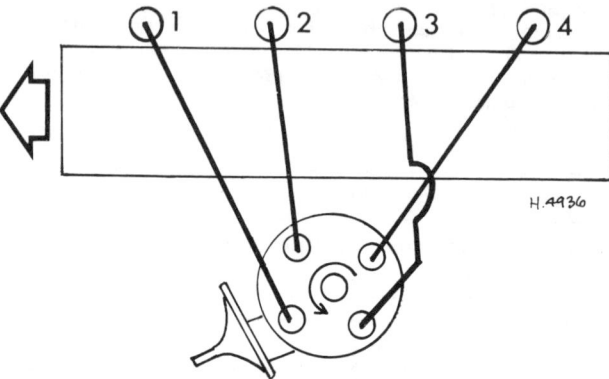

Fig. 4.11. Spark plug lead connection diagram (Sec. 9)

8.1 Location of ignition coil

centre electrode should never be bent as this may crack the insulation and cause plug failure, if nothing worse.

4   The condition and appearance of the spark plugs will tell much about the condition and tune of the engine (page 51).

5   If the insulator nose of the spark plug is clean and white, with no deposits, this is indicative of a weak mixture, or too hot a plug (a hot plug transfers heat away from the electrode slowly - a cold plug transfers it away quickly).

6   If the tip and insulator nose is covered with hard black looking deposits, then this is indicative that the mixture is too rich. Should the plug be black and oily, then it is likely that the engine is fairly worn, as well as the mixture being too rich.

7   If the insulator nose is covered with light tan to greyish brown deposits, then the mixture is correct and it is likely that the engine is in good condition.

8   If there are any traces of long brown tapering stains on the outside of the white portion of the plug, then the plug will have to be renewed, as this shows that there is a faulty joint between the plug body and the insulator, and compression is being allowed to leak away.

9   Every 12,000 miles (19000 km) the spark plugs should be renewed.

10 Always tighten a spark plug to the specified torque - no tighter.

11 Wipe the spark plug leads occasionally with a rag and always connect them in the correct order.

12 The leads are of special carbon cored type and in the event of a terminal becoming detached, renew the lead complete.

10 Fault diagnosis - ignition system

Symptom	Reason
Engine fails to start	Lack of fuel in tank
	Discharged battery
	Loose battery terminals
	Disconnected HT and LT leads
	Faulty condenser
	Damp HT leads or distributor cap
Engine misfires	Faulty spark plug (not sparking under compression)
	HT leads shorting due to faulty insulation
	Cracked distributor cap
	Broken or worn mechanical advance mechanism
	Incorrect spark plug gap
	Incorrect contact breaker points gap
	Faulty coil
	Ignition timing incorrectly set
	Poor earth connection (battery, engine or distributor)

Measuring plug gap. A feeler gauge of the correct size (see ignition system specifications) should have a slight 'drag' when slid between the electrodes. Adjust gap if necessary

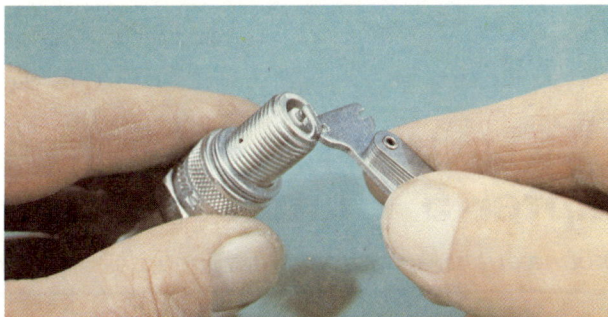

Adjusting plug gap. The plug gap is adjusted by bending the earth electrode inwards, or outwards, as necessary until the correct clearance is obtained. Note the use of the correct tool

Normal. Grey-brown deposits, lightly coated core nose. Gap increasing by around 0.001 in (0.025 mm) per 1000 miles (1600 km). Plugs ideally suited to engine, and engine in good condition

Carbon fouling. Dry, black, sooty deposits. Will cause weak spark and eventually misfire. Fault: over-rich fuel mixture. Check: carburettor mixture settings, float level and jet sizes; choke operation and cleanliness of air filter. Plugs can be re-used after cleaning

Oil fouling. Wet, oily deposits. Will cause weak spark and eventually misfire. Fault: worn bores/piston rings or valve guides; sometimes occurs (temporarily) during running-in period. Plugs can be re-used after thorough cleaning

Overheating. Electrodes have glazed appearance, core nose very white – few deposits. Fault: plug overheating. Check: plug value, ignition timing, fuel octane rating (too low) and fuel mixture (too weak). Discard plugs and cure fault immediately

Electrode damage. Electrodes burned away; core nose has burned, glazed appearance. Fault: pre-ignition. Check: as for 'Overheating' but may be more severe. Discard plugs and remedy fault before piston or valve damage occurs

Split core nose (may appear initially as a crack). Damage is self-evident, but cracks will only show after cleaning. Fault: pre-ignition or wrong gap-setting technique. Check: ignition timing, cooling system, fuel octane rating (too low) and fuel mixture (too weak). Discard plugs, rectify fault immediately

Chapter 5 Clutch

For modifications, and information applicable to later models, see Supplement at end of manual

Contents

Specifications

Clutch type	Single dry plate, diaphragm spring cable actuation
Diameter	7¼ in (184.15 mm)
No. of driven plate torsion springs	4
Free-movement	0.24 in (6.0 mm)
Pedal cross-shaft diameter	0.550 to 0.551 in (13.96 to 14.00 mm)
Pedal cross-shaft clearance in bush	0.005 to 0.009 in (0.12 to 0.23 mm)

Torque wrench setting	lb ft	Nm
Clutch to flywheel bolts	14	19

1 General description

1 The clutch is of single dry plate type with a diaphragm spring. Actuation is by means of a cable through a pendant mounted pedal.

The unit comprises a pressed steel cover which is dowelled to the rear face of the flywheel and bolted to it and incorporates the pressure plate, diaphragm spring and fulcrum rings.

2 The clutch driven plate is free to slide along the splined first motion shaft and is held in position between the flywheel and the pressure plate by the pressure of the pressure plate spring. Friction lining material is riveted to the clutch driven plate and it has a spring cushioned hub to absorb transmission shocks and to help ensure a smooth take-off.

3 The circular diaphragm spring is mounted on shouldered pins held in place in the cover by two fulcrum rings. The spring is also held to the pressure plate by three spring steel clips which are riveted in position.

4 When the clutch pedal is depressed, the cable moves the release arm to which is attached the release bearing and so moves the centre of the diaphragm inwards. The spring is sandwiched between two annular rings which act as fulcrum points. As the centre of the spring is pushed in, the outside of the spring is pushed out, so moving the pressure plate

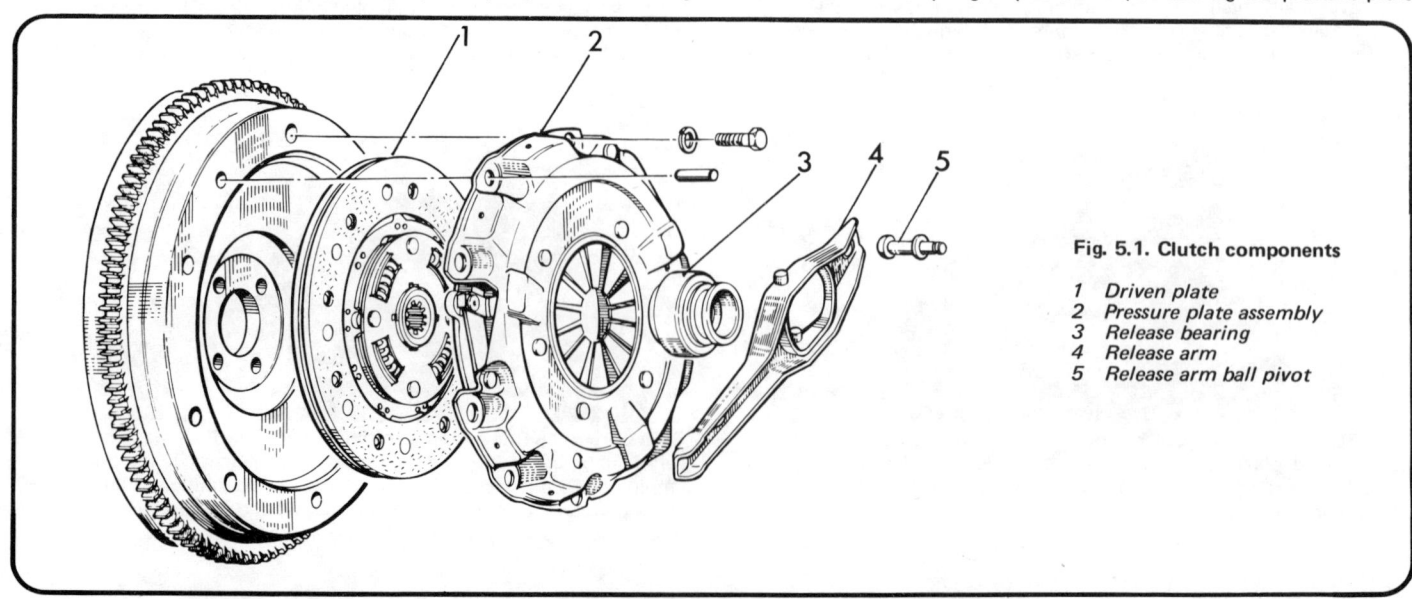

Fig. 5.1. Clutch components

1 Driven plate
2 Pressure plate assembly
3 Release bearing
4 Release arm
5 Release arm ball pivot

backwards and disengaging the pressure plate from the clutch driven plate.

5 When the clutch pedal is released the diaphragm spring forces the pressure plate into contact with the friction linings on the clutch driven plate and at the same time pushes the clutch driven plate a fraction of an inch forwards on its splines, so engaging the clutch driven plate with the flywheel. The clutch driven plate is now firmly sandwiched between the pressure plate and the flywheel so the drive is taken up.

6 As the friction linings wear, the pressure plate friction surface will move closer to the flywheel and the clutch release arm free-movement will increase. Periodic adjustment must therefore be carried out as described in Section 2.

2 Clutch - adjustment

1 Every 3000 miles (5000 km) check and adjust, if necessary, the clutch free movement. One of two methods may be used:

Method (i)
2 Disconnect the release arm return spring. Hold the threaded part of the clutch cable (at the release arm) in its rearmost position and then move the release arm away from the cable adjusting nut. Use only gentle finger pressure, otherwise any greater force will overcome the resistance of the diaphragm spring fingers and give a false indication of the free movement.

3 The amount of travel of the release arm is the free-movement 'A' (Fig. 5.2) and this can be adjusted by releasing the locknut and turning the adjuster nut as required. Reconnect the return spring.

Method (ii)
4 Release the locknut on the threaded end of the clutch cable. Screw up the adjuster nut until the release bearing is just nipped between the diaphragm spring and the release fork. This can be established by inserting a finger through the unused release arm aperture on the opposite side of the clutch bellhousing and spinning the bearing.

5 Set the locknut a distance equal to the specified free-movement away from the adjusting nut and then unscrew the adjuster nut to meet the locknut. Lock the nuts together in this position.

3 Clutch cable - renewal

1 Unscrew and remove the nut and locknut from the release arm end of the cable.

2 Withdraw the rubber bellows and disconnect the cable from the bellhousing.

3 From the top of the clutch pedal, unhook the clutch inner cable and withdraw the complete cable assembly, complete with bulkhead damper and grommet.

4 Installation of the new cable is a reversal of removal but adjust the free-movement as described in the preceding Section. **Note:** during the foregoing operations, do not pull the release arm away from the bellhousing or the release arm clip may become detached from its ball stud pivot. However, the arm can be refitted without any need for dismantling, provided the method of attachment is understood (see Fig. 5.4).

4 Clutch pedal - removal and refitting

1 The clutch and brake pedals operate on a common cross-shaft.

2 Release the clutch cable from the release arm and then unhook it from the top of the clutch pedal.

3 Disconnect the brake pedal from the servo unit pushrod by extracting the spring clip and clevis pin.

4 Unbolt the right-hand pedal support bracket from the bottom of the fascia panel.

5 Unbolt the left-hand pedal support bracket noting that one of the servo mounting studs also serves to secure the bracket.

6 Worn or damaged components may be renewed as necessary, but the cross-shaft bushes must be reamed to accept the cross-shaft if either of these components is renewed (see Specifications for shaft to bush clearance).

7 Apply grease to all moving parts before assembly.

8 When reconnecting the brake pedal, note that the clevis pin must

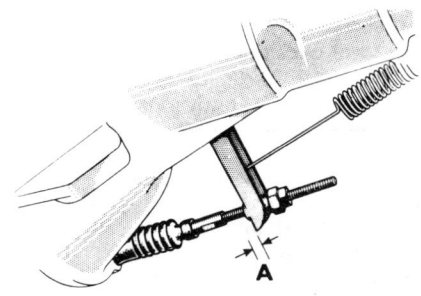

Fig. 5.2. Release arm free movement A = 0.24 in. (6.0 mm) (Sec. 2)

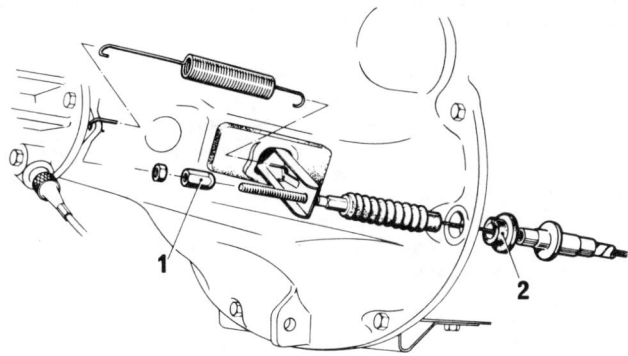

Fig. 5.3. Clutch cable to release arm attachment components (Sec. 2)

1 *Adjuster nut*   2 *Rubber insulator*

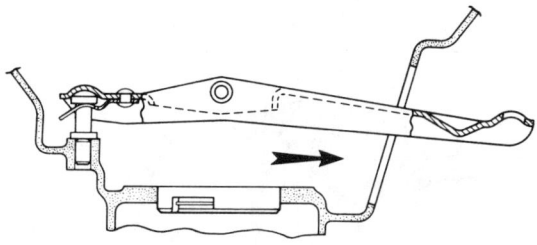

Fig. 5.4. Clutch release arm attachment to ball pivot (Sec. 3)

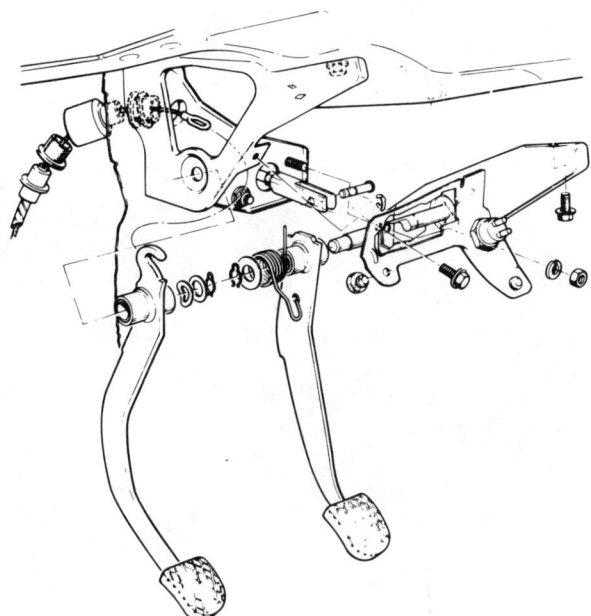

Fig. 5.5. Exploded view of the brake and clutch pedals (Sec. 4)

enter from the right-hand side and that the pedal return spring locates in the notch in the pedal support bracket and in the groove in the clevis pin. Check the stop lamp switch operation as described in Chapter 9, Section 16.

5 Clutch - removal

1 Access to the clutch may be obtained in one of two ways. Either remove the engine (Chapter 1) or remove the gearbox (Chapter 6). Unless the engine requires major overhaul, removal of the gearbox is much the easier and quicker method.
2 Mark the relationship of the clutch cover to the flywheel and unscrew the bolts which secure the clutch pressure plate cover to the flywheel. Unscrew the bolts only a turn at a time, until the pressure of the diaphragm spring is relieved before completely withdrawing them.
3 Lift away the pressure plate/diaphragm spring assembly and the driven plate (friction disc) from the face of the flywheel.

6 Clutch - inspection and renovation

1 The clutch will normally need renewal when all the free-movement adjustment on the cable has been taken up or it can be felt to be slipping under conditions of hard acceleration or when climbing a hill. Sometimes squealing noises are evident when the clutch is engaged. This may be due to the friction linings having worn down to the rivets and/or a badly worn release bearing. A clutch will wear according to the way in which it is used. Much intentional slipping of the clutch while driving - rather than the correct selection of gears - will accelerate wear.
2 Examine the surfaces of the pressure plate and flywheel for signs of scoring. If this is only light it may be left, but if very deep, the pressure plate unit will have to be renewed. If the flywheel is deeply scored it should be taken off and advice sought from an engineering firm.

Providing it may be machined completely across the face the overall balance of engine and flywheel should not be too severely upset. If renewal of the flywheel is necessary the new one will have to be balanced to match the original.
3 Renew the driven plate if the linings are worn down to the rivets (or nearly so) or if the linings appear oil stained. Purchase a new driven plate or one that has been reconditioned professionally; do not waste time and effort trying to rivet new linings yourself - it will not prove satisfactory.
4 If the driven plate and the interior of the clutch bellhousing are saturated with oil, check the gearbox front combined bearing oil seal and the crankshaft rear oil seal and renew whichever has failed.
5 The diaphragm spring and pressure plate should be examined for cracks or scoring. If a new unit is necessary, again purchase a new or reconditioned assembly. Do not attempt to dismantle it yourself.
6 Finally, inspect the condition of the spigot bush in the centre of the flywheel mounting flange. If it is worn, renew it as described in Chapter 1, Section 21.

7 Release bearing - removal and refitting

1 The release bearing is of ball bearing, grease sealed type and although designed for long life it is worth renewing at the same time as the other clutch components are being renewed or serviced.
2 Deterioration of the bearing should be suspected when there are signs of grease leakage or the unit is noisy when spun with the fingers.
3 Remove the rubber dust excluder which surrounds the release arm at the bellhousing aperture.
4 Disconnect and remove the return spring from the release arm.
5 Detach the release lever from the release bearing retaining hub.
6 Withdraw the release bearing/hub assembly from the input shaft (photo).
7 If necessary remove the release arm from its ball pivot.

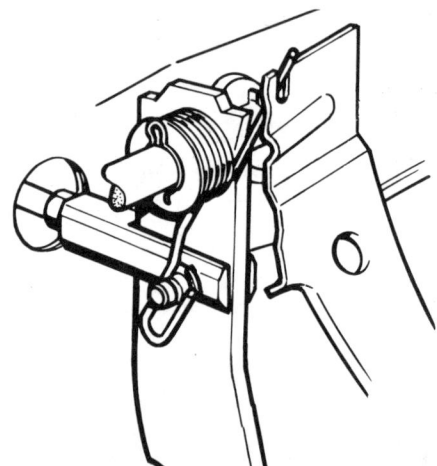

Fig. 5.6. Method of attaching brake pedal return spring (Sec. 4)

Fig. 5.7. Driven plate marking (Sec. 8)

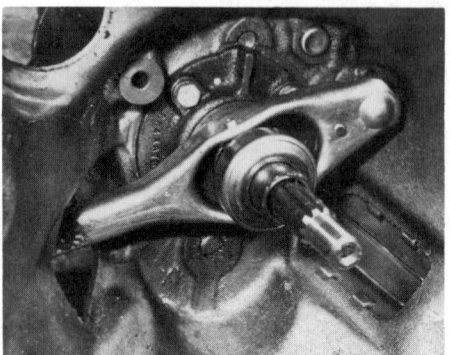

7.6 Clutch release lever and bearing

8.2 Installing clutch to flywheel

8.4 Centralising clutch driven plate

8   Apply a dab of grease to the release arm ball pivot and some to the internal recess of the release bearing.

9   Install the release arm, the release bearing and reconnect the return spring. Refit the dust excluder.

8   Clutch - refitting

1   Refitting the clutch to the flywheel will necessitate centralising the driven plate and for this, either an old input shaft or a suitable piece of dowel (with a step at one end to engage in the input spigot bush in the centre of the flywheel) must be obtained.

2   Locate the driven plate against the face of the flywheel so that the appropriately marked side (**the less projecting side of the torsion spring assembly**) is towards the flywheel (photo).

3, Offer up the pressure plate assembly to the flywheel and engage it with the positioning dowels. Check the alignment marks made before removal, are in line.

4   Insert the guide tool through the splined hub of the driven plate so that the end of the tool locates in the flywheel spigot bush. This action of the guide tool will centralise the driven plate by causing it to move in a sideways direction (photo).

5   Insert and remove the guide tool two or three times to ensure that the driven plate is fully centralised and then tighten the pressure plate securing bolts a turn at a time and in a diametrically opposite sequence, to the specified torque.

6   Refit the gearbox (or engine) whichever was removed and as described in Chapter 6, or Chapter 1, respectively. The purpose of centralising the driven plate is to permit the input shaft of the gearbox to pass through the driven plate and to engage in the spigot bush in the centre of the flywheel. Even so, when installing either the gearbox or the engine, it may be necessary to rotate the crankshaft fractionally to align the splines on the driven plate and the input shaft. To turn the crankshaft, apply a ring spanner to the crankshaft pulley bolt.

7   When installation is completed, adjust the clutch, as described in Section 2.

9   Fault diagnosis - clutch

Symptom	Reason
Judder when taking up drive	Loose engine or gearbox mountings Badly worn friction surfaces or contaminated with oil Worn splines on gearbox input shaft or driven plate hub Worn input shaft spigot bush in flywheel
Clutch spin (failure to disengage) so that gears cannot be meshed	Incorrect release bearing to diaphragm spring finger clearance Driven plate sticking on input shaft splines due to rust. May occur after vehicle standing idle for long period Damaged or misaligned pressure plate assembly
Clutch slip (increase in engine speed does not result in increase in vehicle road speed - particularly on gradients)	Incorrect release bearing to diaphragm spring finger clearance Friction surfaces worn out or oil contaminated
Noise evident on depressing clutch pedal	Dry, worn or damaged release bearing Insufficient pedal free-travel Weak or broken pedal return spring Weak or broken clutch release lever return spring Excessive play between driven plate hub splines and input shaft splines
Noise evident as clutch pedal released	Distorted driven plate Broken or weak driven plate cushion coil springs Insufficient pedal free-travel Weak or broken release lever return spring Distorted or worn input shaft

Chapter 6 Gearbox

For modifications, and information applicable to later models, see Supplement at end of manual

Contents

Specifications

Gearbox type ...	Four forward speeds and reverse. Synchromesh on all forward speeds
Ratios	
1st ...	3.76 : 1
2nd ...	2.213 : 1
3rd ...	1.404 : 1
Top ...	1.0 : 1
Reverse ...	3.707 : 1
Mainshaft diameter ...	1.0990 to 1.0950 in (27.915 to 27.927 mm)
Gear clearance on shaft ...	0.0014 to 0.0028 in (0.036 to 0.071 mm)
Countergear length (overall) ...	6.020 to 6.022 in (152.91 to 152.96 mm)
Thrust washer thickness ...	0.0615 to 0.0635 in (1.562 to 1.613 mm)
Countergear endfloat ...	0.006 to 0.014 in (0.15 to 0.36 mm)
Reverse pinion shaft diameter ...	0.5521 to 0.5528 in (14.023 to 14.041 mm)
Pinion clearance on shaft ...	0.0022 to 0.0039 in (0.056 to 0.099 mm)
Oil capacity ...	0.9 Imp. pint (0.51 litres)

Torque wrench settings	lb ft	Nm
Bellhousing to engine bolts ...	25	35
Gearbox rear mounting to bodyframe ...	28	39
Front cover bolts ...	12	16
Oil filler plug ...	35	48
Gearbox top cover bolts ...	25	35
Gearshift lever housing cover bolts ...	25	35
Gearbox rear extension bolts ...	30	41
Reverse lamp switch locknut ...	16	22
Eccentric pin locknut ...	20	28
Eccentric pin bracket to selector shaft nut ...	30	41
Rear mounting to gearbox ...	32	44

1 General description

The four speed manual gearbox has synchromesh engagement on all forward gears. Gearshift is by means of a short floor mounted remote control lever. The gearbox casing is integral with the clutch bellhousing. A detachable top cover is fitted to the gearbox casing.

A combined filler/level plug is screwed into the left-hand side of the gearbox, but no means of draining the gearbox is provided for when the gearbox is in position in the car.

2 Gearbox - removal and installation

1 Position the car over a pit or on ramps. Alternatively jack-up the car sufficiently high so that the clutch bellhousing will pass beneath the car when the gearbox is withdrawn.
2 Working inside the car, release the flexible boots from the gearshift lever, depress the retaining cap and twist it clockwise. Withdraw the gearshift lever assembly.
3 Working under the car, disconnect the clutch cable from the release

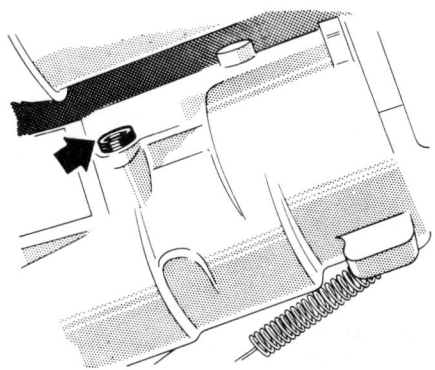

Fig. 6.1. Location of gearbox filler/level plug (Sec. 1)
Use a 3/8 in AF hexagon key

arm.

4   Mark the relationship of the propeller shaft and rear axle pinion flanges and then remove the propeller shaft, as described in Chapter 7. As the propeller shaft is withdrawn from the rear of the gearbox, some loss of oil will occur. This may be restricted by covering the end of the gearbox with a plastic bag and securing it with a strong elastic band.

5   Disconnect the speedometer drive cable from the gearbox.

6   Slacken the gearbox brace bolts at the sump brackets and then unbolt and remove the clutch bellhousing front cover. Disconnect the exhaust downpipes.

7   Unscrew and remove the bolts which secure the clutch bellhousing to the engine (five bolts and two brackets).

8   Place a supporting jack with a wooden block as an insulator under the engine sump.

9   Unbolt and remove the rear mounting from the bodyframe (photo).

10   Lower the jack carefully until the gearbox can be withdrawn from the engine. Do not allow the weight of the gearbox to hang upon the input shaft while the input shaft is still in engagement with the clutch

Fig. 6.2. Removing gearshift control lever (Sec. 2)

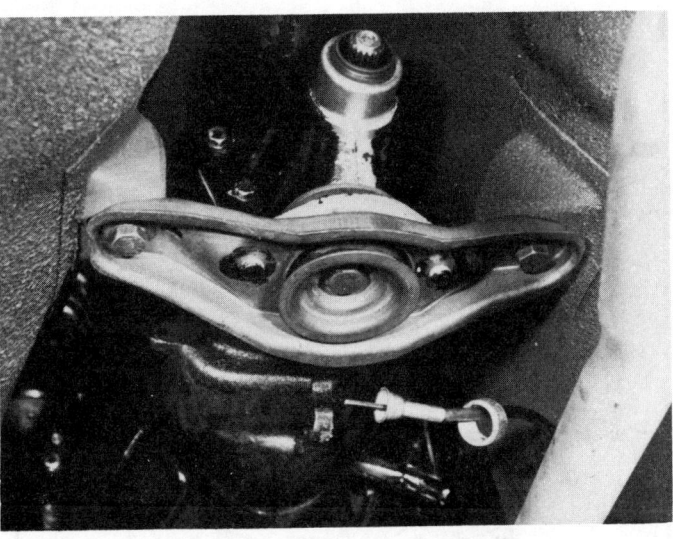

2.9 Gearbox rear mounting

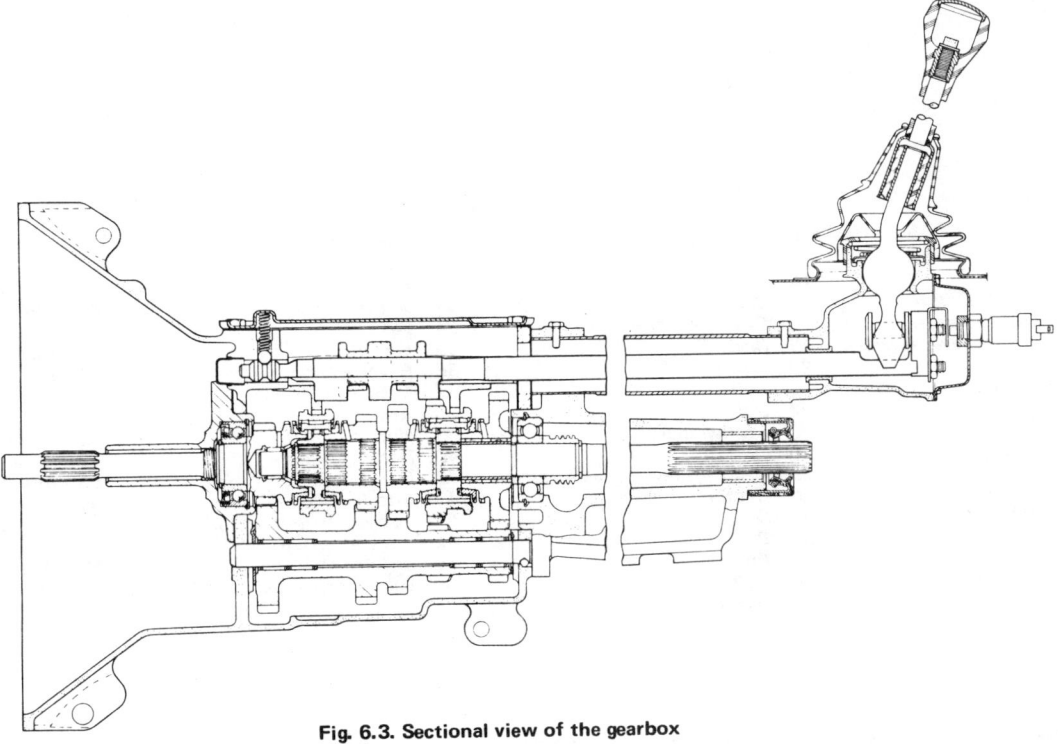

Fig. 6.3. Sectional view of the gearbox

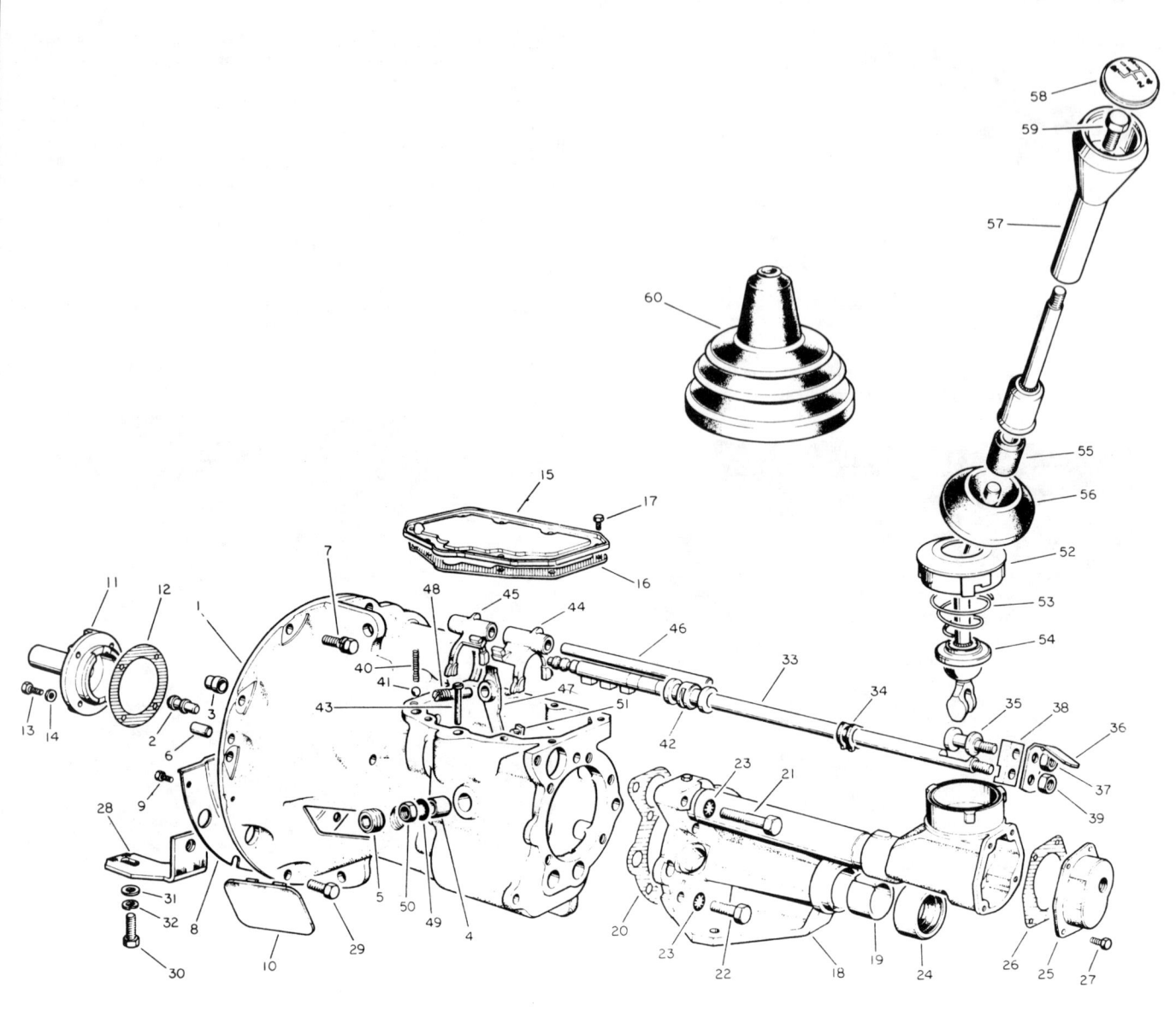

Fig. 6.4. Gearbox components (casing, covers and shift mechanism) (Sec. 3)

1 Gearbox casing	16 Gasket	32 Washer	47 Reverse striking lever
2 Release lever ball stud	17 Bolt	33 Selective shaft	48 Striking lever fulcrum pin
3 Selector shaft cover	18 Gearbox rear extension	34 Bush	49 Lockwasher
4 Reverse striking lever fulcrum bush	19 Bush	35 Eccentric pin	50 Nut
5 Filler/level plug	20 Gasket	36 Reverse lamp switch	51 Reverse striking pad
6 Dowel	21 Bolt	37 Nut	52 Gearshift lever retaining cap
7 Bolt	22 Bolt	38 Arm	53 Spring
8 Bellhousing cover	23 Lockwasher	39 Nut	54 Plate
9 Bolt	24 Oil seal	40 Detent spring	55 Insulator
10 Blanking plate	25 Gearshift lever housing cover	41 Detent ball	56 Flexible coupling
11 Gearbox front cover	26 Gasket	42 Interlock collar	57 Handgrip
12 Gasket	27 Screw	43 Loosely fitting stop pin	58 Cap
13 Bolt	28 Brace	44 1st/2nd selector fork	59 Screw
14 Washer	29 Bolt	45 3rd/4th selector fork	60 Flexible boot
15 Top cover	30 Bolt	46 Selector fork rail	
	31 Washer		

mechanism, but support it adequately (photo).

11 Installation is a reversal of removal but if the clutch mechanism has been removed, make sure to centralise the driven plate, as described in Chapter 5.

12 Adjust the clutch.

13 Check and top-up the gearbox oil level.

3 Gearbox - dismantling into major assemblies

1 With the gearbox removed from the car, wash off all external dirt with paraffin or a water soluble grease solvent.

2 From within the clutch bellhousing, remove the release bearing and arm (Chapter 5).

3 Unbolt and remove the gearbox top cover and invert the unit to drain the oil (the selector shaft detent ball and spring will fall from the casing as this is done and they must not be lost).

4 Unbolt and remove the gearshift lever housing cover.

5 Unbolt and remove the eccentric pin and bracket assembly from the selector shaft, having first bent up the reverse lamp switch contact plate.

6 Withdraw the loose fitting pin '2' (Fig. 6.6). Set the gears in the neutral mode and then using the fingers, rotate the selector shaft '3' so that the key of the shaft clears the selector forks '4'. Withdraw the selector shaft and lift out the interlock collar.

7 Remove the selector fork rail by first unbolting and then rotating the gearbox rear extension until the end of the rail is visible through the hole provided in the rear extension casing, and then driving the rail out so that it emerges from the rear of the gearbox. Withdraw the selector forks.

8 Working within the clutch bellhousing, unscrew and remove the front cover bolts.

9 Pull the input shaft as far forward as possible.

10 Press the 3rd/4th synchro sleeve towards the front of the gearbox without pushing it off the hub. Lift the mainshaft clear of the input shaft and over the countergear.

11 Extract the mainshaft and rear cover assembly from the back of the gearbox.

12 Drive out the countershaft so that it emerges from the rear of the gearbox casing and lower the countergear to the bottom of the casing.

13 Withdraw the front cover and the input shaft and then lift the countergear from the gearbox. Retrieve the thrust washers.

14 Press out the reverse pinion shaft towards the front of the gearbox (a clamp and distance piece can be used to do this) and then withdraw the striking lever from the fulcrum pin.

15 The gearbox is now dismantled into major assemblies and further dismantling should not be carried out unless suitable extractors or pressing facilities are available.

4 Mainshaft - servicing

1 Inspect the gears for worn or chipped teeth. If there has been a history of noisy gearchanges or it has been usual to 'beat' the synchromesh when changing gear, the synchro. units will need renewal.

2 To dismantle the mainshaft, first remove the speedometer driven gear. To do this, drive the centre of the gear inwards with a soft drift; this will eject the blanking plug on the opposite side of the casing and enable the speedometer driven gear to be withdrawn. The speedometer driven gear can be removed in this way when the gearbox is still in the car.

3 Expand the rear bearing circlip and then press the mainshaft through the rear cover. It will facilitate removal if the end cover is first heated in boiling water. (photo)

4 Extract the bearing circlip from the groove in the rear cover.

5 Extract the 3rd/4th synchro. hub circlip.

6 Supporting the rear face of 3rd speed gear, press the mainshaft from the 3rd/4th synchro. unit and 3rd speed gear.

7 Remove the speedometer drive gear circlips.

8 Support the front face of 1st speed gear and press the mainshaft through the speedometer drive gear and mainshaft rear bearing.

9 Withdraw 1st speed gear needle roller bearing.

10 Support the front face of 2nd gear and press the mainshaft through 1st speed gear bush, 1st/2nd synchro. unit and 2nd speed gear.

11 Synchromesh units are supplied as complete assemblies. Do not attempt to renew or mix components. When the synchro. hub and

2.10 Gearbox removed showing engine left in position

Fig. 6.5. Unbolting eccentric pin/bracket assembly from selector shaft (Sec. 3)

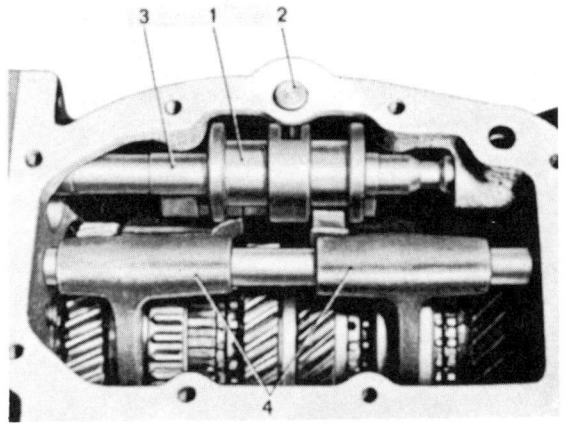

Fig. 6.6. Selector shaft components (Sec. 3)

1 Selector shaft   3 Loose fitting retaining pin
2 Interlock collar   4 Selector forks

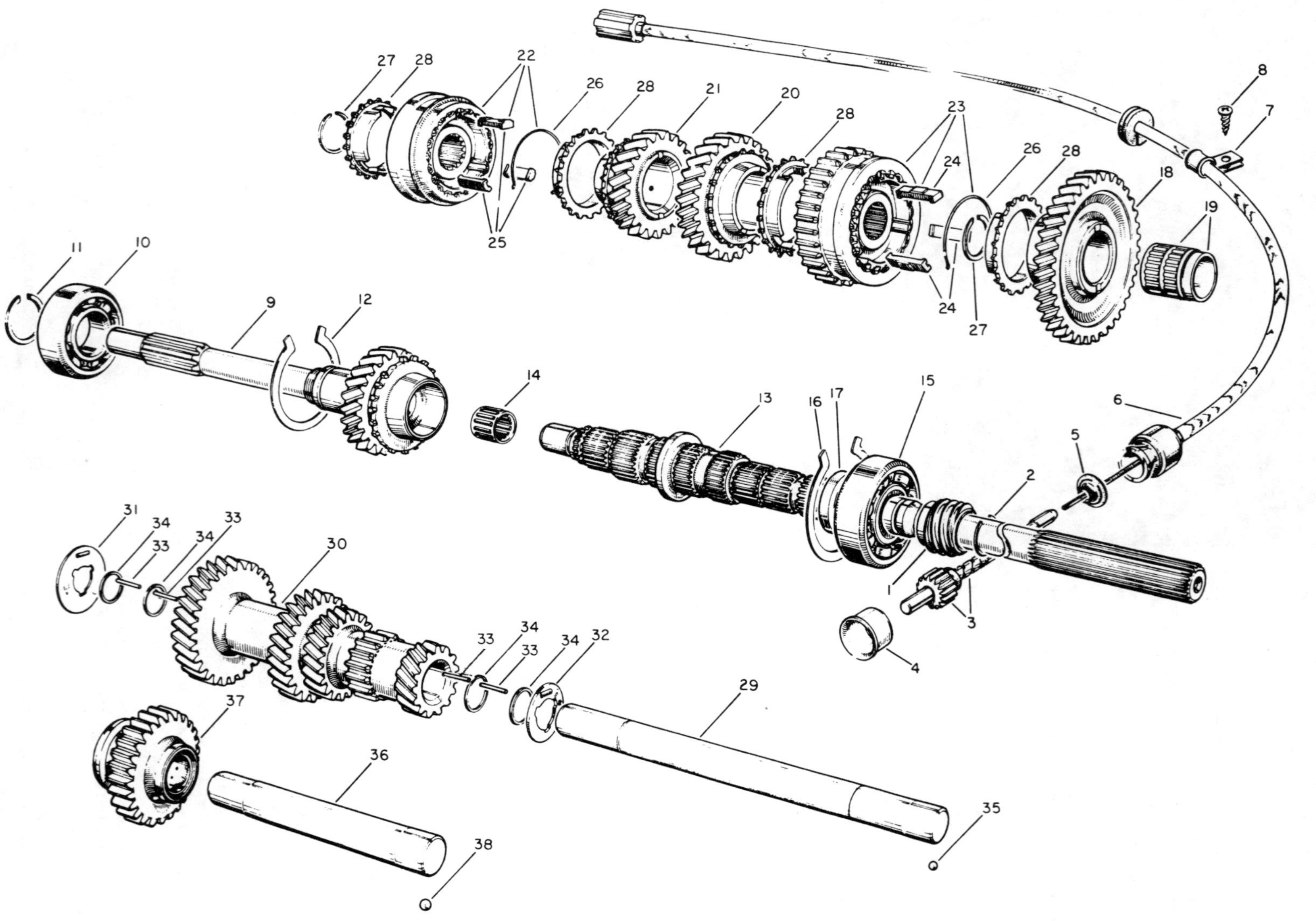

Fig. 6.7. Gearbox internal components (Sec. 4)

1	Speedometer drive gear	9	Input shaft
2	Circlip	10	Combined bearing/oil seal
3	Speedometer driven gear	11	Circlip
4	Cap	12	Circlip
5	Seal	13	Mainshaft
6	Speedometer cable	14	Caged needle roller bearing
7	Clip	15	Mainshaft bearing
8	Self-tapping screw	16	Circlip

17	Thrust washer	25	Sliding keys
18	1st speed gear	26	Sliding key springs
19	Caged needle roller bearing	27	Circlip
20	2nd speed gear	28	Synchro. ring
21	3rd speed gear	29	Countershaft
22	3rd/4th synchro. unit	30	Countergear
23	1st/2nd synchro. unit	31	Thrust washer
24	Sliding keys	32	Thrust washer

33	Needle roller
34	Needle bearing spacers
35	Locking ball
36	Reverse pinion shaft
37	Reverse pinion
38	Locking ball

4.3 Mainshaft rear bearing circlip

sleeve have to be dismantled, first mark their relationship to ensure that they are assembled in their original respective positions. The sliding keys must only engage with those sleeve splines which have keystone contours on both sides. Do not confuse the keystone contours with wear.

The 1st/2nd synchro. sleeve keys have a pip on the outer face of each key and are longer than those for the 3rd/4th synchro. unit. When installing the key springs, the turned out end of both springs must engage in the same key. The springs must also be assembled in an anticlockwise direction when they are viewed from either side of the hub. A synchro. unit in good condition will not have mishapen teeth, a tendency for the ring to rock on the gear cone or any indication of ovality. If these conditions are evident, renew the unit.

12 Before reassembling the mainshaft, check the condition of the rear cover bush and oil seal and renew them if necessary (photo). It is recommended that an anti-scuffing paste is applied to the rear cover bush to provide initial lubrication.

13 During reassembly of the mainshaft, smear all components with gear oil.

14 Install the 3rd speed gear to the front end of mainshaft so that dog teeth are towards the front of the shaft (photo).

15 Install the synchro. ring.

16 Place the 3rd/4th synchro. hub on the front end of the mainshaft so that the longer projecting boss is towards the front of the shaft. Press the hub onto the mainshaft at the same time aligning the slots in the synchro. ring with the sliding keys in the hub. Install a securing circlip from one of the four thicknesses available. The 3rd/4th speed synchro. sleeve must be assembled to the hub so that the stepped outer edge of the sleeve is towards the front of the mainshaft. Make sure that the mating marks made before dismantling are in alignment.

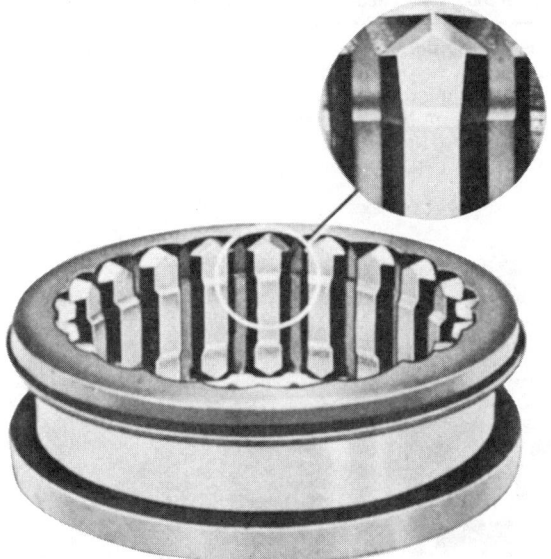

Fig. 6.8. Synchro. sleeve internal splines (Sec. 4)

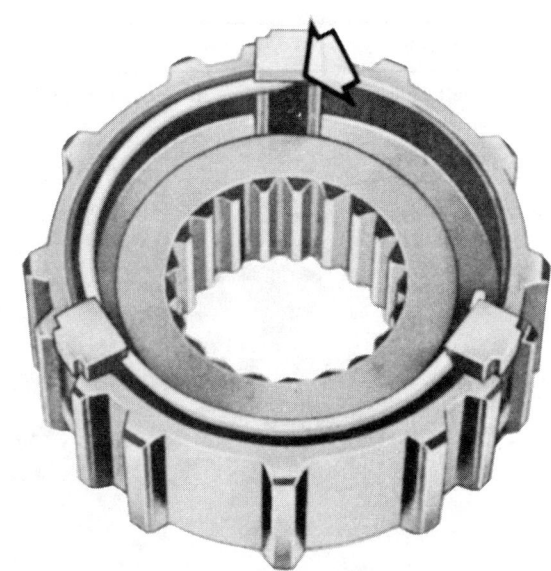

Fig. 6.9. Synchro. hub showing engagement of turned out end of spring (arrowed) (Sec. 4)

4.12 Gearbox rear cover oil seal

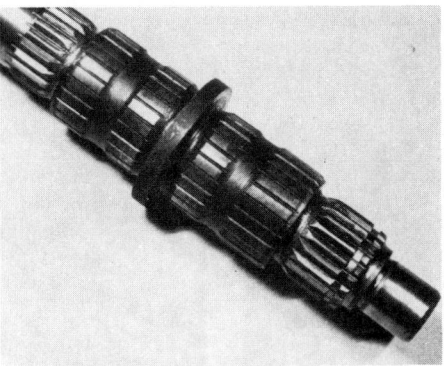

4.14 Mainshaft front end detail

17 Install 2nd speed gear to the rear of the mainshaft so that the plain side of the gear is towards the front of the shaft.

18 Assemble the synchro. ring to the gear and then press 1st/2nd synchro. hub (either way round) onto the mainshaft at the same time aligning the slots in the synchro. ring with the sliding keys in the hub. Make sure that the 2nd speed gear and ring are adequately supported during the pressing operation.

19 Press 1st speed gear bush onto the mainshaft using a suitable piece of tubing (photo).

20 Assemble 1st/2nd speed synchro. sleeve over the synchro. hub so that the selector fork groove is towards the rear and that the hub/sleeve mating marks (see paragraph 11) are in alignment (photo).

21 Position the synchro. ring, 1st speed gear and the caged needle roller bearing onto the mainshaft so that the plain side of the gear is towards the rear of the mainshaft (photo).

22 Align the slots in the synchro. ring with the sliding keys in the synchro. hub. Install the thrust washer and press the rear bearing onto the mainshaft so that the circlip groove is towards 1st speed gear (photo).

23 Install the speedometer drive-gear so that the groove is towards the mainshaft rear bearing. Fit the tightest possible circlip from the ten thicknesses which are available (photo).

24 Push a piece of plastic tubing over the splines at the rear end of the mainshaft to prevent them damaging the lips of the rear cover oil seal as the cover is installed.

25 Install the circlip into its groove in the rear cover, expand it with circlip pliers and press the mainshaft assembly into the rear cover. As when dismantling, warming the cover will facilitate this operation. Make sure that when released, the circlip locates in the bearing groove.

5 Input shaft - servicing

1 The input shaft bearings can be renewed but if the splines or 4th speed gear teeth are worn, then the shaft will have to be renewed as an assembly.

2 To remove the combined bearing/oil seal, extract the circlip and support the rear face of the bearing inner track.

3 Press the input shaft from the bearing.

4 Installation of the bearing is a reversal of removal but apply pressure to the bearing inner track only and make sure that the sealed side of the bearing faces the front of the shaft.

6 Countershaft - servicing

1 The countergear cannot be dismantled and if the teeth are worn or chipped it must be renewed as an assembly.

2 A double row of rollers (25 in number) is incorporated at both ends of the countergear. Three spacers are used to locate and separate the rollers. These components can be renewed and retained in position using thick grease.

3 The endfloat of the countergear must be as specified. Use feeler blades to test this with the countergear temporarily held in position in the gearbox casing with the thrust washers held to the internal faces of the casing with thick grease. The larger thrust washer is located on the front internal face of the gearbox. If the endfloat exceeds that specified, renew the thrust washers.

7 Reverse pinion and gear casing - servicing

1 If the reverse pinion bushes are worn, renew the gear and shaft as a complete set.

2 Now is the time to examine the casing for cracks.

3 The release arm ball pin pivot is an interference fit and if distorted or worn it must be extracted and a new one driven in. Note the unused ball pin hole for LHD cars.

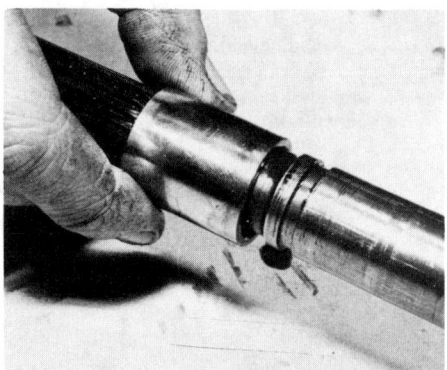

4.19 Installing 1st speed gear bush to mainshaft

4.20 Installing1st/2nd synchro unit to mainshaft

4.21 Installing 1st speed gear, synchro ring and needle roller bearing to mainshaft

4.22 Installing rear bearing and thrust washer to mainshaft

4.23 Installing speedometer drive gear to rear end of mainshaft

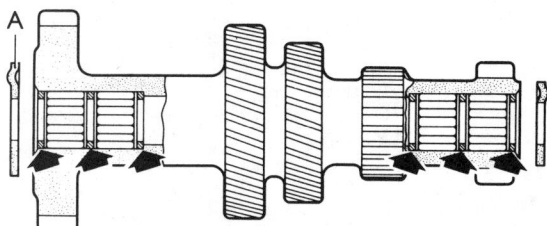

Fig. 6.10. Location of needle rollers, spacers and thrust washers in countergear. A is larger thrust washer at front (Sec. 6)

Fig. 6.12. Clutch release lever ball stud pivot (arrowed) on RHD cars (Sec. 7)

Fig. 6.11. Reverse pinion showing non-renewable bush (Sec. 7)

8 Gearbox - reassembly

1   Install reverse gear striking lever fulcrum pin so that the punch mark which indicates the high side of the eccentric is as near the top of the gearbox casing as possible.

2   Install the striking lever to the fulcrum pin so that the longer side of the boss is towards the casing.

3   Assemble the reverse pinion and shaft so that the pinion groove is towards the front of the gearbox.

4   Engage the reverse striking lever pad in the pinion groove.

5   Assemble the locking ball to the reverse shaft and drive the shaft in so that it is flush with the gearbox casing.

6   If the reverse gear striking lever requires adjustment temporarily install the rear cover without the mainshaft. Insert the selector shaft,

the interlock collar and the retaining pin. Now fit the eccentric pin and bracket assembly to the selector shaft.

Pull the selector shaft fully to the rear and rotate it so that it engages the striking lever in the rear groove of the interlock collar. Insert the gearlever and select reverse gear.

Now release the eccentric pin locknut and turn the pin until a clearance is provided between the rear face of reverse gear and the casing (lower projecting boss) of between 0.002 and 0.012 in. (0.05 and 0.30 mm) (photo).

7   Stick the countershaft thrust washers into the gearbox casing using a dab of thick grease. Make sure that the larger thrust washer is at the front of the casing and that the locating tabs on the washers engage in the casing grooves.

8   With the countergear correctly assembled with its rollers and spacers (see Section 6), carefully lower the countergear to the bottom of the gearbox. Make sure that the larger countershaft end gear is to the front (photo).

9   Stick a new front cover gasket to the front face of the gearbox and assemble the input shaft and front cover to the casing but do not insert the front cover bolts yet (photo).

10 To the rear end of the input shaft install the synchro ring and the needle roller bearing.

11 Carefully lift the countergear so that the thrust washers and roller bearings are not displaced and then drive in the countershaft complete with locking ball through the rear of the gearbox until the end of the shaft is flush with the casing (photo).

12 Stick a new gasket to the rear face of the gear casing and then pull the input shaft as far forward as it will go and install the assembled mainshaft/rear cover through the rear of the gearbox casing. Make sure that the slots in 4th gear synchro ring engages the keys in the synchro hub and that the synchro sleeve is located well forward on its hub in order to clear the countergear (photo), but do not pull the sleeve off or the synchro will fall apart.

13 Insert and tighten the front cover bolts.

14 Install the selector forks making sure that the fork shift lugs are towards the loose-fitting pin hole in the gear casing flange. The 3rd/4th

8.6 Checking reverse gear striking lever adjustment

8.8 Countergear awaiting installing of countershaft

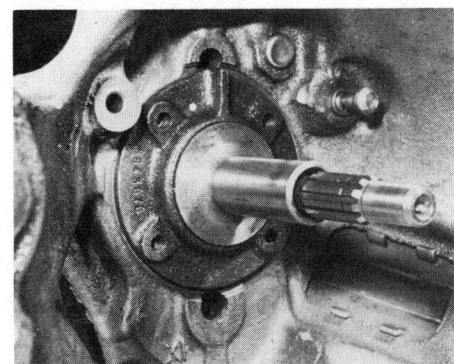

8.9 Front cover correctly aligned

8.11 Countershaft locking ball and groove

8.12 Installing mainshaft/rear cover assembly

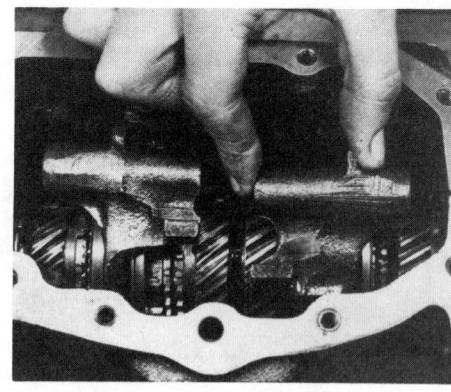

8.14 Installing the selector forks

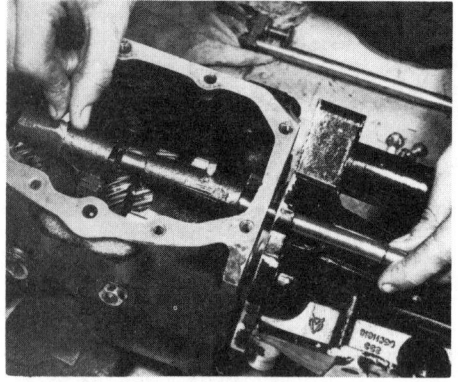

8.16 Installing the selector rail

8.19A Selector shaft engaged with interlock collar

8.19B Installing interlock collar retaining pin

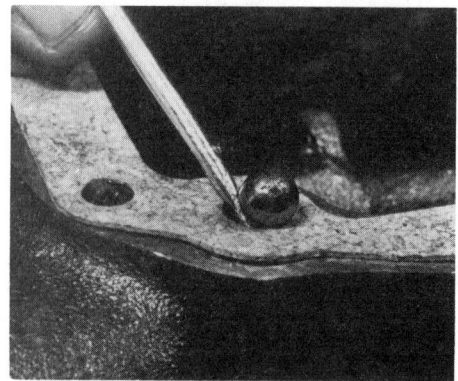

8.20A Installing selector detent ball

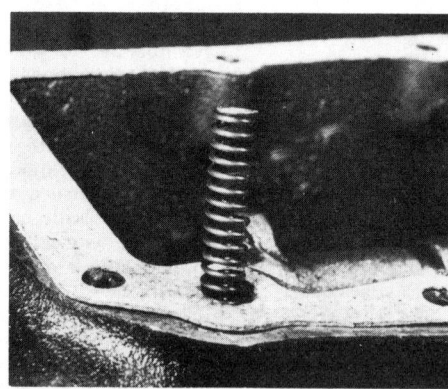

8.20B Installing selector detent spring

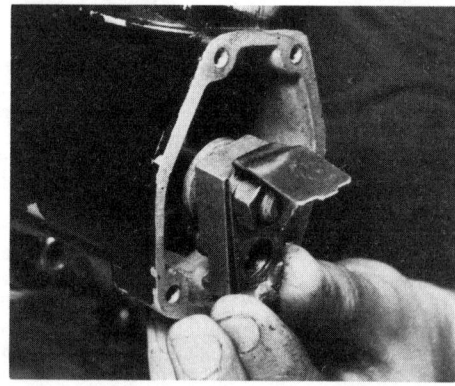

8.21 Installing selector shaft eccentric pin/bracket assembly

8.22 Checking gearshift lever fork to selector shaft clearance

8.24 Installing speedometer drive gear

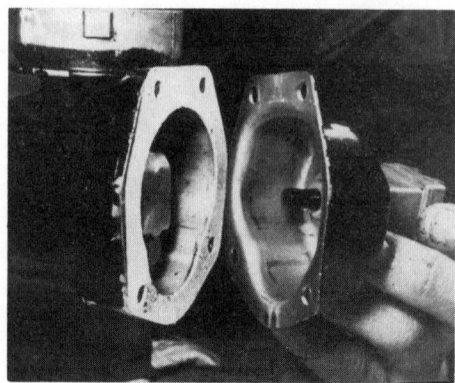

8.26 Fitting gearshift lever housing cover

selector fork has the smaller lug and is located nearer the front of the gearbox (photo).

15 Rotate the rear extension carefully so as not to damage the gasket so that the selector rail holes in the rear extension and rear face of the gearbox casing are in alignment.

16 Drive in the selector rail from the rear of the rear extension. Make sure that the end of the rail which has the groove enters last and is finally positioned flush with the end face of the gearbox casing (photo).

17 Rotate the rear extension until the securing bolts can be screwed in and tightened.

18 Inspect the condition of the plastic bush in the selector shaft housing and renew it if necessary.

19 Set both synchro units and reverse pinion in neutral and then install the selector shaft grooved interlock collar (wider groove to the rear) and the shaft. Rotate the collar and fit the loose fitting collar retaining pin (photos).

20 Insert the detent ball followed by the spring (photos).

21 Install the eccentric pin and bracket assembly, making sure that the slot in the bracket locates correctly on the two flats on the selector shaft (photo).

22 Temporarily install the gearshift control lever and select first gear. Now adjust the eccentric pin to obtain a clearance between the long leg of the lever fork and the selector shaft of between 0.002 and 0.012 in. (0.05 and 0.30 mm). Use feeler blades to check this clearance (photo).

23 When the adjustment has been correctly set, bend the reverse lamp switch contact plate over the eccentric pin locknut and selector shaft nut. Select neutral and withdraw the gearshift control lever.

24 Apply jointing compound to the end cap of the speedometer driven gear and then install the gear using a piece of tubing as a drift (photo).

25 If the reverse lamp switch has been removed from the gearshift lever housing cover, smear the switch threads with jointing compound and adjust the position of the switch in the cover in accordance with the diagram (Fig. 6.13).

26 Install the gearshift lever housing cover and the gearbox top cover using new gaskets (photo).

27 Install the clutch release arm and bearing and check that the starter pinion rubber boot is correctly located in the clutch bellhousing.

28 Refill the gearbox after installation in the car. This will prevent loss of oil from the rear of the unit during refitting operations.

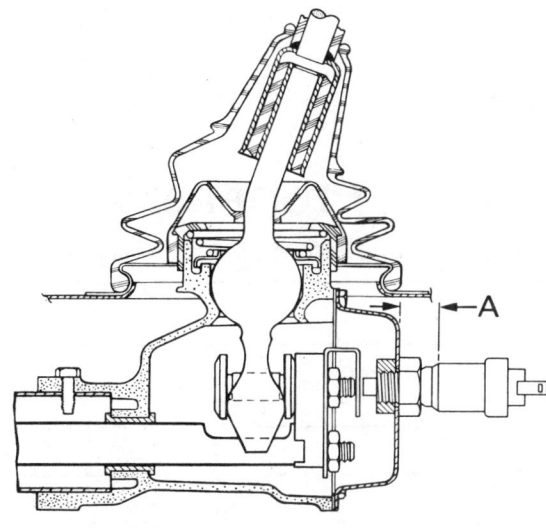

Fig. 6.13. Sectional view of gearshift lever housing (Sec. 8)

A = Reverse lamp switch setting of 0.30 in. (7.5 mm)

Note: *On later models the switch is fitted with fibre and plain washers*

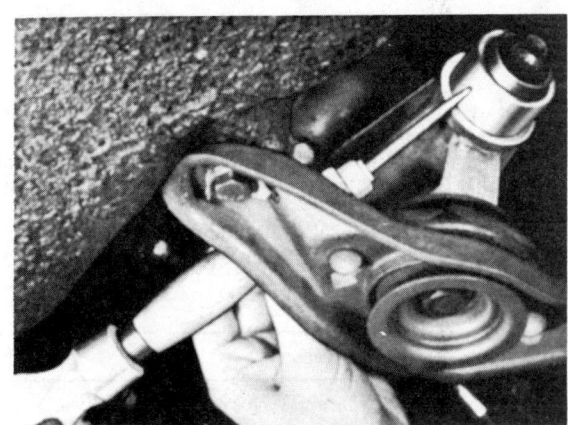

Fig. 6.14. Removing gearbox rear oil seal (Sec. 9)

---

9 Extension housing rear oil seal - renewal without removing gearbox

1 Remove the propeller shaft, as described in Chapter 7.

2 Using a sharp drift applied alternately to each side of the seal outer casing, drive off the oil seal from the rear end of the gearbox extension housing.

3 Smear the lips of the new seal with gear oil and install using a piece of tubing as a drift.

4 Install the propeller shaft, as described in Chapter 7.

---

10 Fault diagnosis - gearbox

Symptom	Reason
Ineffective synchromesh	Worn baulk rings or synchro hubs
Jumps out of one or more gears (on drive or over-run)	Weak detent spring, worn selector forks, worn gears or worn synchro sleeves
Noisy, rough, whining and vibration	Worn bearings and/or thrust washers (initially) resulting in extended wear generally due to play and backlash
Noisy and difficult engagement of gears	Clutch fault

Note: It is sometimes difficult to decide whether it is worthwhile removing and dismantling the gearbox for a fault which may be nothing more than a minor irritant. Gearboxes which howl, or where the synchromesh can be 'beaten' by a quick gear change, may continue to perform for a long time in this stage. A worn gearbox usually needs a complete rebuild to eliminate noise because the various gears, if re-aligned on new bearings will continue to howl when different wearing surfaces are presented to each other.

The decision to overhaul therefore, must be considered with regard to time and money available, relative to the degree of noise or malfunction that the driver can tolerate.

Chapter 7 Propeller shaft

For modifications, and information applicable to later models, see Supplement at end of manual

Contents

Specifications

Type	Single piece, tubular steel with two universal joints and sliding sleeve
Sleeve diameter	1.124 to 1.125 in (28.549 to 28.575 mm)
Sleeve clearance in gearbox extension bush	0.0015 to 0.0040 in (0.038 to 0.102 mm)

Torque wrench settings	lb ft	Nm
Rear flange bolts	24	33

1 General description

The propeller shaft is of single piece tubular steel construction with a universal joint at either end. At the front end of the shaft, an internally splined sliding sleeve connects with the gearbox mainshaft. The sliding sleeve takes care of fore-and-aft movement of the propeller shaft which occurs due to the deflection of the rear axle on the coil type road springs.

The propeller shaft universal joints cannot be serviced as their bearing cups are secured by staking. When wear takes place, a new shaft assembly must be fitted.

2 Universal joints - testing for wear

1 Wear in the needle roller bearings is characterized by vibration in the transmission, 'clonks' on taking up drive, and in extreme cases metallic squeaking and ultimately grating and shrieking sounds as the bearings break up.

2 It is easy to check if the needle roller bearings are worn with the driveshaft in position, by trying to turn the shaft with one hand, the other hand holding the rear axle flange when the rear universal joint is being checked, and the front half coupling when the front universal joint is being checked. Any movement between the driveshaft and the

Fig. 7.1. Propeller shaft universal joint showing staking of bearing cups

3.5 Propeller shaft rear flange

3.7 Withdrawing propeller shaft sliding sleeve from rear of gearbox

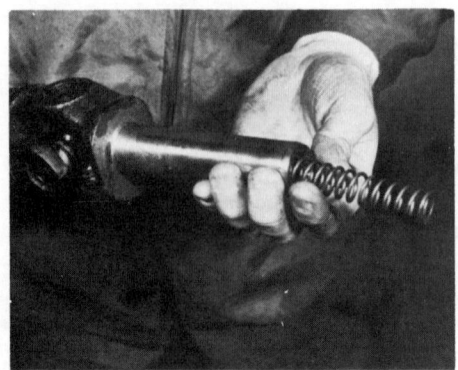

3.8 Extracting coil spring from bore of sliding sleeve

front half couplings, and round the rear half couplings, is indicative of considerable wear.

3 Now lift the shaft and watch for any movement between the yokes of the joints.

4 If wear is evident, fit a new propeller shaft complete.

3 Propeller shaft - removal and installation

1 Jack-up the rear of the car or position the car over a pit.

2 If the rear of the car is jacked-up, supplement the jack with support blocks or axle stands under the bodyframe members so that any danger of the jack collapsing is minimized.

3 If the rear wheels are off the ground, place the car in gear and also apply the handbrake to prevent the propeller shaft turning when the rear flange securing bolts are loosened.

4 The propeller shaft is carefully balanced to fine limits and it is important that it is replaced in exactly the same position it was in prior to removal. Scratch marks on the propeller shaft and rear axle flanges to ensure accurate mating when the time comes for installation.

5 Bend down the rear flange bolt locking tabs and then unscrew and remove the bolts (photo).

6 Push the propeller shaft slightly forward to separate the two flanges and then lower the rear end of the shaft.

7 Pull the propeller shaft to the rear to disengage the sliding sleeve from the rear end of the gearbox. Some loss of oil will occur at this stage, from the rear of the gearbox extension housing. This loss can be restricted by slipping a plastic bag over the end of the housing and securing it with a strong rubber band (photo).

8 Extract the coil spring which is located in the hollow of the sliding sleeve (photo).

9 Installation is a reversal of removal but smear the sliding sleeve with gear oil before pushing it through the gearbox rear seal.

10 Make sure that the coil spring is installed in the hollow of the sliding sleeve.

11 Fit new flange bolt locking plates and tighten the bolts to the specified torque.

12 Check and, if necessary, top-up the gearbox oil level.

4 Fault diagnosis - propeller shaft

Symptom	Reason
Vibration when vehicle running on road	Out of balance or distorted propeller shaft
	Backlash in splined shaft
	Loose flange securing bolts
	Worn universal joint bearings
Knock or 'clink' when taking up drive or shifting gear	Loose rear flange bolts
	Worn universal joint bearings
	Worn rear axle pinion splines
	Excessive backlash in differential gears
	Loose roadwheel nuts

Chapter 8 Rear axle

For modifications, and information applicable to later models, see Supplement at end of manual

Contents

Specifications

Rear axle type	Semi-floating, hypoid
Ratio	4.11 : 1
Oil capacity	1.2 Imp. pints (0.68 litres)

Torque wrench settings		lb ft	Nm
Axleshaft bearing retainer plate nuts		19	26
Pinion extension housing to differential unit		20	28
Pinion extension shaft flange nut		18	25
Pinion extension housing to crossmember bolts		15	21

For rear suspension torque wrench settings, see Specifications, Chapter 11.

1 General description

The rear axle is of hypoid semi-floating type. The differential and the hypoid gear and pinion are carried on taper roller bearings.

The pinion is unusual in the fact that it has an extension shaft splined to it. The extension shaft is supported at its front end by a ball bearing in a housing. The bearing assembly, housing and crossmember are all flexibly mounted.

Fore-and-aft location of the rear axle is provided by suspension arms and the attachment of the pinion extension housing to the bodyframe and crossmember. Side-to-side movement of the rear axle is controlled by a Panhard rod.

The rear axle lubricant cannot be drained unless the rear cover is removed.

2 Axleshafts (halfshafts) - removal

1 Jack-up the rear axle and support it securely under the axle tubes.
2 Remove the relevant roadwheel and brake drum.
3 Using a socket or box spanner inserted through the holes in the axleshaft flange, unscrew and remove the bearing retainer plate nuts.
4 A slide hammer should now be bolted to the wheel studs and the axleshaft withdrawn from the axle casing. It is possible to bolt an old roadwheel to the studs and strike two opposite points on the inner rim simultaneously. On no account use levers to prise the axleshaft. It is useless to try and pull the shaft from the axle casing, you will only succeed in pulling the car off the jacks.

3 Axleshaft - (halfshafts) bearing/oil seal - removal

1 A combined bearing/oil seal assembly is located at the end of each axleshaft. Any leakage of oil from the axle into the brake drum will eventually show on the roadwheel inner rim. This fault necessitates

Fig. 8.1. Removing an axleshaft with a slide hammer (Sec. 2)

renewal of the bearing/oil seal - assuming that the leakage is not from a faulty brake wheel cylinder (much lighter type oil).
2 Having removed the axleshaft as described in the preceding Section, secure the axleshaft in a vice and then cut a section from the retaining ring flange to expose the full width of the bearing retaining rings. (Fig. 8.4).
3 Split the retaining ring with a chold chiel and withdraw the ring. (Fig. 8.5).
4 Using a suitable press, press the axleshaft out of the bearing and extract the bearing retainer plate and dust shield and the gasket.
5 Clean the axleshaft and on it locate the following components:
    (i)   New dust shield with open side away from axleshaft flange.
    (ii)   Gasket and bearing retainer plate.
    (iii) New bearing/oil seal assembly so that the outer sealing ring groove is furthest from the axleshaft flange.

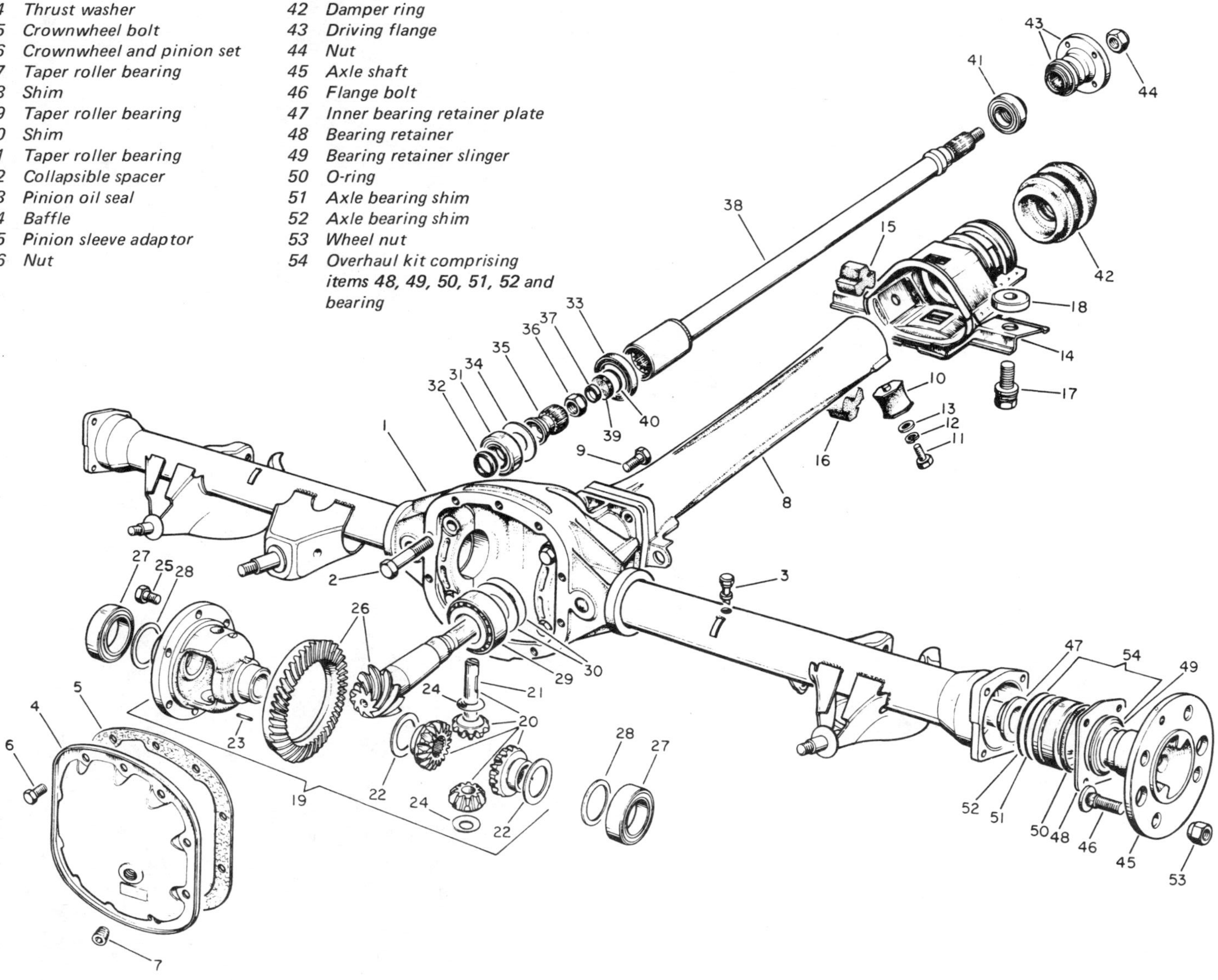

Fig. 8.2 Exploded view of the rear axle

1 Axle casing
2 Bearing cap bolt
3 Breather valve
4 Cover plate
5 Gasket
6 Bolt
7 Filler/level plug
8 Pinion extension housing
9 Bolt
10 Flexible mounting
11 Bolt
12 Lockwasher
13 Plain washer
14 Crossmember assembly
15 Bump stop
16 Bump stop
17 Bolt
18 Washer
19 Differential assembly comprising
20 Side gears, pinions
21 Cross shaft
22 Shim
23 Pin
24 Thrust washer
25 Crownwheel bolt
26 Crownwheel and pinion set
27 Taper roller bearing
28 Shim
29 Taper roller bearing
30 Shim
31 Collapsible spacer
32 Pinion oil seal
33 Baffle
34 Pinion sleeve adaptor
35 Nut
36 Nut
37 Thrust cap
38 Drive pinion extension shaft
39 Buffer
40 Disc
41 Bearing
42 Damper ring
43 Driving flange
44 Nut
45 Axle shaft
46 Flange bolt
47 Inner bearing retainer plate
48 Bearing retainer
49 Bearing retainer slinger
50 O-ring
51 Axle bearing shim
52 Axle bearing shim
53 Wheel nut
54 Overhaul kit comprising items 48, 49, 50, 51, 52 and bearing

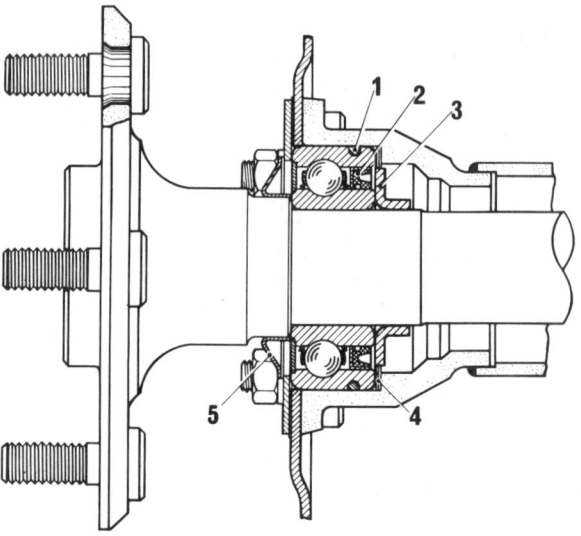

Fig. 8.3. Sectional view of a rear hub

1 'O' ring seal in bearing   3 Bearing retaining ring
  groove   4 Shims
2 Oil seal   5 Dust shield

6   Using a press and a suitable tubular packing piece, apply pressure to the bearing inner track and press it fully into position.
7   Press on a new bearing retaining ring so that its flanged side is towards the bearing.

4   Axleshaft (halfshafts) - installation

1   Locate the 'O' ring seal in the groove of the bearing and apply oil to the axle housing bearing recess in the axle casing.
2   *Where the original bearing has not been disturbed,* make sure that the original shims are in position in the bearing recess and insert the axleshaft, holding it quite horizontally until the splines on the end of the shaft can be felt engaging with the differential gears. Push the axleshaft fully home.
3   *Where a new bearing /oil seal has been fitted,* locate a new gasket on the brake backplate and screw on the nuts slightly more than finger-tight. Using a depth gauge, measure the depth between the face of the gasket and the bottom of the bearing recess. Record this measurement. Now measure the thickness of the axleshaft bearing. Subtract the latter dimension from that recorded earlier and then insert shims into the bearing recess in the axle casing which will equal in thickness the difference between the two measurements taken. The shim thickness can exceed the subtracted figure by not more than 0.006 in (0.15 mm).
4   The bearing retainer plate nuts should be tightened finally to the specified torque.
5   Refit the brake drum and roadwheel, then lower the jacks.

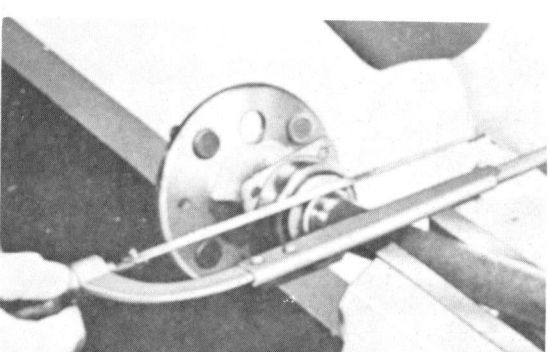

Fig. 8.4. Cutting through axleshaft retaining ring flange (Sec. 3)

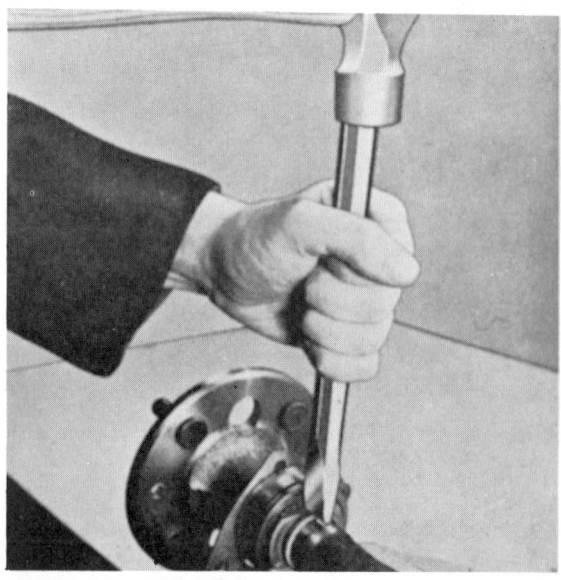

Fig. 8.5. Splitting retaining ring with a cold chisel (Sec. 3)

Fig. 8.6. Installing an axleshaft. Bearing 'O' ring seal (arrowed) (Sec. 4)

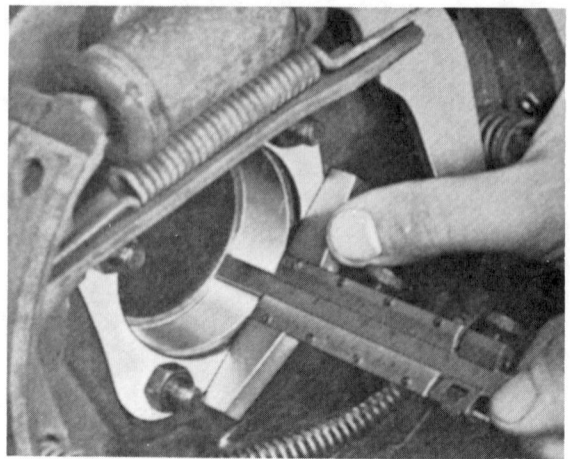

Fig. 8.7. Measuring axleshaft bearing recess depth (Sec. 4)

5 Pinion oil seal - renewal

1 Oil leakage from the pinion oil seal is usually detected by oil streaking along the outside of the differential housing and being thrown to both sides of the underside of the floorpan.

2 A reason for leakage from the pinion oil seal may be a blocked axle casing breather or too high a level of oil in the axle due to having topped it up with the car facing down an incline.

3 The pinion oil seal can be removed and a new one installed without

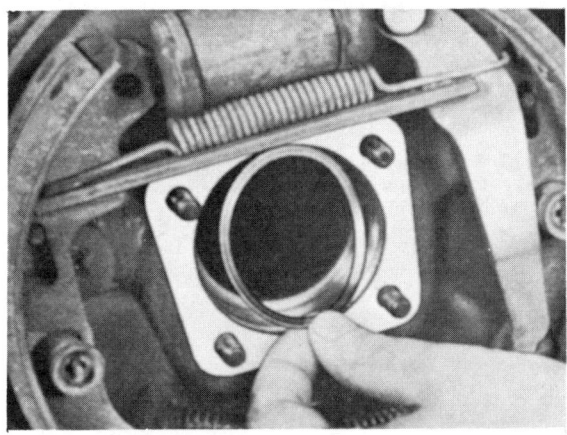

Fig. 8.8. Installing an axleshaft bearing shim (Sec. 4)

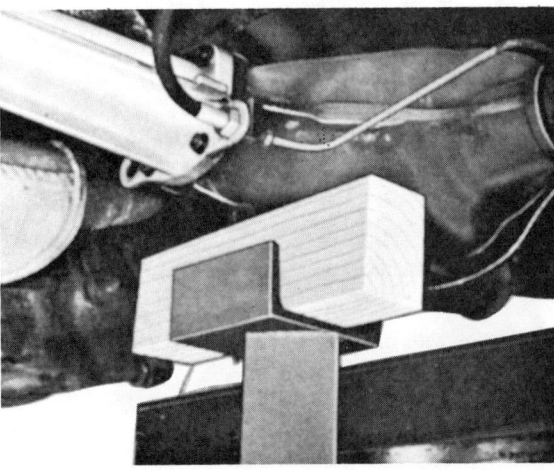

Fig. 8.9. Supporting differential unit prior to disconnecting extension housing crossmember (Sec. 5)

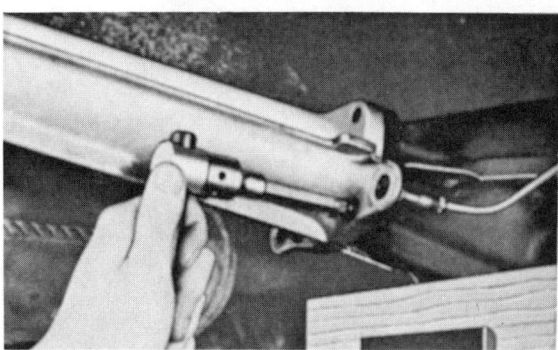

Fig. 8.10. Removing an extension housing to differential unit securing bolt (Sec. 5)

having to remove the rear axle from the car. The action of the rear road springs applies a downward force on the front end of the pinion extension housing and before any work commences support the differential unit immediately behind the pinion extension housing.

4 Disconnect the rear brake flexible hose from the rigid brake pipe at the extension housing flange. Plug the brake lines to prevent loss of fluid.

5 Remove the propeller shaft, as described in Chapter 7.

6 Unbolt the pinion extension front crossmember from the body frame (photo).

7 Unscrew and remove the bolts which secure the pinion extension housing to the differential unit. These bolts are of internally splined socket type and require the use of a M8 tri-square bit.

8 Withdraw the pinion extension housing and prise the defective seal from its recess in the front of the differential unit.

9 Oil the tips of the new seal and install it (closed side visible when installed) using a piece of tubing as a drift.

10 Install the pinion extension housing, the crossmember bolts and propeller shaft, tightening all bolts to the specified torque and having set the suspension as described in Section 7, paragraph 12.

11 Reconnect the brake line and bleed the brakes, as described in Chapter 9.

12 Lower the car to the ground and then check and top-up if necessary, the rear axle oil level.

6 Pinion extension housing crossmember and bearing - dismantling and reassembly

1 Remove the pinion extension housing complete with crossmember support and bearing housing as described in the preceding Section.

5.6 Pinion extension housing and crossmember

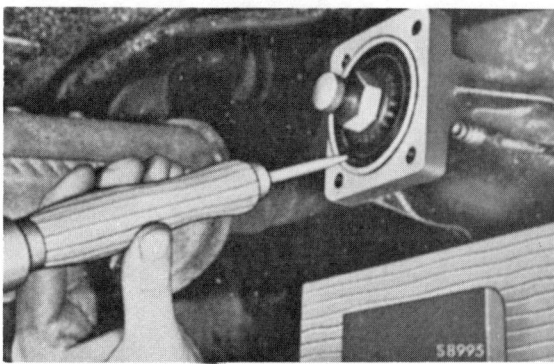

Fig. 8.11. Prising out a pinion oil seal (Sec. 5)

2 The pinion driving flange must now be held still while the shaft flange nut is unscrewed. In the absence of a proper tool, insert two spare bolts into two of the pinion flange holes and pass a long lever between them to prevent the flange rotating.

3 With the pinion flange nut removed, withdraw the flange. The use of a two or three-legged puller will probably be required for this.

4 Rest the rear face of the crossmember bearing housing on the open jaws of a vice and using a soft-faced mallet, drive the pinion extension shaft from the housing and bearing.

5 The bearing assembly can be levered from the rubber insulator and the insulator removed, if required from the crossmember.

6 The crossmember itself can be levered from the pinion extension housing and the rubber mountings unscrewed.

7 Before fitting a new rubber insulator to the crossmember, flatten the retaining tags.

8 The insulator and the bearing can now be installed and the tags bent back to their original position.

9 Pack the space between the dust shield and the bearing with rubber grease as supplied for use in braking systems.

10 Fit the conical flexible mountings to the extension housing and then install the crossmember over them but do not tighten the bolts until the extension housing and crossmember have been installed to the car.

11 Install the pinion extension housing over the extension shaft and drive in the flange using a tubular drift.

12 Hold the flange quite still and using a new nut, tighten it to 18 lb ft (25 Nm). Stake the nut in position.

13 Install the pinion extension housing to the differential unit and attach the crossmember, as described in Section 5, paragraphs 10 to 12.

Fig. 8.12. Removing the pinion driving flange nut. Note tool for holding flange still (Sec. 6)

Fig. 8.14. Removing pinion extension shaft bearing from insulator ring (Sec. 6)

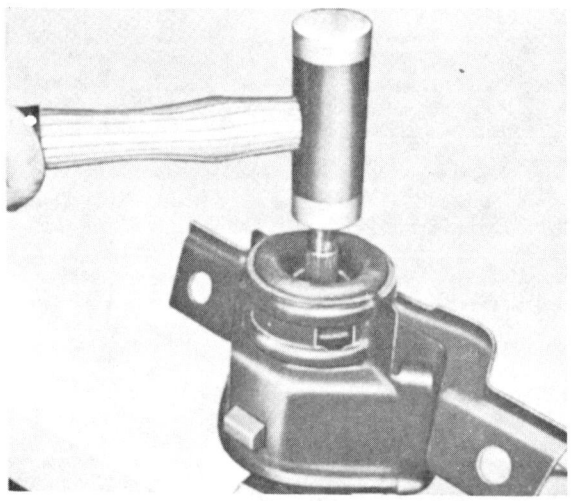

Fig. 8.13. Separating pinion extension shaft from crossmember housing and bearing (Sec. 6)

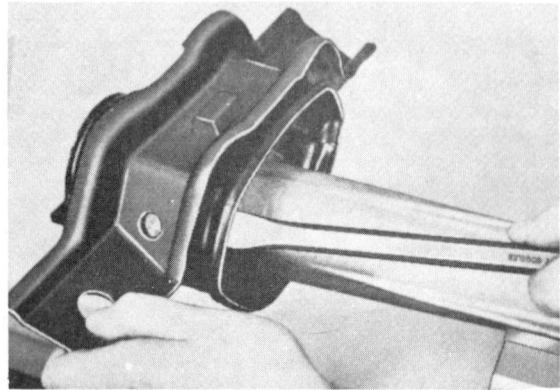

Fig. 8.15. Levering crossmember housing from pinion extension housing (Sec. 6)

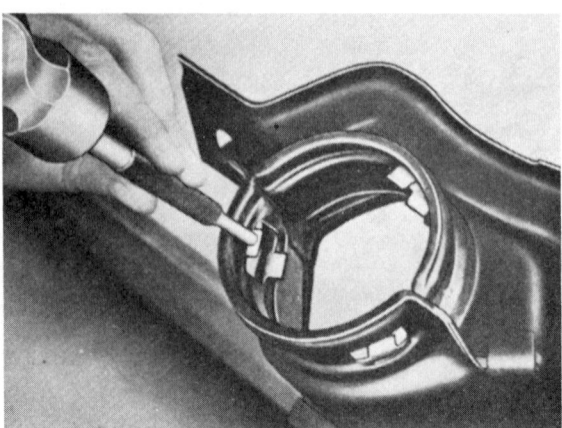

Fig. 8.16. Flattening the insulator retaining tabs in the crossmember housing (Sec. 6)

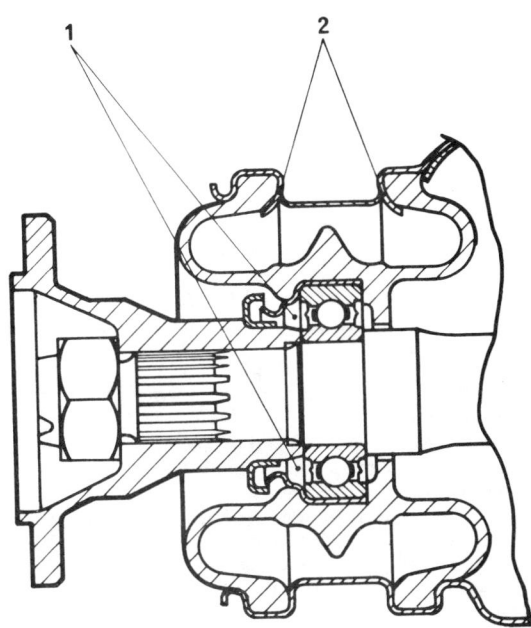

Fig. 8.17. Sectional view of extension housing driving flange and other components (Sec. 6)

1 Space filled with rubber grease

2 Insulator retaining tags

7 Rear axle - removal and installation

1 Removal of the rear axle should be undertaken when, due to wear, the differential unit needs a complete overhaul. Due to special tools and gauges required, it is recommended that your Vauxhall dealer carries out this work or alternatively, a reconditioned or new unit is obtained. If the latter course is chosen, check the extent to which the new unit will represent a complete assembly, as the original axleshafts, extension housing and other items may be required for fitting to the new axle.

2 Jack-up the rear of the car and support it on axle stands placed under the suspension arm front brackets. Support the differential unit on a jack, preferably of trolley type. Remove the rear roadwheels.

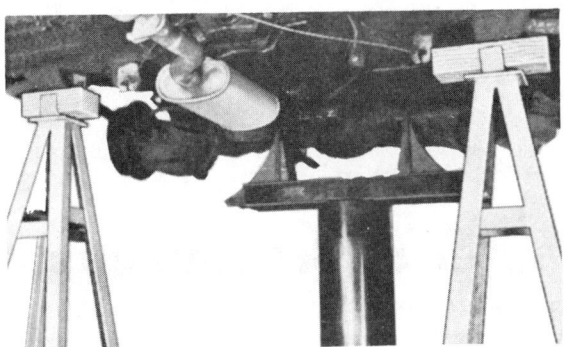

Fig. 8.18. Bodyframe supported prior to removing rear axle (Sec. 7)

3 Disconnect the suspension arm (see Section 11).

4 Disconnect the rear shock absorbers, Panhard rod and anti-roll bar from the axle casing (see Section 11).

5 Disconnect the exhaust system rear mountings so that the parking brake cable can pass over the silencer and tailpipe as the axle is withdrawn.

6 Disconnect the rear flexible brake pipe from the rigid brake pipe and plug them to prevent loss of fluid.

7 Disconnect the handbrake relay rod from the handbrake cable equaliser (see Chapter 9).

8 Disconnect and remove the propeller shaft (Chapter 7).

9 Unbolt the rear axle pinion extension housing from underside of the floor pan.

10 Lower the jack under the differential unit until the coil type roadsprings and their seats can be withdrawn.

11 Withdraw the complete rear axle from beneath and to the rear of the car.

12 Installation is a reversal of removal but the following points must be noted:

Before tightening the suspension bolts and the pinion extension housing to crossmember bolts, the suspension must be set by inserting wooden blocks (4½ in long - 115.0 mm) between the axle casing and each bump stop on the underbody. Now load the rear of the car until the wooden blocks are nipped between the axle casing and the bump stops. Tighten the bolts to the specified torque settings given in Specifications Sections (this Chapter and Chapter 11).

13 Bleed the brakes, as described in Chapter 9.

14 Check and if necessary, top-up the rear axle oil level.

8 Fault diagnosis - rear axle

Symptom*	Reason
Vibration	Worn axleshaft bearing
	Loose pinion flange bolts
	Roadwheels out of balance
	Propeller shaft out of balance
Noise on turns	Worn differential gear
	Worn or incorrectly adjusted crownwheel and pinion
'Clunk' on acceleration or deceleration	Excessive backlash in differential gears
	Worn axleshaft splines
	Worn propeller shaft joints
	Loose pinion flange bolts

*It must be appreciated that tyre noise, wear in the rear suspension bushes and worn or loose shock absorber mountings can all mislead the mechanic into thinking that components of the rear axle are the source of trouble.

Chapter 9 Braking system

For modifications, and information applicable to later models, see Supplement at end of manual

Contents

Specifications

System type	Four wheel hydraulic with servo assistance. Discs on front, drums on rear with self adjusting shoes. Handbrake mechanical on rear wheels. Dual circuit with pressure regulating valve

Discs

Diameter	9.4 in (238.76 mm)
Maximum run-out	0.004 in (0.1 mm)
Minimum thickness after resurfacing	0.39 in (9.9 mm)
Minimum pad friction material thickness	0.06 in (1.5 mm)
Swept area	185 sq. in (1193.5 sq. cm)

Drums

Internal diameter	7.87 in (199.89 mm)
Shoe width	1.75 in (44.45 mm)
Maximum internal diameter after regrinding	7.913 in (201.0 mm)
Swept area	87.5 sq. in (564.57 sq. cm)

Torque wrench settings

	lb ft	Nm
Caliper to stub axle bolts	72	100
Disc to hub bolts	30	41
Master cylinder secondary port connector	27	37
Rear brake backplate nuts	19	26

1 General description

The four wheel braking system is of dual circuit, hydraulic type with discs at the front and self-adjusting drum brakes at the rear. A vacuum servo unit is fitted to most models as standard equipment.

A pressure regulating valve is installed in the hydraulic circuit to prevent the rear wheels locking in advance of the front wheels during heavy applications of the brakes. The handbrake is mechanically operated on the rear wheels only and incorporates an 'ON' warning lamp switch.

2 Disc pads - inspection and renewal

1 Every 6000 miles (9600 km) inspect the disc friction pads for wear. To do this, jack-up the front roadwheels and remove them.
2 Withdraw the clips and remove the pad retaining pins (photos).
3 Extract the spring retainer plates.

4 Inspect the thickness of the friction material on each of the disc pads. If it is 0.06 in (1.5 mm) or less, or will be before the next service, then the pads must be renewed.
5 Using a pair of pliers, withdraw the disc pads together with their anti-squeal shims (photo).
6 Syphon some fluid from the front circuit reservoir on the master cylinder so that the fluid will not overflow when the caliper pistons are depressed. Syphoning can be carried out using a poultry baster or old hydrometer.
7 Brush any dust or dirt from the disc pad recesses in the calipers (try not to inhale the dust) and then using a flat bar or piece of wood, depress the caliper pistons squarely into their housings to accommodate the extra thickness of the new pads.
8 Install the new friction pads making sure that the friction surface is towards the disc and the anti-squeal shims are located on the rear of the pad backing plates with their directional arrows facing upwards. Always renew the front disc pads as a complete axle set.
9 When all the disc pads have been installed, give the footbrake pedal several hard applications and then check and, if necessary, top-up the fluid level in the master cylinder reservoir.

2.2A Extracting a disc caliper pin clip

2.2B Caliper pin and spring retainer plate

2.5 Removing disc pad and anti-squeal shim

3 Rear brake shoes - inspection and renewal

1   Jack-up the rear of the car and remove the roadwheels. Fully release the handbrake control.

2   Although the rear shoes are adjusted automatically by application of the foot or handbrake, two eccentric cam adjusters are fitted to the brake backplates and these should be turned to release the shoes from contact with the drum so that the drum can be more easily withdrawn. Turn the rear adjuster in the direction of forward roadwheel rotation and the front adjuster in the opposite direction.

3   Remove the two drum retaining clips and withdraw the drum (photo).

4   Brush away any accummulated dust and inspect the linings, if the friction material is worn down to, or nearly down to the rivets, renew the shoes as a complete axle set. If the linings are in good condition, clean the interior of the brake drum and refit it (photo).

5   Where the shoes must be renewed, obtain new or reconditioned ones. Do not re-line them yourself as this seldom proves satisfactory.

6   Unhook the handbrake cable from the rear shoe lever.

7   Remove the shoe steady posts. To do this, grip the dished washer with a pair of pliers, depress it and rotate it through 90° then release it and withdraw the washer and spring from the 'T' shaped post.

8   Release the front shoe from the lower anchor block.

9   Detach the lower shoe return spring.

10 Using a pair of pliers, unhook the upper shoe return spring and withdraw the shoes and the strut.

11 Clean the brake backplate and check for oil leakage which may be from a faulty axleshaft bearing/seal (see Chapter 8) or a leaking wheel cylinder. Trace and rectify the fault.

Fig. 9.1. Rear brake shoe adjusters showing rotational direction to withdraw linings from drum (Sec. 3)

3.3 Brake drum securing clip

3.4 View of rear brake assembly

12 Do not touch the brake pedal or handbrake lever while the shoes are removed.

13 Detach the parking brake lever from the rear brake shoe (circlip) and fit the lever to the new shoe.

14 Smear a little brake grease on the rubbing surfaces of the backplate; also on the ends of the shoe webs which will contact the wheel cylinder pistons and the anchor block. Rotate the cam adjusters to their retracted positions.

15 Locate the rear shoe on the backplate and attach the handbrake cable.

16 Install the strut, the front shoe, and attach the lower return spring.

17 Attach the upper return spring making sure that the larger hook engages with the rear shoe.

18 Check that the shoes are correctly positioned with respect to the leading and trailing ends of their linings.

19 Install the shoe steady posts by reversing the removal process.

20 Install the drum and roadwheel.

21 After the car has been lowered to the ground, apply the foot and handbrake several times each to bring the new shoes into the closest possible contact with the drums.

4 Disc caliper - removal, servicing and refitting

1 Jack-up the front of the car and remove the roadwheel.

2 Withdraw the disc pads, as described in Section 2.

3 Unscrew and remove the bolts which secure the caliper to the stub axle.

4 Lift the caliper from its location and if no further operations are to be carried out to the unit, it should be tied up to the suspension to prevent strain on the flexible hydraulic hose.

5 If the caliper is to be overhauled or renewed, remove the cap from the master cylinder reservoir and place a piece of polythene sheet over the opening and then press the cap on again. This will create a vacuum and prevent loss of fluid when the hydraulic line is disconnected.

6 The flexible hose to the caliper can either be removed as described

Fig. 9.2. Left-hand rear backplate and shoe assembly (Sec. 3)

Fig. 9.3. Assembling brake shoe upper return spring (Sec. 3)

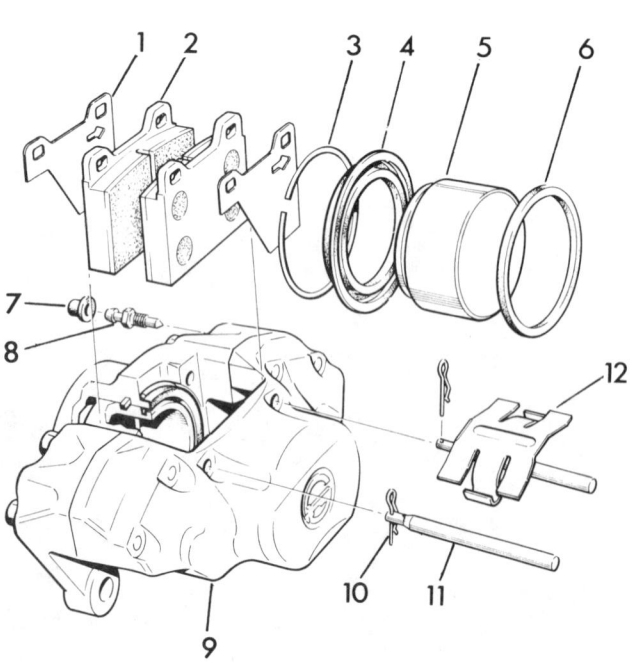

Fig. 9.4. Exploded view of a front disc caliper (Sec. 4)

1   Anti-squeal shim
2   Disc pad
3   Dust excluder retaining ring
4   Dust excluder
5   Piston
6   Seal
7   Dust cap
8   Bleed nipple
9   Caliper body
10 Clip
11 Retaining pin
12 Spring retainer

As the caliper is of dual piston type, items 3 to 6 are also incorporated in the opposing cylinder

in Section 10, or a simpler method is to hold the union at the caliper end of the hose in a spanner and unscrew the caliper from the hose. Make sure when using this method that the hose is not twisted. Retain the sealing washer and plug the end of the hose to prevent loss of fluid.

7 With the caliper removed, clean the external surfaces. **On no account remove or loosen the bolts that secure the two halves of the caliper body together.**

8 Extract the spring retaining rings and dust excluders from the ends of the caliper pistons.

9 Using two screwdrivers as levers and taking care not to scratch the pistons, prise the pistons from the caliper body. Mark each piston in relation to its respective bore.

10 Inspect the surfaces of the pistons and cylinder bores. If these appear scratched or show any 'bright' wear areas, the complete caliper unit must be renewed.

11 If the components are in good condition, ease the seals from the cylinder bores taking care not to damage the surfaces of the bores.

12 Discard the seals and obtain new ones in the form of a repair kit.

13 Install the new seals using the fingers only to manipulate them into their grooves.

14 Dip the pistons in clean hydraulic fluid and insert them squarely into their cylinder bores. Install the new dust excluders and spring retainers.

15 Reconnect the caliper to the flexible hose, install the caliper and tighten the securing bolts to the specified torque. Refit the disc pads.

16 Bleed the front braking circuit as described in Section 12, having first removed the polythene sheet from the master cylinder (if this device was employed).

17 Refit the roadwheel and lower the car.

5 Brake disc - examination, removal and refitting

1 Detach the caliper from the stub axle and tie it up out of the way, as described in the preceding Section, paragraphs 1 to 4.

2 The disc should now be inspected for deep scoring or grooving (light scoring is normal). If severe, the disc should be removed and either renewed or ground provided the thickness will not be reduced below the minimum specified in the Specifications Section.

3 Finally check for run-out (buckling or distortion) of the disc. Ideally a dial gauge should be used to measure this but feeler blades can be used against a fixed block as the hub/disc is slowly rotated.

4 If the disc is to be removed, first withdraw the hub/disc assembly, as described in Chapter 11.

5 Unscrew and remove the four socket type bolts which secure the disc to the hub and separate the two components.

6 Reassembly and refitting are reversals of dismantling and removal but make sure that the disc to hub mating surfaces are clean and tighten the securing bolts to the specified torque.

7 Lubricate and adjust the hub bearings, as described in Chapter 11.

6 Rear brake operating (slave) cylinders - removal, servicing and refitting

1 Jack-up the rear of the car and remove the roadwheel and brake drum.

2 Rotate each of the backplate adjusters until the brake shoes are clear of the operating cylinder.

3 Remove the cap from the master cylinder reservoir and place a piece of polythene sheeting over the opening and then press the cap on again. This will create a vacuum and prevent loss of fluid when the hydraulic line is disconnected.

4 Disconnect the hydraulic line at the operating cylinder union and plug the line.

5 Unscrew the two bolts which secure the cylinder to the backplate and then withdraw the cylinder.

6 Clean the external surfaces of the cylinder and peel off the dust

Fig. 9.6. Removing a disc to hub securing bolt (Sec. 5)

Fig. 9.5. Extracting a caliper piston (Sec. 4)

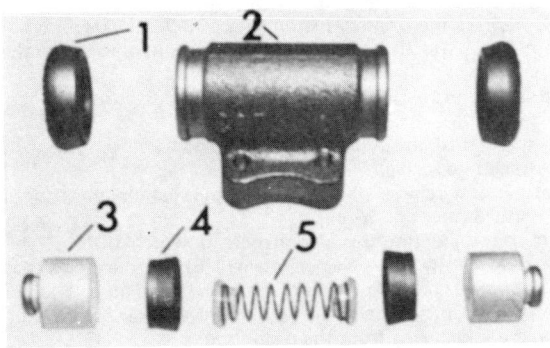

Fig. 9.8. Exploded view of a wheel operating cylinder (Sec. 6)

1	Dust excluder	3	Piston
2	Body	4	Seal
		5	Spring

Fig. 9.7. Brake shoes withdrawn from wheel operating cylinder (Sec. 6)

excluders. If the pistons cannot be shaken out, release the bleed screw and apply air pressure from a tyre pump.

7   Inspect the surfaces of the pistons and cylinder bores. If any scoring or 'bright' wear areas are evident, renew the complete assembly.

8   If the components are in good condition, discard the rubber seals and obtain new ones in the form of a repair kit.

9   Install the new seals using the fingers only to manipulate them into position. Dip the pistons into clean hydraulic fluid before installing them and then fit the dust excluders.

10 Installation is a reversal of removal but make sure that the locating boss on the cylinder body is engaged correctly in the hole in the backplate.

11 Turn the backplate adjusters to their maximum retracted positions and install the brake drum.

12 Remove the polythene sheeting from the master cylinder reservoir and bleed the rear hydraulic circuit as described in Section 12.

13 Refit the roadwheel and lower the car to the ground.

14 The action of bleeding will have adjusted the shoes but check that this has in fact taken place by applying both the foot pedal and the handbrake lever several times.

7   Brake drum - inspection and renovation

1   The brake drums are of composite cast iron and pressed steel construction. Whenever they are removed examine the areas round the bolt holes for cracks and the friction surfaces for scoring or grooves.

2   After a high mileage, the drums may become slightly oval internally and this condition or grooving caused by neglect in renewing the shoes can only be rectified by renewal or surface grinding provided the latter will not increase the drum internal diameter by more than the maximum specified in Specifications.

8   Master cylinder - removal, servicing and installation

1   The master cylinder is of tandem type and is mounted on the front face of the servo unit. Should a drop in pressure occur in either the front or rear circuit, a pressure warning switch will indicate this by means of a warning lamp mounted on the instrument panel. The switch comprises a double ended piston which is kept in balance in a separate bore within the master cylinder body. When one circuit pressure drops, the piston is displaced and makes contact to complete the warning lamp electrical circuit (photos).

2   Disconnect the leads from the master cylinder pressure warning lamp switch.

3   Disconnect the brake pipes from the master cylinder and allow the fluid to drain into a suitable container.

4   Unscrew and remove the nuts which secure the master cylinder to the front face of the servo unit and release the front support bracket. Remove the master cylinder.

5   Tip out fluid from the reservoirs and using suitable pliers, extract the retaining circlips and seals and remove the reservoirs.

6   Extract the stop pin from its recess.

7   Now depress the primary piston about 0.40 in (10.0 mm) and insert a piece of wire into the primary piston bypass hole to retain the piston in this position.

8   Extract the primary piston circlip and then withdraw the temporary wire and withdraw the piston assembly.

9   Tap the end of the cylinder on a block of wood to eject the secondary piston and its spring.

10 Unscrew and remove the secondary port connector and withdraw the non-return valve and spring.

11 To extract the pressure warning lamp switch piston, remove the contact head (3), pin (4), carrier retainer (5) and the plug (7) as shown in Fig. 9.15 and then tap the end of the cylinder on a block of wood.

12 The primary piston can only be dismantled after compressing it and extracting the lock ring from the piston rod.

13 Examine the piston and cylinder bore surfaces for scoring or 'bright' wear areas. Where these are evident, renew the complete master cylinder.

14 If the components are in good order, discard the seals and obtain new ones, preferably in the form of a repair kit.

15 Install the new primary and secondary pistons seals as shown in Fig. 9.16, using the fingers only to manipulate them into position. Make

8.1A Location of master cylinder and pressure regulating valve

8.1B Close up of pressure regulating valve showing bleed nipple

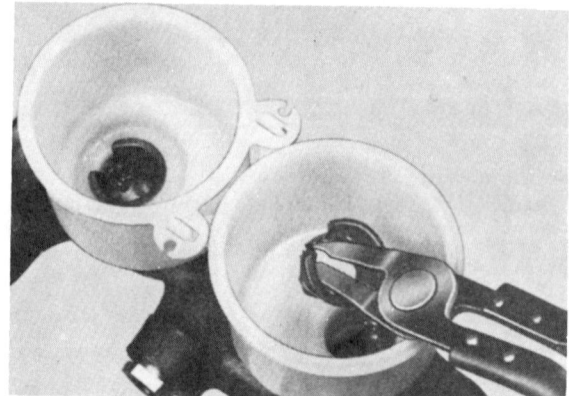

Fig. 9.9. Extracting a master cylinder reservoir securing circlip (Sec. 8)

sure that the seal protecting shims are located **behind** the front seals of the pistons.

16 Compress the primary piston spring and install the new lock ring (supplied), to the piston rod.

17 Install the pistons to the master cylinder body by reversing the removal procedure and again using the temporary restraining wire.

18 Refitting of the remaining components is a reversal of removal but tighten the secondary port connector to 27 lb/ft (37 Nm) after first installing the non-return valve and spring.

19 Installation of the master cylinder is a reversal of removal but bleed the hydraulic system, as described in Section 12.

20 Before installing the reservoir top cover, make sure that the dirt excluding diaphragms are returned to their original shapes (Fig. 9.17).

Fig. 9.10. Extracting master cylinder stop pin (Sec. 8)

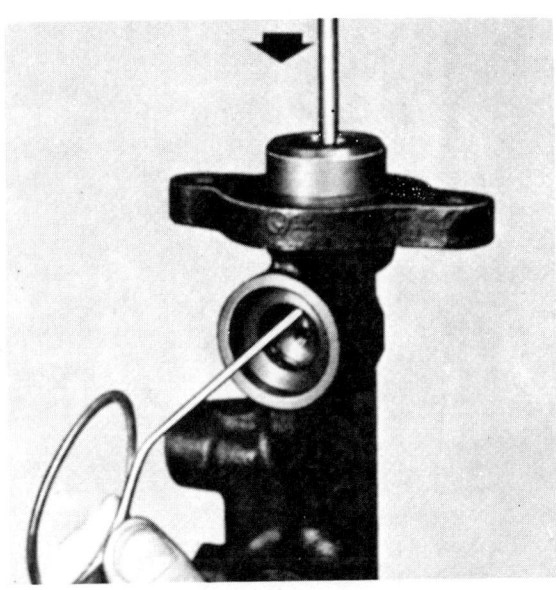

Fig. 9.11. Depressing master cylinder primary piston and inserting restraining wire (Sec. 8)

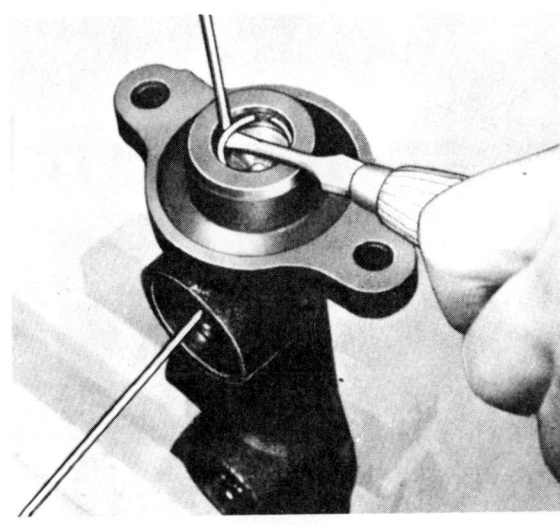

Fig. 9.12. Extracting primary piston circlip from master cylinder (Sec. 8)

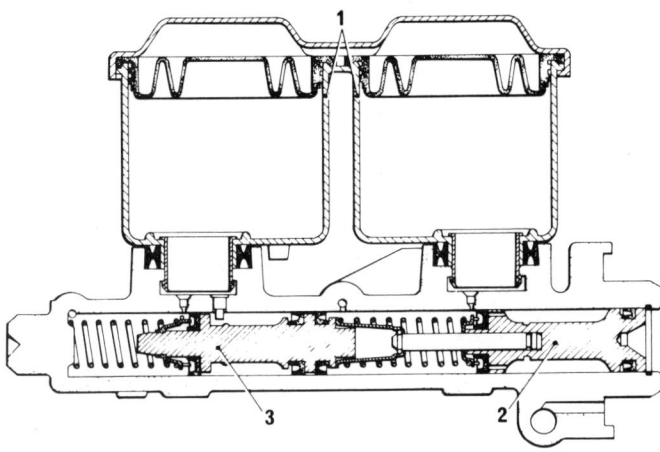

Fig. 9.13. Sectional view of the master cylinder (Sec. 8)

1 Reservoirs
2 Primary piston
3 Secondary piston

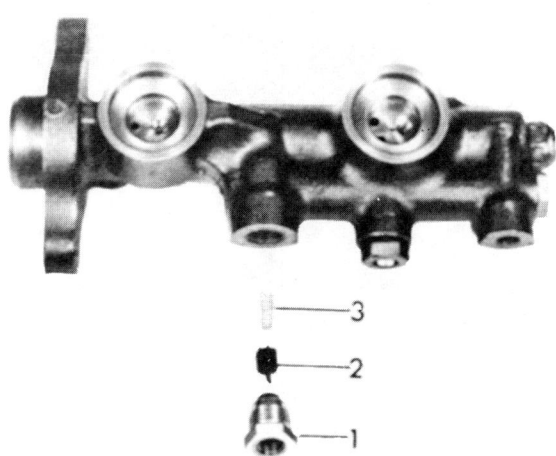

Fig. 9.14. Master cylinder non-return valve (Sec. 8)

1 Secondary port   2 Non-return valve   3 Spring
   connector

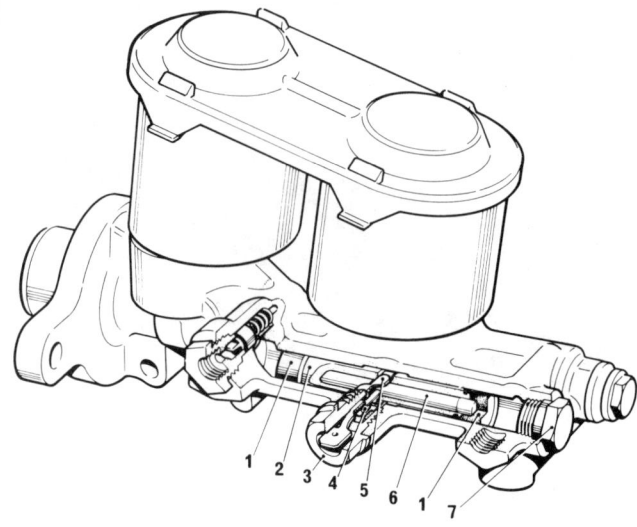

Fig. 9.15. Cutaway view of master cylinder pressure warning lamp switch (Sec. 8)

1   Diaphragms   4   Pin
2   Carrier   5   Carrier
3   Contact head   6   Piston
                           7   Plug

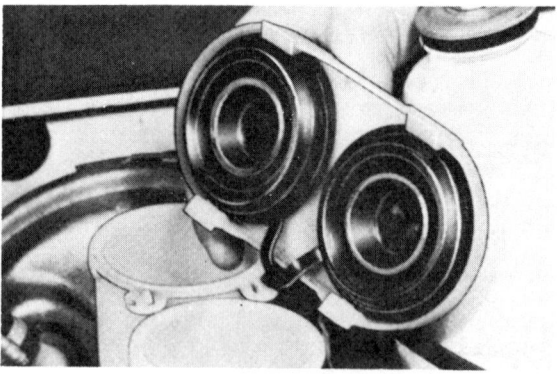

Fig. 9.17. Installing master cylinder reservoir caps (Sec. 8)

Fig. 9.19. Pressure regulating valve flow diagram (Sec. 9)

LHD cars   –   Fluid pressure to front calipers through ports A
                and B
RHD cars   –   Fluid pressure to front calipers through port A
                (a bleed nipple is installed in port B)
All cars   –   Fluid pressure to rear brakes through port C and
                modified before it leaves port D

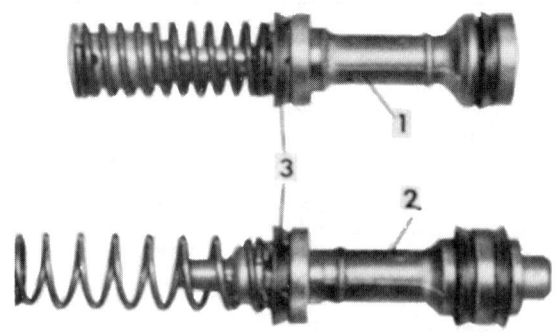

Fig. 9.16. Master cylinder piston assemblies (Sec. 8)

1   Primary piston   2   Secondary piston   3   Cup seals

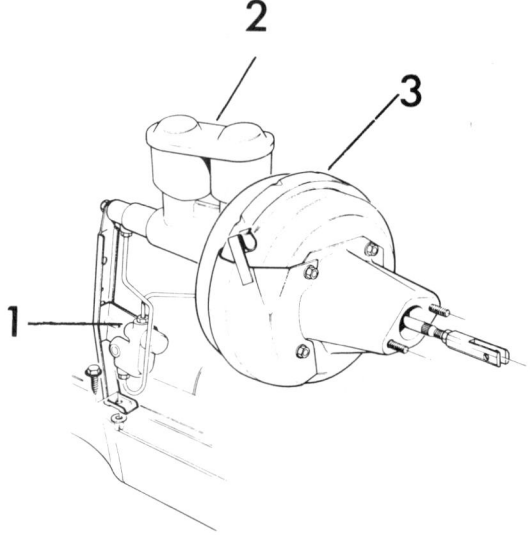

Fig. 9.18. Location of major brake units

1   Pressure regulating   2   Master cylinder   3   Vacuum servo
    valve   unit

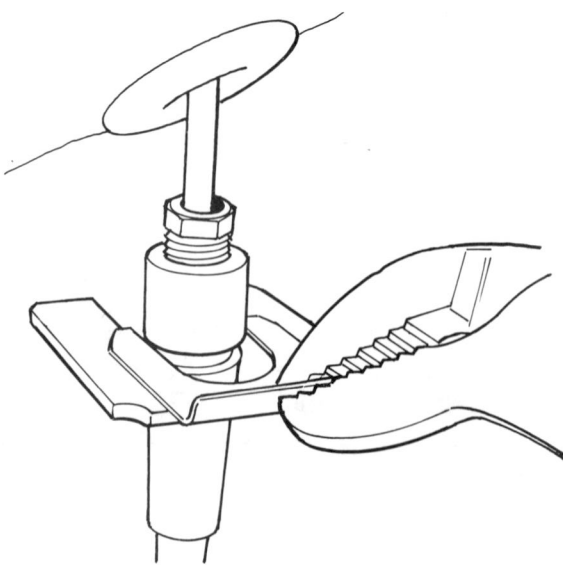

Fig. 9.20. Extracting a brake line support bracket clip (note bent tag
points away from flexible hose) (Sec. 10)

9 Pressure regulating valve - description, removal and refitting

1 The valve is mounted on the master cylinder support bracket.
2 The valve is a pressure sensing device and is quite automatic in its operation to permit front brake pressure to increase but to modify this increase in the case of the rear brakes during periods of heavy brake application. Should pressure drop in the rear hydraulic circuit due to a leak, then the valve maintains full pressure to the front wheels. Conversely, if a leak develops in the front circuit then full pressure is maintained to the rear wheels and the normal pressure regulating action of the valve is bypassed.
3 The valve cannot be repaired and in the event of a fault developing, it must be renewed complete.
4 To remove the valve, disconnect the fluid lines from it.
5 Refitting is a reversal of removal, the system must then be bled (Section 12) and in the case of RHD cars, the valve must also be bled after having first bled the rest of the hydraulic system.

10 Flexible hoses - inspection, removal and refitting

1 Regularly inspect the condition of the flexible hydraulic hoses. If they are perished, chafed or swollen they must be renewed.
2 To remove a flexible hose, extract the clip from the support bracket.
3 Hold the flats of the flexible hose end fitting quite still with a spanner and unscrew the union nut which couples it to the rigid brake line.
4 Disconnect the flexible hose from the rigid line and from the support bracket and then unscrew the hose from the component at its opposite end.
5 Refitting is a reversal of removal. Screw the hose into the caliper or tee piece using the sealing washer supplied and then connect it to the rigid line having first passed it through the opening in the support bracket. Install the securing clip so that the bent tag is pointing away from the flexible hose.
6 It is important to note that all pipe unions and connections are to metric standards **and hoses or unions with other threads should on no account be used.**
7 Always bleed the hydraulic system if a flexible hose has been disconnected or renewed.

11 Rigid brake lines - inspection, removal and refitting

1 At regular intervals wipe the steel brake pipes clean and examine them for signs of rust or denting causing by flying stones.
2 Examine the securing clips to prevent wear to the pipe surface. Bend the tongues of the clips if necessary to ensure that they hold the brake pipes securely without letting them rattle or vibrate.
3 Check that the pipes are not touching any adjacent components or rubbing against any part of the vehicle. Where this is observed, bend the pipe gently away to clear.
4 Although the pipes are plated, any section of pipe may become rusty through chafing and should be renewed. Brake pipes are available to the correct length and fitted with end unions from most Vauxhall dealers and can be made to pattern by many accessory suppliers. When installing the new pipes use the old pipes as a guide to bending and do not make any bends sharper than is necessary.
5 The system will of course have to be bled when the circuit has been reconnected.

12 Hydraulic system - bleeding

1 Removal of all the air from the hydraulic system is essential to the correct working of the braking system, and before undertaking this, examine the fluid reservoir cap to ensure that the vent holes, one on top and the second underneath but not in line, are clear; check the level of fluid and top up if required.
2 Check all brake line unions and connections for possible seepage, and at the same time check the condition of the rubber hoses, which may be perished.
3 If the condition of the wheel cylinders is in doubt, check for possible signs of fluid leakage.

4 If there is any possibility of incorrect fluid having been put into the system, drain all the fluid out and flush through with methylated spirit. Renew all piston seals and cups since these will be affected and could possible fail under pressure.
5 Gather together a clean jar, a length of tubing which fits tightly over the bleed nipples, and a tin of correct brake fluid.
6 Depress the brake pedal several times in order to destroy the vacuum in the servo system.
7 As the front and rear circuits are independent, it will be obvious that only one circuit need be bled if only one hydraulic line has been disconnected.
8 Bleed the calipers and wheel operating cylinders working on the principle of bleeding the unit first which is furthest from the master cylinder then the next furthest away, and so on, in sequence.
9 To do this, fit the rubber tube to the nipple and immerse its open end in a little brake fluid contained in the jar. Keep the open end of the tube submerged throughout the operation.
10 Open the bleed nipple about one half of a turn and then have an assistant depress the brake pedal fully. The foot should then be removed quickly from the pedal so that it returns unobstructed. Pause and then repeat the operation until no more air bubbles can be seen emerging from the end of the bleed tube which is submerged in the jar. Tighten the bleed nipple (do not force it) when the pedal is held in the fully depressed position.
11 It is vital that the reservoir supplying the circuit which is being bled, is kept topped-up throughout the operation with clean hydraulic fluid which has been stored in an airtight container and has remained unshaken for the previous 24 hours.
12 Always discard fluid which is expelled into the jar - never use it for topping-up.
13 On RHD cars, when the calipers and wheel cylinders have been bled, bleed the nipple on the pressure regulating valve (see Section 9).

13 Handbrake - adjustment

1 The handbrake is normally adjusted automatically by the action of the rear shoe internal adjustment mechanism. However, due to cable stretch or after renewal of the cable, additional adjustment may be needed to ensure that the handbrake is fully on after having passed over four notches of its lever ratchet.
2 Release the handbrake lever fully and jack-up the rear axle.
3 Release the locknut on the rod at the cable equaliser and turn the adjuster nut until all slackness has been eliminated from the cables but when the roadwheels are turned, the brake linings cannot be heard to rub on the drums. Retighten the locknut.
4 Lower the car to the ground.

14 Handbrake cable - renewal

1 The handbrake cable is of one piece design and incorporates the equaliser which is captive on the cable.
2 To remove the cable assembly, disconnect the relay rod from the equaliser by removing the adjuster nut and detaching the return spring.

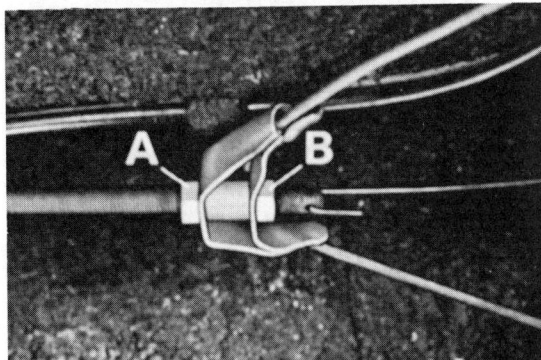

Fig. 9.21. Attachment of handbrake relay rod to cable equaliser (Sec. 13)

A Locknut   B Adjuster nut

3 Jack-up the rear of the car, remove the roadwheels and brake drums.
4 Remove the leading and trailing shoes and disconnect the handbrake cables from their operating levers (see Section 3).
5 The handbrake cables may now be released from the backplates by extracting the 'E' clips.
6 Pull the handbrake cable assembly forward, drawing the cables through the nylon bushed support brackets.
7 Installation is a reversal of removal but finally adjust the handbrake cable **after** the shoes have first been automatically adjusted by repeated applications of the footbrake pedal.

15 Handbrake control lever - removal and installation

1 The centrally positoned, floor mounted handbrake lever is bolted to a plate which is welded to the underside of the transmission tunnel. A handbrake 'ON' warning lamp switch is incorporated.
2 To remove the control lever, disconnect the relay rod from the cable equaliser. This rod is riveted to the handbrake lever.
3 Remove the left-hand front seat and raise the carpet.
4 Disconnect the lead and grommet from the warning lamp switch and unbolt the control lever from the floor.
5 Installation is a reversal of removal but adjust the cables, as described in Section 13.

16 Footbrake pedal - removal and refitting

1 The brake pedal operates on a common cross-shaft with the clutch pedal and removal and refitting operations are fully described in Chapter 5, Section 4.
2 The stoplamp switch is mounted on the pedal support and should be

adjusted so that the stoplamps come on when the brake pedal is depressed by between 0.80 and 1 in (20.0 to 25.0 mm). Always disconnect the switch leads before screwing the switch body in or out as required.

17 Vacuum servo unit - description

1 A vacuum servo unit is fitted into the brake hydraulic circuit in series with the master cylinder, to provide assistance to the driver when the brake pedal is depressed. This reduces the effort required by the driver to operate the brakes under all braking conditions.
2 The unit operates by vacuum obtained from the induction manifold and comprises basically a booster diaphragm and non-return valve. The servo unit and hydraulic master cylinder are connected together so that the servo unit piston rod acts as the master cylinder pushrod. The driver's braking effort is transmitted through another pushrod to the servo unit piston and its built-in control system. The servo unit piston does not fit tightly into the cylinder, but has a strong diaphragm to keep its edges in constant contact with the cylinder wall, so assuring an air tight seal between the two parts. The forward chamber is held under vacuum conditions created in the inlet manifold of the engine and,

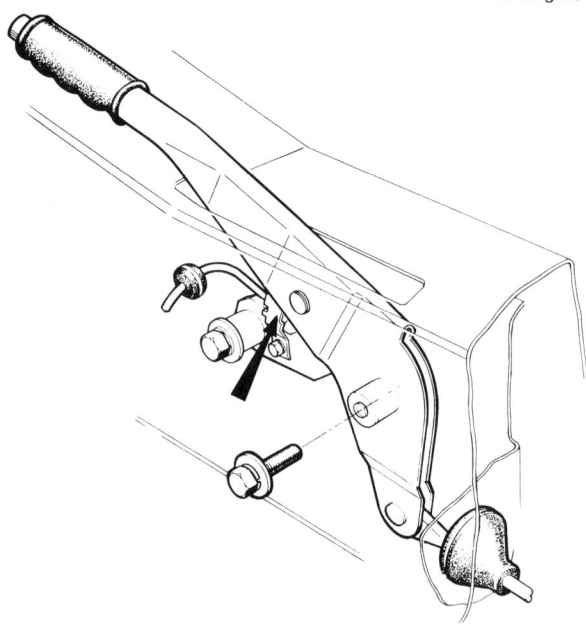

Fig. 9.23. Handbrake control lever (warning switch arrowed) (Sec. 15)

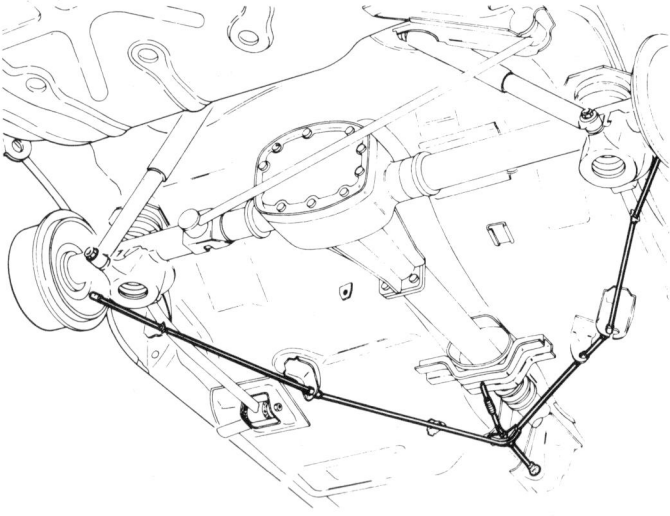

Fig. 9.22. Handbrake cable layout (Sec. 14)

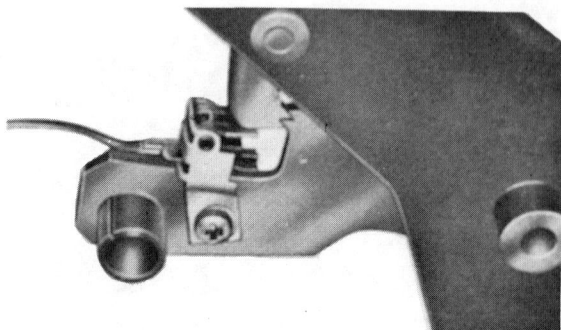

Fig. 9.24. Detailed view of handbrake control lever warning switch (Sec. 15)

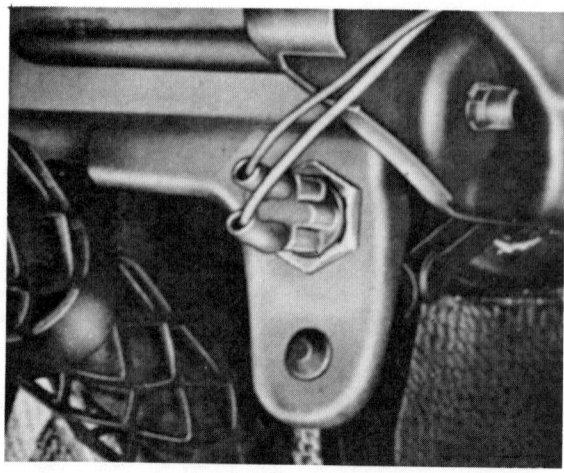

Fig. 9.25. Footbrake stop lamp switch location (Sec. 16)

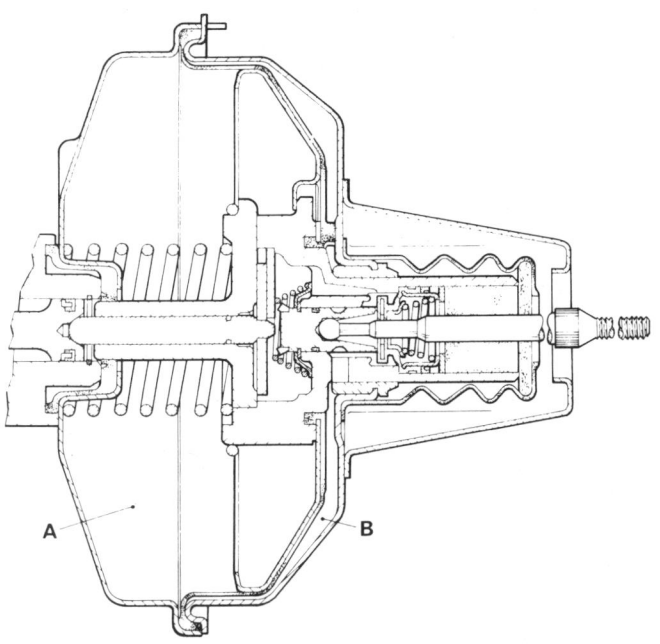

Fig. 9.26. Sectional view of vacuum servo unit (Sec. 17)

A   Chamber under vacuum
B   Chamber open to atmosphere when brake pedal depressed

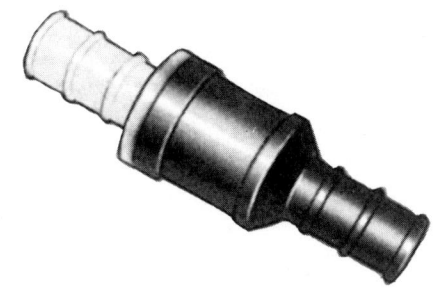

Fig. 9.27. Brake servo vacuum pipe non-return valve (Sec. 18)

Fig. 9.28. Components removed for access to servo air filter (Sec. 19)

1 Mounting bracket	3 Retainer felt
2 Dust excluding boot	4 Air filter

during periods when the brake pedal is not in use, the controls open a passage to the rear chamber so placing it under vacuum conditions as well. When the brake pedal is depressed, the vacuum passage to the rear chamber is cut off and the chamber opened to atmospheric pressure. The consequent rush of air pushes the servo piston forward in the vacuum chamber and operates the main pushrod to the master cylinder.
3   The controls are designed so that assistance is given under all conditions and, when the brakes are not required, vacuum in the rear chamber is established when the brake pedal is released. All air from the atmosphere entering the rear chamber is passed through a small air filter.
4   Under normal operating conditions the vacuum servo unit is very reliable and when a fault does occur, the unit should be renewed on an exchange basis and no attempt made to dismantle it beyond renewing the air filter, as described in Section 19.
5   It is emphasised, that the servo unit assists in reducing the braking effort required at the foot pedal and in the event of its failure, the hydraulic braking system is in no way affected except that the need for higher pedal pressures will be noticed.

18 Vacuum servo unit - removal and installation

1   Dissipate the vacuum in the servo unit by repeated applications of the brake pedal.
2   Disconnect the hose which runs between the servo unit and the intake manifold.
3   Remove the master cylinder from the front face of the master cylinder, as described in Section 8.
4   Disconnect the operating pushrod from the brake pedal and then

unbolt the servo unit and remove it from the support bracket.
5   Installation is a reversal of removal but adjust the pushrod clevis to provide a pedal free-movement (measured at the pedal pad) of between 0.25 and 0.35 in (6.0 and 9.0 mm).
6   If the non-return valve in the servo to manifold hose has been removed or is renewed because of a fault, make sure that the arrow marked on the valve body points towards the intake manifold and the white part of the valve nearest the servo unit.

19 Vacuum servo unit air filter - renewal

1   At intervals of 48000 miles (77000 km) the servo air filter should be renewed. In dusty climates renew it more frequently.
2   Remove the servo unit as described in the preceding Section.
3   Withdraw the mounting bracket, rubber boot and the retainer felt.
4   Extract the filter and discard it.
5   Reassembly is a reversal of dismantling.
6   Installation of the servo unit is as described in the preceding Section with particular reference to paragraph 5.

For 'Fault diagnosis - braking system' - see next page

20 Fault diagnosis - braking system

Symptom	Reason
Pedal travels almost to floor before brakes operate	Brake fluid level too low Caliper leaking Master cylinder leaking (bubbles in master cylinder fluid) Brake flexible hose leaking Brake line fractured Brake system unions loose Pad or shoe linings over 75% worn Rear brake badly out of adjustment (automatic adjusters seized)
Brake pedal feels springy	New linings not yet bedded-in Brake discs or drums badly worn or cracked Master cylinder securing nuts loose
Brake pedal feels 'spongy' and 'soggy'	Caliper or wheel cylinder leaking Master cylinder leaking (bubbles in master cylinder reservoir) Brake pipe line or flexible hose leaking Unions in brake system loose
Excessive effort required to brake car	Faulty vacuum servo unit Pad or shoe linings badly worn New pads or shoes recently fitted - not yet bedded in Harder linings fitted than standard causing increase in pedal pressure Linings and brake drums contaminated with oil, grease or hydraulic fluid
Brakes uneven and pulling to one side	Linings and discs or drums contaminated with oil, grease or hydraulic fluid Tyre pressures unequal Brake caliper loose Brake pads or shoes fitted incorrectly Different type of linings fitted at each wheel Anchorages for front suspension or rear suspension loose Brake discs or drums badly worn, cracked or distorted
Brakes tend to bind, drag or lock-on	Rear brakes overadjusted (release automatic adjuster) Air in system Handbrake cables overtightened

Chapter 10 Electrical system

For modifications, and information applicable to later models, see Supplement at end of manual

Contents

Specifications

System type ... 12v negative earth

Battery rating
Standard	40 amp/hr
Heavy duty	55 amp/hr

Alternator
Type	Delco-Remy DN 460
Output	28, 35 or 45 amp
Field resistance	2.8 ohms ($\pm$ 5%)
Minimum brush length	0.4 in (10.0 mm)

Starter motor (inertia type)
Type	Lucas M35J/1
Minimum brush length	0.38 in (9.5 mm)
Minimum commutator thickness	0.08 in (2.0 mm)

Starter motor (pre-engaged type)
Type	Lucas 5M90/PE
Minimum brush length	0.38 in (9.5 mm)
Minimum commutator thickness	0.08 in (2.0 mm)
Armature shaft endfloat	0.010 in (0.25 mm)

Fuses ... 6 x 16 amp (continuous rating — UK equivalent 32 amp)

Fusible links ... Two

Bulbs
	Wattage
Headlamp	45/40
Front parking	4
Tail/stop	5/21
Direction indicator	21
Side repeater	4
Rear number plate:	
Hatchback and Saloon	5
Estate	10
Reversing lamps	21
Fog lamps	55
Fog rear guard lamp	21

Bulbs (continued)

Interior	10
Warning and instrument lamps	1.2
Alternator failure warning lamp	3
Heated rear window indicator	0.75

Torque wrench settings

	lb in	lb ft	Nm
Alternator tie bolts	62	—	7.0
Alternator pulley nut	—	50	69
Starter motor bolts	—	30	41

1 General description

The electrical system is of 12 volt negative earth type. The battery is charged by a belt-driven alternator which incorporates a regulator.

The starter motor fitted as standard is of inertia type but a pre-engaged type is available as an option.

Although repair procedures and methods are fully described in this Chapter, in view of the long life of the major electrical components, it is recommended that when a fault does develop, consideration should be given to exchanging the unit for a factory reconditioned assembly rather than renew individual components of a well worn unit.

2 Battery - removal and installation

1 The battery is located at the rear of the engine compartment on the right-hand side.
2 Remove the lead from the negative (—) terminal followed by the positive (+) one.
3 Disconnect the battery clamp and lift the battery from its mounting platform, taking care not to spill any electrolyte on the bodywork.
4 Installation is a reversal of removal but make sure that the polarity is correct before connecting the leads and to not overtighten the clamp bolts.

3 Battery - maintenance

1 Carry out the regular weekly maintenance described in the Routine Maintenance Section at the front of this manual.
2 Clean the top of the battery, removing all dirt and moisture.
3 As well as keeping the terminals clean and covered with petroleum jelly, the top of the battery, and especially the top of the cells, should be kept clean and dry. This helps prevent corrosion and ensures that the battery does not become partially discharged by leakage through dampness and dirt.
4 Once every three months, remove the battery and inspect the battery securing bolts, the battery clamp plate, tray and battery leads for corrosion (white fluffy deposits on the metal which are brittle to touch). If any corrosion is found, clean off the deposits with ammonia and paint over the clean metal with an anti-rust/anti-acid paint.
5 At the same time inspect the battery case for cracks. if a crack is found, clean and plug it with one of the proprietary compounds marketed for this purpose. If leakage through the crack has been excessive then it will be necessary to refill the appropriate cell with fresh electrolyte as detailed later. Cracks are frequently caused to the top of the battery case by pouring in water in the middle of winter *after* instead of *before* a run. This gives the water no chance to mix with the electrolyte and so the former freezes and splits the battery case.
6 If topping-up the battery becomes excessive and the case has been inspected for cracks that could cause leakage, but none are found, the battery is being over-charged and the alternator will have to be tested and if necessary the internal regulator renewed (see Section 8, paragraph 13).
7 With the battery on the bench at the three monthly interval check, measure its specific gravity with a hydrometer to determine the state of charge and condition of the electrolyte. There should be very little variation between the different cells and if a variation in excess of 0.025 is present it will be due to either:

a) Loss of electrolyte from the battery at some time caused by spillage or a leak, resulting in a drop in the specific gravity of the electrolyte when the deficiency was replaced with distilled water instead of fresh electrolyte.
b) An internal short circuit caused by buckling of the plates or a similar malady pointing to the likelihood of total battery failure in the near future.

8 The specific gravity of the electrolyte for fully charged conditions at the electrolyte temperature indicated, is listed in Table A. The specific gravity of a fully discharged battery at different temperatures of the electrolyte is given in Table B.

Table A
Specific Gravity - Battery Fully Charged

1.268 at 100° F or 38° C electrolyte temperature
1.272 at 90° F or 32° C electrolyte temperature
1.276 at 80° F or 27° C electrolyte temperature
1.280 at 70° F or 21° C electrolyte temperature
1.284 at 60° F or 16° C electrolyte temperature
1.288 at 50° F or 10° C electrolyte temperature
1.292 at 40° F or 4° C electrolyte temperature
1.286 at 30° F or -1.5° C electrolyte temperature

Table B
Specific Gravity - Battery Fully Discharged

1.098 at 100° F or 38° C electrolyte temperature
1.102 at 90° F or 32° C electrolyte temperature
1.106 at 80° F or 27° C electrolyte temperature
1.110 at 70° F or 21° C electrolyte temperature
1.114 at 60° F or 16° C electrolyte temperature
1.118 at 50° F or 10° C electrolyte temperature
1.122 at 40° F or 4° C electrolyte temperature
1.126 at 30° F or -1.5° C electrolyte temperature

4 Electrolyte - replenishment

1 If the battery is in a fully charged state and one of the cells maintains a specific gravity reading which is 0.025 or more lower than the others, and a check of each cell has been made with a voltage meter to check for short circuits (a four to seven second test should give a steady reading of between 1.2 to 1.8 volts), then it is likely that electrolyte has been lost from the cell with the low reading at some time.
2 Top-up the cell with a solution of 1 part sulphuric acid to 2.5 parts of water. If the cell is already fully topped-up draw some electrolyte out of it with a hydrometer.
3 When mixing the sulphuric acid and water **never add water to sulphuric acid** - always pour the acid slowly onto the water in a glass container. **If water is added to sulphuric acid it will explode.**
4 Continue to top up the cell with freshly made electrolyte and then recharge the battery and check the hydrometer readings.

5 Battery charging

1 In winter time when heavy demand is placed upon the battery, such as when starting from cold, and much electrical equipment is continually in use, it is a good idea to occasionally have the battery

fully charged from an external source at the rate of 3.5 or 4 amps.

2   Continue to charge the battery at this rate until no further rise in specific gravity is noted over a four hour period.

3   Alternatively, a trickle charger charging at the rate of 1.5 amps can be safely used overnight.

4   Specially rapid 'boost' charges which are claimed to restore the power of the battery in 1 to 2 hours are most dangerous as they can cause serious damage to the battery plates.

7.2 Alternator and mountings

Fig. 10.1. Alternator rotor showing slip rings (Sec. 8)

Fig. 10.2. Alternator stator (Sec. 8)

6   Alternator - maintenance and special precautions

1   Occasionally wipe away any drit or grease which has accumulated on the outside of the unit and check the security of the leads.

2   Every 3000 miles (48000 km) check the tension of the drivebelt and adjust it if necessary as described in Section 12, of Chapter 2.

3   No lubrication is required as the bearings are grease sealed for life.

4   Take extreme care when making circuit connections to a vehicle fitted with an alternator and observe the following. When making connections to the alternator from a battery always match correct polarity. Before using electric-arc welding equipment to repair any part of the vehicle, disconnect the connector (output) from the alternator and disconnect the battery terminals. Never start the car with a battery charger connected. Always disconnect both battery leads before using a mains charger. If boosting from another battery, always connect in parallel using heavy cable. It is not recommended that testing of an alternator should be undertaken at home due to the testing equipment required and the possibility of damaged occurring during testing. It is best left to automotive electrical specialists.

7   Alternator - removal and installation

1   Pull out the connector plugs from the rear of the alternator.

2   Slacken the mounting and adjustment strap bolts and push the alternator in towards the engine so that the drivebelt can then be slipped off the alternator pulley (photo).

3   Remove the mounting and adjustment strap bolts and lift the engine from the support bracket.

4   Installation is a reversal of removal but make sure that the drive end bracket bolt is tightened before the slip ring end bracket bolt which incorporates a split sliding bush.

5   Adjust the belt tension, as described in Chapter 2, Section 12.

8   Alternator - dismantling, servicing and reassembly

1   Scratch a mating mark across the end brackets and the stator so that they can be reassembled in their original relative positions.

2   Unscrew and remove the three tie-bolts.

3   Prise apart the drive end bracket and rotor assembly from the stator; also lever off the slip-ring end bracket.

4   If the drive end bearing is to be renewed or the rotor is faulty, remove the pulley and fan. The pulley nut can most easily be removed by placing an old drivebelt in the pulley groove and then gripping the belt in a vice as close to the pulley as possible. This method will prevent damage to the pulley and effectively stop it turning while the nut is unscrewed. Alternatively, an Allen key may be inserted in the socket end of the rotor shaft to stop it turning.

5   Withdraw the rotor from the drive end bracket.

6   Inspect the brush gear for free-movement in their guides and renew them if they have worn below their minimum specified length.

7   Examine the surfaces of the slip rings, these should be smooth and clean. If not, clean them with white spirit applied with a cloth.

8   If an ohmmeter is available, connect it across the slip-rings. Where a reading lower than 2.8 ohms is indicated, there is probably a short circuit between the rotor coils. A high reading usually indicates dirty slip-rings and infinity means an open circuit.

9   To test the stator, connect an ohmmeter between a stator lead and its core. If a low reading is indicated, the stator windings are earthed. The windings can also be tested for continuity by connecting the ohmmeter between any two of the stator leads. Repeat the foregoing test by substituting the lead not previously used, for one of the two other leads. Readings during both tests should be similar otherwise the insulation is defective and the stator must be renewed.

10   The rectifier bridge and the Diode Trio are located within the slip-ring end bracket and if they are to be tested, they must first be removed.

11   To check the field diodes of the Diode Trio, connect an ohmmeter (having a 1½ volt cell and set to the lowest range) to the single, larger connector of the Diode Trio and to one of the three smaller connectors. Note the reading and then reverse the ohmmeter leads between the same two connectors. If the diode is in good condition, it will indicate a high reading in one direction and a much lower one in the reverse direction. Repeat this test between the large connector and each of the

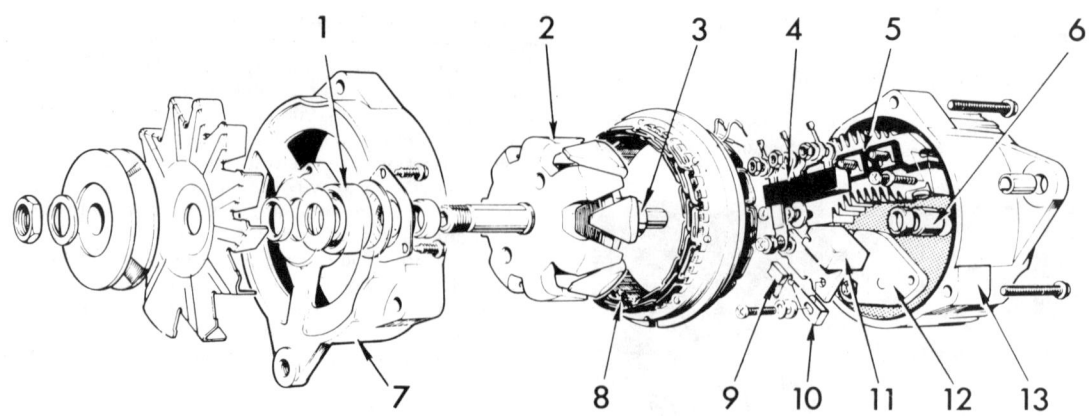

Fig. 10.3. Exploded view of the alternator

1 Drive end bearing	4 Diode trio	7 Drive end bracket	10 Brush lead clip
2 Rotor	5 Rectifier	8 Stator	11 Brush holder
3 Slip rings	6 Slip ring end bracket	9 Brush	12 Regulator
			13 Slip ring end bracket

Fig. 10.4. Alternator diode trio (Sec. 8)

Fig. 10.5. Alternator rectifier bridge (Sec. 8)

1 Heat sink   2 Insulated heat sink   3 Terminals

Fig. 10.6. Identification of alternator heat sink attachment components - for key see text (Sec. 8)

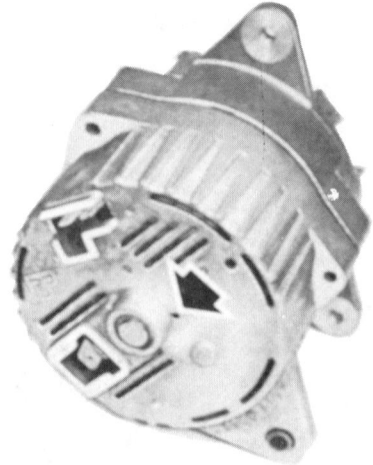

Fig. 10.7. Hole in alternator slip ring end bracket for inserting brush retracting rod (Sec. 8)

other two smaller connectors in turn.

12 To test the diodes of the rectifier bridge, connect the ohmmeter to the earthed heat sink and to one of the three terminals. Record the reading and then reverse the ohmmeter leads between the terminals. A diode in good condition will give a high reading in one direction and a much lower one in the reverse direction. Repeat this test for the other two terminals when the readings for all of them should be similar, otherwise renew the rectifier bridge.

13 The voltage regulator which is located inside the slip-ring end bracket is a sealed unit and if there has been under or overcharging during previous operation of the alternator, it must be renewed as a unit.

14 End bracket bearings can be renewed by pressing them out using suitable pieces of tubing as distance pieces and supporting the brackets squarely. The slip-ring end bearing should be pressed in from the outside and set flush with the bearing housing outside face. Always install a new seal at the same time as the slip-ring end bracket bearing is renewed. The drive end bracket bearing should be filled a quarter full with wheel bearing grease before installation and the bearing retainer plate renewed if the seal incorporated in it has hardened or worn.

15 Reassembly is a reversal of dismantling but observe the following points:

    (i)   *Install insulating spacer on screw (1) between heat sink and end bracket (Fig. 10.6).*

    (ii) *Install insulating sleeves to unthreaded parts of screws (3) and (4).*

    (iii) *Locate insulating washers under the metal washers on screws (1), (3) and (4). Screws (2) and (5) do not have any insulators.*

16 The brushes can be retained in the retracted position (so that they will pass over the slip-rings during assembly of the end bracket) by inserting a thin rod through the hole in the slip-ring and bracket, arrowed in Fig. 10.7.

9 Starter motor (inertia type) - description

1 The starter is a series-wound, four pole unit having a face type moulded commutator. Armature endfloat is controlled by thrust washers. The field winding is one continuous aluminium strip, earthed at one end to the yoke and at the other end joined to a pair of brushes. The starter drive incorporates a thrust spring to counter shock loading during engagement and a light spring to prevent the pinion vibrating into mesh with the ring gear when the engine is running (photo).

10 Starter motor (inertia type) - removal and installation

1 Open the bonnet and remove the air cleaner.
2 Place a jack with an insulating wooden block under the sump and take the weight of the engine.
3 Unscrew and remove the nut which secures the right-hand engine mounting stud to the crankcase bracket (see Chapter 1, Section 37).
4 Raise the engine slightly, unbolt the crankcase bracket and then unscrew and remove the flexible mounting together with cup from the crossmember.
5 Disconnect the lead from the starter motor.
6 Unscrew and remove the starter motor securing bolts and withdraw the starter in a straight line from beneath the alternator.
7 Installation is a reversal of removal.

11 Starter motor (inertial type) - overhaul

1 Using a suitable proprietary compressor, compress the main starter drive spring so that the retaining jump ring can be prised off.
2 Remove the commutator end bracket bolts, withdraw the end bracket from the yoke making sure that the thrust washer is retained.
3 Unscrew the two tie bolts from the drive end bracket and withdraw the bracket and armature from the yoke.
4 Inspect the dismantled components for wear or damage and renew as necessary. If the brush springs are weak or broken, the complete commutator end bracket will have to be renewed. If the brushes are worn, they are supplied new complete with terminal together with two field coil brushes.
5 To renew the field brushes, there is no need to remove the field coils

9.1 Starter motor (inertia type) with gearbox removed

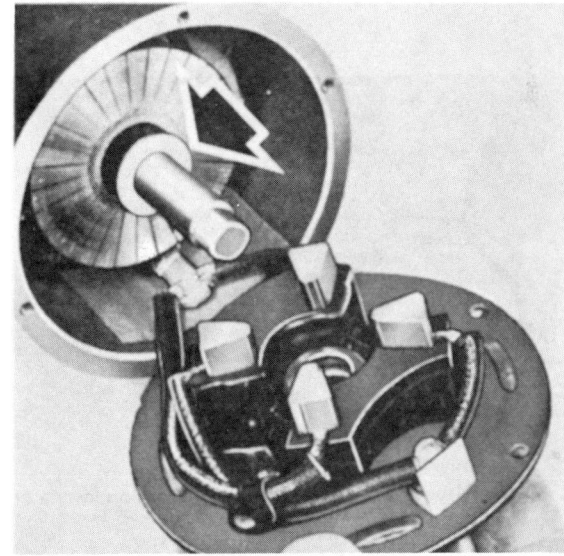

Fig. 10.8. Location of thrust washer at commutator end of inertia type starter motor (Sec. 11)

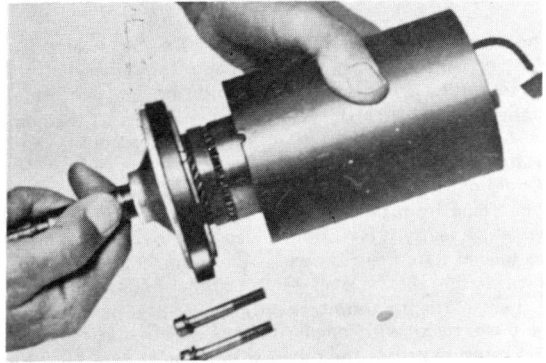

Fig. 10.9. Removing drive end bracket and armature from inertia type starter motor (Sec. 11)

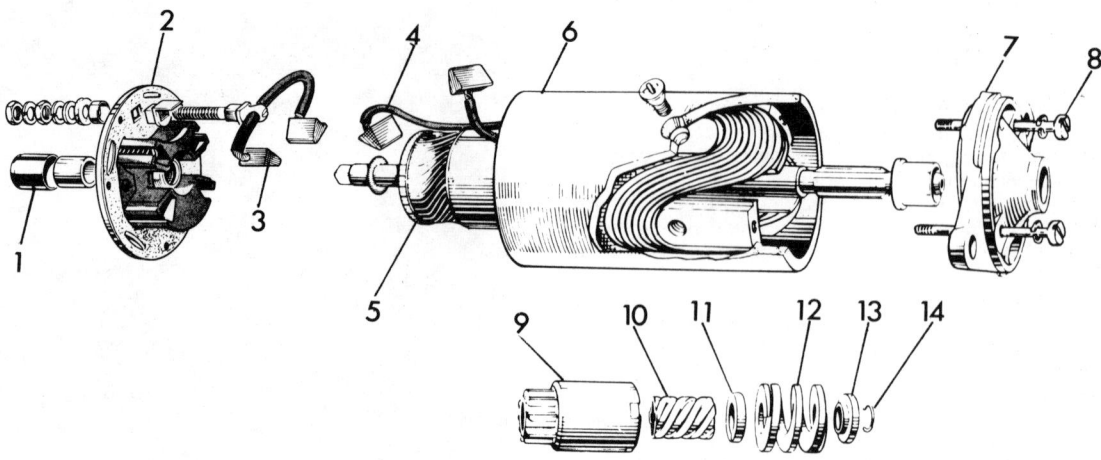

Fig. 10.10. Exploded view of the inertia type starter motor

1	Plastic cap covering squared end of shaft	4	Brushes
2	Commutator end bracket	5	Commutator
3	Brushes	6	Yoke

7	Drive end bracket	10	Screwed sleeve
8	Tie bolts	11	Buffer washer
9	Pinion and barrel	12	Main spring
		13	Retaining cup
		14	Jump ring

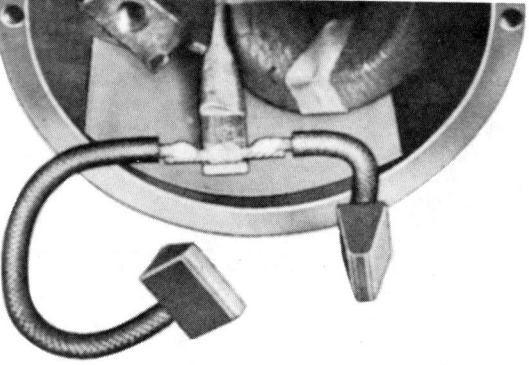

Fig. 10.11. Method of attaching field brush leads on inertia type starter (Sec. 11)

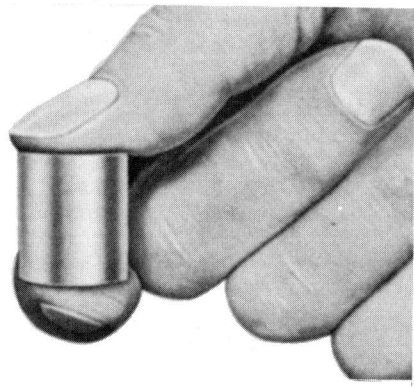

Fig. 10.12. Using the fingers to create hydraulic pressure and permeate starter motor bush with oil (Sec. 11)

from the yoke, simply cut off the original brush leads 0.30 in (8.0 mm) from the connecting tag and solder the new brush leads to the original stubs.

6 If the commutator is burnt or dirty it may be cleaned with a fuel soaked rag or a piece of very fine glass paper (not emery). If the face of the commutator is in very bad condition, it can be skimmed professionally, provided that the reduced thickness of the commutator will not be below 0.08 in (2.0 mm). On no account undercut the commutator insulators.

7 The field coils can be tested for open circuit by first disconnecting the earthed lead from the yoke and then using a test lamp and battery. If the coils are faulty it is recommended that they are renewed by your dealer as special equipment is necessary to remove the pole screws.

8 If the armature shaft bushes are to be renewed, use a tubular drift to remove them. With the thumb and forefinger at either end of the bush and the bush filled with engine oil, press with the fingers until the hydraulic pressure causes the oil to seep through the walls of the bush.

9 Press the new bush into the commutator end bracket until it stands proud of the outside face of the bracket by 0.22 in (5.5 mm).

10 Reassembly is a reversal of dismantling but use a new jump ring on the armature shaft to retain the starter drive components.

12 Starter motor (pre-engaged type) - description

The starter motor has a face type moulded commutator and a series field of continuously wound aluminium strip one end of which is earthed to the yoke and the other to a pair of brushes.

The drive end bracket is secured by two bolts which screw into the end of the pole shoes.

The commutator end bracket is secured to the yoke by four screws. Armature endfloat is controlled by a thrust plate and shims on the armature shaft extension. These thrust components are secured to the shaft by a split pin which also locks them so that they rotate with the shaft.

A solenoid, secured to the drive end bracket engages the pinion with the flywheel ring gear through the medium of an engagement lever as soon as the ignition key is turned to the 'start' position. As the solenoid reaches the end of its stroke and with the pinion by now almost fully engaged with the flywheel ring gear, the main contacts close and energise the starter motor to rotate the flywheel. To prevent over-speeding of the armature, when the engine fires, the drive from the motor to the pinion incorporates a one-way roller clutch.

13 Starter motor (pre-engaged type) - removal and installation

1 The procedure is similar to that described in Section 10 except that the securing bolts are of socket headed type.

14 Starter motor (pre-engaged type) - overhaul

1 From the face of the solenoid, detach the connecting link.
2 Unscrew and remove the two solenoid securing nuts, extract the heat shield (fitted to protect the solenoid from the exhaust pipe) and then withdraw the solenoid from the drive bracket.
3 Remove the securing screws and withdraw the commutator end bracket from the yoke making sure to retain the thrust washer.
4 Unscrew and remove the two bolts from the drive end bracket and withdraw the bracket from the yoke.
5 Drive the engagement lever pin out of its retaining ring and then withdraw the armature from the drive end bracket.
6 Using a piece of tubing, tap down the thrust collar which is located on the armature shaft, prise off the jump ring and withdraw the drive assembly. If this is worn or faulty, it can only be renewed as an assembly.

Fig. 10.13. Withdrawing solenoid from drive end bracket of pre-engaged type starter motor (Sec. 14)

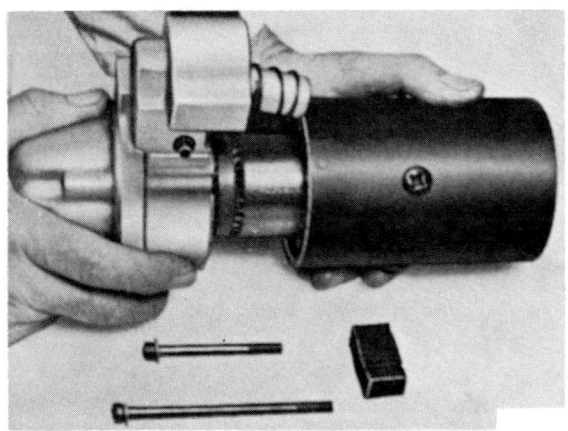

Fig. 10.14. Withdrawing drive end bracket complete with armature from yoke of pre-engaged starter motor (Sec. 14)

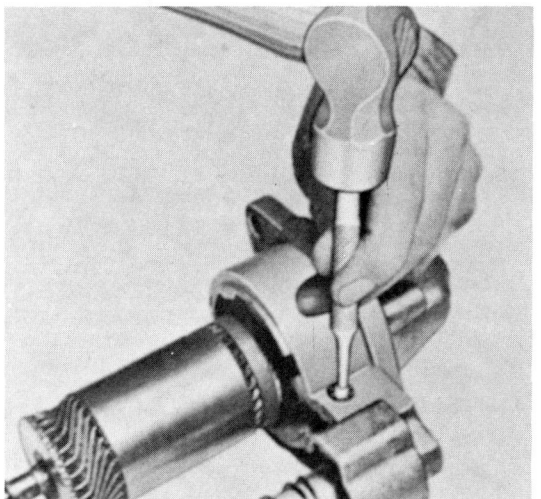

Fig. 10.15. Removing engagement lever pivot pin (pre-engaged starter) (Sec. 14)

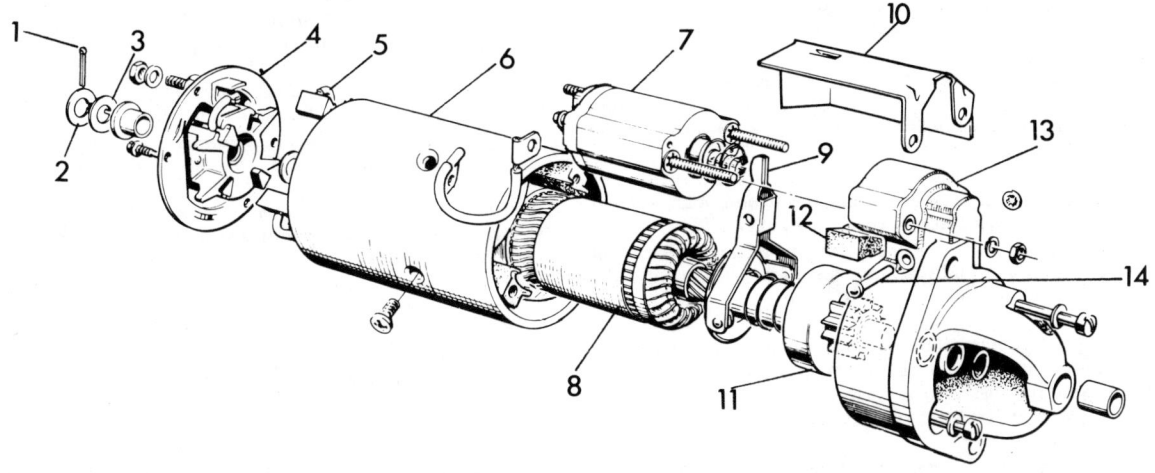

Fig. 10.16. Exploded view of the pre-engaged type starter motor

1 Split pin
2 Thrust washer
3 Shim
4 Commutator end bracket
5 Field brush
6 Yoke
7 Solenoid
8 Armature
9 Engagement lever
10 Exhaust pipe heat shield
11 Drive pinion/clutch assembly
12 Rubber grommet
13 Drive end housing
14 Engagement lever pivot pin

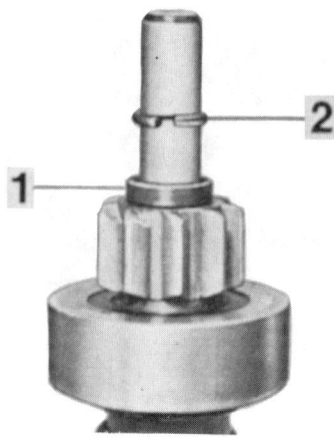

Fig. 10.17. Pre-engaged starter drive

1 *Thrust collar*   2 *Jump ring*

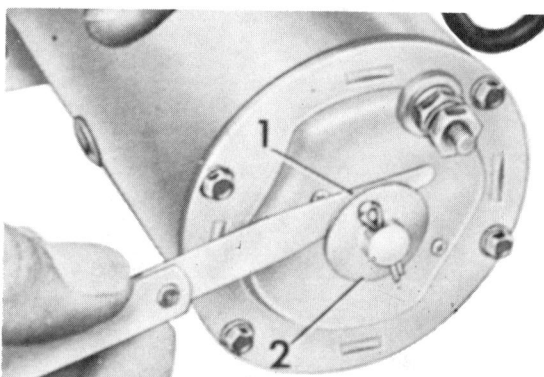

Fig. 10.18. Checking armature endfloat on pre-engaged type starter (Sec. 14)

1 *Feeler gauge*   2 *Thrust plate*

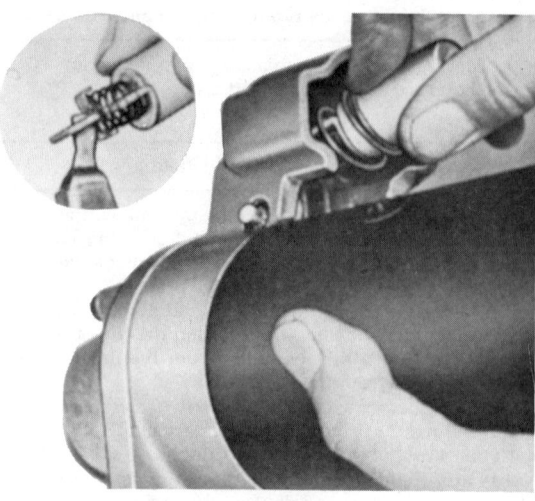

Fig. 10.19. Connecting solenoid plunger to engagement lever on pre-engaged type starter (Sec. 14)

Fig. 10.20. Installing rubber grommet (pre-engaged starter) (Sec. 14)

7 The brushes, commutator and armature shaft bushes should be serviced as described in Section 11, paragraphs 4 to 8. Press the drive end bush into the bracket until it is quite flush. Press the commutator end bush into the bracket until the shoulder contacts the bracket.

8 Reassembly is largely a reversal of dismantling but observe the following essential procedures.

9 The engagement lever is attached to the drive assembly and when assembling to the armature shaft, if the pinion is nearest the thrust collar then the engagement lever will automatically be the correct way round.

10 Use a new retaining ring to secure the engagement lever pivot pin.

11 Make sure that the thrust washer is located on the armature shaft before assembling commutator end bracket to the yoke.

12 After commutator end bracket is installed, fit the thrust plate and split pin and check that the endfloat does not exceed 0.010 in (0.25 mm) otherwise install extra shims between the thrust plate and the split pin.

13 Engage the solenoid plunger with the engagement lever having first applied a little grease to their rubbing surfaces.

14 Fit the rubber grommet between the drive end bracket and the yoke and then install the solenoid and the heat shield.

15 Fuses and fusible links

1 The fuse box is located at the bottom of the instrument panel, between the steering column and the driver's door (photo).

2 Six circuits are protected by 16 amp (continuous rating) fuses as follows:

(1) *RH sidelamps and taillamps, instrument panel illumination lamps, cigar lighter bulb, fog lamps and fog rear guard lamps.*

(2) *LH sidelamps and taillamps, rear number plate lamp, engine compartment lamp.*

(3) *Interior lamp, horn, headlamp flasher, hazard warning system, clock.*

(4) *Heated rear window, reversing lamps.*

(5) *Stoplamps, direction indicator lamps, instrument panel warning lamps, instrument voltage stabiliser, fuel and temperature gauges, heater motor, brake pressure warning system.*

(6) *Windscreen wiper and washer, radio, cigar lighter element.*

3 Always renew a fuse with one of similar rating and never renew it more than once without finding the source of the trouble (usually broken or deteriorated wiring insulation causing it to short circuit).

4 Fusible links are incorporated in the main battery feed at the starter solenoid switch. One of the two links protects all circuits routed through the ignition switch with the exception of the starter motor, while the other link protects the lighting circuits.

5 The fusible links will burn out only in the event of a heavy overload caused probably by a direct short circuit. Always trace and rectify the fault before renewing the links which are supplied in kit form.

6 Cut away the fusible link from its soldered junction at point 'A', also from the ring terminal at point 'B' (Fig. 10.21). Strip back the insulation on the end of the new fusible link and double back the exposed wire. Strip back the insulation from the end of the harness cable. Insert both bare ends of the cables into the connector and crimp securely. Attach the other end of the fusible link to the solenoid switch terminal.

15.1 Fuse box

Fig. 10.22. Location of direction indicator flasher unit (Sec. 15)

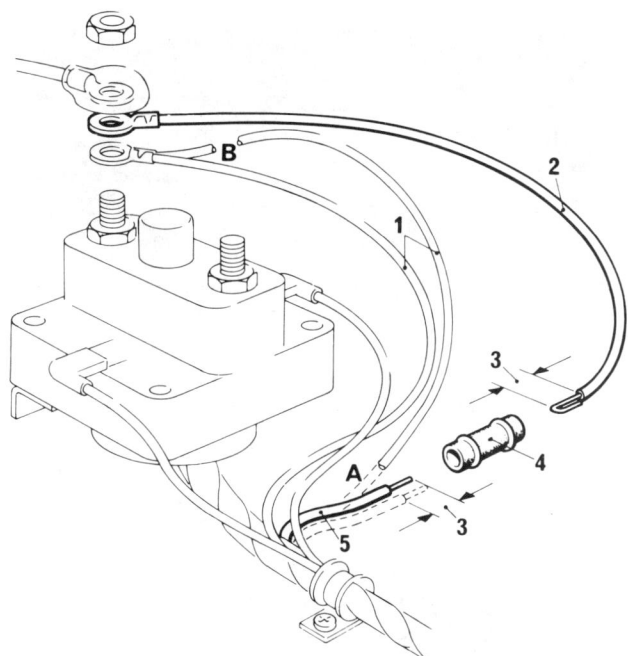

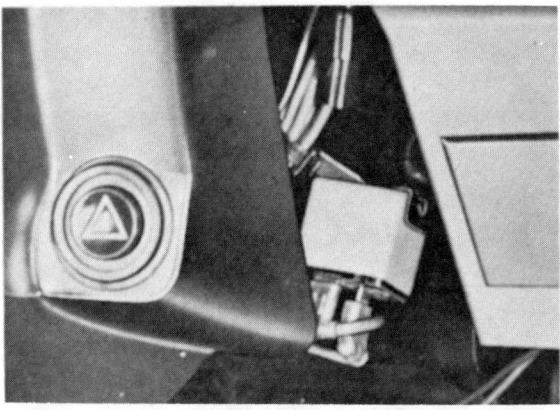

Fig. 10.23. Location of hazard warning flasher unit (Sec. 16)

Fig. 10.21. Fusible link renewal diagram

1 *Original links*
2 *New link*
3 *0.5 in. (12.0 mm)*
4 *Connector*
5 *Existing cables (brown or brown/blue)*

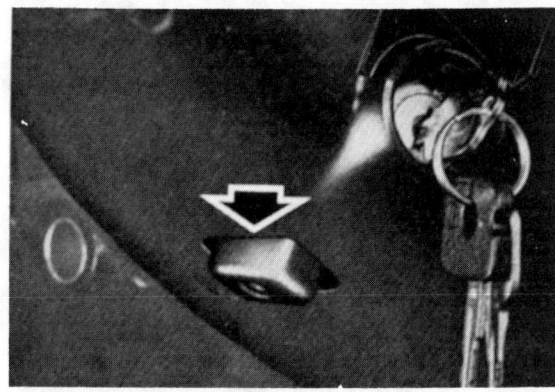

Fig. 10.24. Location of steering column lock safety button (Sec. 17)

7   The foregoing operation can be applied to either fusible link according to the circuit which has 'blown'.

16 Direction indicator flasher system

1   The flasher unit is clipped to the steering column bracket. It may be cylindrical or rectangular in shape according to make or of hot wire type. In the case of the latter, when installed, terminal 'B' must lie in the horizontal plane.
2   Should the flashers become faulty in operation, carry out a check of the bulbs and for security of the connecting leads. If these are in order and the fuse has not 'blown' the unit is at fault and should be renewed.

17 Hazard warning flasher system

1   The hazard warning flasher unit is located adjacent to the direction indicator flasher unit on the steering column bracket.
2   Failure of the system may be due to bulb failure in the flasher lamp units or disconnected wiring or a blown circuit fuse. If these are in order, renew the flasher unit.

18 Ignition/steering column lock switch - removal and refitting

1   The four position switch is marked '0', '1', '11' and '111' and the

key can only be inserted or withdrawn when it is in the '0' position. When the key has been withdrawn, the steering lock will engage when the steering column has been turned to align the bolt and slot. The key cannot be turned from position '1' to '0' for withdrawal unless the safety button is first depressed (Fig. 10.24).

2   To remove the switch, first withdraw the steering column lower shroud (six screws) and then extract the two switch securing screws. The wiring harness can be disconnected by separating the plug and socket connector (photos).

3   Installation of the switch is a reversal of removal.

4   Removal and installation of the steering column lock is described in Chapter 11.

19 Combination switch - removal and installation

1   Disconnect the lead from the battery negative terminal.

2   Remove the steering wheel, as described in Chapter 11.

3   Remove the steering column upper and lower shrouds.

4   Disconnect the multi-pin plugs and then release the screw which clamps the switch to the steering column.

5   Withdraw the switch complete with mounting plate.

6   The direction indicator and wiper switches are supplied as complete

assemblies which include the mounting plate and striker bush. Do not remove the direction indicator switch from the mounting plate or it will separate into many small items. The wiper switch can be renewed as a separate item from its mounting plate but the securing rivets will have to be drilled out and the new switch secured with the screws supplied with the new switch.

7   Access to the horn button contacts can be obtained by prising off the stalk end cap.

8   Installation is a reversal of removal but make sure that the spigot on the switch engages with the slot in the steering column before tightened the clamp screw.

20 Lighting switches - removal and refitting

1   The lighting switches are retained to the instrument panel by a screw at the upper end of the escutcheon. Having removed the screw, prise the top of the escutcheon away and lift slightly to disengage the tag at the lower end.

2   The switches can be released from the escutcheon by depressing the retaining clips.

3   Reconnect the switch leads according to the diagram which applies (Figs. 10.29 to 10.32).

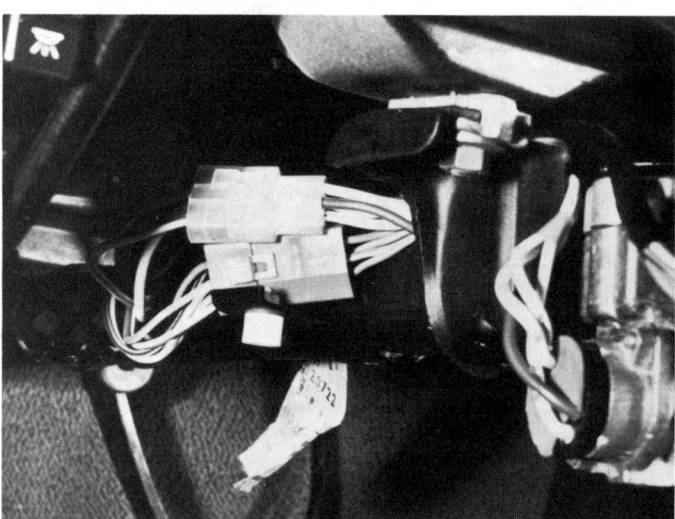

18.2A Steering column switch wiring plugs

18.2B Steering column lock and combination switch (right)

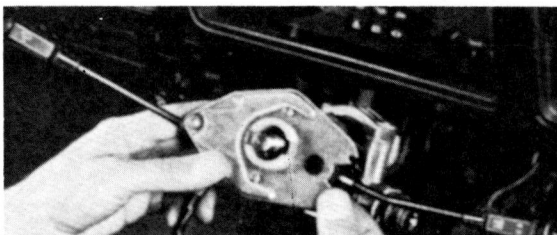

Fig. 10.25. Withdrawing the combination switch from the steering column (Sec. 19)

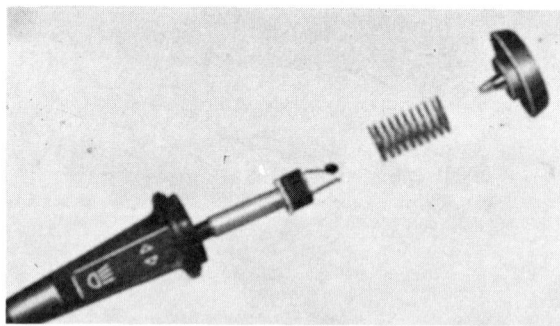

Fig. 10.26. Horn button components (Sec. 19)

Fig. 10.27. Combination switch spigot and slot (Sec. 19)

Fig. 10.28. Lighting switch securing screw (Sec. 20)

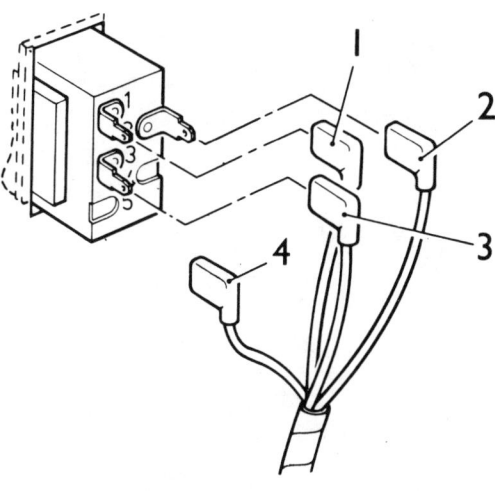

Fig. 10.29. Lighting switch connections (Sec. 20)

1	Blue	3	Red/green
2	Brown/blue	4	Red/blue

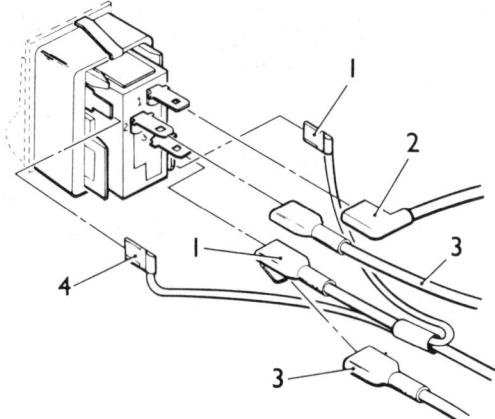

Fig. 10.30. Fog lamp switch connections (Sec. 20)

1	Red/green	3	Red/yellow
2	Red/orange	4	Black

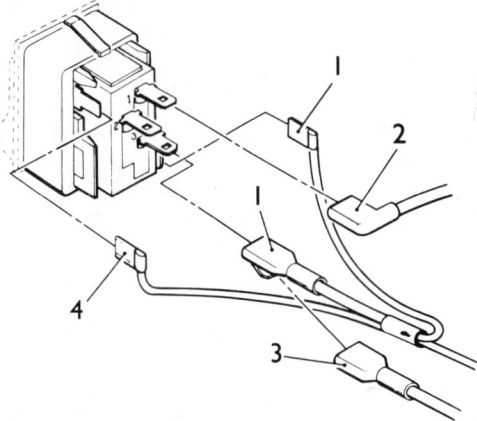

Fig. 10.31. Fog rear guard lamp switch connections (Sec. 20)

1	Red/green	3	Red/blue
2	Red/orange	4	Black

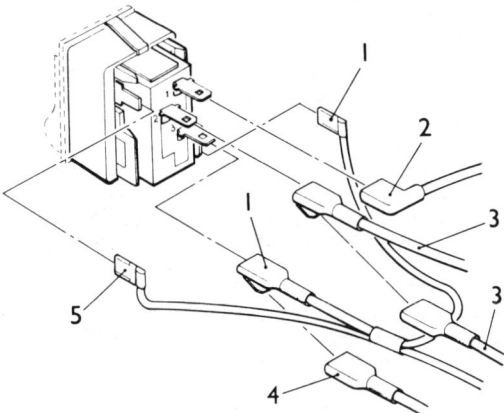

Fig. 10.32. Fog lamp and rear guard lamp combination switch connections (Sec. 20)

1	Red/green	4	Red/blue
2	Red/orange	5	Black
3	Red/yellow		

21 Interior lamp and heated rear window switches - removal and refitting

1 The switches are retained in the heater control panel by clips. To remove a switch, press it downwards and ease the top from the panel (Fig. 10.33).

2 The switch terminals are numbered; the following guide will make reconnection of the leads easy:

Interior lamp switch	Heated rear window switch
Purple/white to terminal '2'	*Green to terminal '2'*
Black to terminal '3'	*White/black to terminal '3'*
	Black to left-hand side
	White/black to right-hand side

22 Heater booster fan switch - removal and installation

1 This rotary type switch is mounted in the heater control panel.

2 To remove the switch, depress the spring securing clips using a small screwdriver inserted between the switch bezel and the panel. Pull the multi-pin plug from the rear of the switch (Fig. 10.34).

Fig. 10.33. Removing heated rear window switch (Sec. 21)

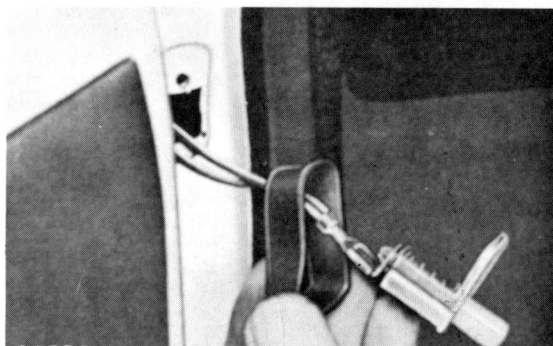

Fig. 10.35. Withdrawing a courtesy lamp switch (Sec. 23)

25.2 Speedometer head cable connection

23 Courtesy lamp switch - removal and refitting

1 These switches are secured to the door pillars by a single screw.
2 Failure of the switch can often be traced to the screw making poor earth contact due to rust or to corrosion of the switch plunger. A little petroleum jelly applied to the plunger will help to prevent this.

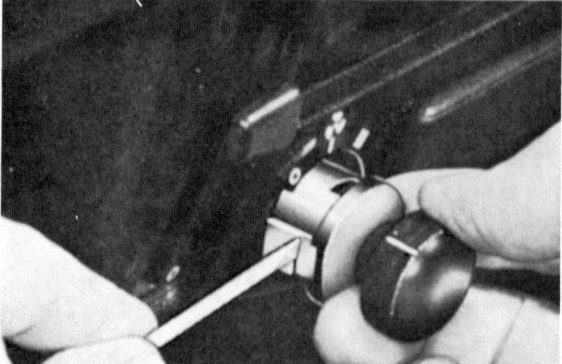

Fig. 10.34. Removing heater booster fan switch (Sec. 22)

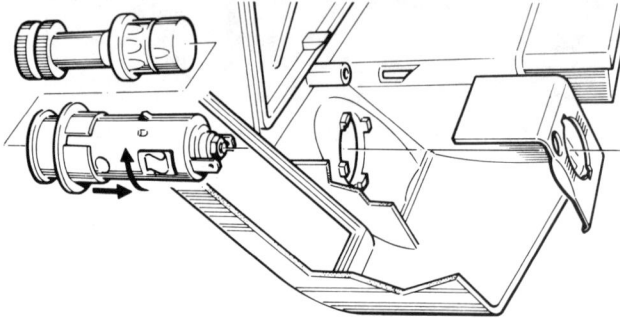

Fig. 10.36. Cigar lighter components and mounting (Sec. 24)

24 Cigar lighter - removal and refitting

1 The cigar lighter is mounted in the heater control panel.
2 The bulb holder can be unclipped from the mounting plate by reaching up under the control panel.
3 To remove the lighter, first withdraw the element and then turn the outer casing clockwise one quarter of a turn and withdraw it. Disconnect the leads.
4 Refitting is a reversal of removal but make sure that the white/green lead connects with the central terminal and the black lead to the outer one.

25 Instrument cluster - removal and installation

1 Disconnect the lead from the battery negative terminal.
2 Reach up under the instrument panel and release the bayonet type speedometer cable connector. On RHD models the demister duct will first have to be moved aside (photo).
3 Again reach up under the instrument panel and release the instrument cluster from the four retaining tabs and two spring clips.
4 Pull the instrument cluster far enough forward so that the connecting plugs and leads can be disconnected and then lift the cluster away. There is no need to remove the steering wheel for this operation. An alternative method of removing the instrument cluster is to insert a piece of wire about 9 inches long and suitably bent, between the shroud and cluster, then turn it to engage the spring clips and pull to release the cluster. The speedometer cable can be disconnected with the cluster pulled forward away from the instrument panel.
5 The instrument assembly can be separated from the hood and lens by removing the two securing screws.
6 Pull out the bulb holders, remove the securing screws and separate the printed circuit board and gauges from the casing.
7 Before detaching the fuel contents and water temperature gauges from their backplate, remove the mask (two screws).
8 The clock and its plastic housing can only be removed after first withdrawing the other instruments.
9 A voltage stabiliser is plugged into the printed circuit and its purpose is to prevent fluctuation in readings on the fuel and water temperature gauges, which are caused by fluctuations of battery voltage.

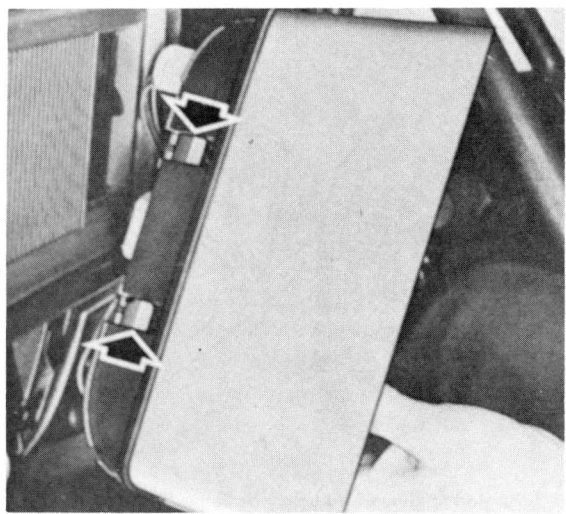

Fig. 10.37. Instrument cluster spring clips (Sec. 25)

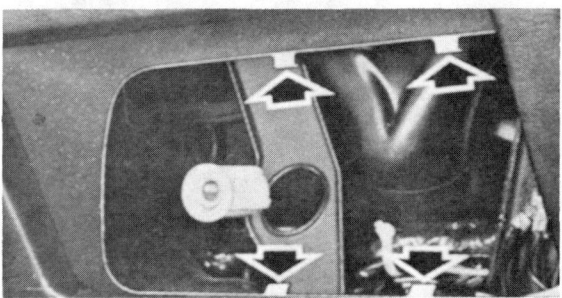

Fig. 10.38. Instrument cluster retaining tabs (Sec. 25)

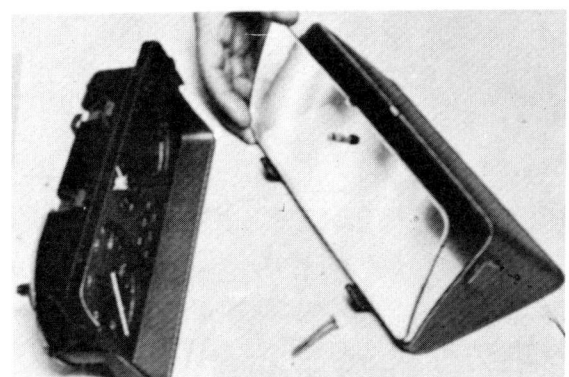

Fig. 10.39. Separating instrument cluster, lens and hood (Sec. 25)

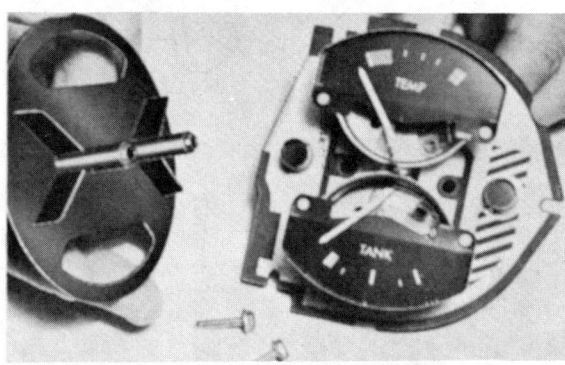

Fig. 10.40. Removing mask from water temperature and fuel gauges (Sec. 25)

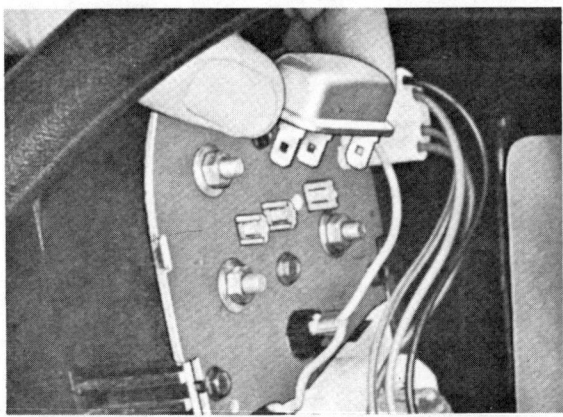

Fig. 10.41. Removing instrument voltage stabiliser (Sec. 25)

10 To test the stabiliser, connect a battery and voltmeter as shown in Fig. 10.42. After a warming-up period, the voltmeter needle should give regular pulsations, the centre of the deflection range being 10 volts. If these indications are not obtained, renew the stabiliser as a sealed unit.

11 If a warning or illumination lamp within the instrument panel fails, it can be renewed only after the cluster has been pulled forward as described in paragraphs 1 to 4 of this Section. The warning lamp bulb carrier can be withdrawn after depressing the carrier side clips. The bulbs are of wedge-base capless type and are simply pulled from their holders (photo).

12 Installation is a reversal of removal but make sure that any loose collars originally fitted to the instrument mounting studs are refitted and also make sure that the instrument cluster securing spring clips are in position before fitting the clock casing and before mating the gauges and circuit board to the instrument casing (photo).

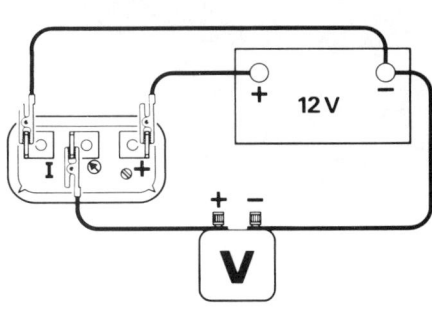

Fig. 10.42. Instrument voltage stabiliser test circuit (Sec. 25)

25.11 Instrument cluster lamp carrier

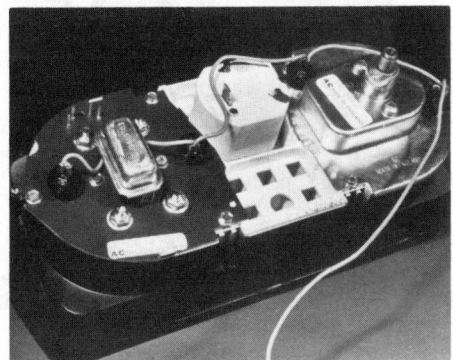

25.12 Rear view of instrument cluster

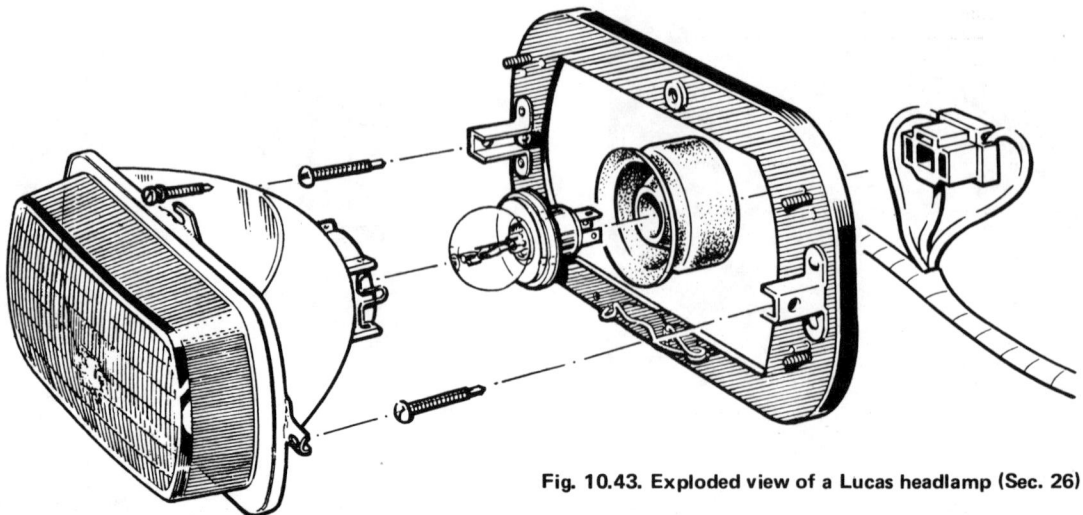

Fig. 10.43. Exploded view of a Lucas headlamp (Sec. 26)

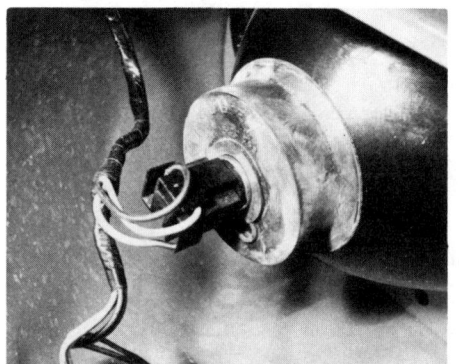

26.1 Rear view of a headlamp

26.2 Removing a headlamp bulb

26.4 Removing a headlamp surround

Fig. 10.44. Removing a Lucas headlamp unit (Sec. 26)

13 It should be noted that the speedometer cable is of grease-sealed type and no attempt should be made to extract the inner cable from the outer conduit.

26 Headlamps (Lucas) - bulb renewal and lamp unit removal

1   To renew a bulb, open the bonnet and pull the plug connector from the back of the headlamp unit (photo).
2   Peel off the rubber dust cover and release the two wire clips. Lift the bulb from its holder (photo).
3   Installation is a reversal of removal but make sure that the projection on the bulb flange engages correctly in the cut out in the holder.

26.6 Headlamp body securing bolts

4   To remove a headlamp unit, first detach the lamp surround (three screws) (photo).
5   Release the retaining spring at the bottom of the lamp and ease the bracket from the top alignment screw (do not alter the position of this screw otherwise the headlamp beam will be altered).
6   The mounting plate can be removed after unscrewing the four mounting nuts (photo).

27 Headlamps (Cibie) - bulb renewal and lamp unit removal

1 The procedure is similar to that described in the preceding Section except that the lamp unit is removed by easing it from its beam adjustment screws. The unit is held to these screws by captive plastic clips.

28 Headlamps - alignment

1 It is recommended that headlamp alignment is carried out by your dealer using modern beam setting equipment. However, in an emergency, the following procedure will provide an acceptable light pattern.

2 Position the car on a level surface with tyres correctly inflated. The adjustment will of course be carried out during the hours of darkness. Set the headlamps to dipped beam.

3 The adjustment screws are accessible at the rear of the lamp unit and the bonnet will have to be opened and a special key used to rotate them (photo).

4 On right-hand drive cars, obtain a light pattern as illustrated in Fig. 10.47. On left-hand drive cars the pattern must be reversed so that the sloping part is to the right.

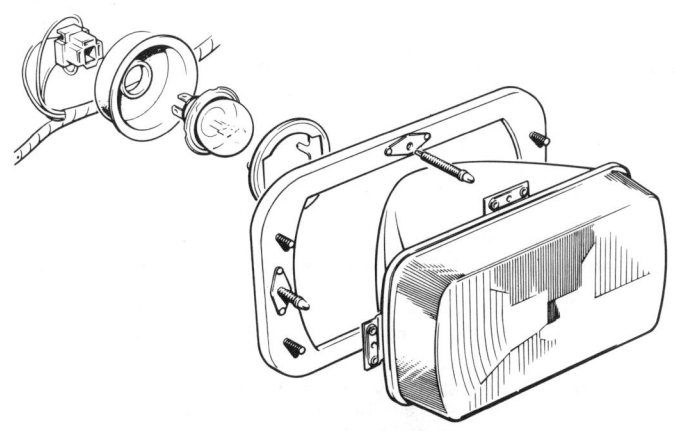

Fig. 10.45. Exploded view of a Cibie headlamp (Sec. 27)

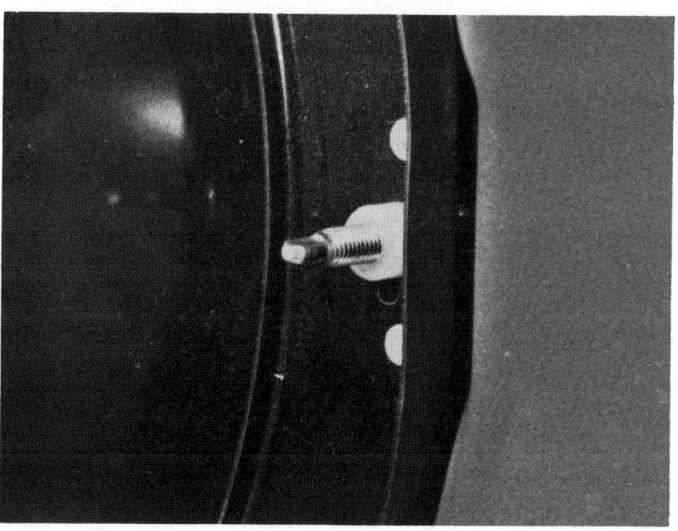

28.3 Headlamp adjuster screw

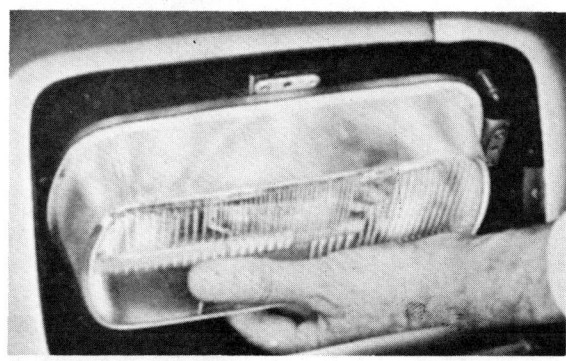

Fig. 10.46. Removing a Cibie headlamp unit (Sec. 27)

Fig. 10.47. Headlamp beam pattern (RHD) (Sec. 28)

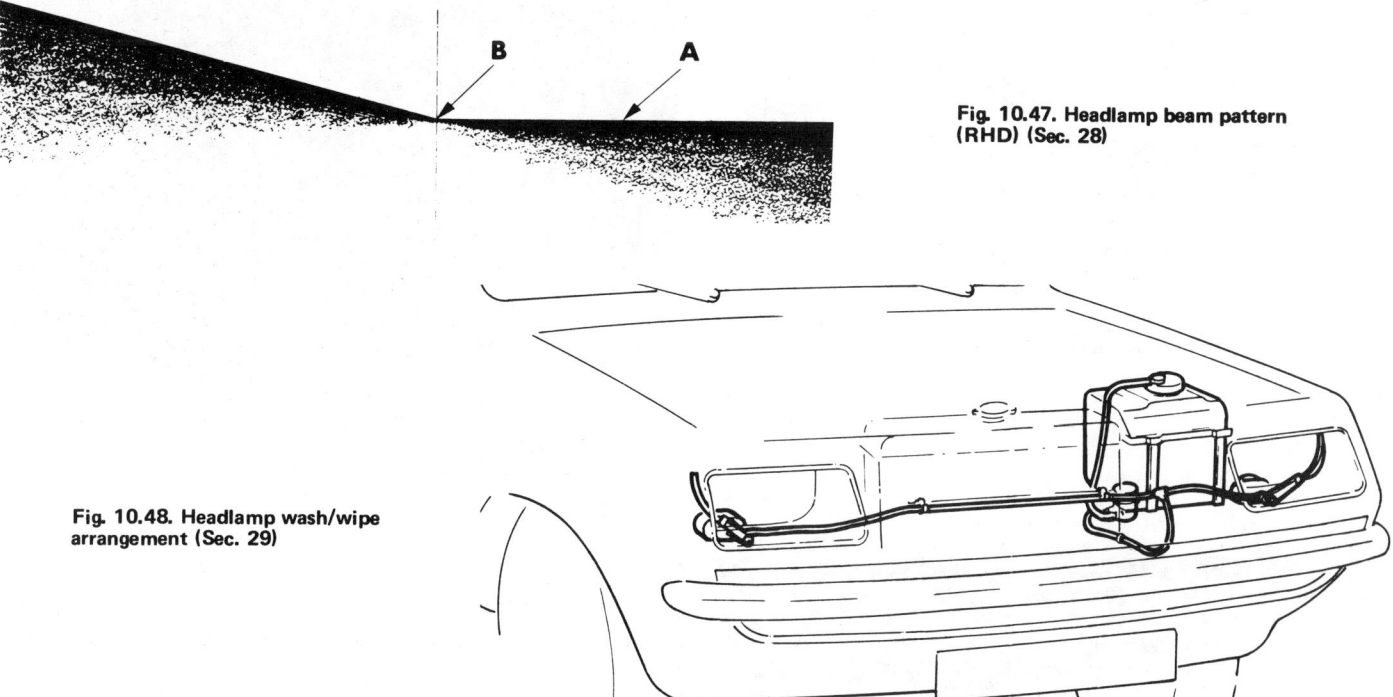

Fig. 10.48. Headlamp wash/wipe arrangement (Sec. 29)

29 Headlamp lens washer/wiper - description and servicing

1 This device is installed on cars destined for certain overseas territories. It comprises a reservoir/pump washer unit, wiper blades powered by individual electric motors and washer jets attached to the wiper blades. The blades are self-parking type (Fig. 10.48).

2 Electrical power is taken from no. 6 fuse to a relay mounted on the left-hand side of the engine compartment. A line fuse is incorporated in the wiring.

3 Access to the wiper blades is obtained after removing the headlamp surround (three screws). The left-hand motor can only be removed after first withdrawing the reservoir/pump unit.

4 The motors are sealed units and can only be renewed as such.

5 The blades unclip from the wiper arms and the arms are secured to the motor shafts by nuts.

6 When refitting components, make sure that with the motors in the parked position, the arms and blades are located on the outer rims of the lenses before tightening the securing nuts. The jet fluid tube must be wound round the motor shaft twice to provide flexibility during operation.

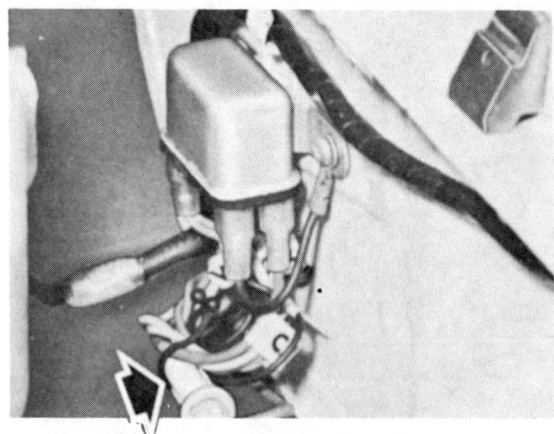

Fig. 10.49. Headlamp wash/wiper relay and line fuse (arrowed) (Sec. 29)

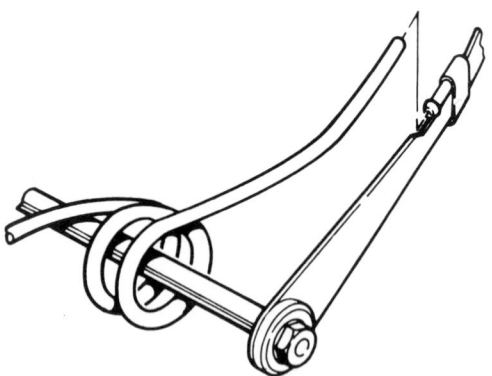

Fig. 10.51. Method of routing headlamp washer jet tube (Sec. 29)

30 Lamp bulbs - renewal

1 Lamp bulbs should always be renewed with ones of similar type and rating as listed in Specifications Section.

Front parking/direction indicator lamps

2 The bulbs are accessible after removal of the lens (two screws) (photo).

Side repeater lamps

3 The bulbs are accessible after removal of the lens (one screw).

Rear lamp cluster

4 The bulbs are accessible after removal of the lens (two screws). If the lamp bodies are to be removed, the rear internal trim panel will have to be detached (four screws). The lamp bodies are secured by two nuts each (photo).

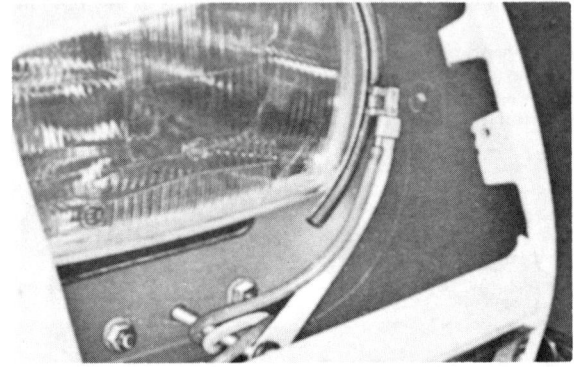

Fig. 10.50. Parked position of headlamp wash/wipe arm and blade (Sec. 29)

30.2 Flasher/side lamp (lens removed)

Fig. 10.52. Rear trim panel securing screws (Sec. 30)

5 When reconnecting the leads to the lamp terminals, note that the sequence is:

Green/white to direction indicator lamp
Red/orange (RH), red/black (LH) to taillamp
Green/purple to stoplamp
Green/brown to reverse lamp

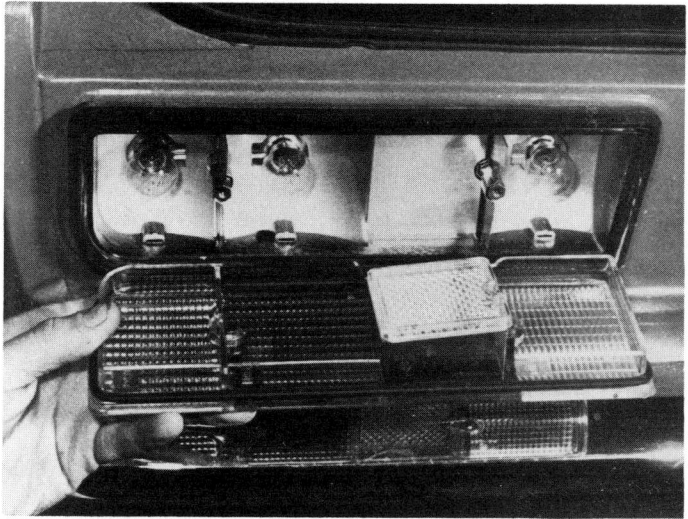

30.4 Rear lamp cluster

Rear number plate lamp
6 To renew the bulb, remove the two screws which secure the lens and ease the lens downward until it clears the lamp body.
7 Pull the bulb holder towards you and extract the wedge-base capless bulb.
8 If the complete lamp assembly must be withdrawn, then the left-hand floor panel from the luggage area must first be removed.

Interior lamp
9 The festoon type bulb is accessible after moving the lamp lens in the same relative direction as the side of the car to which the steering wheel is fitted and then pulling it from the head lining.

31 Wiper blades - renewal

1 Whenever the wiper blades no longer clean the windscreen effectively, the flexible inserts should be renewed.
2 On 'SWF' type arms and blades, depress the blade catch and withdraw the blade towards the wiper arm pivot.
3 On 'Trico' type arms and blades, insert a screwdriver between the spring catch and the arm and then tilt the end of the blade connecting sleeve in the direction of the windscreen and withdraw it (photo).
4 Carefully slide out the flexible inserts and install the new ones and refit the blades to the arms.

32 Wiper linkage - removal and installation

1 Remove the wiper blades, as described in the preceding Section.
2 Remove the wiper arms from the driving spindles by prising them off with a screwdriver which simultaneously holds back the spring clip

Fig. 10.53. Removing rear number plate lamp lens (Sec. 30)

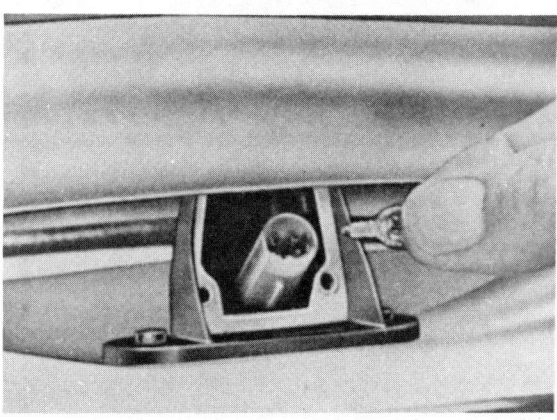

Fig. 10.54. Removing rear number plate lamp bulb (Sec. 30)

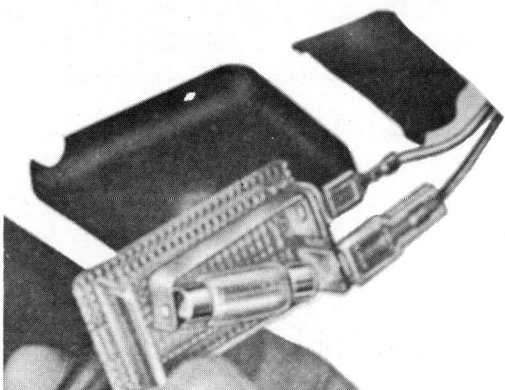

Fig. 10.55. Withdrawing interior lamp (Sec. 30)

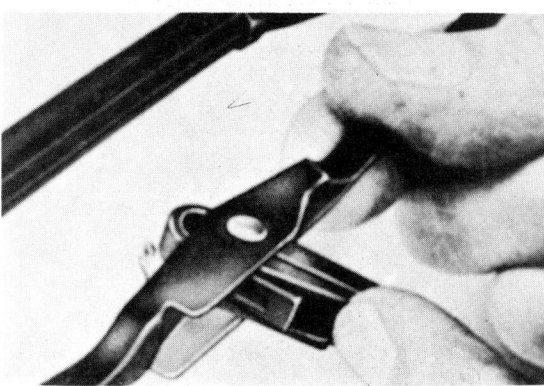

Fig. 10.56. Disconnecting wiper blade (SWF type) (Sec. 31)

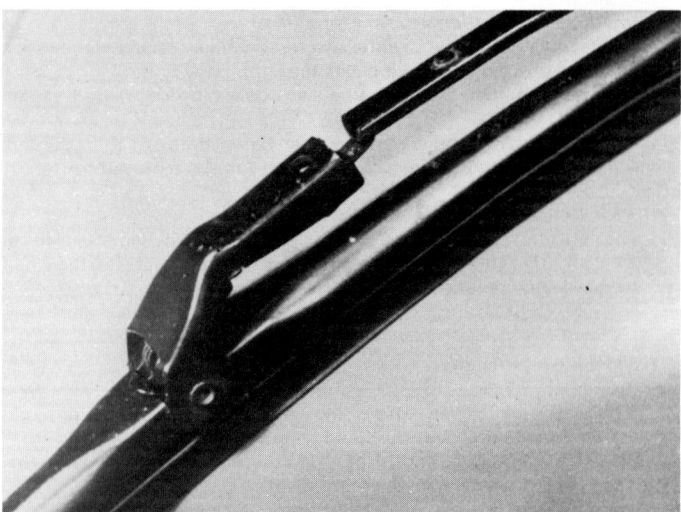

31.3 Wiper blade attachment

32.2 Wiper arm attachment

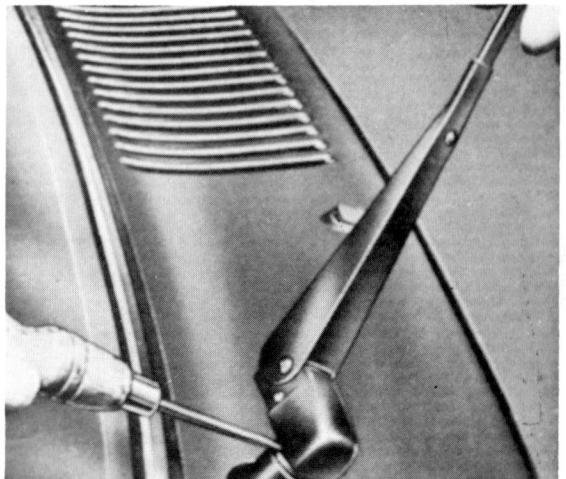

Fig. 10.57. Prising off a wiper arm (Sec. 32)

from engagement with the wiper arm boss (photo).

3   Remove the steering wheel and column shrouds (see Chapter 11).

4   Remove the instrument cluster (Section 25, this Chapter), the lighting switch and the parcels shelf.

5   Remove the instrument panel cover (two nuts and six clips).

6   Unscrew and remove the nut which secures the crank arm to the wiper motor cross-shaft.

7   Unscrew and remove the bolts which secure the wiper arm driving spindles and withdraw the complete linkage assembly from behind the instrument panel downwards into the car interior.

8   Installation is a reversal of removal but make sure that the wiper arms are set so that the blades take up the positions shown in the diagram (Fig. 10.60) when the motor is in the self-parked position.

9   Should any judder occur when the wiper arms are moving across a wet screen in one direction, this can usually be rectified by twisting the flat section of the arm slightly until the condition disappears.

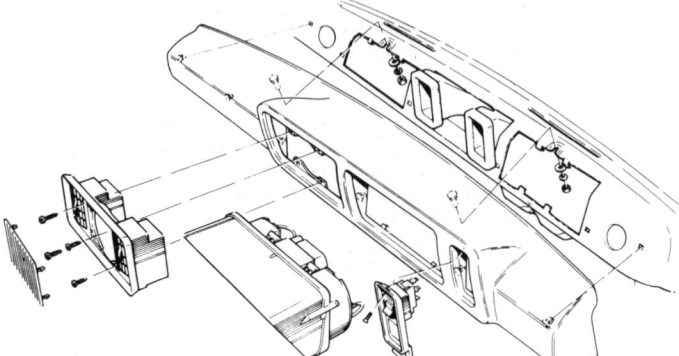

Fig. 10.58. Instrument panel cover showing securing nuts and clips (Sec. 32)

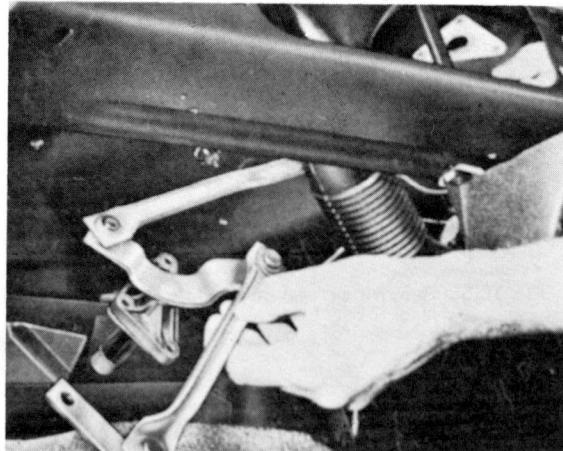

Fig. 10.59. Withdrawing windscreen wiper arm linkage (Sec. 32)

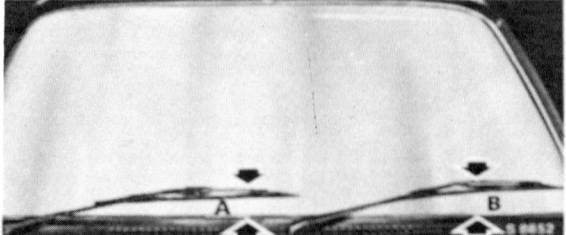

Fig. 10.60. Correct setting of wiper arms and blades (Sec. 32)

RHD   A = 1.2 in. (30.0 mm)   B = 1.8 in. (45.0 mm)
LHD   Transpose dimensions A and B

33 Windscreen wiper motor - removal, overhaul and installation

1 Remove the parcels shelf.

2 Unscrew the nut which secures the crank arm to the wiper motor cross-shaft.

3 Working within the engine compartment, disconnect the multi-pin plug and then unscrew and remove the three mounting nuts and withdraw the motor and bracket (photo).

4 Remove the mounting bracket from the motor (three screws) making sure that its relative position is marked to facilitate reassembly (Fig. 10.63).

5 Detach the endframe from the gear housing by prising out the retaining clips (Fig. 10.64).

6 Remove the gear housing cover (four screws).

7 Withdraw the gear and cross-shaft, taking care not to lose the thrust washer (Fig. 10.65).

8 Using a small screwdriver, hook the brush leads over the brush holders to keep the brushes in a retracted position pending withdrawal of the armature (Fig. 10.66).

9 Slacken the bearing retainer nut and withdraw the armature and bearing (Figs. 10.67 and 10.68).

10 Remove the brush plate assembly together with the gear housing cover (three screws) (Fig. 10.69).

11 Inspect all components for wear. Any wear in the bushes will necessitate renewal of the support component as the bushes are not supplied separately.

12 Reassembly is a reversal of dismantling but the following points must be observed:

(i) *Before inserting cross-shaft, pack housing half full with grease.*

(ii) *Apply a smear of grease to the cross-shaft thrust button.*

(iii) *Make sure that the brushes are retracted before inserting the armature but are released before installing the endframe.*

33.3 Location of windscreen wiper motor and washer assembly

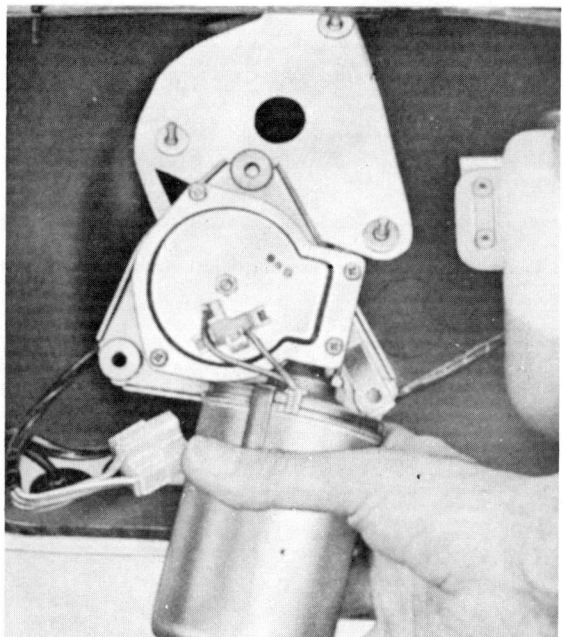

Fig. 10.61. Removing windscreen wiper motor (Sec. 33)

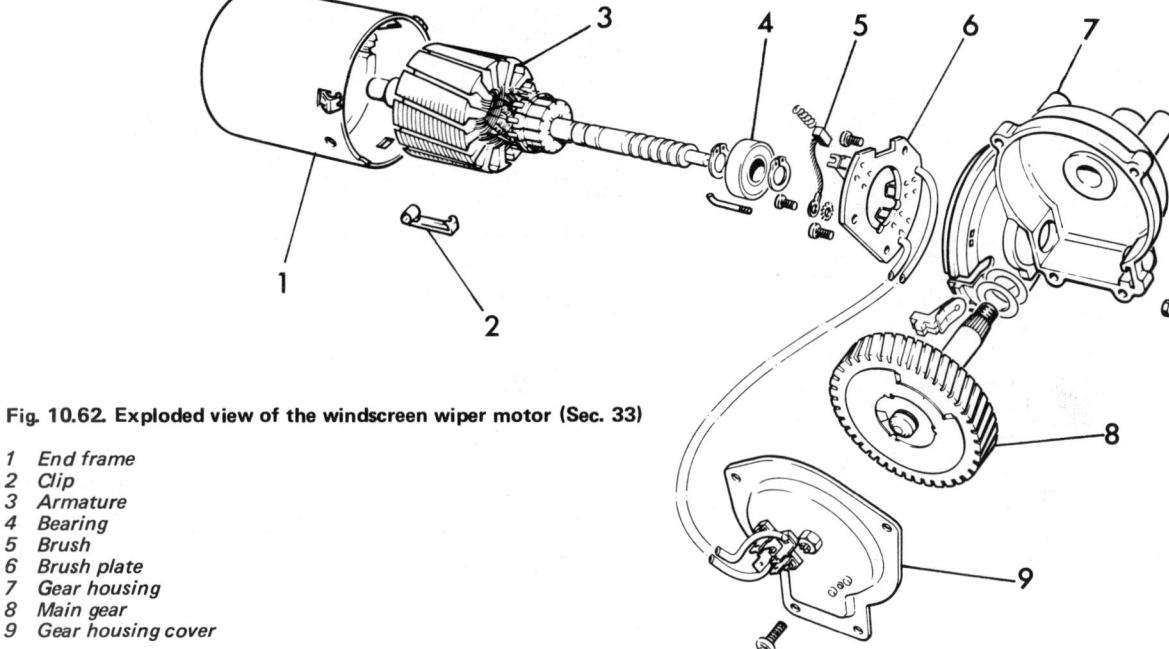

Fig. 10.62. Exploded view of the windscreen wiper motor (Sec. 33)

1 End frame
2 Clip
3 Armature
4 Bearing
5 Brush
6 Brush plate
7 Gear housing
8 Main gear
9 Gear housing cover

(iv) *When the unit is fully assembled, slacken the locknut in the centre of the gear housing cover and with the motor temporarily connected to a 12 volt supply with an ammeter in circuit, tighten the adjuster screw until current consumption increases by not more than 0.1 amp. Tighten the locknut without moving the position of the adjuster screw.*

13 Install the motor, connect the crankarm making sure that the key engages correctly with the keyway in the cross-shaft. Reconnect the multi-pin plug.

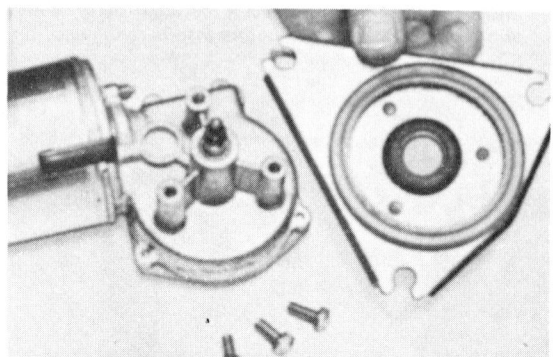

Fig. 10.63. Removing wiper motor mounting bracket (Sec. 33)

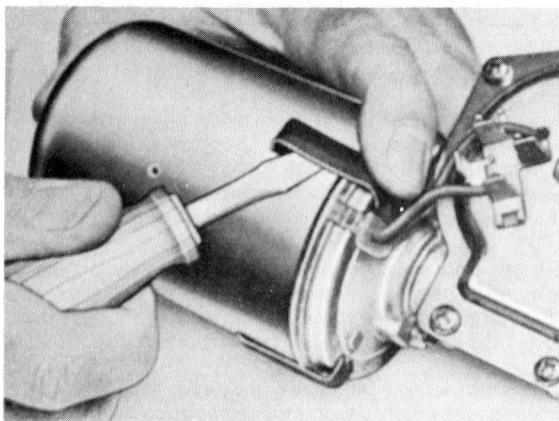

Fig. 10.64. Releasing a wiper motor end frame clip (Sec. 33)

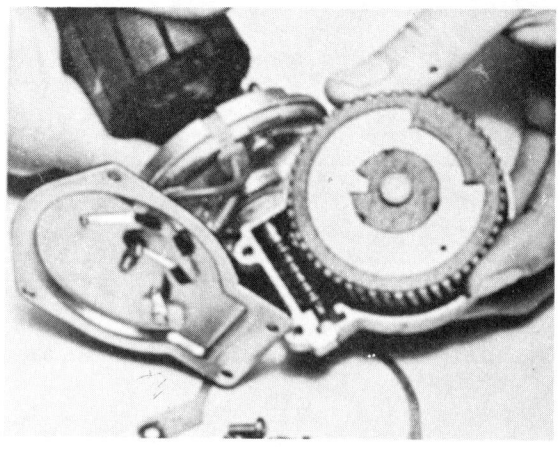

Fig. 10.65. Withdrawing wiper motor main gear and cross shaft (Sec. 33)

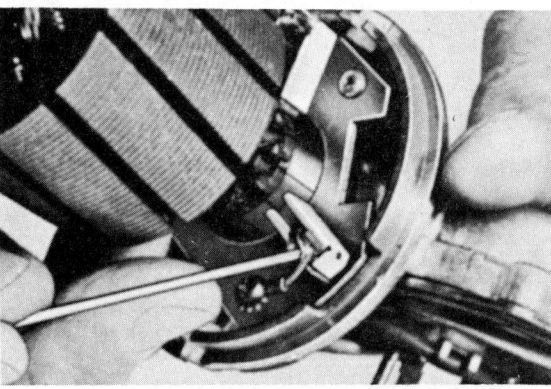

Fig. 10.66. Method of retracting wiper motor brushes pending removal of armature (Sec. 33)

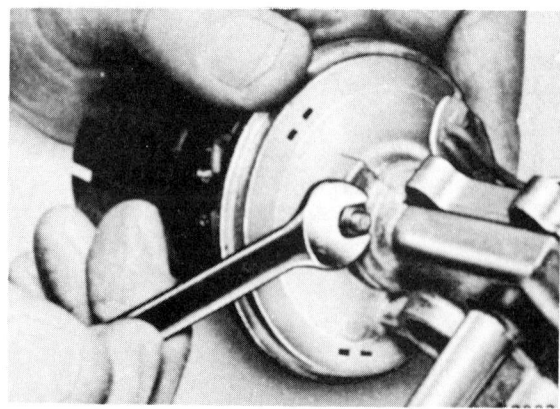

Fig. 10.67. Slackening wiper motor bearing retainer nut (Sec. 33)

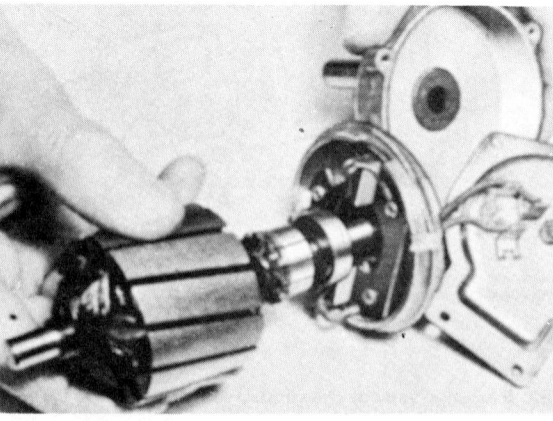

Fig. 10.68. Withdrawing wiper motor armature and bearing (Sec. 33)

Fig. 10.69. Removing wiper motor brush plate and gear housing cover (Sec. 33)

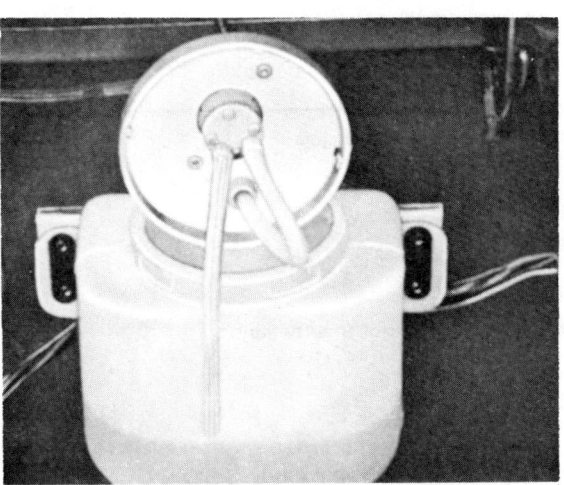

Fig. 10.70. Windscreen washer reservoir and pump unit (Sec. 34)

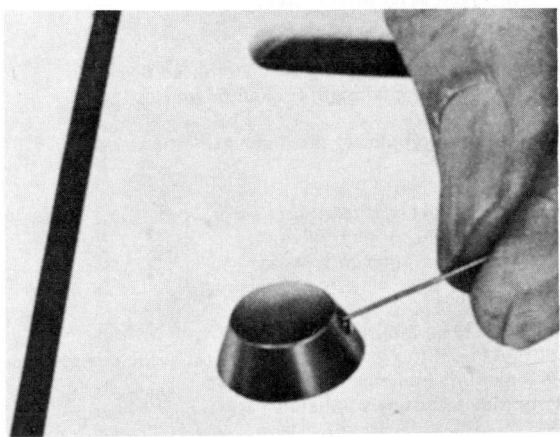

Fig. 10.71. Adjusting a windscreen washer jet (Sec. 34)

2 The fluid in the washer reservoir should be kept topped-up during the weekly routine maintenance checks. To fill the reservoir, unscrew the lid to which the pump is mounted.

3 It is an advantage to keep the reservoir filled with water to which a recommended cleaning solvent has been added. This will also reduce the chance of freezing during winter conditions.

4 Access to the pump impeller can be obtained, if clogging is suspected, by removing the cover and seal (four screws).

5 The washer jets can be adjusted as required by inserting a pin into them and moving them to the desired angle.

35 Horn - description, removal and installation

1 A single low-note horn is mounted adjacent to the radiator.

2 Access to the horn is obtained after removal of the radiator grille as described in Chapter 12.

3 The horn is not adjustable but any fault may be due to a poor earth connection which is made through the mounting bracket to the body.

4 The horn button operation can be checked by reference to Section 19, paragraph 7.

34 Windscreen washer - maintenance

1 Occasionally check that the electrical connections and the fluid pipelines are secure.

See next page for 'Fault diagnosis - electrical system'.

36 Fault diagnosis - electrical system

Symptom	Reason
Starter motor fails to turn engine	
No electricity at starter motor	Battery discharged
	Battery defective internally
	Battery terminal leads loose or earth lead not securely attached to body
	Loose or broken connections in starter motor circuit
	Starter motor switch or solenoid faulty
Electricity at starter motor: faulty motor	Starter motor pinion jammed in mesh with flywheel gear ring
	Starter brushes badly worn, sticking, or brush wire loose
	Commutator dirty, worn or burnt
	Starter motor armature faulty
	Field coils earthed
Starter motor turns engine very slowly	
Electrical defects	Battery in discharged condition
	Starter brushes badly worn, sticking, or brush wires loose
	Loose wires in starter motor circuit
Starter motor operates without turning engine	
Dirt or oil on drive gear	Starter motor pinion sticking on the screwed sleeve
	Pinion or flywheel gear teeth broken or worn
Electrical defect	Battery almost completely discharged (inertia starters)
Starter motor noisy or excessively rough engagement	
Lack of attention or mechanical damage	Pinion or flywheel gear teeth broken or worn
	Starter drive main spring broken
	Starter motor retaining bolts loose
Battery will not hold charge for more than a few days	
Wear or damage	Battery defective internally
	Electrolyte level too low or electrolyte too weak due to leakage
	Plate separators no longer fully effective
	Battery plates severely sulphated
Insufficient current flow to keep battery charge	Battery plates severely sulphated
	Fan belt slipping
	Battery terminal connections loose or corroded
	Alternator not charging
	Short in lighting circuit causing continual battery drain
	Alternator regulator unit nor working correctly
Ignition light fails to go out, battery runs flat in a few days	
Alternator not charging	Fan belt loose and slipping or broken
	Brushes worn, sticking, broken or dirty
	Brush springs weak or broken
	Slip rings dirty, greasy, worn or burnt
	Alternator stator coils burnt, open, or shorted
Horn	
Horn operates all the time	Horn push either earthed or stuck down
	Horn cable to horn push earthed
Horn fails to operate	Blown fuse
	Cable or cable connection loose, broken or disconnected
	Horn has an internal fault
Horn emits intermittent or unsatisfactory noise	Cable connections loose
Lights	
Lights do not come on	If engine not running, battery discharged
	Light bulb filament burnt out or bulbs broken
	Wire connections loose, disconnected or broken
	Light switch shorting or otherwise faulty
Lights come on but fade out	If engine not running battery discharged
	Light bulb filament burnt out or bulbs or sealed beam units broken
	Wire connections loose, disconnected or broken
	Light switch shorting or otherwise faulty

Symptom	Reason
Lights give very poor illumination	Lamp glasses dirty Lamps badly out of adjustment
Lights work erratically - flashing on and off, especially over bumps	Battery terminal or earth connection loose Lights not earthing properly Contacts in light switch faulty
Wipers Wiper motor fails to work	Blown fuse Wire connections loose, disconnected or broken Brushes badly worn Armature worn or faulty Field coils faulty
Wiper motor works very slowly and takes excessive current	Commutator dirty, greasy or burnt Armature bearings dirty or unaligned Armature badly worn or faulty
Wiper motor works slowly and takes little current	Brushes badly worn Commutator dirty, greasy or burnt Armature badly worn or faulty
Wiper motor works but wiper blades remain static	Wiper motor gearbox parts badly worn

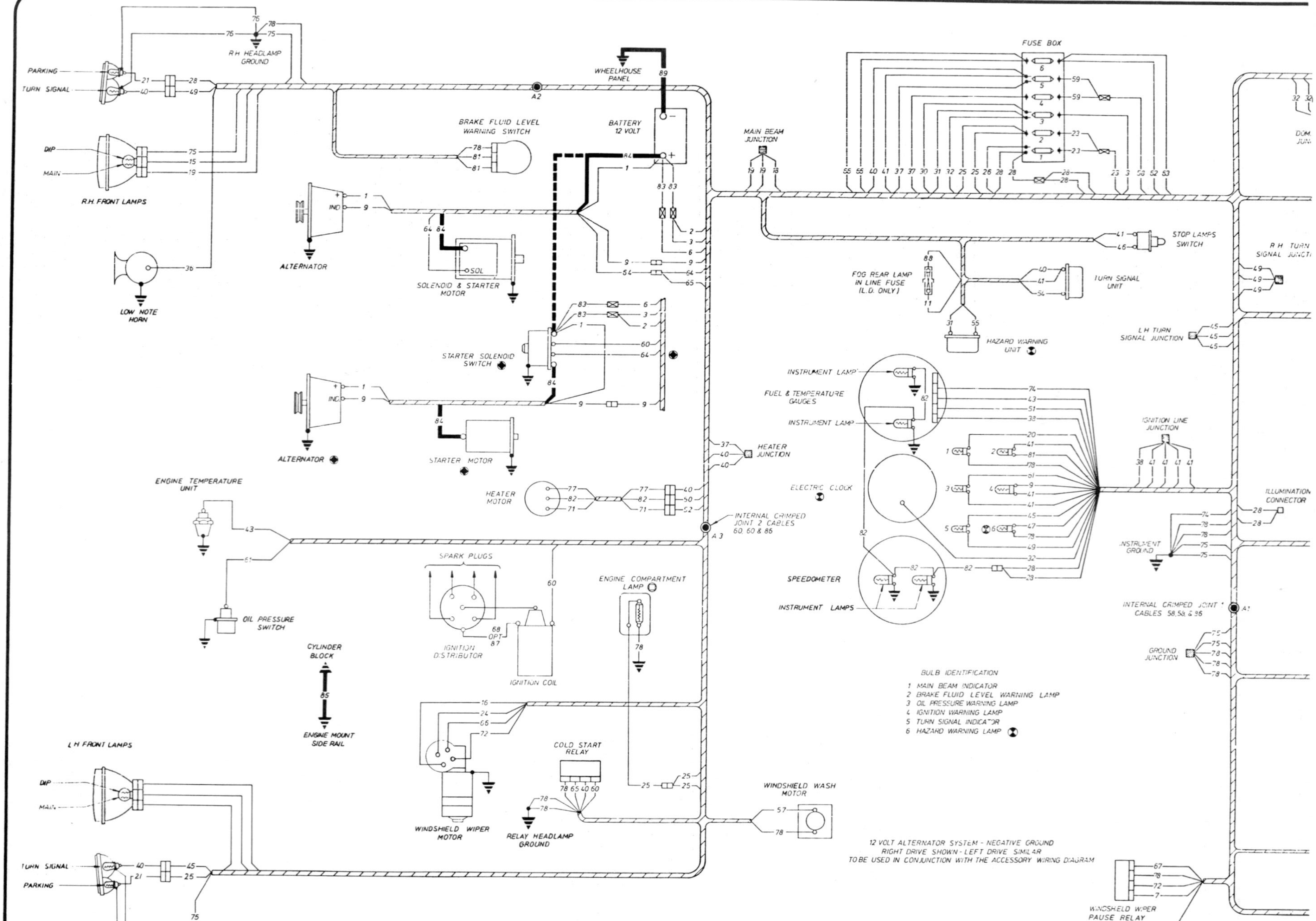

Fig. 10.71. Wiring diagram. For option and accessory circuits see Figs 10.72, 13.70 & 13.71
Note: Not all items shown are applicable to all models

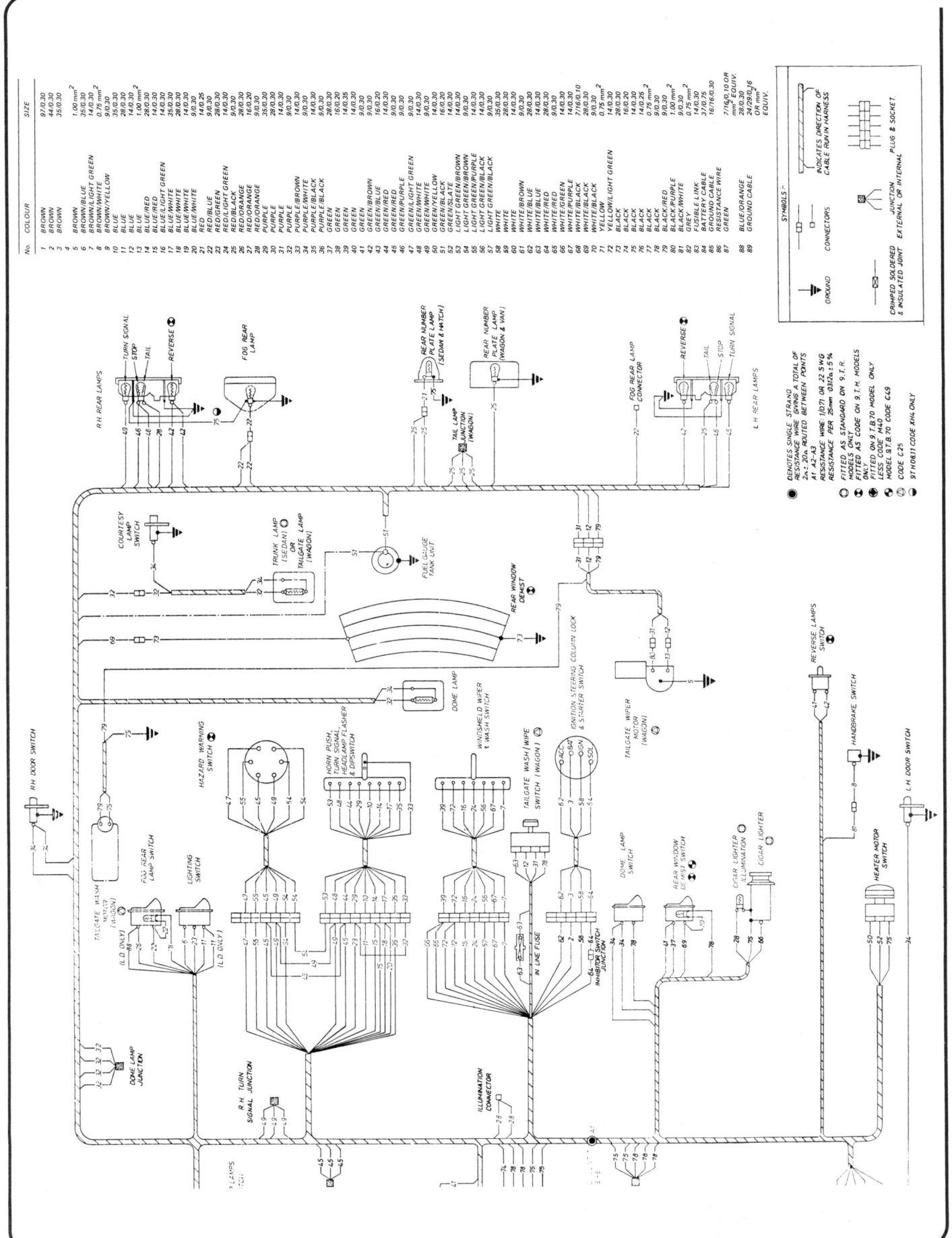

No.	COLOUR	SIZE
1	BROWN	9/0.30
2	BROWN	44/0.30
3	BROWN	35/0.30
4	BROWN	1.00 mm²
5	BROWN/BLUE	35/0.30
6	BROWN/LIGHT GREEN	14/0.30
7	BROWN/WHITE	0.75 mm²
8	BROWN/YELLOW	14/0.30
9	BLUE	35/0.30
10	BLUE	28/0.30
11	BLUE	1.00 mm²
12	BLUE	14/0.30
13	BLUE/RED	1.00 mm²
14	BLUE/RED	14/0.30
15	BLUE/LIGHT GREEN	14/0.30
16	BLUE/LIGHT GREEN	35/0.30
17	BLUE/WHITE	28/0.30
18	BLUE/WHITE	14/0.30
19	BLUE/WHITE	9/0.30
20	BLUE/WHITE	9/0.30
21	RED	9/0.25
22	RED/BLUE	14/0.30
23	RED/GREEN	9/0.30
24	RED/LIGHT GREEN	14/0.30
25	RED/BLACK	9/0.30
26	RED/ORANGE	28/0.30
27	RED/ORANGE	9/0.30
28	RED/ORANGE	9/0.30
29	PURPLE	35/0.30
30	PURPLE	9/0.30
31	PURPLE	14/0.30
32	PURPLE/BROWN	9/0.30
33	PURPLE/WHITE	14/0.30
34	PURPLE/BLACK	14/0.30
35	PURPLE/PURPLE	9/0.30
36	PURPLE/BLACK	9/0.30
37	GREEN	14/0.30
38	GREEN	16/0.20
39	GREEN	14/0.30
40	GREEN	9/0.30
41	GREEN	9/0.30
42	GREEN/BROWN	16/0.20
43	GREEN/LIGHT GREEN	14/0.30
44	GREEN/RED	9/0.30
45	GREEN/RED	9/0.30
46	GREEN/PURPLE	9/0.30
47	GREEN/LIGHT GREEN	9/0.30
48	GREEN/WHITE	14/0.30
49	GREEN/WHITE	9/0.30
50	GREEN/YELLOW	9/0.30
51	GREEN/BLACK	16/0.20
52	GREEN/SLATE	14/0.30
53	LIGHT GREEN/BROWN	9/0.30
54	LIGHT GREEN/BROWN	14/0.30
55	LIGHT GREEN/PURPLE	7/0.30
56	LIGHT GREEN/BLACK	14/0.30
57	LIGHT GREEN/BLACK	9/0.30
58	WHITE	35/0.30
59	WHITE	28/0.30
60	WHITE	9/0.30
61	WHITE/BROWN	28/0.30
62	WHITE/BLUE	14/0.30
63	WHITE/RED	28/0.30
64	WHITE/RED	9/0.30
65	WHITE/GREEN	14/0.30
66	WHITE/PURPLE	14/0.30
67	WHITE/PURPLE	14/0.30
68	WHITE/BLACK	7/0.30
69	WHITE/BLACK	28/0.30
70	WHITE/BLACK	9/0.30
71	YELLOW	0.75 mm²
72	YELLOW/LIGHT GREEN	9/0.30
73	BLACK	28/0.30
74	BLACK	28/0.30
75	BLACK	16/0.20
76	BLACK	14/0.30
77	BLACK	9/0.30
78	BLACK	9/0.30
79	BLACK/RED	28/0.30
80	BLACK/PURPLE	14/0.30
81	BLACK/PURPLE	14/0.30
82	BLACK/WHITE	14/0.25
83	GREY	0.75 mm²
84	FUSIBLE LINK	9/0.30
85	BATTERY CABLE	1.00 mm²
86	GROUND CABLE	14/0.30
87	RESISTANCE WIRE	37/0.75
	GREEN	16/16/0.30
88	BLUE/ORANGE	7/16,0.10 OR 24/29x16 mm² EQUIV.
89	GROUND CABLE	0.8 mm² EQUIV.

SYMBOLS:-

INDICATES DIRECTION OF CABLE RUN IN HARNESS

CONNECTORS

PLUG & SOCKET

GROUND

JUNCTION EXTERNAL OR INTERNAL

CRIMPED SOLDERED & INSULATED JOINT

● DENOTES SINGLE STRAND

RESISTANCE WIRE = 1(107) OR 22 SWG RESISTANCE PER 25mm ·03Ω·±·5%

○ FITTED AS STANDARD ON 9.T.B70 MODELS ONLY

◐ FITTED AS CODE ON 9.T.H. MODELS ONLY

⊕ FITTED ON 9.T.B70 MODEL ONLY

◑ LESS CODE M40

⊖ MODEL 9T.B.70 CODE C69

⊘ CODE C25

◒ 9TH0811 CODE XH4 ONLY

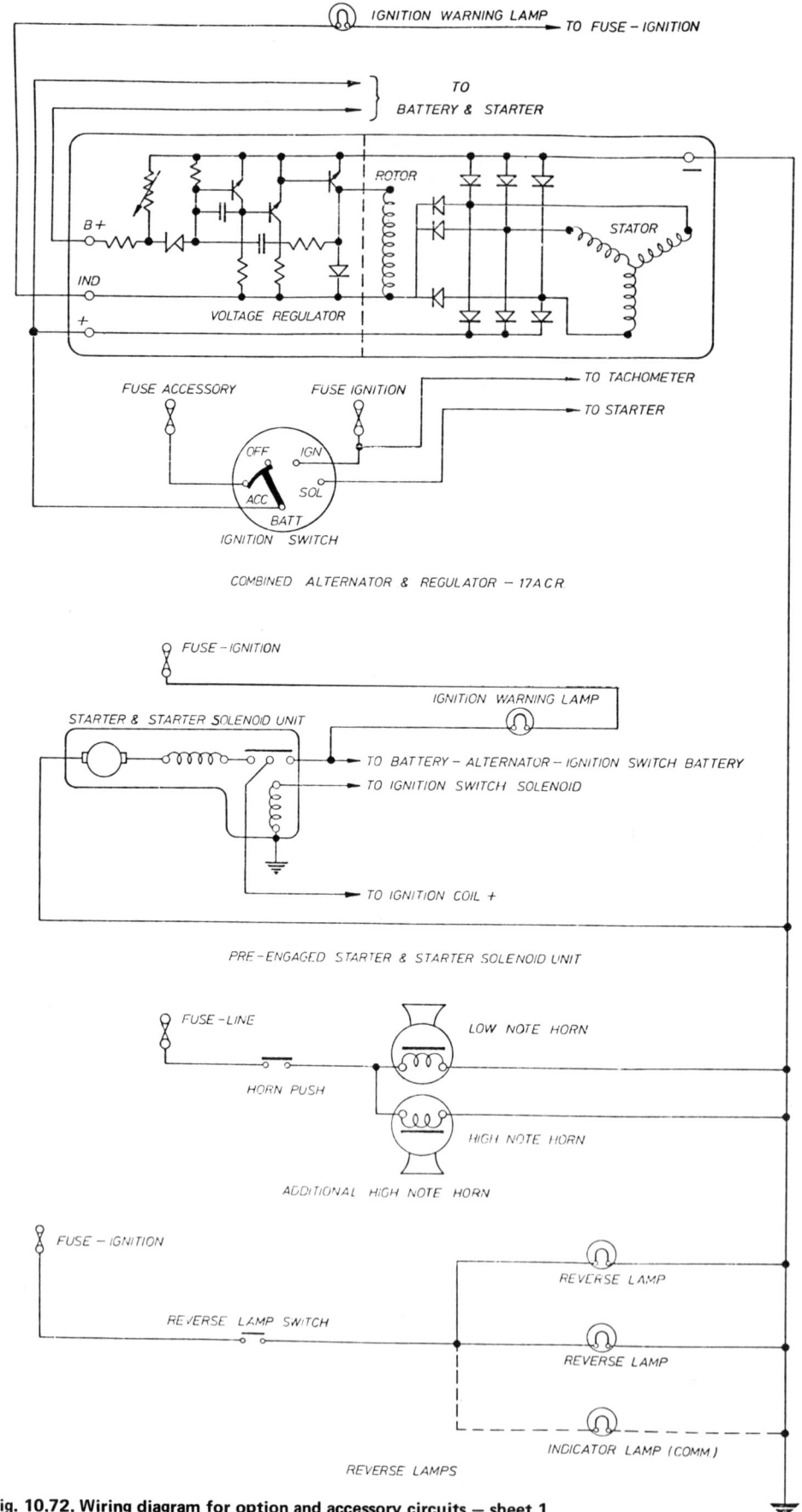

Fig. 10.72. Wiring diagram for option and accessory circuits — sheet 1
See Figs. 13.70 and 13.71 for sheets 2 and 3

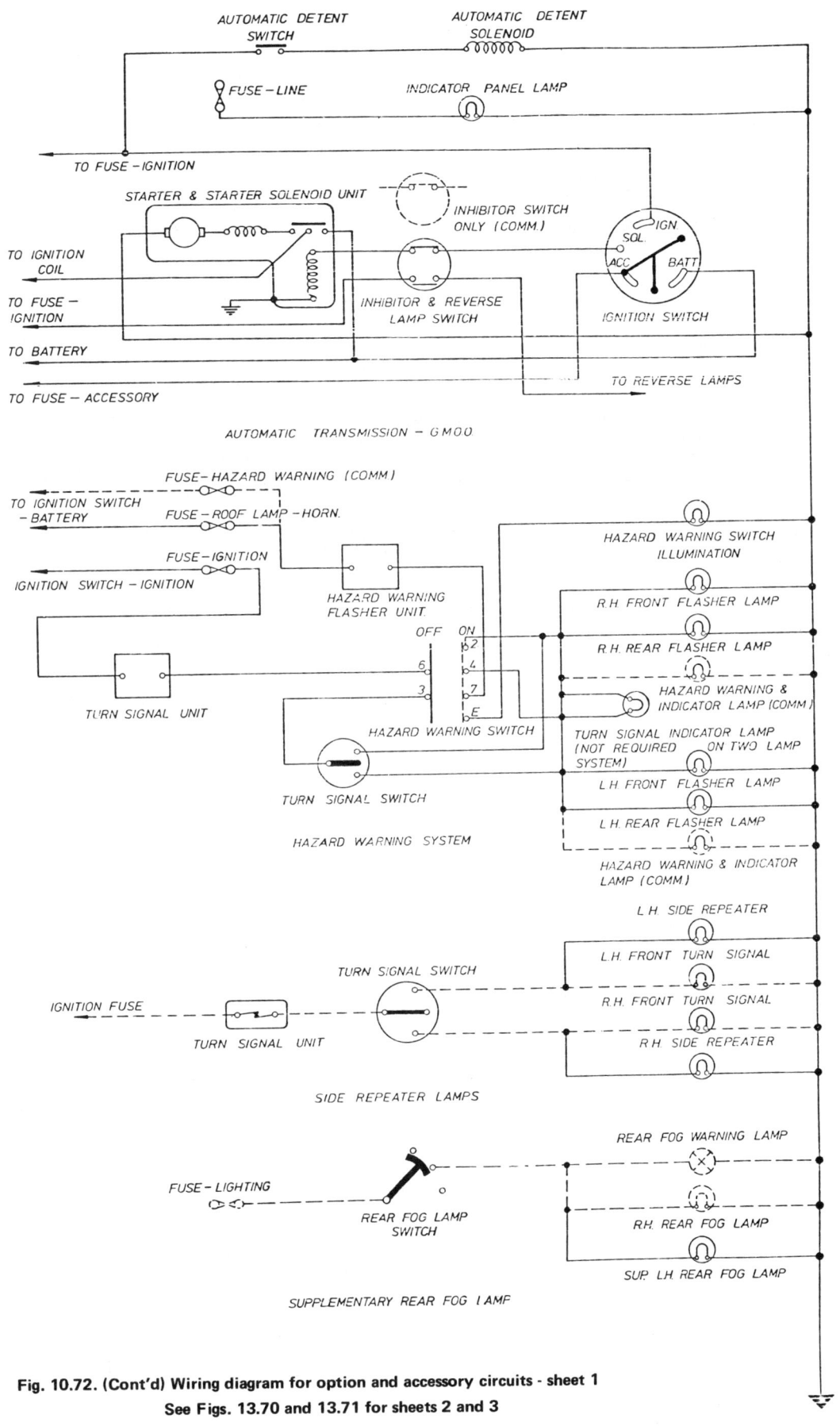

Fig. 10.72. (Cont'd) Wiring diagram for option and accessory circuits - sheet 1
See Figs. 13.70 and 13.71 for sheets 2 and 3

Chapter 11 Suspension and steering

For modifications, and information applicable to later models, see Supplement at end of manual

Contents

Specifications

Front suspension

Type	Upper and lower wishbone, coil spring telescopic shock absorbers, stabiliser bar
Hub bearing endfloat	0.001 to 0.004 in (0.02 to 0.10 mm)
Steering angles:	
Camber	0° 15' positive to 1° 15' negative
Castor	2° 30' to 5° positive
Steering axis inclination	8°
Toe-in	0.16 to 0.24 in (4.0 to 6.0 mm)

Rear suspension

Type	Trailing arm, coil spring, Panhard rod and stabiliser bar. Telescopic shock absorbers

Steering

Type	Rack and pinion with collapsible column and flexible coupling
Turning circle (between kerbs)	30.2 ft (9.2 m)
Number of turns (lock-to-lock)	3.5
Steering wheel diameter	14¾ in (374.7 mm)

Wheels and tyres

Roadwheels	Pressed steel 5 in (127.0 mm) rim
Tyres:	
Standard and 'L'	Radial 155SR-13
'GL'	Radial 175/70SR x 13
Pressures:	
Normal speed range:	
Front	21 lb/sq. in (1.48 kg/sq. cm)
Rear	24 lb/sq. in (1.69 kg/sq. cm)
High speeds:	
Front	25 lb/sq. in (1.76 kg/sq. cm)
Rear	28 lb/sq. in (1.97 kg/sq. cm)

Torque wrench settings

	lb ft	Nm
Front suspension		
Upper arm pivot bolts	59	80
Lower arm pivot bolts	49	68
Crossmember inner bolts	47	65
Crossmember outer bolts	55	76
Upper swivel balljoint flange nuts	30	41
Stabiliser bar clamp bolts	15	21
Shock absorber lower mounting bolts	30	41

Torque wrench settings (continued)

Rear suspension

								lbf ft	Nm
Panhard rod to body	...	...	...	...	...	...	...	72	100
Panhard rod to axle casing	...	...	...	...	...	...	...	47	65
Suspension arm pivot bolts	...	...	...	...	...	...	...	50	69
Pinion extension to crossmember	...	...	...	...	...	...	...	15	21
Shock absorber lower mountings	...	...	...	...	...	...	...	32	44

Steering

Steering wheel nut	...	...	...	...	...	...	...	44	61
Column upper bracket nuts	...	...	...	...	...	...	...	10	14
Column lower shear bolt (initially)	...	...	...	...	...	...	15	21
Flexible coupling pinch bolt	...	...	...	...	...	...	...	13	18
Pinion shaft retaining nut	...	...	...	...	...	...	...	11	15
Rack preload adjuster screw locknut	...	...	...	...	...	...	50	69
Trackrod inner balljoint to rack	...	...	...	...	...	...	66	91
Trackrod-end taper pin nuts	...	...	...	...	...	...	...	35	48
Trackrod-end locknuts	...	...	...	...	...	...	...	30	41
Steering gear mounting bolts	...	...	...	...	...	...	...	15	21

Wheels

Roadwheel nuts	...	...	...	...	...	...	...	48	65

1 General description

1 The front suspension is of independent, upper and lower wishbone type incorporating coil springs and double acting shock absorbers. The suspension arms are mounted to a crossmember at their inner ends and balljoints at their outer ends carry the stub axle. A stabiliser bar is mounted on the underbody and linked to the lower suspension arms (photo).

2 The rear suspension is of coil spring type and the rear axle is located by two suspension arms attached to the axle tubes and a short crossmember supporting the front of the pinion extension housing. A Panhard rod controls side movement of the axle and a stabiliser bar and double acting shock absorbers are incorporated in the suspension system (photos).

3 The steering gear is of rack and pinion type, mounted on the front suspension crossmember. The steering column is of energy absorbing type and incorporates a flexible coupling at its point of attachment to the steering pinion (photos).

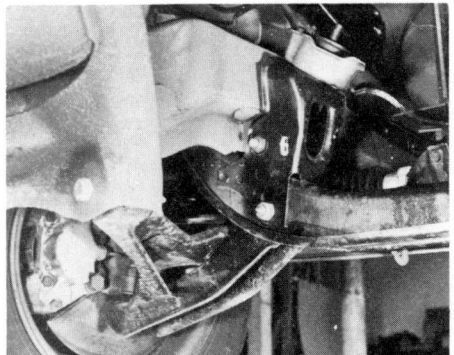

1.1 View of one side of the front suspension

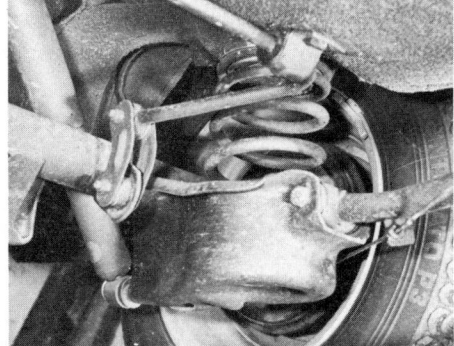

1.2A Front view of one side of the rear suspension

1.2B Rear view of one side of the rear suspension

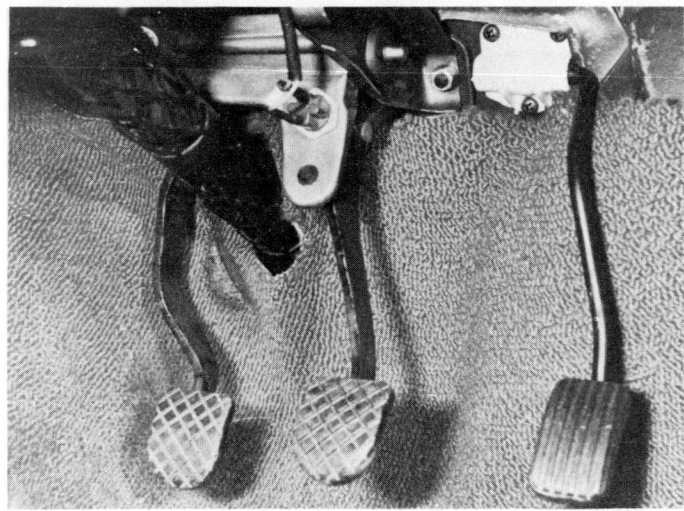

1.3A Collapsible type steering column and location of brake stop lamp switch

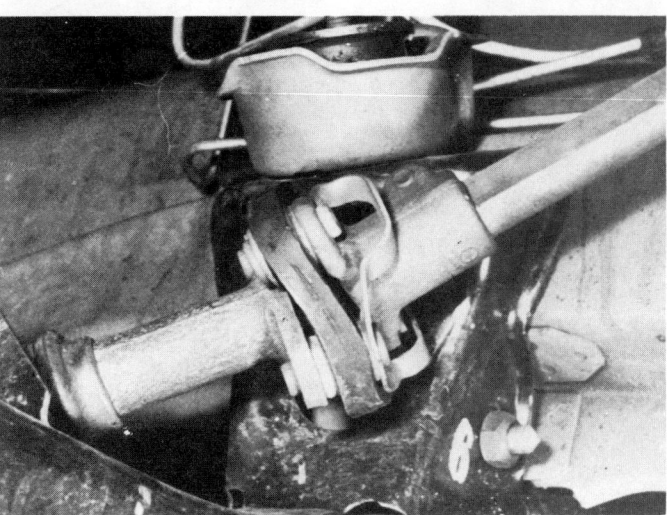

1.3B Flexible steering coupling

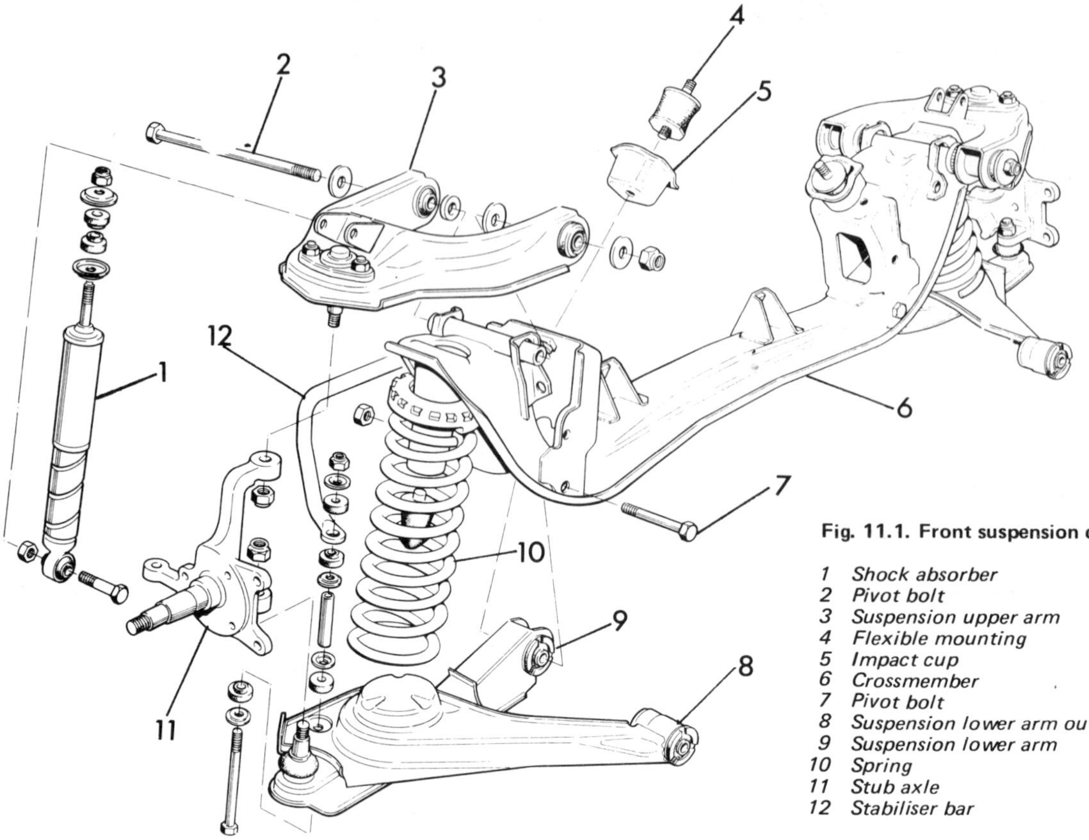

Fig. 11.1. Front suspension components

1   Shock absorber
2   Pivot bolt
3   Suspension upper arm
4   Flexible mounting
5   Impact cup
6   Crossmember
7   Pivot bolt
8   Suspension lower arm outrigger
9   Suspension lower arm
10 Spring
11 Stub axle
12 Stabiliser bar

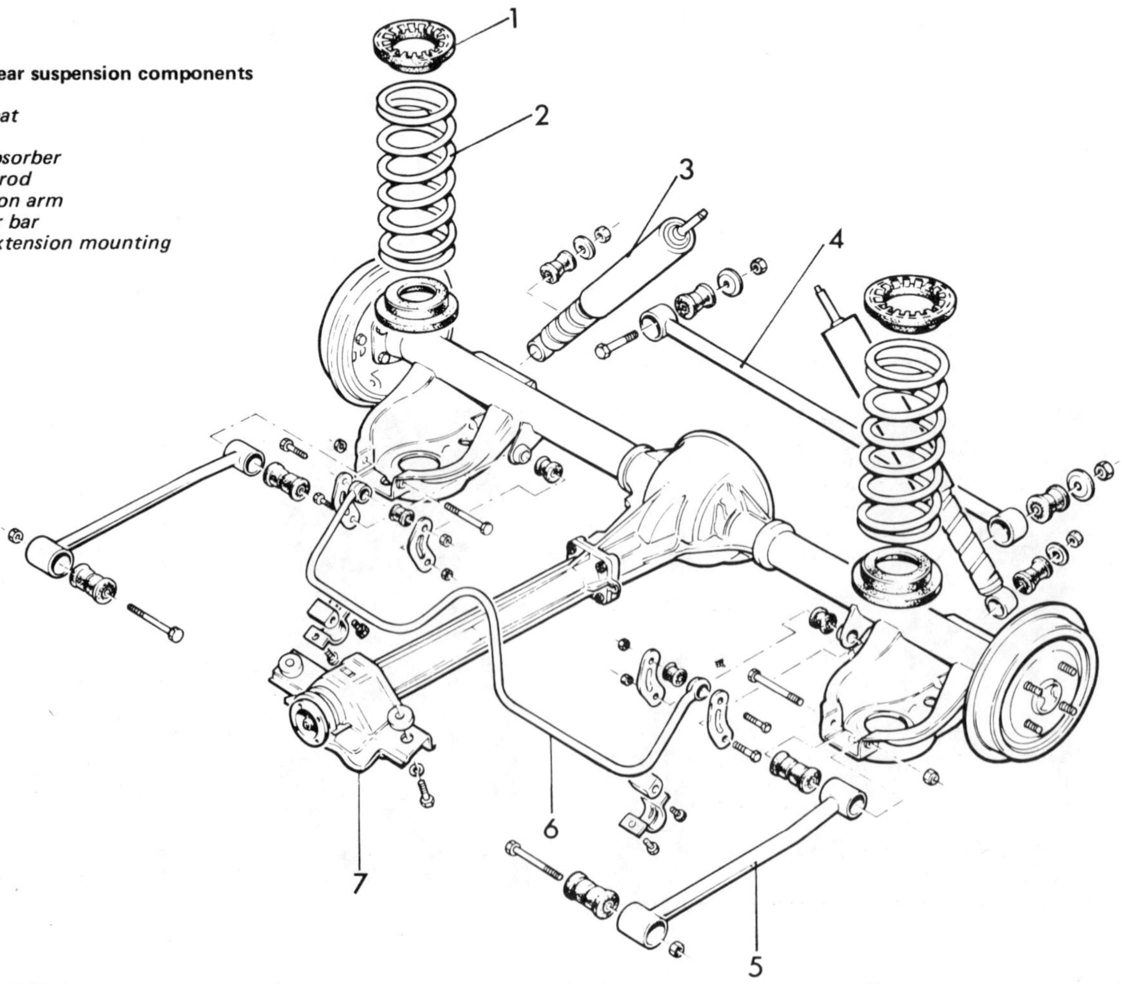

Fig. 11.2. Rear suspension components

1   Spring seat
2   Spring
3   Shock absorber
4   Panhard rod
5   Suspension arm
6   Stabiliser bar
7   Pinion extension mounting

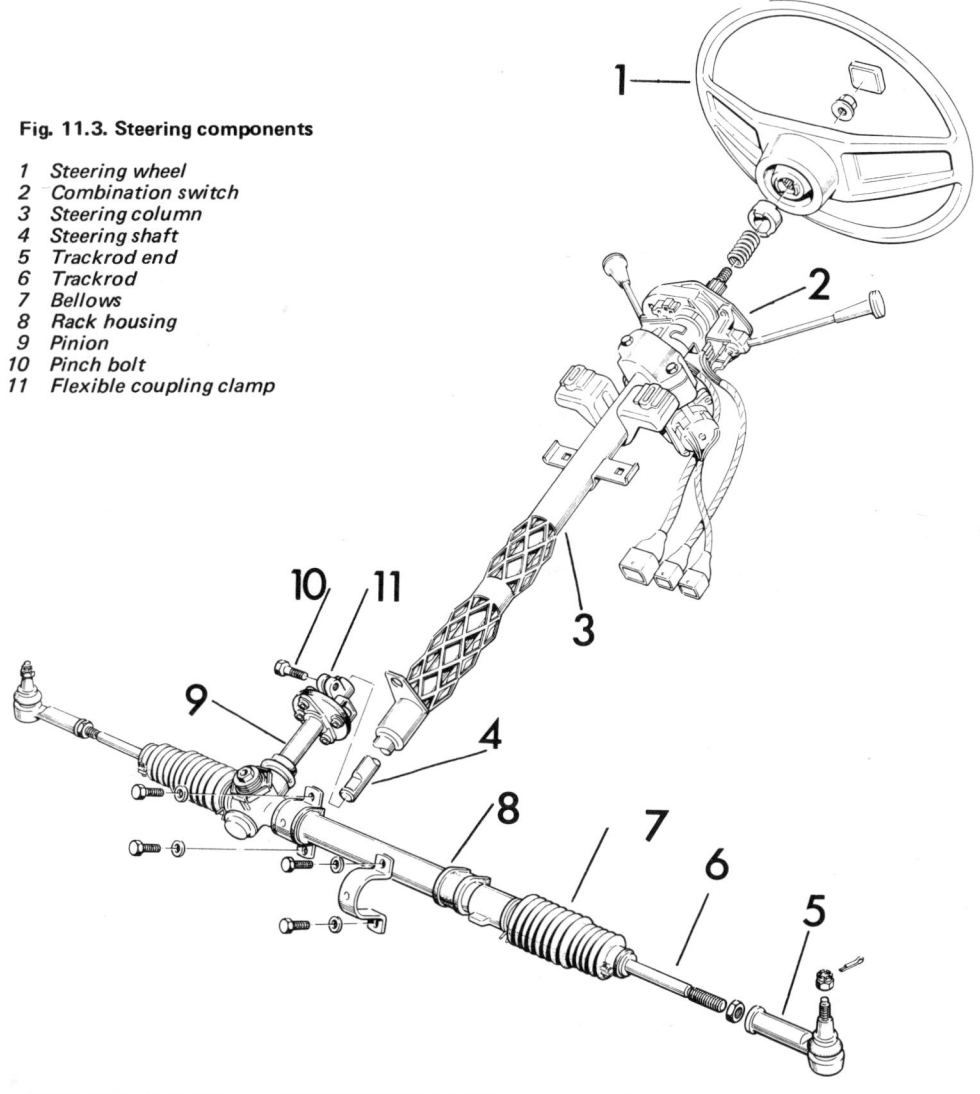

Fig. 11.3. Steering components

1 *Steering wheel*
2 *Combination switch*
3 *Steering column*
4 *Steering shaft*
5 *Trackrod end*
6 *Trackrod*
7 *Bellows*
8 *Rack housing*
9 *Pinion*
10 *Pinch bolt*
11 *Flexible coupling clamp*

2 Maintenance and inspection

1 At regular intervals, inspect the condition of all flexible gaiters, balljoint dust excluders and rubber suspension bushes. Renew any that have split or deteriorated, as described in the appropriate Section of this Chapter.
2 At the same time, check the torque of all nuts and bolts on suspension components and steering assemblies in accordance with those listed in Specifications.
3 At the intervals specified in 'Routine Maintenance', adjust or re-lubricate the front hubs and check the front wheel alignment.

3 Front shock absorbers - removal, testing and installation

1 Do not remove a front shock absorber if the front roadwheels are hanging free with the front-end jacked up under the crossmember. Either remove a shock absorber when the roadwheels are on the ground or if the front end is jacked-up, place a supporting jack under the suspension lower arm.
2 Unscrew and remove the pivot bolt from the shock absorber lower mounting eye.
3 Working within the engine compartment, unscrew and remove the shock absorber upper mounting nut.
4 To test the shock absorber for serviceability, grip the lower mounting eye in the jaws of a vice so that the shock absorber is held vertically and then fully extend and retract the unit ten or twelve times. There should be a considerable resistance in both directions during

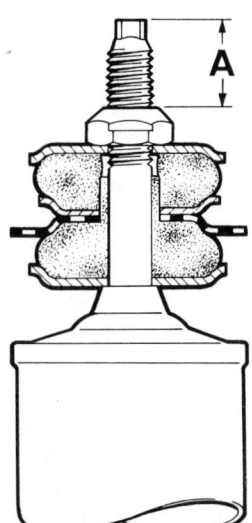

Fig. 11.4. Front shock absorber upper mounting (Sec. 3)

A = 0.6 in (16.0 mm)

every movement. Any jerkiness or lack of resistance will indicate the need for renewal.

5　The rubber mounting bushes can be renewed simply by detaching them.

6　Installation is a reversal of removal, tighten the lower pivot bolt to the specified torque and the upper mounting nut so that the threaded spindle is exposed by the amount shown in the diagram (Fig. 11.4).

4　Front hub - adjustment and lubrication

1　Jack-up the front roadwheel and remove the hub cap and the road-wheel.

2　Prise off the dust cap and withdraw the split pin.

3　Withdraw the caliper disc pads as described in Chapter 9.

4　Spin the roadwheel in the forward direction of rotation at the same time, tightening the hub nut to a torque of 20 lb ft (27 Nm).

5　Unscrew the hub nut until a feeler blade (0.001 to 0.004 in. - 0.02 to 0.10 mm) can be inserted between the rear face of the nut and the thrust washer.

6　Insert a new split pin, bending its ends well over and refit the dust cap.

7　Refit the disc pads, roadwheel and hub cap and lower the car to the ground.

8　If the bearings are to be repacked with grease, carry out the operations described in paragraphs 1 and 2 and then remove the disc caliper, as described in Chapter 9 and tie it up out of the way with a piece of wire to avoid straining the brake flexible hose. There is no need to disconnect the hydraulic line.

9　Unscrew and remove the hub nut and extract the thrust washer.

10 Pull the hub/disc assembly slightly towards you. This will eject the outer bearing race which can be removed. Now pull the hub/disc from the stub axle.

11 All old grease should now be wiped carefully from the bearings and hub recesses and fresh grease worked into the rollers. Take care not to damage the oil seal and do not pack any grease into the recess in the hub interior between the bearings.

12 Installation is a reversal of removal but offer the hub squarely to the stub axle so as not to damage the lips of the seal.

13 Adjust the bearings as previously described.

5　Front hub bearings and seal - renewal

1　Remove the hub/disc, as described in the preceding Section.

2　Lever out the oil seal from the inner hub recess.

3　Withdraw the inner roller race.

4　The bearing tracks may now be drifted from the hub using a suitable rod.

5　Do not mix bearing components as they are supplied as matched sets. Install the tracks by reversing the removal process and always install a new oil seal.

6　Pack grease into the bearings, install the hub/disc and adjust as described in the preceding Section.

6　Front stabiliser bar - removal and installation

1　Disconnect the links which secure the ends of the stabiliser bar to the suspension lower arms.

2　Unscrew and remove the bolts which secure the clamps to the body-frame and withdraw the stabiliser bar from the car.

3　Installation is a reversal of removal, but make sure that the marking on the stabiliser bar faces upwards and that the clamp insulating rubbers have their split facing the front of the car.

4　Assemble the end link rubber bushes as shown in the diagram and tighten the link nuts so that the overall dimension of the mounting bush components is also as specified in the diagram (Fig. 11.7).

7　Front road springs - removal and installation

1　Jack-up the front of the car and support it securely under the front crossmember.

2　Slacken the suspension lower arm inner pivot bolts and disconnect the stabiliser bar end link bolts from the suspension arms.

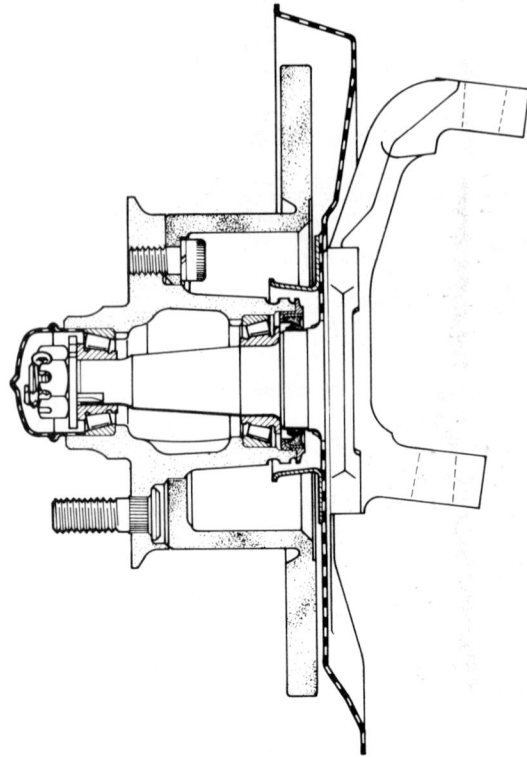

Fig. 11.5. Sectional view of a front hub (Sec. 4)

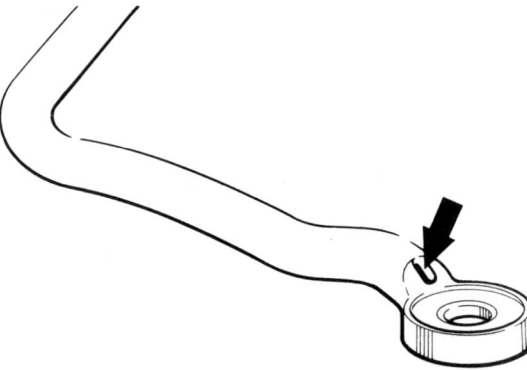

Fig. 11.6. Front stabiliser bar top marking (Sec. 6)

3　Using a suitable compressor, compress the coil spring onto the suspension lower arm.

4　Disconnect the suspension lower arm balljoint from the stub axle.

5　Remove the pivot bolts from the inner ends of the suspension arm and withdraw the arm complete with coil spring still in its compressed state.

6　The compressor can be carefully released and the spring separated from the suspension arm.

7　Reassembly is a reversal of removal but make sure that the end of the coil spring which is straight, locates correctly in the suspension lower arm recess.

8　Fit the rubber insulator to the top end of the spring before installing it.

9　Tighten all suspension nuts and bolts to the specified torque settings given in Specifications Section at the beginning of this Chapter.

8　Front suspension arm balljoints - checking for wear and renewal

1　Raise the front of the car and support its weight under the suspension lower arms.

2　Hold each of the balljoints in turn and rock the roadwheel in the vertical plane. Any slackness must not be confused with incorrect hub

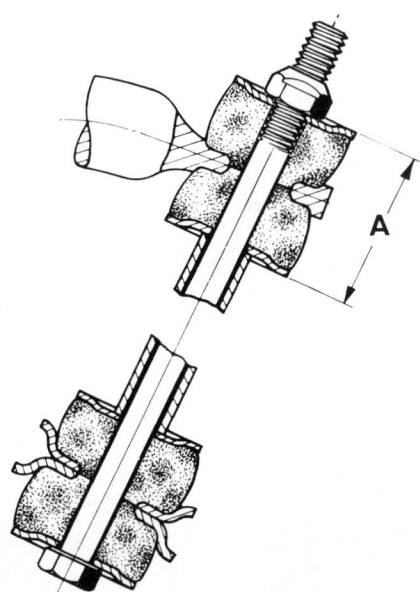

Fig. 11.7. Front stabiliser bar end link installation diagram

A = 1.50 in. (38.0 mm) (Sec. 6)

endfloat.

3 The upper balljoint has a pre-loaded seating and there should therefore be no perceptible clearance, but the lower balljoint is of the pendant type and the maximum vertical clearance may be up to 0.008 in (0.2 mm); a dial gauge will be required to check the lower balljoint clearance. Should either joint require renewal, follow the instructions given in the following paragraphs.

4 Remove the roadwheel and partially compress the roadspring as described in the preceding Section.

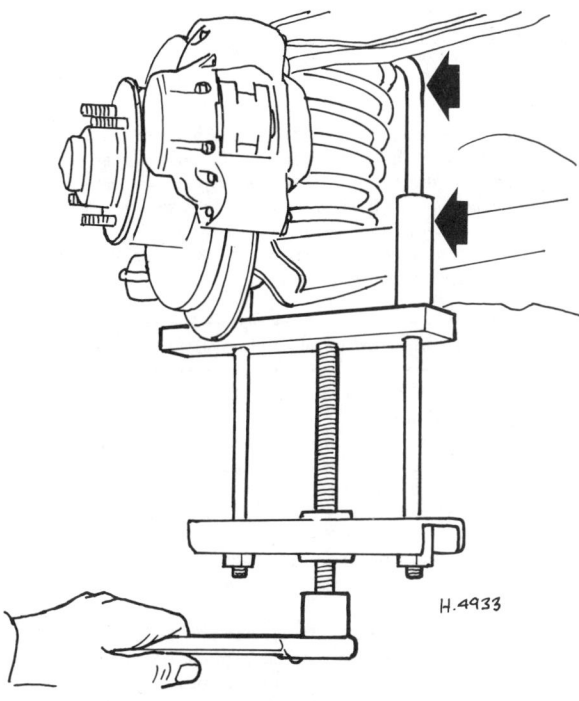

Fig. 11.8. Front coil spring compressed onto suspension lower arm prior to removal (Sec. 7)

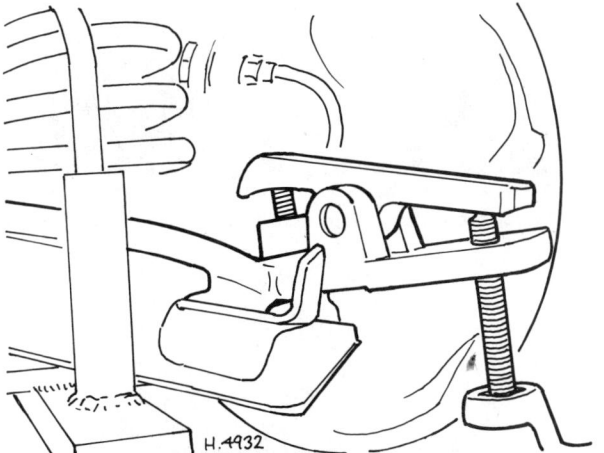

Fig. 11.9. Disconnecting a front suspension lower balljoint (Sec. 7)

Fig. 11.11. Installing front coil spring in suspension lower arm seat (Sec. 7)

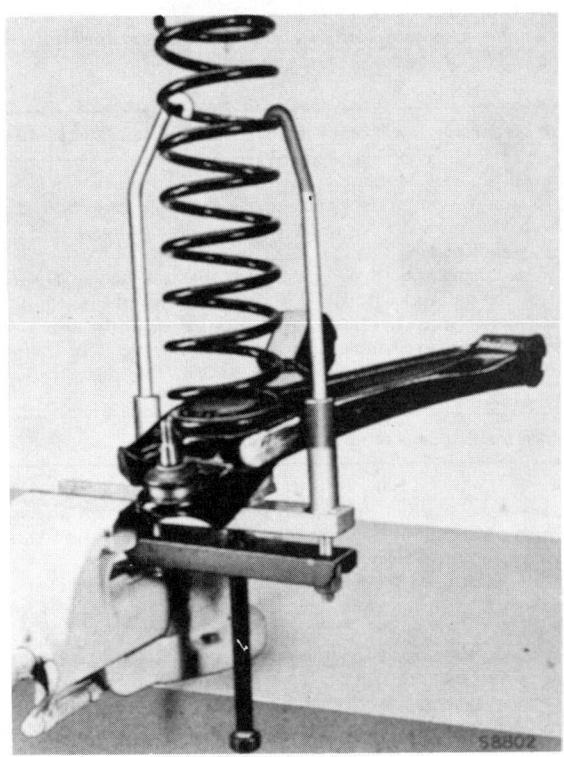

Fig. 11.10. Coil spring removed complete with suspension lower arm (Sec. 7)

Upper balljoint

5   Scribe round the balljoint mounting plate to mark its position in relation to the suspension upper arm. Failure to do this will mean that the new joint will not take up the setting of the original and the camber will be altered (see Section 24).

6   Disconnect the balljoint taper pin from the stub axle using a suitable separator.

7   Unscrew and remove the nuts which secure the balljoint to the upper arm.

8   Installation is a reversal of removal, but tighten the retaining nuts to specified torque. Check the front wheel alignment and steering angles at the first opportunity.

Lower balljoint

9   Remove the suspension lower arm, as described in Section 7.

10 The lower balljoint is splined externally and is pressed with considerable force into the suspension lower arm. Unless suitable pressing facilities are available it is best to take the arm to your dealer to have the old balljoint removed and the new one installed.

11 After installation, check the front wheel alignment and steering angles at the first opportunity.

9   Front suspension upper arm - removal, servicing and installation

1   Raise the front of the car and support it under the suspension lower arm. Remove the roadwheel.

2   Partially compress the roadspring as described in Section 7.

3   Disconnect upper balljoint from the stub axle.

4   Disconnect the shock absorber lower mounting.

5   Support the front hub on a block to avoid straining the flexible brake hose.

6   Unscrew and remove the suspension arm inner pivot bolt and withdraw the arm, taking great care to observe the positions of the castor spacers (see Section 24).

7   Renewal of the suspension arm bushes can be carried out using a press or a bolt and nut with suitable tubular distance pieces. When installing the new bushes note their correct locations in relation to the front of the car (Fig. 11.16).

8   Installation is a reversal of removal, but refit the castor spacers in their original positions and have the front wheel alignment and steering angles checked at the first opportunity.

9   Tighten the suspension arm pivot bolt to the specified torque only when the weight of the car is on the roadwheels.

10 Front suspension lower arm - removal, servicing and installation

1   Removal of the arm complete with spring is described in Section 7. Gently release the compressor and remove the roadspring from the arm.

2   If the bushes are worn, a press will be required or a bolt and nut and suitable distance pieces.

3   The new bushes should be installed so that the flanges are towards the rear of the car and with the cut-outs as shown in Fig. 11.19. Make sure that the flanges of the bushes are in contact with the arm.

4   Installation is a reversal of removal but tighten the pivot bolts to the specified torque when the weight of the car is on the roadwheels.

11 Front crossmember - removal and installation

1   Unscrew the pinch bolt from the steering column flexible coupling and separate the steering shaft from the pinion, after withdrawing the bolts which hold the rack and pinion assembly to the crossmember and pulling the assembly downwards.

2   With the weight of the car on the roadwheels, disconnect the shock absorber lower mountings and detach the stabiliser bar clamps from the bodyframe.

3   Disconnect both front flexible hoses from the rigid brake lines and extract the clips from the support brackets.

4   Support the weight of the engine (either by attaching a hoist or placing a jack with insulating wooden block under the sump) and disconnect the engine front mountings.

5   Remove the suspension lower arm to crossmember pivot bolts and the crossmember inner and outer mounting bolts.

6   The crossmember outer mounting bolt threads are coated with a locking compound and the bolts should be renewed before installing the crossmember. The threads in the bolt holes should be cleared of old compound using a tap or old bolt having a longitudinal slot cut in it.

7   When installation is complete, tighten all bolts to the specified torque when the weight of the car is on the roadwheels.

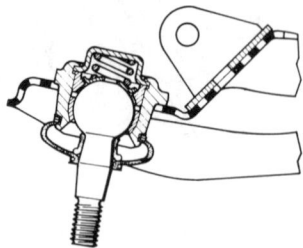

Fig. 11.12. Sectional view of front suspension upper balljoint (Sec. 8)

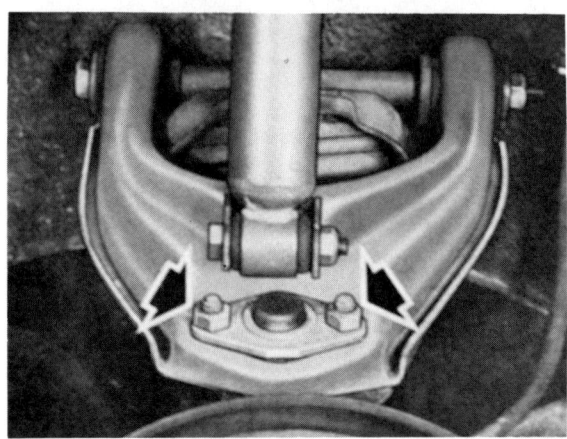

Fig. 11.13. Front suspension upper balljoint mounting (Sec. 8)

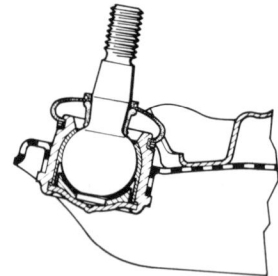

Fig. 11.14. Sectional view of front suspension lower balljoint (Sec. 8)

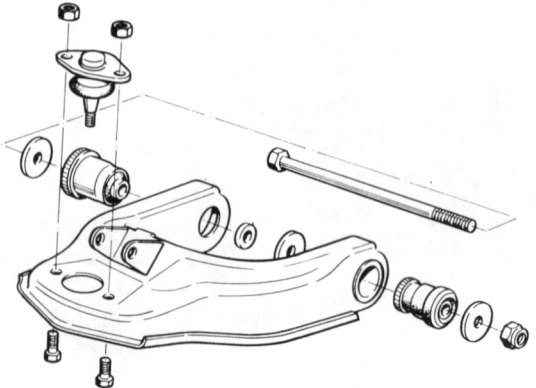

Fig. 11.15. Suspension upper arm components (Sec. 9)

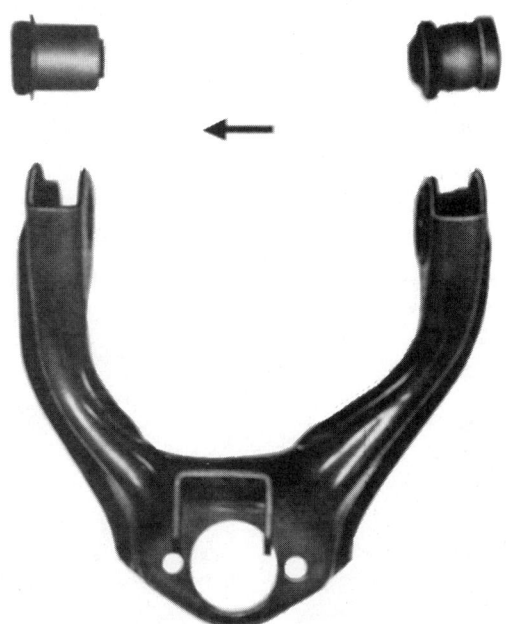

Fig. 11.16. Suspension upper arm bush installation (arrow to front of car)(Sec. 9)

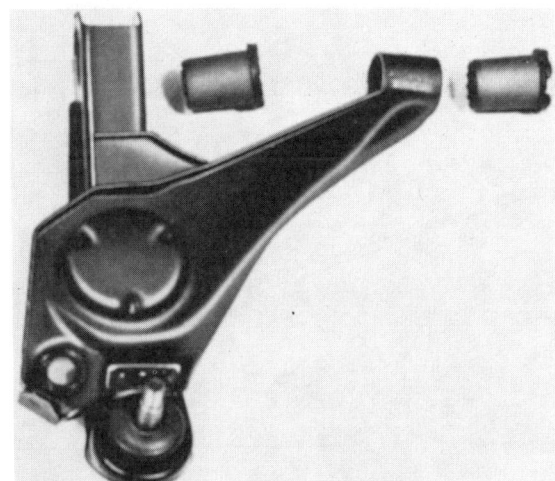

Fig. 11.18. Front suspension lower arm bush installation (Sec. 10)

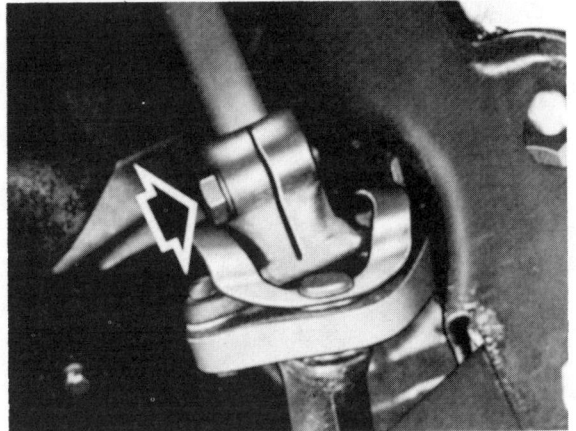

Fig. 11.20. Steering shaft flexible coupling pinch bolt (Sec. 11)

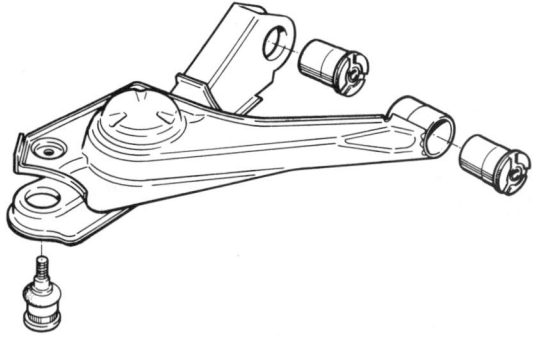

Fig. 11.17. Front suspension lower arm components (Sec. 10)

Fig. 11.19. Position of bush flange cut-out on front suspension lower arm (Sec. 10)

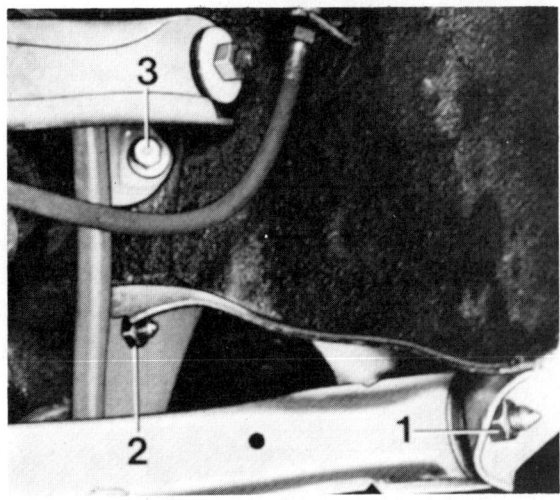

Fig. 11.21. Front crossmember inner mounting bolts (2) outer mounting bolts (3) and suspension lower arm pivot bolt (1) (Sec. 11)

12 Rear shock absorber - removal, testing and installation

1 Jack-up and support the weight of the car under the rear axle.

2 Disconnect the lower mounting by removing the pivot nut.

3 The shock absorber upper mounting nuts are accessible after removing the floor panels. The right-hand trim panel must first be removed before the right-hand floor panel can be removed (see Chapter 3, Section 6).

4 Withdraw the shock absorber and test it in a similar way to that described in Section 3, of this Chapter.

5   Installation is a reversal of removal but make sure that the rubber
cups and bushes are correctly positioned and tighten the mounting nut
so that the exposed portion of the spindle is as specified in Fig. 11.22.

13 Rear stabiliser bar - removal and installation

1   Unscrew and remove the end link bolts from the axle tube brackets.
2   Unbolt the rubber insulated clamps which secure the stabiliser bar
to the underbody.
3   Installation is a reversal of removal.

14 Panhard rod - removal, servicing and installation

1   The Panhard rod is located between a bodyframe anchorage and a
bracket on the left-hand axle tube.
2   Removal is simply a matter of unscrewing and removing the securing
nuts.
3   If the flexible bushes are worn, press the old ones out or draw them
out using a nut and bolt and a tubular distance piece. To facilitate
insertion of the new ones, dip them in soapy water or brake fluid.
4   Installation is a reversal of removal but tighten the two nuts to the
specified torque with the weight of the car on the roadwheels.

15 Rear suspension arm - removal and installation

1   Release the handbrake control lever and prise the handbrake cable
from the small clip which is located on the underside of the suspension
arm. If there is not enough slack in the cable, release the equaliser on
the relay rod (Chapter 9).
2   Unscrew and remove the two suspension arm pivot bolts and remove

the arm from its anchorages.
3   If the flexible bushes are worn or have deteriorated, press them out
or draw them out using a bolt, nut and tubular distance piece.
Installation of the new bushes will be facilitated if they are dipped in
soapy water or brake fluid.
4   Installation is a reversal of removal but remember to pull the
handbrake cable beneath the arm before inserting the pivot bolts.
5   Tighten the suspension arm bolts to the specified torque only after
wooden gauge blocks have been inserted between the axle casing and
bump stops and the rear of the car loaded as described in Chapter 8,
Section 7, paragraph 12.

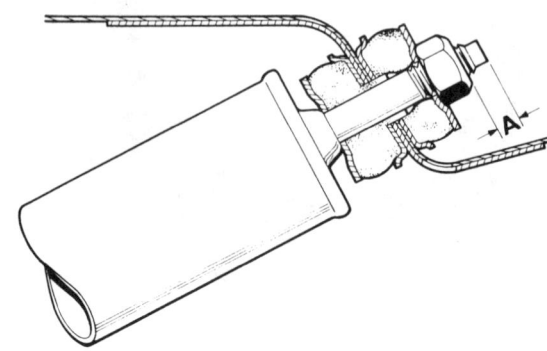

Fig. 11.22. Rear shock absorber upper mounting diagram (Sec. 12)

A = 0.31 in. (8.0 mm)

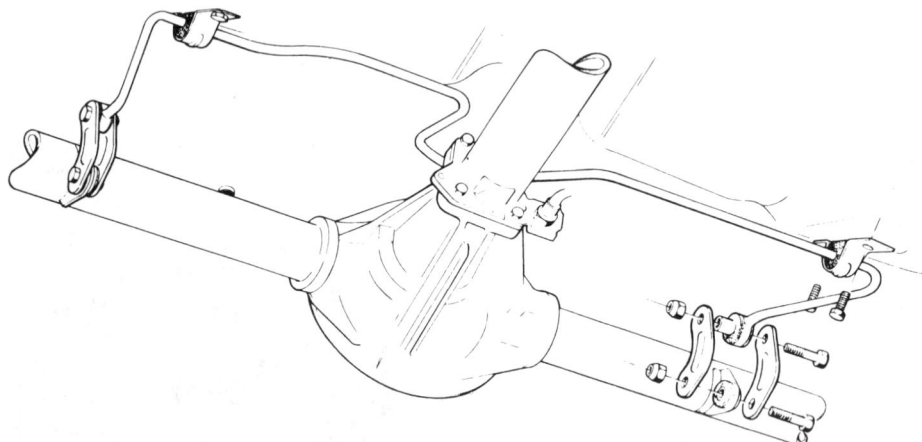

Fig. 11.23. Rear stabiliser bar mountings (Sec. 13)

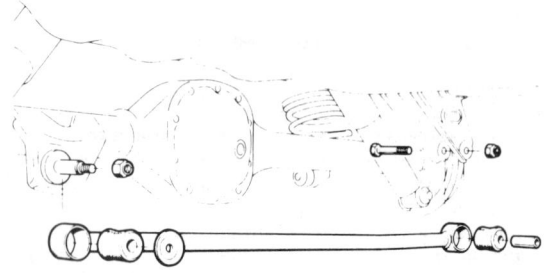

Fig. 11.24. Panhard rod mountings (Sec. 14)

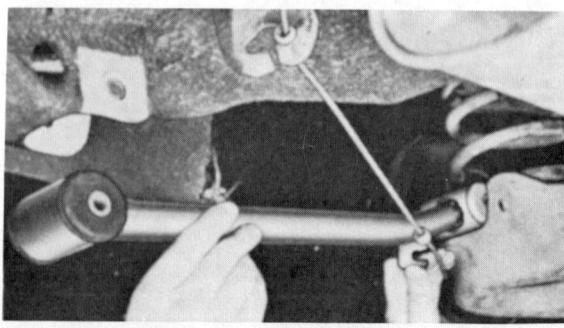

Fig. 11.25. Rear suspension arm showing handbrake cable clip (Sec. 15)

16 Rear roadspring - removal and installation

1   Jack-up the rear of the car and support the bodyframe side members on stands. Place a jack under the rear axle differential unit.
2   Disconnect the stabiliser bar 'U' shaped clamps from the underbody.
3   Slacken the suspension arm pivot bolts.
4   Disconnect the shock absorber lower mounting on the side from which the spring is being removed. If both springs are being removed, disconnect one shock absorber at a time.

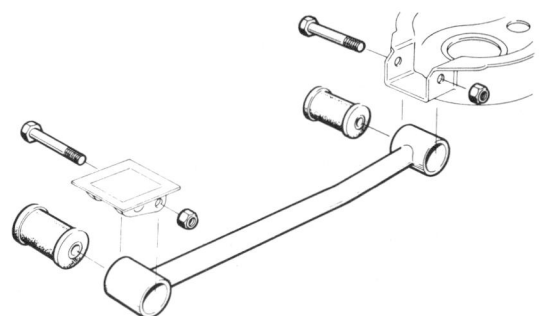

Fig. 11.26. Rear suspension arm and mountings (Sec. 15)

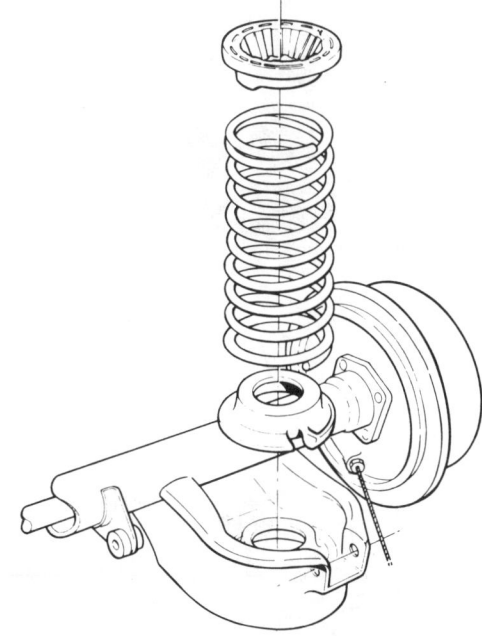

Fig. 11.27. A rear roadspring (Sec. 16)

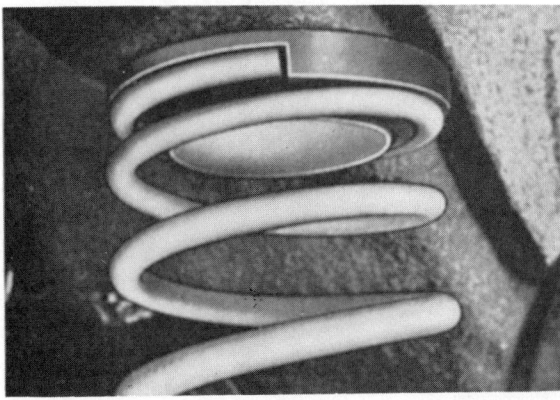

Fig. 11.29. Rear roadspring correctly installed in upper seat (Sec. 16)

5   Now lower the axle gently, avoiding any strain on the flexible brake hose. Pull downwards on the spring and extract it together with flexible seats.
6   When installing a spring make sure that the straightened end of the spring locates in the axle tube seat, also that the step in the upper seat is in contact with the end of the spring coil.
7   Tighten the suspension arm pivot bolts using the wooden blocks and weighting the car as described in Chapter 8, Section 7, paragraph 12.

17 Steering wheel - removal and installation

1   Set the front roadwheels in the straight-ahead position.
2   Prise out the medallion located in the centre of the steering wheel.
3   Unscrew and remove the now exposed steering wheel retaining nut.
4   Mark the relative position of the wheel to the steering shaft by dot punching the end faces.
5   Maintaining pressure with the thumbs on the end of the shaft, pull the steering wheel off its splines. On no account attempt to jar it off, as this may damage the inbuilt column collapsible plastic retainers. If the wheel is excessively tight, use a suitable puller.
6   When installing the steering wheel, mate the alignment marks before pressing it fully home on the splines. When correctly installed, the longer part of the rim between the spokes should be at the top when the roadwheels are in the 'straight-ahead' position.
7   Ensure that the projections and slots of the striker bush, cancelling sleeve and lugs are correctly engaged before tightening the steering wheel retaining nut to the specified torque.

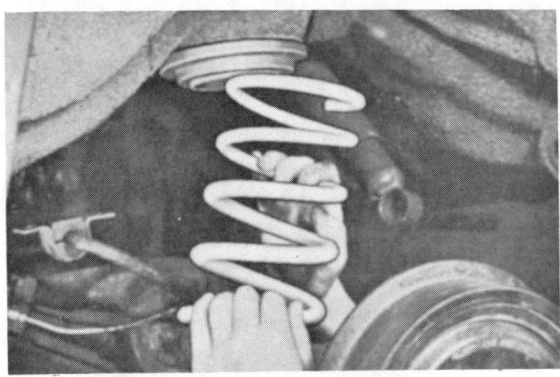

Fig. 11.28. Removing a rear roadspring (Sec. 16)

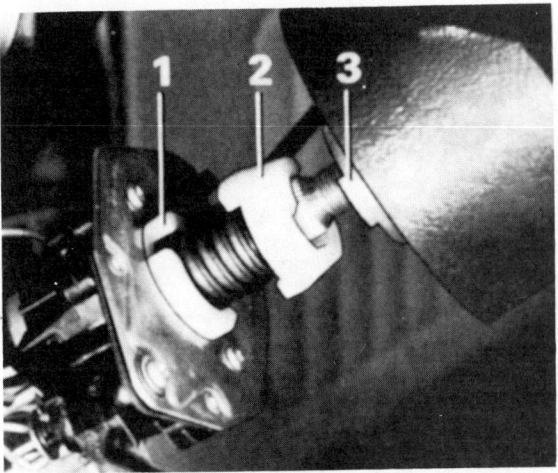

Fig. 11.30. Steering column upper components (Sec. 17)

1   Striker bush   3   Lugs on steering
2   Indicator switch cancelling sleeve   wheel boss

18 Steering column shrouds - removal and refitting

1   The two halves of the steering column upper shroud can be removed without having to withdraw the steering wheel.
2   Unscrew and remove the securing screws and lift the shrouds away. In the case of the lower shroud, if it is to be removed completely then the choke control will have to be disconnected and withdrawn as described in Chapter 3, Section 8.

19 Steering column - inspection for damage

1   In the event of a front end collision, however slight, the collapsible type steering column should be examined for damage.
2   Check for gaps between the column upper mounting pads and bracket. If gaps similar to those shown in Fig. 11.32 are to be seen, then the column has partially collapsed due to the plastic retainers having sheared.
3   If the overall length of the lattice section of the column is less than 10.37 in. (263.5 mm) then again the column has suffered partial collapse.
4   Where damage to the steering column has been proved, then the column must be renewed.
5   Checking the steering shaft can only be carried out after its removal from the column, as described in Section 20.

Fig. 11.31. Removing steering column lower shroud (Sec. 18)

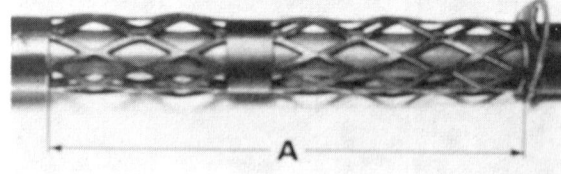

Fig. 11.33. Measurement of undamaged steering column (Sec. 19)

A = 10.37 in. (263.5 mm)

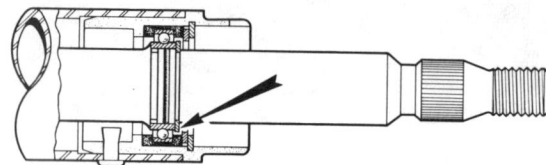

Fig. 11.35. Sectional view of steering column upper bearing. Circlip arrowed (Sec. 20)

20 Steering column - removal, servicing and installation

1   Remove the flexible coupling pinch bolt.
2   Remove the column lower mounting bolt by drilling a hole in its centre (1/8 in. - 3.0 mm twist drill) and unscrewing it with a screw extractor. Access to this bolt can only be gained after removal of the clutch and brake pedal assemblies as described in Chapter 5.
3   Remove the steering column upper shrouds.
4   Disconnect the lead from the battery negative terminal and then disconnect the plugs to the column switches.
5   Remove the column upper bracket bolts and withdraw the column assembly into the car interior. If the flexible coupling will not disengage easily, do not attempt to tap it off but turn the steering wheel from side-to-side fractionally and also insert a thick bladed screwdriver in the coupling clamp slot.
6   Remove the steering wheel (Section 17).
7   Withdraw the combination switch (Chapter 10).
8   Unlock the steering column lock by turning the ignition key to position 'I', 'II', or 'III'.
9   Extract the upper bearing inner circlip and gently tap the upper end of the shaft to partially eject it from the column.
10 With the shaft in this position, release the lower bearing locating pips and withdraw the bearing, then the shaft.

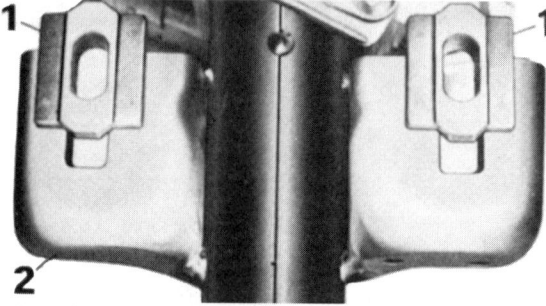

Fig. 11.32. Steering column upper bracket (2) and pads (1) (Sec. 19)

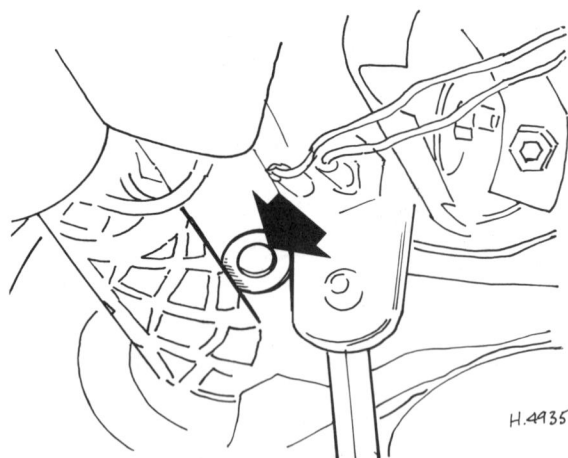

Fig. 11.34. Steering column lower mounting bracket shear bolt (Sec. 20)

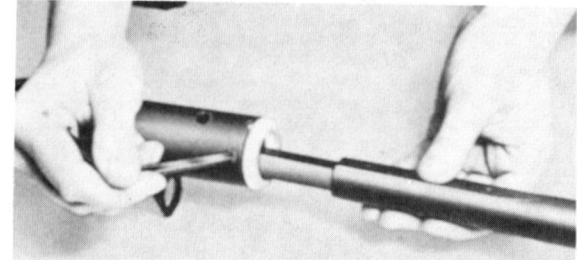

Fig. 11.36. Releasing steering column lower bearing (Sec. 20)

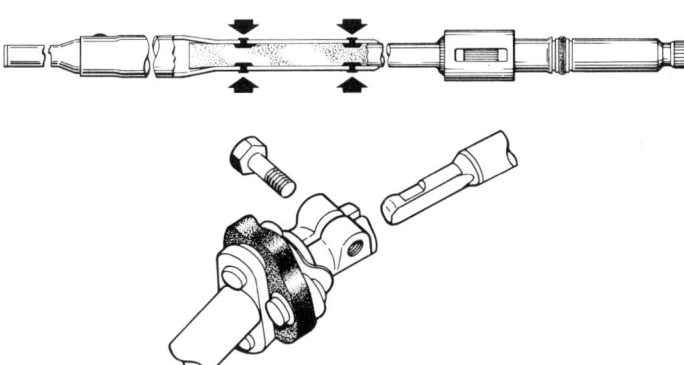

Fig. 11.37. Steering shaft showing plastic shear type retainers (Sec. 20)

Overall length of shaft must be between 38.64 and 38.68 in. (981.5 and 982.5 mm)

Fig. 11.38. Steering flexible coupling assembly (RHD cars) (Sec. 20)

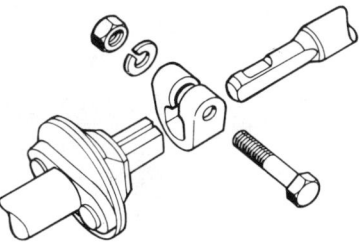

Fig. 11.39. Steering flexible coupling assembly (LHD cars) (Sec. 20)

Fig. 11.40. Steering column lock shear head bolts (Sec. 21)

11 The column upper bearing and rubber sleeve can be extracted after removing the circlip and washer.

12 Renew any worn components and check that the shaft has not partially collapsed due to impact or collision. To do this, measure the overall length and if this is outside the dimensions specified, the shaft must be renewed (see Fig. 11.37).

13 Commence reassembly, by packing the upper bearing with grease and placing the rubber sleeve over it before pressing them into the column.

14 Install a new 'O' ring in the centre of the three grooves at the upper end of the shaft.

15 Work grease well into the felt ring at the shaft lower bearing and then install the shaft to the column until its waisted section permits the lower bearing to be fitted to the column. Make sure that the bearing pips are fully located.

16 Press the shaft fully into the column using hand pressure only, pulling on the upper end of the shaft. Do not be tempted to tap the shaft into the column as this will cause the plastic inserts of the

collapsible mechanism to shear.

17 Check that the steering column gaiter is in good condition and fitted securely to the aperture in the toe board.

18 Lower the column into position making sure that the cut-out in the shaft is towards the pinch bolt side of the flexible coupling clamp. The different designs of the couplings and direction of entry of the clamp pinch bolt between LHD and RHD cars should be noted.

19 Install the mounting bracket bolts and the pinch bolt finger-tight and then install a new lower mounting bolt to a torque of 15 lb ft (11 Nm) only.

20 Tighten the upper mounting bracket bolts and the coupling pinch bolt to the specified torque and then return to the lower mounting bolt and tighten it until its head shears off.

21 Install the steering column combination switch, the steering wheel and the column shrouds.

22 Reconnect the electrical harness plugs and battery.

23 Reassemble the clutch and brake pedals.

21 Steering column lock - removal and installation

1 Remove the steering column, as described in the preceding Section.

2 Drill the centre of each bolt which secures the lock clamp to the column with a 1/8 in. (3.0 mm) twist drill. Remove the bolts with a screw extractor.

3 When installing the lock use new shear bolts but only tighten them enough to hold the lock securely to the column and then check the operation of the lock by inserting the ignition key and ensuring that the tongue of the lock engages smoothly and positively in the shaft cut-out. Adjust the position of the lock if necessary and then finally tighten the bolts fully until the heads shear off.

22 Steering gear - removal, overhaul and installation

1 Disconnect the trackrod ends from the steering arms using a suitable separator.

2 Unscrew and remove the pinch bolt from the steering shaft flexible coupling.

3 Unscrew and remove the bolts which hold the steering gear to the crossmember and lift the gear away. If the flexible coupling is difficult to disengage, do not tap it from the steering shaft but turn the steering wheel from side to side and also insert a thick bladed screwdriver in the coupling clamp slot to expand it slightly.

4 Release the trackrod-end locknuts and unscrew and remove the trackrod-ends and the locknuts.

5 Release the clamps and withdraw the dust excluding bellows.

6 Using two open-ended spanners, hold the rack quite still and unscrew the inner balljoint assemblies.

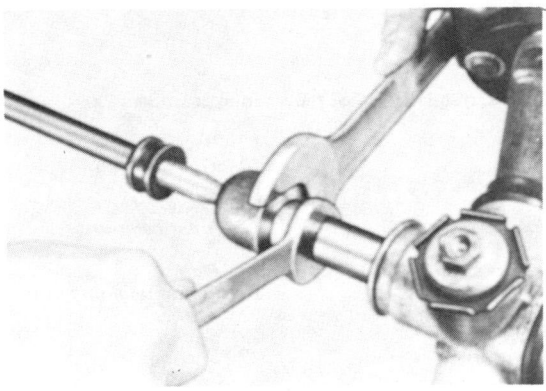

Fig. 11.41. Releasing steering rack inner balljoint (Sec. 22)

7 Release the locknut and withdraw the adjusting screw, spring, washer and thrust bearing.

8 Withdraw the dust cover, hold the pinion shaft quite still and unscrew the pinion retaining nut.

9 Extract the pinion shaft.

10 Extract the rack from the pinion end of the steering gear housing to avoid damaging the housing bushes.

11 Extract the circlip and drive out the lower pinion shaft housing.

12 Examine all components for wear and renew as necessary. If the upper pinion shaft needle bearing must be renewed, press it out using a suitable tubular drift or spacer and install the new one in a similar way.

13 Commence reassembly by installing the pinion shaft lower bearing and securing with a new circlip.

14 Fill the rack housing between the bushes with 2 oz (50 g) of recommended grease.

15 Install the rack from the pinion end of the housing and then centralise it so that it protrudes an equal amount at each end of the housing.

16 Apply grease to the pinion shaft and housing and install the shaft so that the slot in the coupling is aligned with the rack thrust bearing adjusting screw. Install the thrust washer to the pinion shaft, tighten the retaining nut to a torque of 11 lb ft (15 Nm) only.

17 Install the rack thrust bearing, spring and adjusting screw and with the rack still centralised, tighten the adjusting screw until a slight resistance is felt and then back off the screw between 30 and 60°. Tighten the locknut to a torque of 50 lb ft (68 Nm) and check that the pinion will move the rack over its full length of travel without binding.

18 Fit the inner balljoint assemblies and tighten to 66 lb ft (90 Nm) torque and stake securely.

19 Install the flexible bellows but do not tighten the outer clamps at this stage.

20 Spin on the trackrod-end locknuts and then screw on the trackrod-ends an equal amount.

21 Centre the rack and offer up the steering gear so that the flat on the steering shaft is in alignment with the pinion coupling flange.

22 Tighten the steering gear mounting bolts to the specified torque.

23 Install the flexible coupling pinch bolt and tighten to the specified torque.

24 Connect the trackrod-end balljoints to the steering arms and then adjust the front wheel toe-in, as described in Section 24.

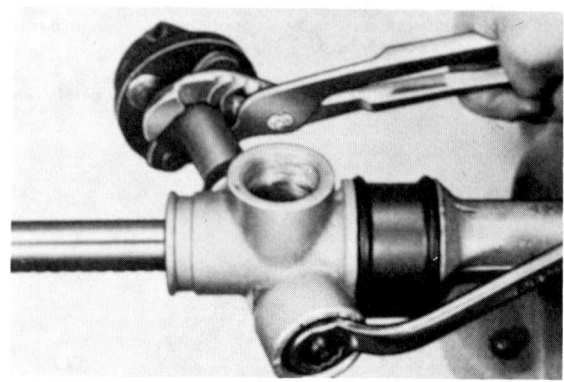

Fig. 11.42. Unscrewing the pinion retaining nut (Sec. 22)

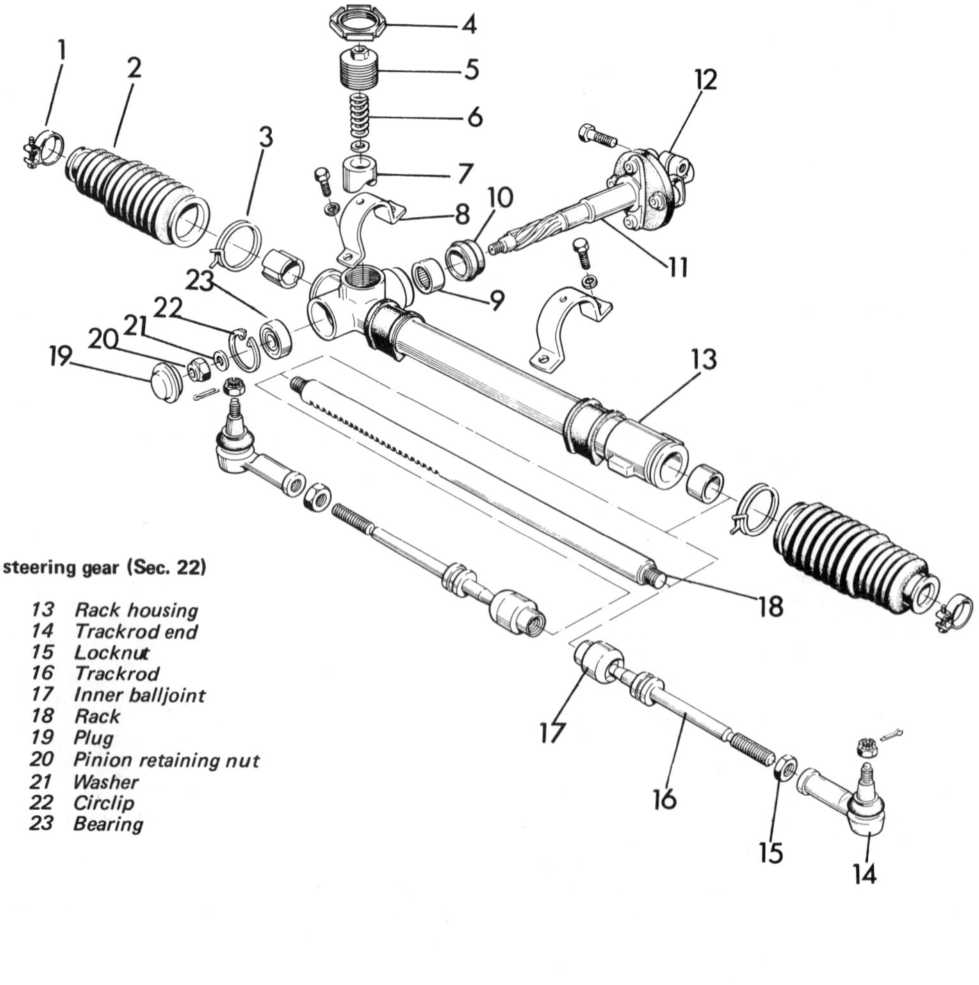

Fig. 11.43. Exploded view of the steering gear (Sec. 22)

1	Clip	13	Rack housing
2	Bellows	14	Trackrod end
3	Clip	15	Locknut
4	Locknut	16	Trackrod
5	Adjusting screw	17	Inner balljoint
6	Spring	18	Rack
7	Thrust bearing	19	Plug
8	Rack housing clip	20	Pinion retaining nut
9	Pinion shaft upper needle	21	Washer
	bearing	22	Circlip
10	Dust cover	23	Bearing
11	Pinion		
12	Flexible coupling		

23 Trackrod-end balljoints - testing and renewal

1   Periodically inspect the condition of the trackrod-end balljoint dust excluding boots. If they are split, the complete joint will have to be renewed as the boots are not supplied separately.

2   The balljoints are spring loaded with nylon seats and require no lubrication.

3   If any free movement in a vertical direction can be felt when the trackrod is gripped and moved up and down, then the balljoint is worn and must be renewed.

4   Release the trackrod-end locknut one quarter turn only.

5   Disconnect the trackrod-end from the steering arm using a suitable separator.

6   Unscrew and remove the trackrod-end at the same time holding the trackrod quite still so that the rack bellows are not twisted.

7   Screw on the new trackrod-end to the same relative position as the old one, so that the locknut will require one quarter turn only to lock it. Hold the trackrod-end in its correct attitude using the flats provided.

8   Make sure that the balljoint taper pin is clean and unlubricated and connect it to the steering arm.

9   Check the front wheel alignment, as described in Section 24.

24 Steering angles and front wheel alignment

1   Accurate front wheel alignment is essential for good steering and slow tyre wear. Before considering the steering angle, check that the tyres are correctly inflated, that the front wheels are not buckled, the hub bearings are not worn or incorrectly adjusted and that the steering linkage is in good order, without slackness or wear at the joints.

2   Wheel alignment consists of four factors:
   Camber, is the angle at which the front wheels are set from the vertical when viewed from the front of the car. Positive camber is the amount (in degrees) that the wheels are tilted outwards at the top from the vertical.
   Adjustment of the camber angle is carried out by rotating the suspension upper swivel joint flange through 180º. This movement will alter the camber angle by 0º50' (see Fig. 11.13).

3   *Castor* is the angle between the steering axis and a vertical line when viewed from each side of the car. Positive castor is when the steering axis is inclined rearward.
   Adjustment of the castor angle is carried out by varying the thickness of the spacers located between the suspension upper arm and crossmember. Due to the need for special gauges, it is not recommended that either the camber or castor angles are altered by the home mechanic.

4   *Steering axis inclination* is the angle, when viewed from the front of the car, between the vertical and an imaginary line drawn between the upper and lower suspension pivots.

5   *Toe-in* is the amount by which the distance between the front inside edges of the roadwheels (measured at hub height) is less than the diametrically opposite distance measured between the rear inside edges of the front roadwheels.

6   Front wheel tracking (toe-in) checks are best carried out with modern setting equipment but a reasonably accurate alternative and adjustment procedure may be carried out as follows:

7   Place the car on level ground with the wheels in the straight-ahead position.

8   Obtain or make a toe-in gauge. One may be easily made from tubing, cranked to clear the sump and bellhousing, having an adjustable nut and setscrew at one end.

9   Using the gauge, measure the distance between the two inner wheel rims at hub height at the rear of the wheels.

10   Rotate the wheels (by pushing the car backwards or forwards) through 180º (half a turn) and again using the gauge, measure the distance of hub height between the two inner wheel rims at the front of the wheels. This measurement should be between 0.16 and 0.24 in. (4.0 to 6.0 mm) **less** than that previously taken at the rear of the wheel and represents the correct toe-in.

11   Where the toe-in is found to be incorrect, slacken the trackrod-end locknuts and the rack bellows outer clips.

12   Rotate each of the trackrods **an equal amount** and then recheck the toe-in. When adjustment is correct, tighten the locknuts, holding the trackrod-ends in the centres of their arcs of travel.

13   Check that the rack bellows are not twisted and then retighten the clips.

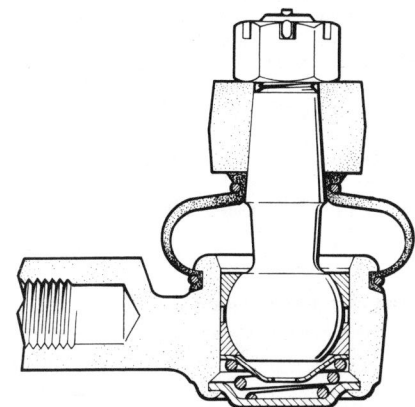

Fig. 11.44. Sectional view of a trackrod-end balljoint (Sec. 23)

Fig. 11.45. Trackrod-end showing flats for spanner (Sec. 23)

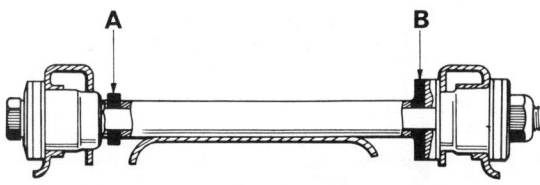

Fig. 11.46. Front suspension upper arm spacers which control castor angle (Sec. 24)

A   *Nearest front of car*   B   *Towards rear of car*

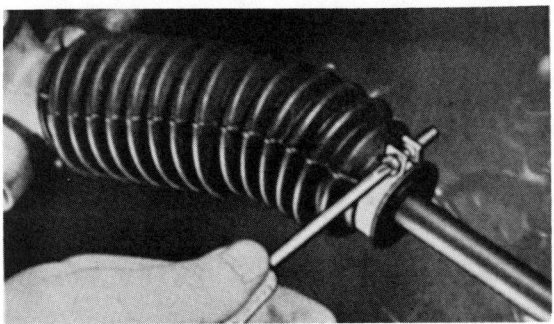

Fig. 11.47. Slackening a steering bellows clip prior to adjusting track (Sec. 24)

25 Roadwheels and tyres

1   Whenever the roadwheels are removed it is a good idea to clean the insides of the wheels to remove accumulations of mud and in the case of the front ones, disc pad dust.
2   Check the condition of the wheel for rust and repaint if necessary.
3   Examine the wheel stud holes. If these are tending to become elongated or the dished recesses in which the nuts seat have worn or become overcompressed, then the wheel will have to be renewed.
4   With a roadwheel removed, pick out any embedded flints from the tread and check for splits in the sidewalls or damage to the tyre carcass generally.

5   Where the depth of tread pattern is 1 mm or less, the tyre must be renewed.
6   Rotating of the roadwheels to even out wear is a worthwhile idea if the wheels have been balanced off the car. Include the spare wheel in the rotational pattern.
7   If the wheels have been balanced on the car then they cannot be moved round the car as the balance of wheel, tyre and hub will be upset.
8   It is recommended that wheels are re-balanced halfway through the life of the tyres to compensate for the loss of tread rubber, due to wear.
9   Finally, always keep the tyres (including the spare) inflated to the recommended pressures and always replace the dust caps on the tyre valves. Tyre pressures are best checked first thing in the morning when the tyres are cold.

26 Fault diagnosis - suspension and steering

Symptoms	Reasons
Lost motion at steering wheel	Wear in rack and pinion Wear in trackrod-end balljoints
Steering wander	Wear in gear or linkage Incorrect front wheel alignment Incorrectly adjusted or worn front hub bearings Worn suspension swivel balljoints
Heavy or stiff steering	Incorrect front wheel alignment Seized balljoint Dry rack assembly Distorted shaft/column
Wheel wobble and vibration	Roadwheels out of balance Roadwheel buckled Incorrect front wheel alignment Faulty shock absorber Weak coil spring
Excessive pitching or rolling on corners or during braking	Faulty shock absorber Weak or broken coil spring

Chapter 12 Bodywork and fittings

For modifications, and information applicable to later models, see Supplement at end of manual

Contents

1 General description

The bodyshell and underframe is of all-steel welded construction. The front wings are bolted in position and are detachable should renewal be necessary after a front end collision.

2 Maintenance - bodywork and underframe

1 The general condition of a car's bodywork is the one thing that significantly affects its value. Maintenance is easy but needs to be regular and particular. Neglect, particularly after minor damage, can lead quickly to further deterioration and costly repair bills. It is important also to keep watch on those parts of the car not immediately visible, for instance the underside, inside all the wheel arches and the lower part of the engine compartment.
2 The basic maintenance routine for the bodywork is washing - preferably with a lot of water, from a hose. This will remove all the loose solids which may have stuck to the car. It is important to flush these off in such a way as to prevent grit from scratching the finish. The wheel arches and underbody need washing in the same way to remove any accumulated mud which will retain moisture and tend to encourage rust. Paradoxically enough, the best time to clean the underbody and wheel arches is in wet weather when the mud is thoroughly wet and soft. In very wet weather the underbody is usually cleaned of large accumulations automatically and this is a good time for inspection.
3 Periodically it is a good idea to have the whole of the underside of the car steam cleaned, engine compartment included, so that a thorough inspection can be carried out to see what minor repairs and renovations are necessary. Steam cleaning is available at many garages and is necessary for removal of accumulation of oily grime which sometimes is allowed to cake thick in certain areas near the engine, gearbox and back axle. If steam facilities are not available, there are one or two excellent grease solvents available which can be brush applied. The dirt can then be simply hosed off.
4 After washing paintwork, wipe off with a chamois leather to give an unspotted clear finish. A coat of clear protective wax polish will give added protection against chemical pollutants in the air. If the paintwork sheen has dulled or oxidised, use a cleaner/polisher combination to restore the brilliance of the shine. This requires a little effort, but is usually caused because regular washing has been neglected.

Always check that the door and ventilator opening drain holes and pipes are completely clear so that water can drain out. Bright work should be treated the same way as paintwork. Windscreens and windows can be kept clear ot the smeary film which often appears if a little ammonia is added to the water. If they are scratched, a good rub with a proprietary metal polish will often clear them. Never use any form of wax or other body or chromium polish on glass.

3 Maintenance - upholstery and carpets

1 Mats and carpets should be brushed or vacuum cleaned regularly to keep them free of grit. If they are badly stained remove them from the car for scrubbing or sponging and make quite sure they are dry before replacement. Seats and interior trim panels can be kept clean by a wipe over with a damp cloth. If they do become stained (which can be more apparent on light coloured upholstery) use a little liquid detergent and a soft nailbrush to scour the grime out of the grain of the material. Do not forget to keep the headlining clean in the same way as the upholstery. When using liquid cleaners inside the car do not over-wet the surfaces being cleaned. Excessive damp could get into the seams and padded interior causing stains, offensive odours or even rot. If the inside of the car gets wet accidentally it is worthwhile taking some trouble to dry it out properly, particularly where carpets are involved. **Do not** leave oil or electric heaters inside the car for this purpose.

4 Minor body damage - repair

See photo sequence on pages 134 and 135

Repair of minor scratches in the car's bodywork

If the scratch is very superficial, and does not penetrate to the metal of the bodywork, repair is very simple. Lightly rub the area of the scratch with a paintwork renovator, or a very fine cutting paste, to remove loose paint from the scratch and to clear the surrounding body-work of wax polish. Rinse the area with clean water..

Apply touch-up paint to the scratch using a thin paintbrush, continue to apply thin layers of paint until the surface of the paint in the scratch is level with the surrounding paintwork. Allow the new paint at least two weeks to harden; then blend it into the surrounding paintwork by rubbing the paintwork, in the scratch area with a paint-work renovator, or a very fine cutting paste. Finally apply wax polish.

Where the scratch has penetrated right through to the metal of the bodywork, causing the metal to rust, a different repair technique is required. Remove any loose rust from the bottom of the scratch with a penknife, then apply rust inhibiting paint to prevent the formation of rust in the future. Using a rubber nylon applicator, fill the scratch with bodystopper paste. If required, this paste can be mixed with cellulose thinners to provide a very thin paste which is ideal for filling narrow scratches. Before the stopper-paste in the scratch hardens, wrap a piece of smooth cotton rag around the top of a finger. Dip the finger in cellulose thinners and then quickly sweep it across the surface of the stopper-paste in the scratch; this will ensure that the surface of the stopper-paste is slightly hollowed. The scratch can now be painted over as described earlier in this Section.

Repair of dents in the car's bodywork

When deep denting of the car's bodywork has taken place, the first task is to pull the dent out, until the affected bodywork almost attains its original shape. There is little point in trying to restore the original shape completely, as the metal in the damaged area will have stretched on impact and cannot be reshaped fully to its original contour. It is better to bring the level of the dent up to a point which is about 1/8 inch (3 mm) below the level of the surrounding bodywork. In cases where the dent is very shallow anyway, it is not worth trying to pull it out at all.

If the underside of the dent is accessible, it can be hammered out gently from behind, using a mallet with a wooden or plastic head. Whilst doing this, hold a suitable block of wood firmly against the impact from the hammer blows and thus prevent a large area of bodywork from being 'belled-out'.

Should the dent be in a section of the bodywork which has a double skin or some other factor making it inaccessible from behind, a different technique is called for. Drill several small holes through the metal inside the dent area - particularly in the deeper sections, then screw long self-tapping screws into the holes just sufficiently for them to gain a good purchase in the metal. Now the dent can be pulled out by pulling on the protruding heads of the screws with a pair of pliers.

The next stage of the repair is the removal of the paint from the damaged area, and from an inch or so of the surrounding 'sound' bodywork. This is accomplished most easily by using a wire brush or abrasive pad on a power drill, although it can be done just as effectively by hand using sheets of abrasive paper. To complete the preparations for filling, score the surface of the bare metal with a screwdriver or the tang of a file, or alternatively, drill small holes in the effected area. This will provide a really good 'key' for filler paste.

To complete the repair see the sub-Section on filling and respraying.

Repair of rust holes or gashes in the car's bodywork

Remove all paint from the affected area and from an inch or so of the surrounding 'sound' bodywork, using an abrasive pad or a wire brush on a power drill. If these are not available a few sheets of abrasive paper will do the job just as effectively. With the paint removed you will be able to gauge the severity of the corrosion and therefore decide whether to replace the whole panel (if this is possible) or to repair the affected area. Replacement body panels are not as expensive as most people think and it is often quicker and more satisfactory to fit a new panel than to attempt to repair large areas of corrosion.

Remove all fittings from the affected area except those which will act as a guide to the original shape of the damaged bodywork (eg; headlamp shells etc.). Then, using tin snips or a hacksaw blade, remove all loose metal and any other metal badly affected by corrosion. Hammer the edges of the hole inwards in order to create a slight depression for the filler paste.

Wire brush the affected area to remove the powdery rust from the surface of the remaining metal. Paint the affected area with rust inhibiting paint; if the back of the rusted area is accessible treat this also.

Before filling can take place it will be necessary to block the hole in some way. This can be achieved by the use of one of the following materials: Zinc gauze, Aluminium tape or Polyurethane foam.

Zinc gauze is probably the best material to use for a large hole. Cut a piece to the appropriate size and shape of the hole to be filled, then position it in the hole so that its edges are below the level of the surrounding bodywork. It can be retained in position by several blobs of filler paste around its periphery.

Aluminium tape should be used for small or very narrow holes. Pull a piece off the roll and trim it to the approximate size and shape required, then pull off the backing paper (if used) and stick the tape over the hole; it can be overlapped if the thickness of one piece is insufficient. Burnish down the edges of the tape with the handle of a screwdriver or similar, to ensure that the tape is securely attached to the metal underneath.

Polyurethane foam is best used where the hole is situated in a section of bodywork of complex shape, backed by a small box section (eg; where the sill panel meets the rear wheel arch - most cars). The unusual mixing procedure for this foam is as follows: Put equal amounts of fluid from each of the two cans provided in the kit, into one container. Stir until the mixture begins to thicken, then quickly pour this mixture into the hole, and hold a piece of cardboard over the larger apertures. Almost immediately the polyurethane will begin to expand, gushing frantically out of any small holes left unblocked. When the foam hardens it can be cut back to just below the level of the surrounding bodywork with a hacksaw blade.

Bodywork repairs - filling and re-spraying

Before using this sub-Section, see the sub-Section on dent, deep scratch, rust hole, and gash repairs.

Many types of bodyfiller are available, but generally speaking those proprietary kits which contain a tin of filler paste and a tube of resin hardener are best for this type of repair. A wide, flexible plastic or nylon applicator will be found invaluable for imparting a smooth and well contoured finish to the surface of the filler.

Mix up a little filler on a clean piece of card or board - use the hardener sparingly (follow the maker's instructions on the packet) otherwise the filler will set very rapidly.

Using the applicator, apply the filler paste to the prepared area; draw the applicator across the surface of the filler to achieve the correct contour and to level the filler surface. As soon as a contour that approximates to the correct one is achieved, stop working the paste - if you carry on too long the paste will become sticky and begin to 'pick-up' on the applicator. Continue to add thin layers of filler paste at twenty-minute intervals until the level of the filler is just 'proud' of the surrounding bodywork.

Once the filler has hardened, excess can be removed using a Surform plane or Dreadnought file. From then on, progressively finer grades of abrasive paper should be used, starting with a 40 grade production paper and finishing with 400 grade 'wet-and-dry' paper. Always wrap the abrasive paper around a flat rubber, fork, or wooden block - otherwise the surface of the filler will not be completely flat. During the smoothing of the filler surface the 'wet-and-dry' paper should be periodically rinsed in water. This will ensure that a very smooth finish is imparted to the filler at the final stage.

At this stage the 'dent' should be surrounded by a ring of bare metal which in turn should be encircled by the finely 'feathered' edge of the good paintwork. Rinse the repair area with clean water, until all the dust produced by the rubbing-down operation is gone.

Spray the whole repair area with a light coat of grey primer - this will show up any imperfections in the surface of the filler. Repair these imperfections with fresh filler paste or bodystopper and once more smooth the surface with abrasive paper. If bodystopper is used, it can be mixed with cellulose thinners to form a really thin paste which is ideal for filling small holes. Repeat this spray and repair procedure until you are satisfied that the surface of the filler, and the feathered edge of the paintwork are perfect. Clean the repair area with clean water and allow to dry fully.

The repair area is now ready for spraying. Paint spraying must be carried out in a warm, dry, windless and dust free atmosphere. This condition can be created artificially if you have access to a large indoor working area, but if you are forced to work in the open, you will have to pick your day very carefully. If you are working indoors, dousing the floor in the work area with water will 'lay' the dust which would otherwise be in the atmosphere. If the repair is confined to one body panel, mask off the surrounding panels; this will help to minimise the effects of a slight mis-match in paint colours. Bodywork fittings (eg; chrome strips, door handles etc.), will also need to be masked off. Use genuine masking tape and several thicknesses of newspaper for the masking operation.

Before commencing to spray, agitate the aerosol can, thoroughly, then spray a test area (an old tin, or similar) until the technique is mastered. Cover the repair area with a thick coat of primer; the thickness should be built up using several thin layers of paint rather than one thick one. Using 400 grade 'wet-and-dry' paper, rub down the surface of the primer until it is really smooth. While doing this, the work area should be thoroughly doused with water, and the 'wet-and-dry' paper periodically rinsed in water. Allow to dry before spraying on more paint.

Spray on the top coat, again building up the thickness by using several thin layers of paint. Start spraying in the centre of the repair area and then, using a circular motion, work outwards until the whole repair area and about 2 inches of the surrounding original paintwork is covered. Remove all masking material 10 to 15 minutes after spraying on the final coat of paint.

Allow the new paint at least 2 weeks to harden fully; then, using a paintwork renovator or a very fine cutting paste, blend the edges of the new paint into the existing paintwork. Finally, apply wax polish.

5 Major bodywork damage - repair

Where serious damage has occurred or large areas need renewal due to neglect, it means certainly that completely new sections or panels will need welding in and this is best left to professionals. If the damage is due to impact it will also be necessary to completely check the alignment of the bodyshell structure. Due to the principle of construction the strength and shape of the whole can be affected by damage to a part. In such instances the services of a Vauxhall agent with specialist checking jigs are essential. If a body is left misaligned it is first of all dangerous as the car will not handle properly and secondly uneven stresses will be imposed on the steering, engine and transmission, causing abnormal wear or complete failure. Tyre wear may also be excessive.

6 Maintenance - hinges and locks

1 Oil the hinges of the bonnet, boot and doors with a drop or two of light oil periodically. A good time is after the car has been washed.
2 Oil the bonnet release, the catch pivot pin and the safety catch pivot pin periodically.
3 Do not over lubricate door latches and strikers. Normally a little oil on the rotary cam spindle alone is sufficient.

7 Doors - tracing rattles and their rectification

1 Check first that the door is not loose at the hinges and that the latch is holding the door firmly in position. Check also that the door lines up with the aperture in the body.
2 If the hinges are loose or the door is out of alignment it will be necessary to reset the hinge positions, as described in Section 15.
3 If the latch is holding the door properly it should hold the door

tightly when fully latched and the door should line up with the body. If it is out of alignment, it needs adjustment as described in Section 12. If loose, some part of the lock mechanism must be worn out and requires renewal.

4 Other rattles from the door would be caused by wear or looseness in the window winder, the glass channels and sill strips or the door buttons and interior latch release mechanism.

8 Front wing - removal and installation

1 Remove the headlamp surround and the headlamp unit (see Chapter 10). Wing securing screw (1) is then accessible and can be removed (Fig. 12.1).
2 From under the wing, unscrew and remove the filler panel securing screws. Removal of the roadwheel will provide better access to these.
3 Working within the car, unclip and remove the scuttle side trim and then unscrew and remove the screws (3) (photo).
4 At the rear of the wing, the screw (4) can be removed from its lower edge.
5 The wing securing screws can now be removed from the upper edge and the wing withdrawn.
6 Installation is a reversal of removal but renew any mastic sealing compound and apply protective coating to the under surface. The upper surface can be resprayed to match the body colour.

8.3 Upper wing securing bolt on front door pillar

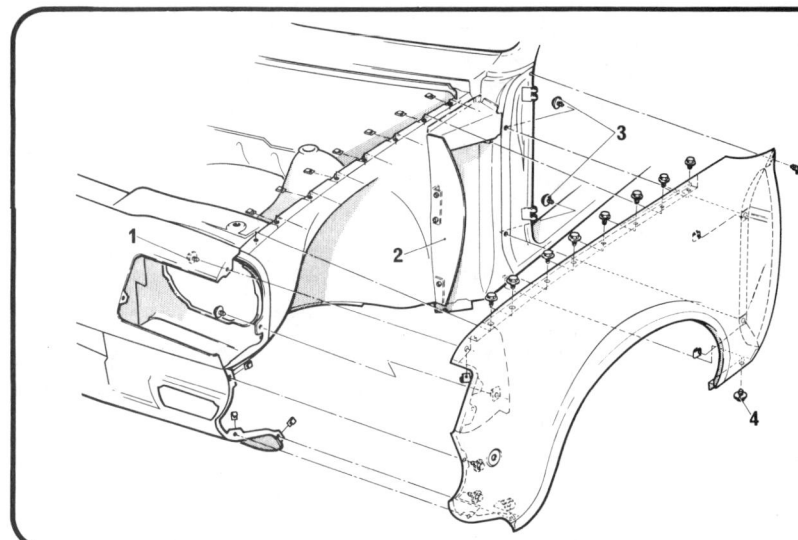

Fig. 12.1. Front wing securing screws (Sec. 8)

1 *Screw accessible after removal of headlamp surround*
2 *Filler panel*
3 *Screws accessible after removal of scuttle side panel*
4 *Lower edge screw*

9 Windscreen glass - removal and installation

1 Where a windscreen is to be replaced then if it is due to shattering, the facia air vents should be covered before attempting removal. Adhesive sheeting is useful to stick to the outside of the glass to enable large areas of crystallised glass to be removed.

2 Where the screen is to be removed intact or is of laminated type then an assistant will be required. First release the rubber surround from the bodywork by running a blunt, small screwdriver around and under the rubber weatherstrip both inside and outside the car. This operation will break the adhesive of the sealer originally used. Take care not to damage the paintwork or catch the rubber surround with the screwdriver. Remove the windscreen wiper arms and interior mirror and place a protective cover on the bonnet.

3 Have your assistant push the inner lip of the rubber surround off the flange of the windscreen body aperture. Once the rubber surround starts to peel off the flange, the screen may be forced gently outwards by careful hand pressure. The second person should support and remove the screen complete with rubber surround and metal beading as it comes out.

4 Remove the bright moulding from the rubber surround.

5 Before fitting a windscreen, ensure that the rubber surround is completely free from old sealant and glass fragments, and has not hardened or cracked. Fit the rubber surround to the glass and apply a bead of suitable sealant between the glass outer edge and sealing strip.

6 Clean old sealant from the bodyflange.

7 Cut a piece of strong cord greater in length than the periphery of the glass and insert it into the body flange locating channel of the rubber surround.

8 Apply a thin bead of sealant to the face of the rubber channel which will eventually mate with the body.

9 Offer the windscreen to the body aperture and pass the ends of the cord, previously fitted and located at bottom centre into the vehicle interior.

10 Press the windscreen into place, at the same time have an assistant pulling the cords to engage the lip of the rubber channel over the body flange.

11 Remove any excess sealant with a paraffin soaked rag.

12 Refit the bright moulding to the rubber surround. A special tool will facilitate this operation but take care not to tear the lips of the rubber.

10 Rear quarter light (fixed type) - glass renewal

1 The procedure is similar to that described in the preceding Section, the glass being pushed from inside as the rubber surround is peeled from the body flange.

11 Rear quarter light (opening type) - removal and installation

1 To remove the quarterlight, unscrew the three self-tapping screws which hold the link type fastener to the body side panel.

2 Pull the glass hinges out of engagement with the rubber grommets located in the door lock pillar.

3 If a new body flange weatherstrip is being fitted, make sure that the lip is to the outside and that the ends of the strip butt together at the centre of the bottom run.

4 If new rubber hinge grommets are being installed, make sure that their flat sides are outwards and when inserting the hinges, take care not to push the grommets into the pillar cavity.

12 Door lock - removal and installation

1 Open the door to its fullest extent and remove the armrest (two screws) (photo).

2 Remove the door lock remote control handle escutcheon by prising it carefully with a broad-bladed lever (photo).

3 Press the trim panel inwards slightly and extract the clip which secures the window regulator handle. In the absence of the correct tool, a hooked piece of wire can be used.

4 Insert the broad-bladed lever between the door trim panel and the door, moving it up or down to position it as close as possible to each retaining clip in turn and then prising the clip from the door. When all

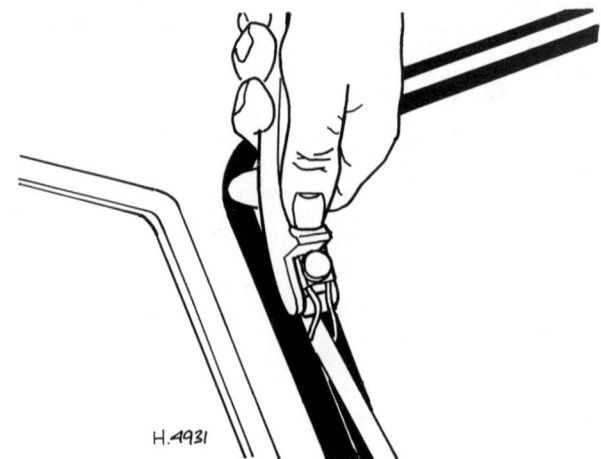

Fig. 12.2. Installing windscreen bright trim using special tool (Sec. 9)

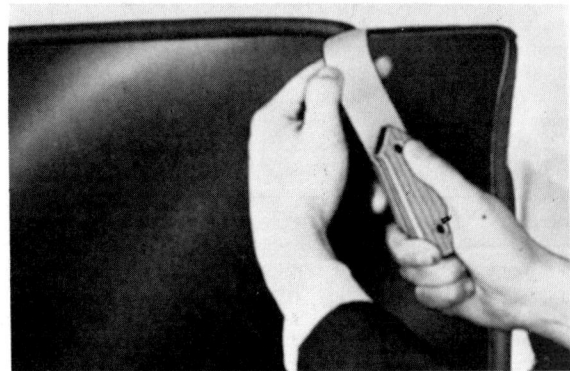

Fig. 12.3. Peeling back fixed rear quarterlight rubber surround (Sec. 10)

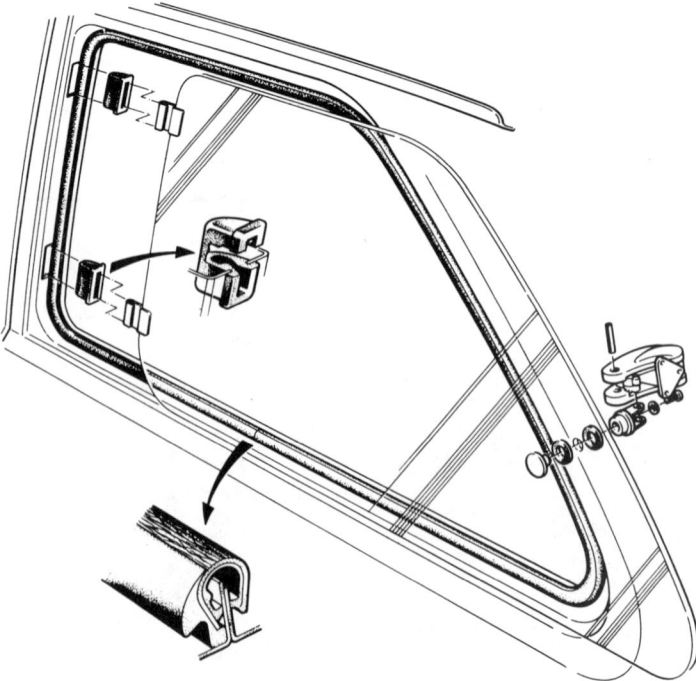

Fig. 12.4. Opening type rear quarterlight detail (Sec. 11)

12.1 Removing a door arm rest

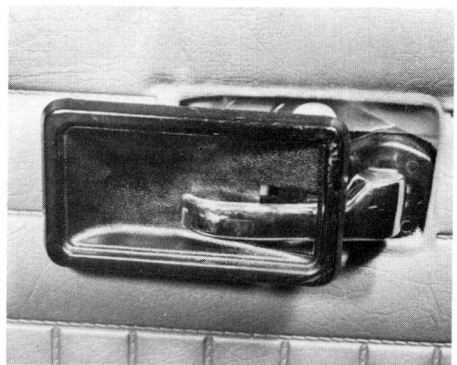

12.2 Removing a remote control handle escutcheon

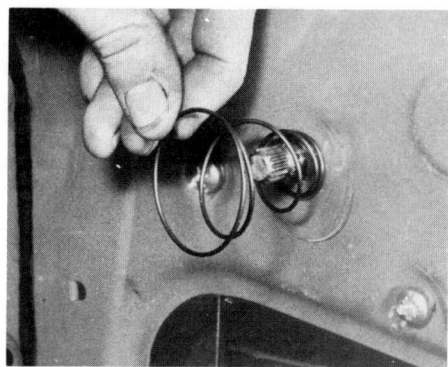

12.4 Removing window winder handle door spring (after door trim has been withdrawn)

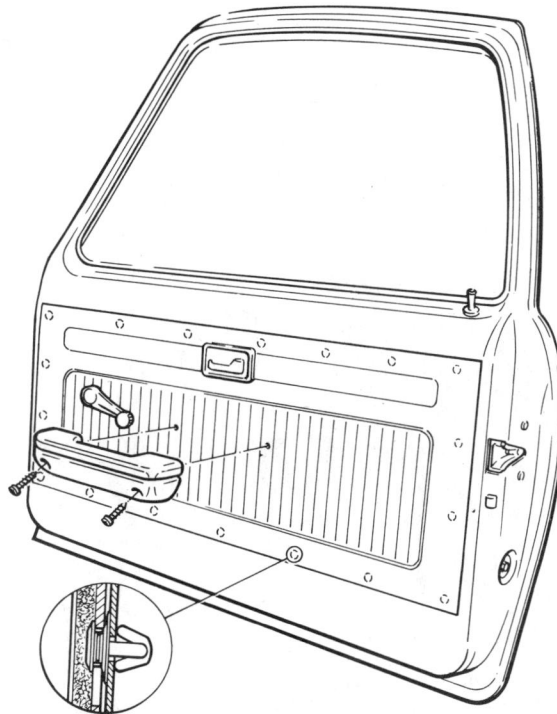

Fig. 12.5. Interior of door showing trim panel fasteners (Sec. 12)

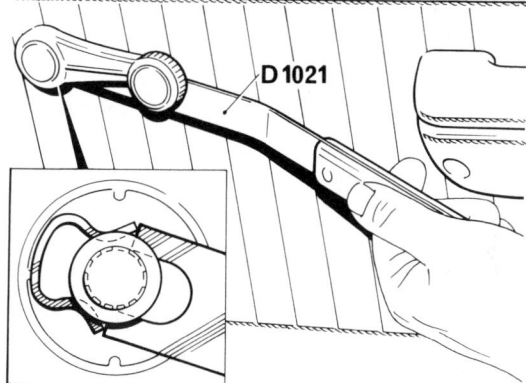

Fig. 12.6. Removing window regulator handle clip (Sec. 12)

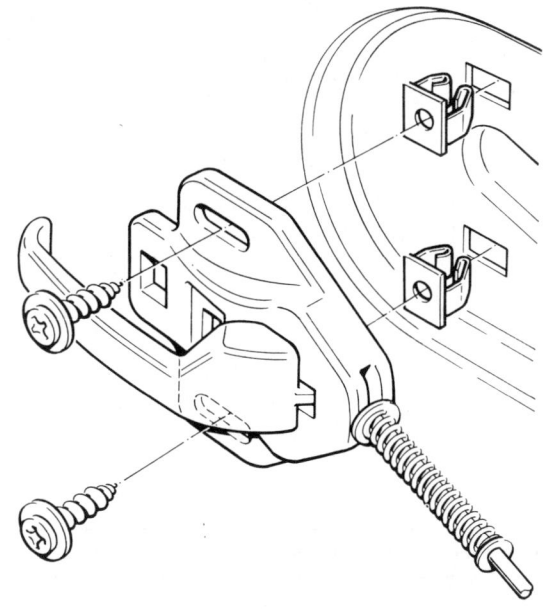

Fig. 12.7. Remote control handle securing screws (Sec. 12)

the clips have been released, remove the panel and carefully peel away the waterproof sheet and extract the window regulator handle coil spring (photo).

5   The remote control handle can be removed after extracting the two screws.

6   Unscrew the knob from the locking rod.

7   Temporarily replace the window regulator handle and wind the glass fully up.

8   Unscrew and remove the two nuts which secure the outside door handle. Prise the adjusting nut '2' (Fig. 12.9) from its retaining clip '1' and withdraw the handle assembly.

9   To remove the lock cylinder, extract the sliding clip '1' (Fig. 12.10) and disconnect the rod '3'. The lock assembly can now be withdrawn from within the door.

10 Installation is a reversal of removal but carry out the following adjustments.

11 When fitting the outside handle, adjust the nut on the release rod so that all free movement is eliminated. Apply a little grease to rubbing surfaces.

12 Before tightening remote control handle mounting plate screws, press the mounting forward with the finger to eliminate any free-movement. The holes in the mounting plate are elongated for this purpose.

13 If adjustment of the door lock striker plate is required to provide smooth, positive closure, an Allen key will be required to release the striker. The contact point of the door lock striker fork should be at the centre of the striker and this can be adjusted by varying the thickness or number of packing washers.

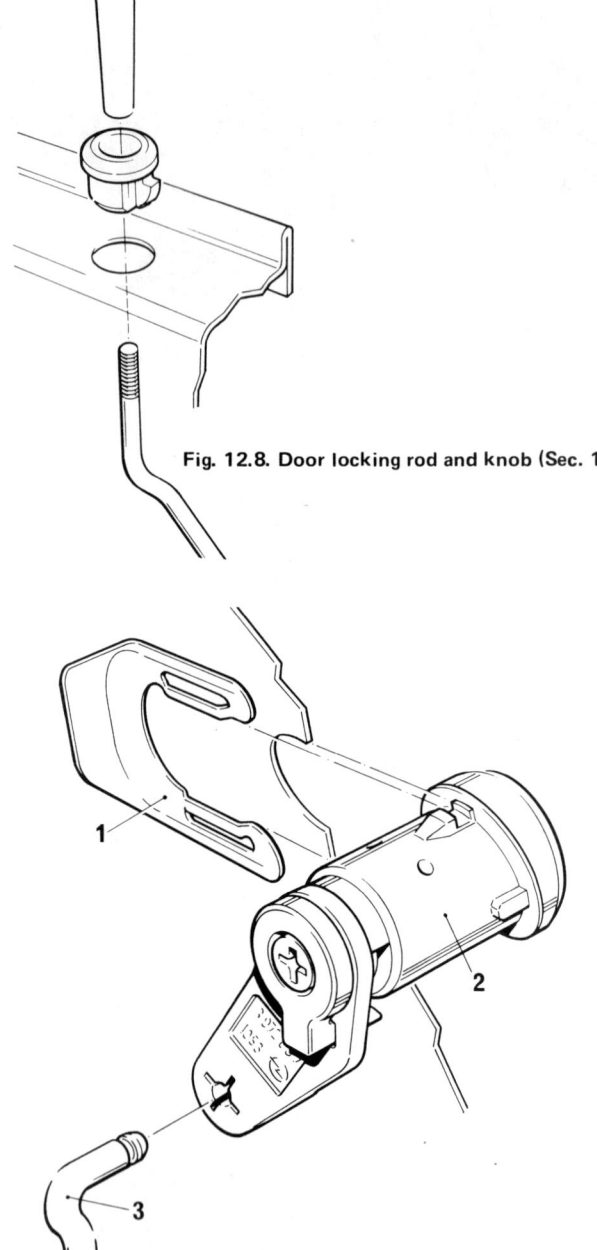

Fig. 12.8. Door locking rod and knob (Sec. 12)

Fig. 12.10. Door lock cylinder (Sec. 12)

1   Sliding clip   2   Cylinder   3   Connecting rod

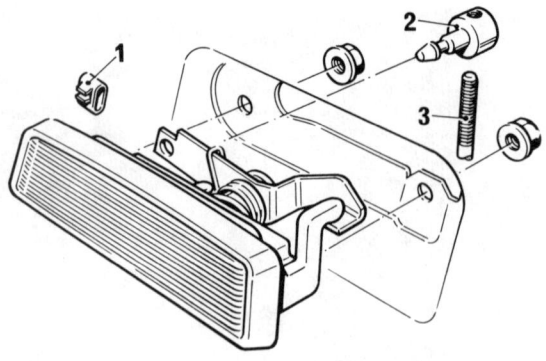

Fig. 12.9. Door exterior handle (Sec. 12)

1   Retaining clip   2   Adjusting nut   3   Release rod

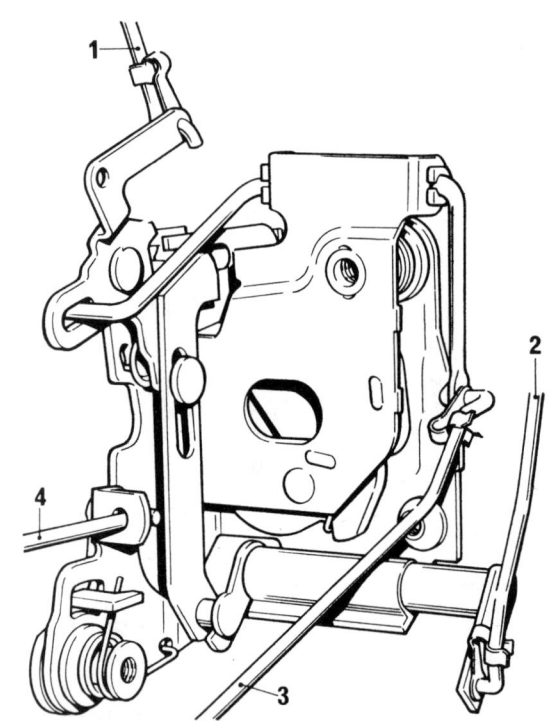

Fig. 12.11. The door lock (Sec. 12)

1   Internal lock plunger   3   Cylinder lock connecting
    connecting rod   rod
2   Exterior handle connecting rod 4   Remote control rod

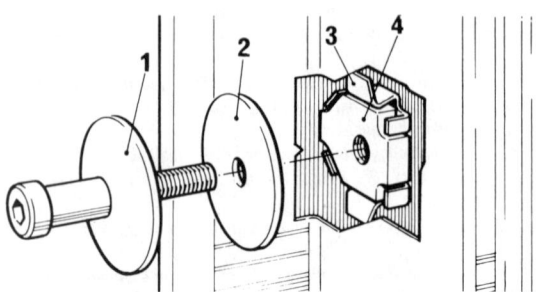

Fig. 12.12. Door striker plate components (Sec. 12)

1   Striker   3   Retainer
2   Packing washer   4   Anchor plate

13 Door glass - removal and installation

1   Remove the door interior trim panel as described in the preceding Section.
2   Temporarily refit the window regulator handle and wind down the glass until the cable to glass support clamps come into view in the door apertures.
3   Unscrew the clamp bolts to release the glass support channel (photo).
4   Remove the door waist inner and outer weatherstrips.
5   Unscrew and remove the two lower bolts from the glass front channel guide and slacken the upper one (Fig. 12.14).

Fig. 12.13. Unscrewing a door glass support channel to cable clamp bolt (Sec. 13)

13.3 Window regulator cable clamp

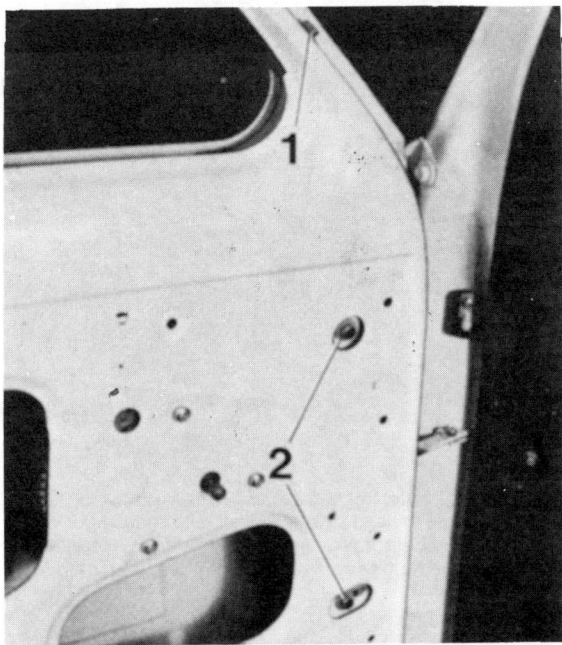

Fig. 12.14. Door glass guide channel bolts (1) upper (2) lower, adjustable (Sec. 13)

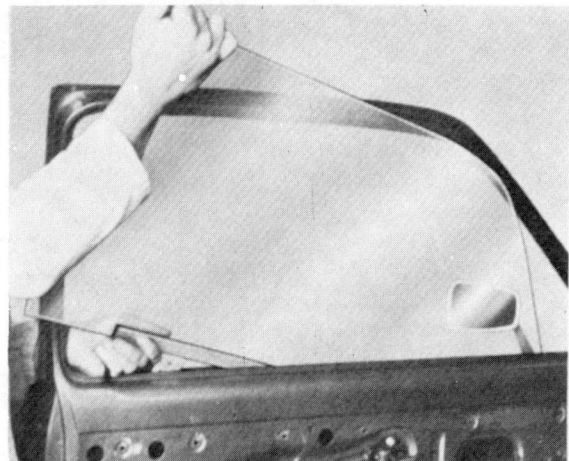

Fig. 12.15. Removing door glass (Sec. 13)

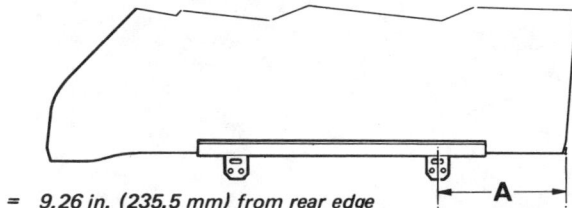

A = 9.26 in. (235.5 mm) from rear edge

Fig. 12.16. Door glass and correct location of support channel (Sec. 13)

Fig. 12.17. Window regulator cable drum notch (Sec. 13)

6   Lift the glass, turn it slightly and withdraw it towards the inner side of the door frame.

7   If a new glass is being installed, fit the support channel to its lower edge in accordance with the diagram (Fig. 12.16).

8   Turn the window regulator handle until it can be rotated no further (anticlockwise on right-hand door clockwise on left-hand door). Now turn the handle in the opposite direction until the notch on the cable drum appears in the door aperture. Continue turning until it appears for the second time. Do not move the regulator from this position.

9   Install the glass squarely so that it engages in the rear guide channel and then bolt the support channel to cable clamps into position by inserting a socket wrench through the door apertures.

10 Install the glass front guide channel bolts.

11 Any adjustment to the glass can be carried out by moving the cable clamps slightly or by moving the position of the front guide channel. The rear guide channel is secured at its lower end by a bolt and at its upper end by a clip.

This sequence of photographs deals with the repair of the dent and paintwork damage shown in this photo. The procedure will be similar for the repair of a hole. It should be noted that the procedures given here are simplified — more explicit instructions will be found in the text

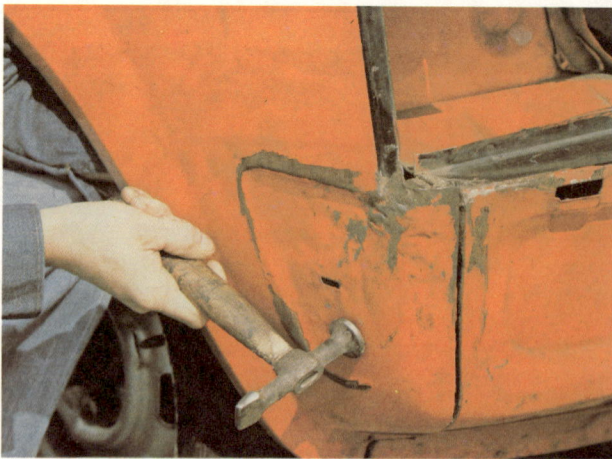

In the case of a dent the first job — after removing surrounding trim — is to hammer out the dent where access is possible. This will minimise filling. Here, the large dent having been hammered out, the damaged area is being made slightly concave

Now all paint must be removed from the damaged area, by rubbing with coarse abrasive paper. Alternatively, a wire brush or abrasive pad can be used in a power drill. Where the repair area meets good paintwork, the edge of the paintwork should be 'feathered', using a finer grade of abrasive paper

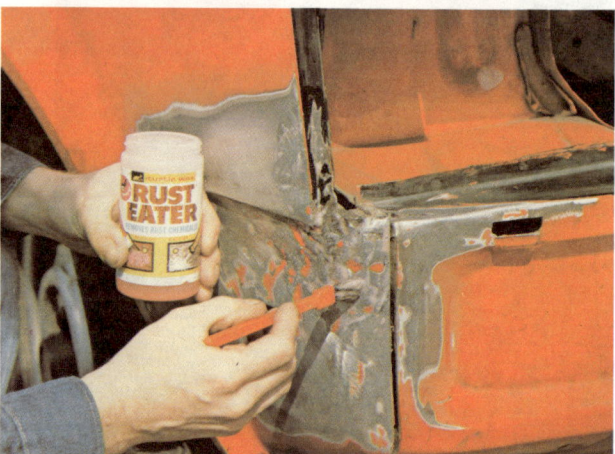

In the case of a hole caused by rusting, all damaged sheet-metal should be cut away before proceeding to this stage. Here, the damaged area is being treated with rust remover and inhibitor before being filled

Mix the body filler according to its manufacturer's instructions. In the case of corrosion damage, it will be necessary to block off any large holes before filling — this can be done with zinc gauze or aluminium tape. Make sure the area is absolutely clean before...

...applying the filler. Filler should be applied with a flexible applicator, as shown, for best results; the wooden spatula being used for confined areas. Apply thin layers of filler at 20-minute intervals, until the surface of the filler is slightly proud of the surrounding bodywork

Initial shaping can be done with a Surform plane or Dreadnought file. Then, using progressively finer grades of wet-and-dry paper, wrapped around a sanding block, and copious amounts of clean water, rub down the filler until really smooth and flat. Again, feather the edges of adjoining paintwork

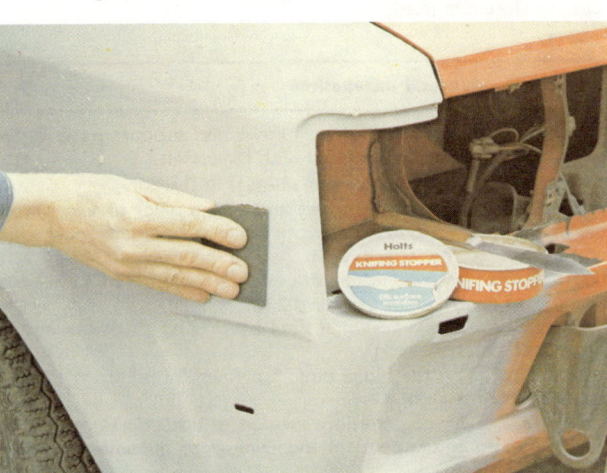

Again, using plenty of water, rub down the primer with a fine grade of wet-and-dry paper (400 grade is probably best) until it is really smooth and well blended into the surrounding paintwork. Any remaining imperfections can now be filled by carefully applied knifing stopper paste

The top coat can now be applied. When working out of doors, pick a dry, warm and wind-free day. Ensure surrounding areas are protected from over-spray. Agitate the aerosol thoroughly, then spray the centre of the repair area, working outwards with a circular motion. Apply the paint as several thin coats

The whole repair area can now be sprayed or brush-painted with primer. If spraying, ensure adjoining areas are protected from over-spray. Note that at least one inch of the surrounding sound paintwork should be coated with primer. Primer has a 'thick' consistency, so will fill small imperfections

When the stopper has hardened, rub down the repair area again before applying the final coat of primer. Before rubbing down this last coat of primer, ensure the repair area is blemish-free – use more stopper if necessary. To ensure that the surface of the primer is really smooth use some finishing compound

After a period of about two weeks, which the paint needs to harden fully, the surface of the repaired area can be 'cut' with a mild cutting compound prior to wax polishing. When carrying out bodywork repairs, remember that the quality of the finished job is proportional to the time and effort expended

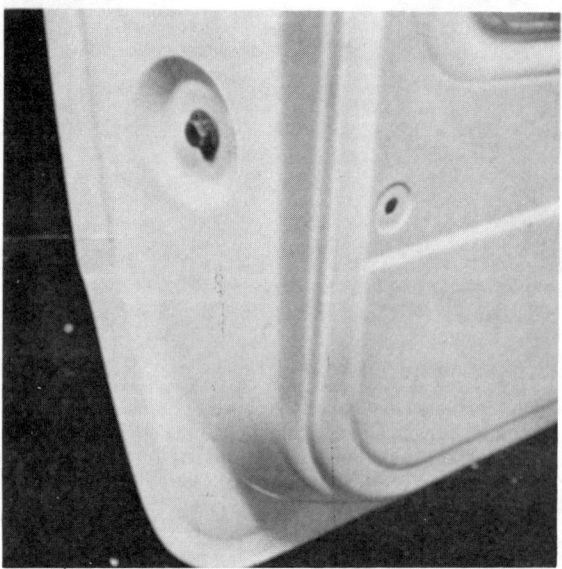

Fig. 12.18. Door rear glass guide securing bolt (Sec. 13)

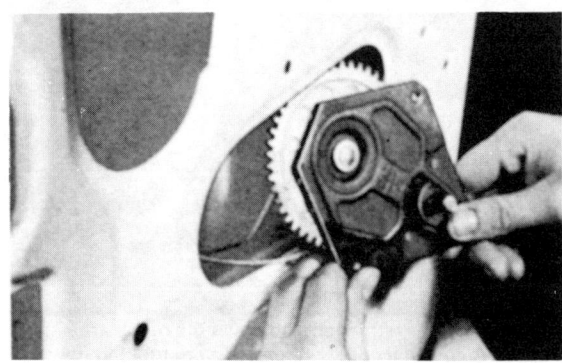

Fig. 12.19. Withdrawing window regulator and cable from door cavity (Sec. 14)

Fig. 12.21. Attachment of window winding cable to regulator drum (viewed from inside door cavity in the interest of clarity) (Sec. 14)

14 Door window regulator and cable - removal and installation

1   Remove the glass as described in the preceding Section.
2   Slacken the bolt which secures the cable tension roller.
3   Unscrew and remove the three screws which secure the regulator assembly to the door inner panel. Withdraw the assembly from the door cavity, complete with the continuous cable, having lifted the cable from the rollers.
4   The regulator assemblies are not interchangeable and are marked 'L' or 'R' on the inside face of the drum.
5   Commence installation by fitting the regulator to the door panel making sure that the rubber sealing ring is located between the panel and the regulator spindle.
6   The cable should be installed so that as shown in Figs. 12.21 and 12.22 it runs from tension roller '4' to the groove adjacent to the toothed sprocket of the regulator drum, fills four grooves and then leaves the outer groove to link with roller '2'.
7   When the cable is correctly installed, apply hand-pressure to the tension roller '4' and tighten the roller locking bolt.
8   Carry out the operations described in paragraphs 8 and 9, of the preceding Section.
9   Check for smooth operation and apply oil to the cable rollers and grease to the cable itself.

15 Door - removal and installation

1   Open the door to its fullest extent and support its lower edge on jacks or blocks suitably insulated with rag or felt.
2   Prise out the hinge pin sealing plugs (Fig. 12.23).
3   Drill out the check strap rivet and pass a piece of wire through the hole in the strap to prevent it from being accidentally pushed into the door cavity. If the check strap has to be renewed, then it can be unbolted and removed after the door interior trim panel has been detached, as described in Section 12 (Fig. 12.24).
4   Extract the roll type hinge pins by driving them out towards the centre of the door.
5   When installing the hinge pins, tap them in as shown in Fig. 12.25 before hanging the door.
6   As the door hinge plates are welded to both the door pillar and the door frame, no adjustment for incorrect door alignment can be carried

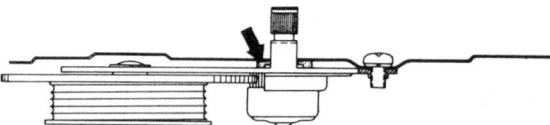

Fig. 12.20. Location of window regulator rubber sealing ring (Sec. 14)

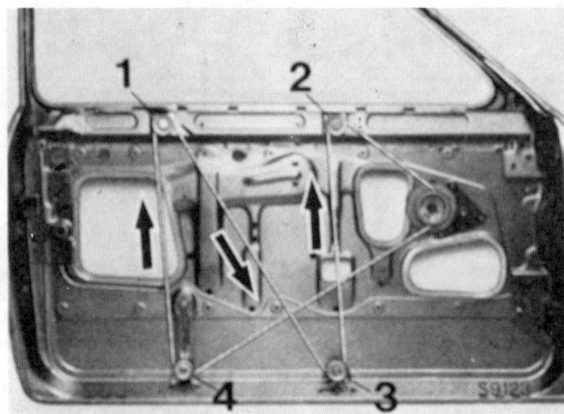

Fig. 12.22. Correct layout of window winding cable (viewed from inside door cavity for clarity) (Sec. 14)

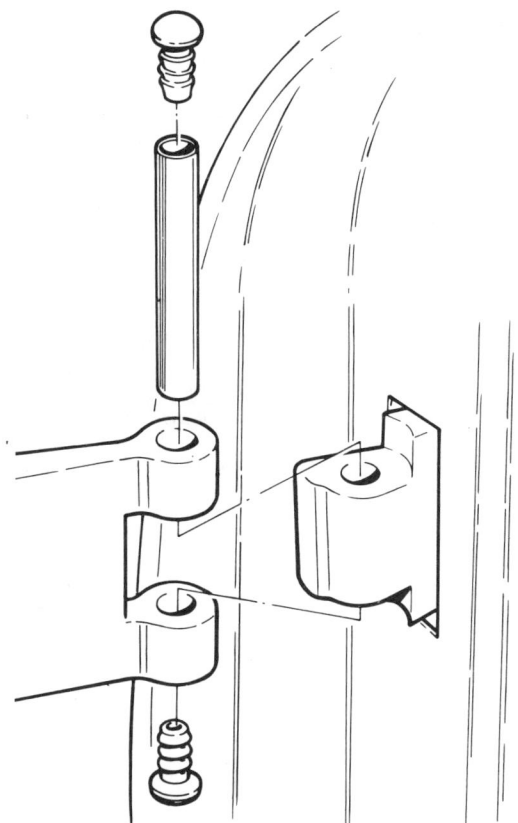

Fig. 12.23. Door hinge components (Sec. 15)

Fig. 12.25. Installation of door hinge pins prior to hanging door (Sec. 15)

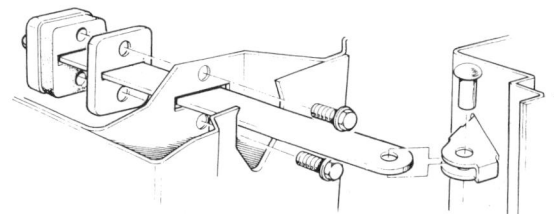

Fig. 12.24. Door check strap (Sec. 15)

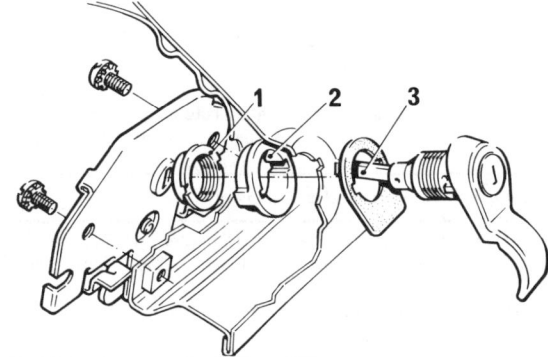

Fig. 12.26. The tailgate lock (Sec. 16)

1 Slotted nut   2 Spacer   3 Cylinder lock operating tang

Fig. 12.27. Exploded view of the tailgate lock cylinder (Sec. 16)

1 Circlip   2 Cylinder

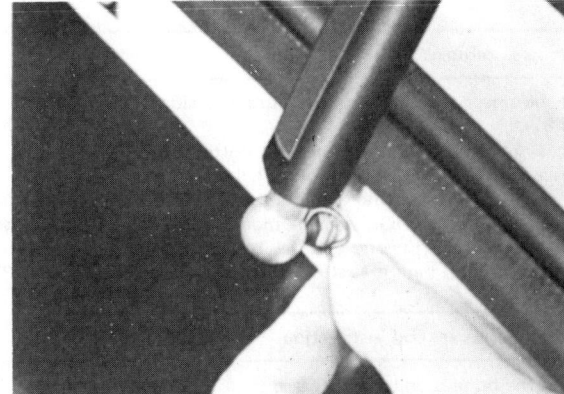

Fig. 12.28. Extracting a tailgate counterbalance piston securing clip (Sec. 16)

out other than by prising the pillar hinge plates using an adjustable wrench. This should be done very carefully and only a fraction at a time before re-checking the alignment.

7   Wear in the hinge pin holes will cause a door to drop and if the condition cannot be remedied by drilling and fitting oversize pins, then new hinge plates will have to be installed — very definitely a job for your Vauxhall dealer.

16 Tailgate lock - removal and refitting

1   Remove the interior trim panel in a similar manner to that described for the door (Section 12).
2   Unscrew and remove the lock securing bolts and withdraw the lock assembly.
3   The cylinder and exterior handle can be removed after unscrewing the slotted retaining nut. The cylinder can be separated from the handle after removing the circlip and inserting and turning the key to align the lock tangs.
4   The tailgate striker is adjustable after releasing its securing bolt. The tailgate should close smoothly and positively with firm hand-pressure.

17 Tailgate glass - removal and installation

1   This is similar to the procedure described, in Section 9, for the windscreen but the leads must be disconnected from the heating element.
2   If the glass is being removed in order to renew the rubber surround, take care not to scratch the printed circuit. In the event of a break in the printed circuit, a special paint can be applied to repair it.

18 Tailgate - removal and installation

1   Have an assistant hold the tailgate in its fully open position.
2   Disconnect the two counter-balance pistons by extracting the spring clips from the balljoints.
3   Pull down a section of the weatherstrip and carefully peel back the roof lining to gain access to one of the hinge plates which are bolted to the roof rail.
4   Unbolt one of the hinge plates and then slide the tailgate sideways to disengage the other hinge pin from the hinge plate.
5   Installation is a reversal of removal but lubricate the tailgate hinges with gear oil.
6   Do not be tempted to dismantle the counter-balance pistons as they contain heavy springs under compression. When refitting the pistons, grease the balljoints.

19 Radiator grille moulding - removal and refitting

1   The grille mouldings are retained by a combination of threaded clips '1' and friction bushes '2' (Fig. 12.30).
2   Unscrew the nuts from the clips first and then ease the moulding carefully away so that the bushes are left in the front panel.
3   Refitting is a reversal of removal.

20 Bumpers - removal and installation

1   The bumpers are secured by centre and side brackets (Figs. 12.31 and 12.32).
2   Access to the rear bumper bracket bolts is gained by removing the load area floor panels (see Section 23).
3   Make sure when refitting the side brackets that the rubber insulators are correctly located. On certain models (dependent upon date of production), access to one of the rear bumper bolts can only be obtained if the fuel tank is first moved forward slightly (Chapter 3).

21 Bonnet - removal and installation

1   Open the bonnet and support it in its fully open position.
2   Mark round the position of the hinge plates on the underside of the bonnet to ease the job of refitting.
3   Unscrew and remove the bolts from the hinge plates and with the

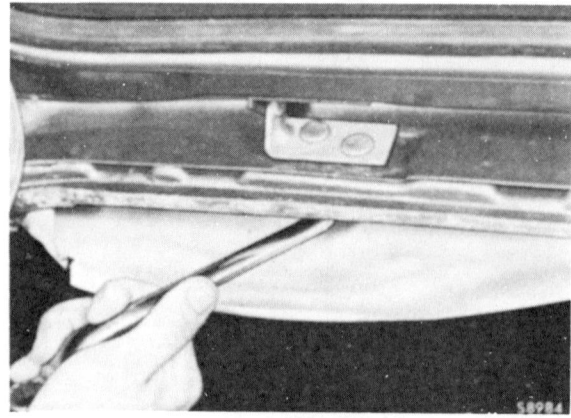

Fig. 12.29. Unscrewing a tailgate hinge securing nut (Sec. 18)

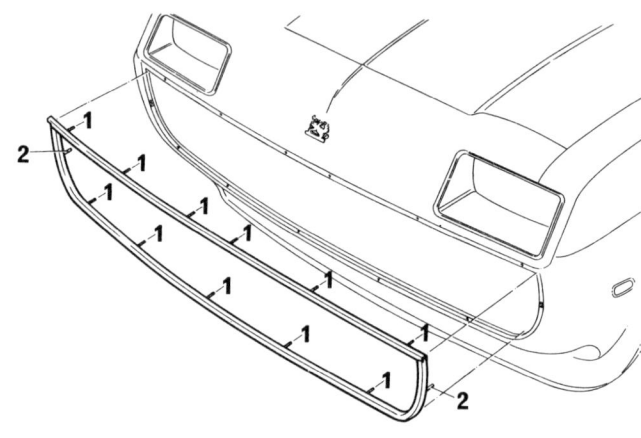

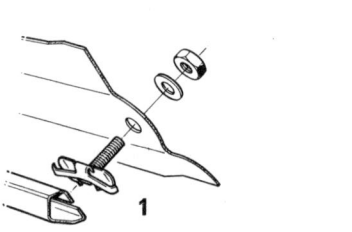
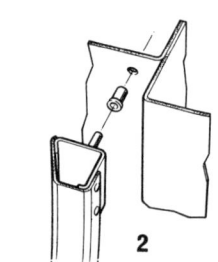

Fig. 12.30. Attachment of radiator grille moulding (Sec. 19)

1   Clip/threaded stud   2   Friction bushes

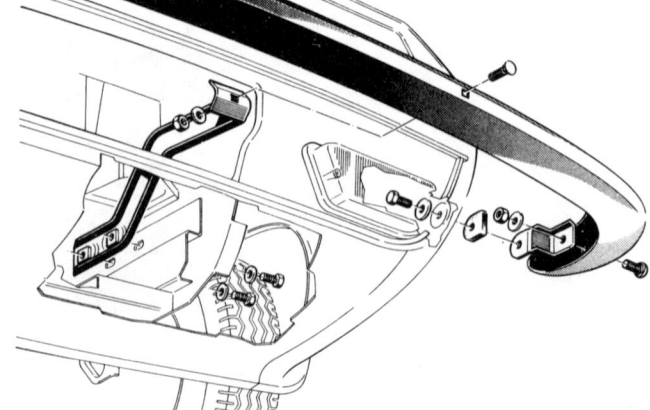

Fig. 12.31. Attachment of front bumper (Sec. 20)

help of an assistant, lift the bonnet away.

4 Installation is a reversal of removal but any adjustment for alignment can be carried out by moving the bonnet within the range of the elongated slots in the hinge plates, having first slackened the retaining bolts.

22 Bonnet lock - removal, refitting and adjustment

1 Open the bonnet and remove the cable clip '2' (Fig. 12.33).
2 Ease the cable nipple from the bonnet locking spring.
3 The complete cable assembly can be removed after unscrewing the back nut from the instrument panel support bracket.

4 The locking spring can be removed after releasing its end from the anchor slot.
5 Smooth positive closure can be obtained by adjusting the height of the bonnet front rubber buffers in conjunction with the dovetail bolt. The surface of the bonnet should be level with upper surfaces of the front wings.

23 Body interior trim panels - removal and installation

1 The quarter trim panels at the rear of the car interior are held in

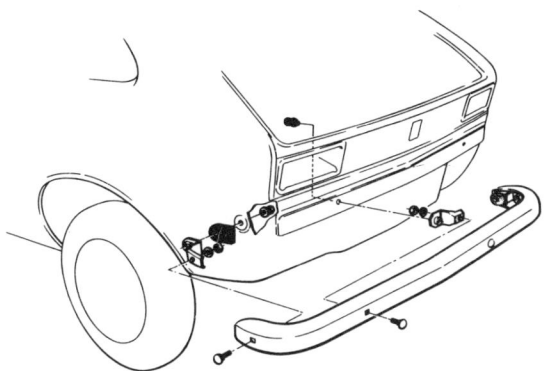

Fig. 12.32. Attachment of rear bumper (Sec. 20)

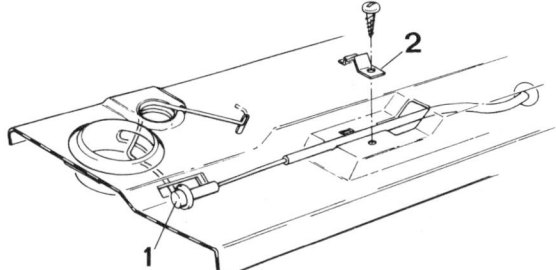

Fig. 12.33. Bonnet lock cable attachment (Sec. 22)

1 Cable nipple   2 Outer cable clip

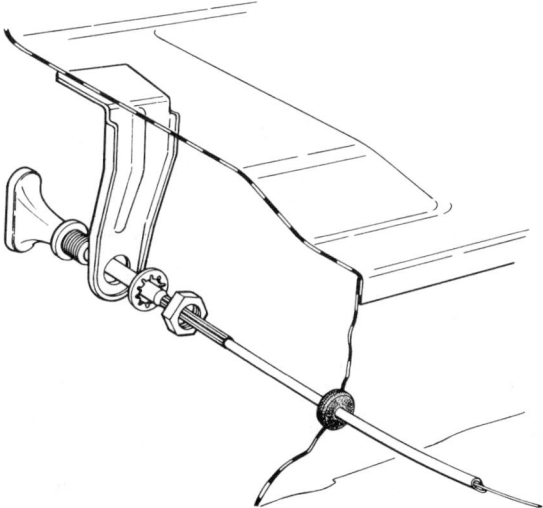

Fig. 12.34. Bonnet lock release and bracket (Sec. 22)

Fig. 12.35. Adjusting bonnet lock dovetail bolt (Sec. 22)

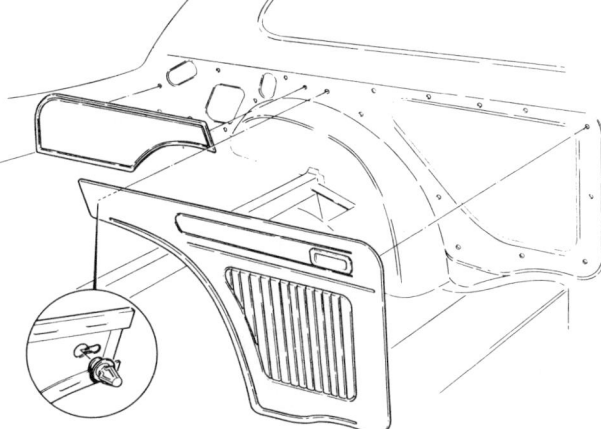

Fig. 12.36. Interior quarter trim panels and type of retainer (Sec. 23)

Fig. 12.37. Suitable tool for releasing trim panel clips (Sec. 23)

position by press clips. Use a broad bladed lever with a cut-out to release the panel.

2   The scuttle side trim panels are secured by press fasteners. Prise the fastener out and withdraw the panel from the pillar channel. On the side where the parcels shelf is fitted, also extract the shelf bracket screw and slide the panel downwards.

3   The left-hand load area floor panel is secured by two tongues and a cam type catch.

4   The right-hand panel is secured by self-tapping screws but the side trim panel must first be removed to gain access to the fuel filler pipe protective cover screw (see Chapter 3, fuel tank removal).

24 Fresh air ducts and grilles - removal and installation

1   Insert a thin blade and prise the radio speaker grille from the ventilator grille assembly.

2   The four screws which hold the ventilator assembly to the instrument panel are now accessible.

3   If one or both of the fresh air ducts must be removed, then the parcels shelf (four screws) will have to be removed, also the instrument assembly, the light switch and the instrument panel cover, as described in Sections 25 and 32, of Chapter 10.

4   Installation is a reversal of removal, but check that the duct seal lips are correctly located.

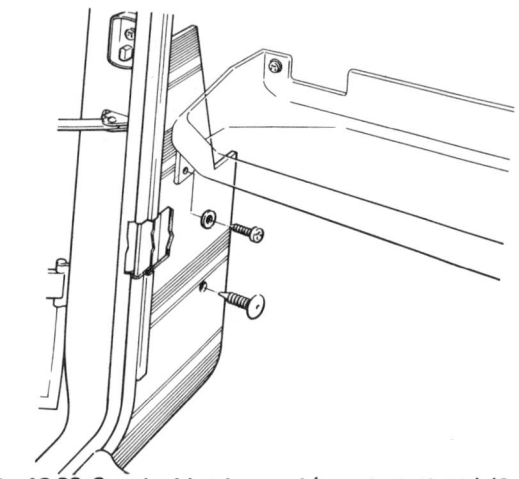

Fig. 12.38. Scuttle side trim panel (parcels shelf side) (Sec. 23)

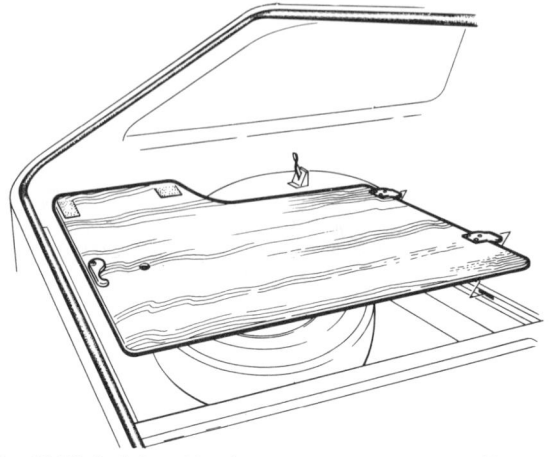

Fig. 12.39. Left-hand load carrying area floor panel (Sec. 23)

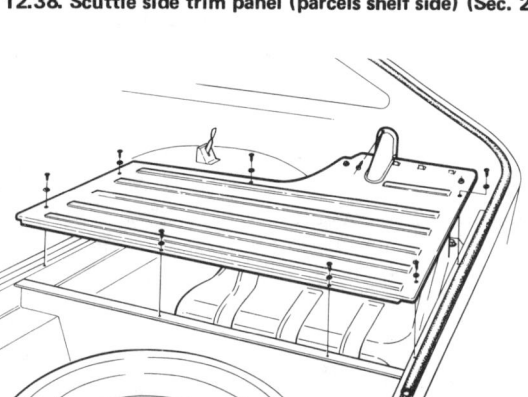

Fig. 12.40. Right-hand load carrying area floor panel (Sec. 23)

Fig. 12.41. Prising radio speaker grille from ventilator grille assembly (Sec. 24)

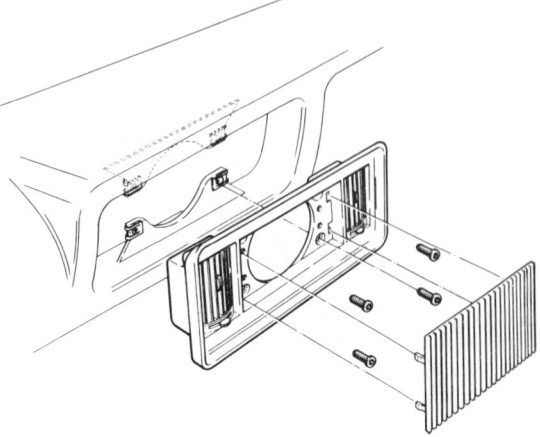

Fig. 12.42. Components of the ventilator assembly (Sec. 24)

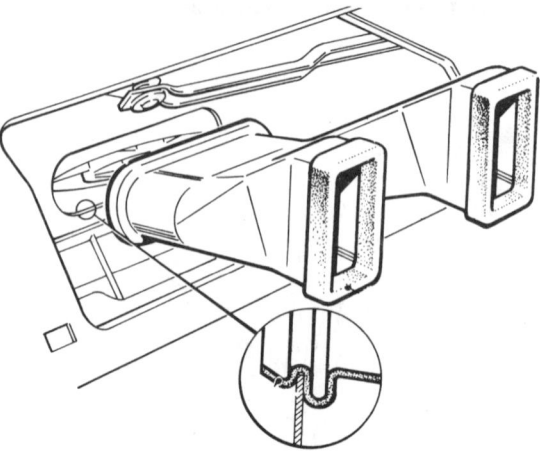

Fig. 12.43. Correct installation of ventilator duct seals (Sec. 24)

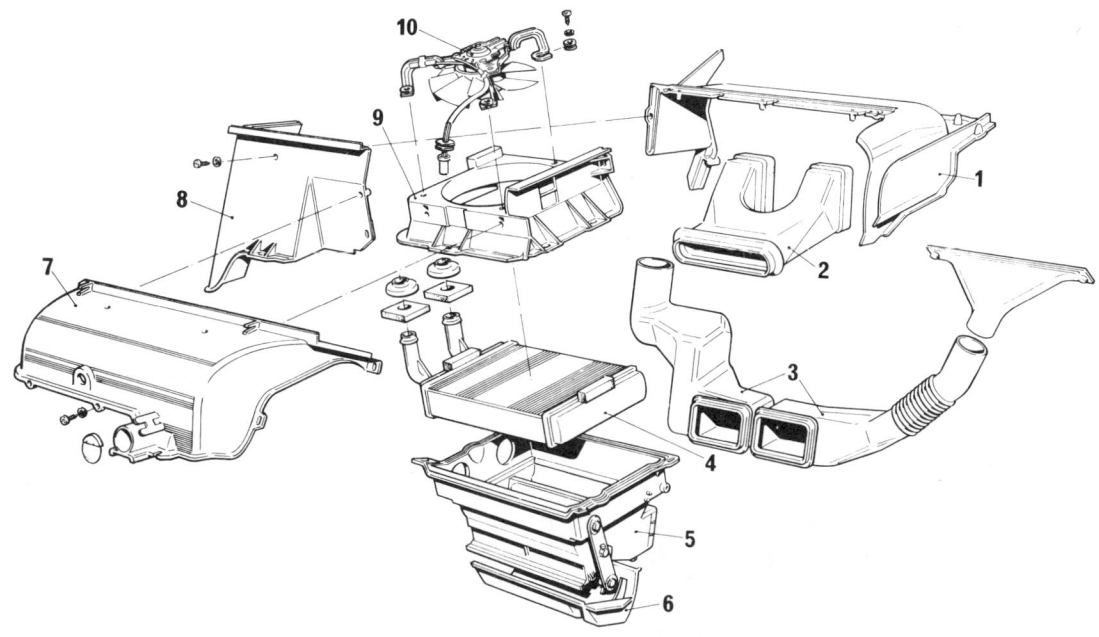

Fig. 12.44. Major components of the heater (Sec. 25)

1	Weatherproof cover	4	Matrix
2	Duct	5	Lower casing
3	Demister ducts	6	Outlet deflector

7	Weatherproof cover	10	Fan/motor assembly
8	Weatherproof cover		
9	Upper casing		

Fig. 12.45. Heater controls (Sec. 25)

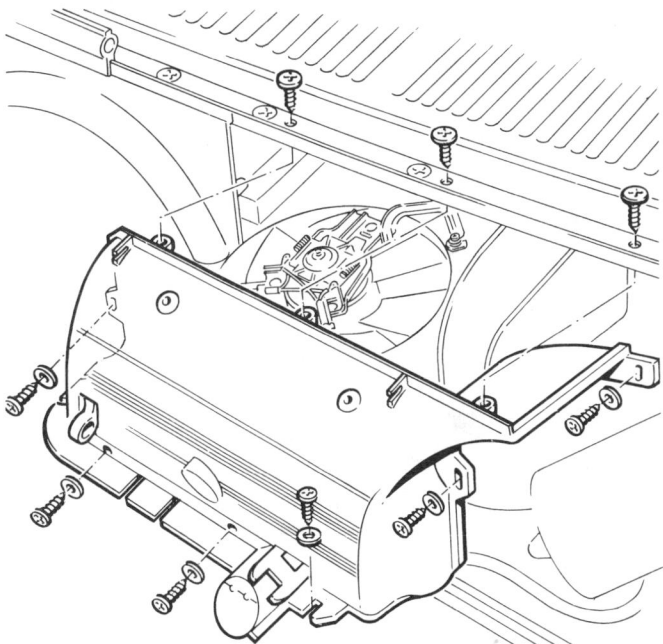

Fig. 12.46. Removing under bonnet heater cover (Sec. 26)

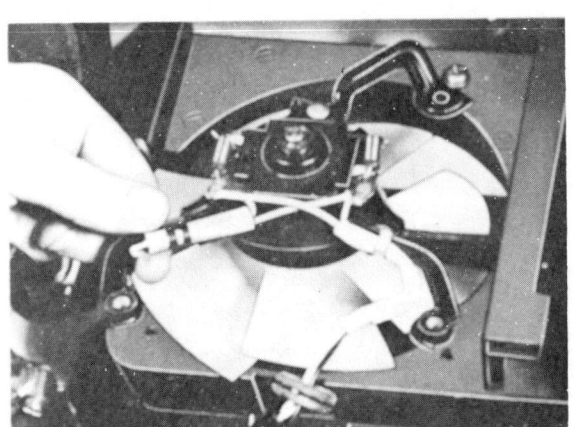

Fig. 12.47. Removing heater fan/motor assembly (Sec. 26)

25 Heater and ventilation system - description

1 The system is of fresh air type, the air entering from the grilles located at the base of the windscreen. The heat is provided by the engine cooling system through an adjustable water flow valve. Temperature control and adjustment of the air deflectors for interior heating or screen demisting or defrosting are set by the instrument panel controls. A booster fan is fitted to the heater unit and this has a three position control switch.

An entirely independent face-level cold air system is provided, having adjustable grilles on the instrument panel (Section 24).

26 Heater fan - removal and refitting

1 Open the bonnet and prop it securely in its fully open position.
2 From the engine compartment rear bulkhead, unscrew and remove the cover assembly (nine screws) to expose the fan and motor.
3 Unscrew and remove the two most accessible motor mounting screws.
4 Loosen the remaining screw and withdraw the forked end of mounting strut from the rubber grommet.
5 Withdraw the motor/fan unit after disconnecting the electrical leads.
6 If the motor is to be renewed, it will be supplied complete with fan. The fan and mounting struts are however supplied separately.
7 Installation is a reversal of removal, but seal the edges of the cover to the bulkhead with sealant when the screws have been fully tightened.

27 Heater matrix - removal and installation

1 Drain the cooling system, as described in Chapter 2.

Fig. 12.48. Removing heater air outlet deflector (Sec. 27)

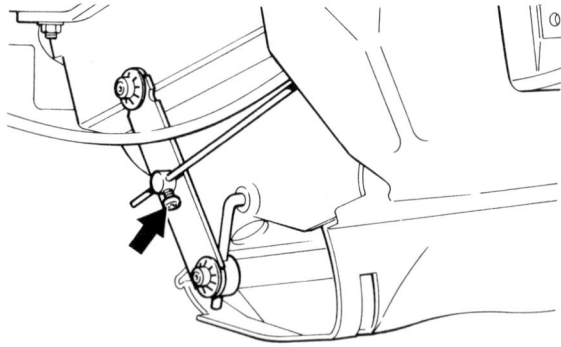

Fig. 12.50. Attachment of heater air distribution flap control rod (Sec. 27)

Fig. 12.52. Heater unit securing nuts (Sec. 27)

2 Remove the parcels shelf (four screws).
3 Detach the air outlet deflector by pinching in the sides to disengage the pegs and then slide it to the left-hand side.
4 Disconnect the heater hoses from the nozzles on the matrix. If they are tight, do not twist them roughly or the nozzles may fracture but ease the interiors of the hoses with a thin screwdriver.
5 Disconnect the control cable from the water valve.
6 Disconnect the control rod from the air distribution flap.
7 Disconnect the demister ducts from the heater casing apertures.
8 Unscrew and remove the heater casing nuts and lower the heater/

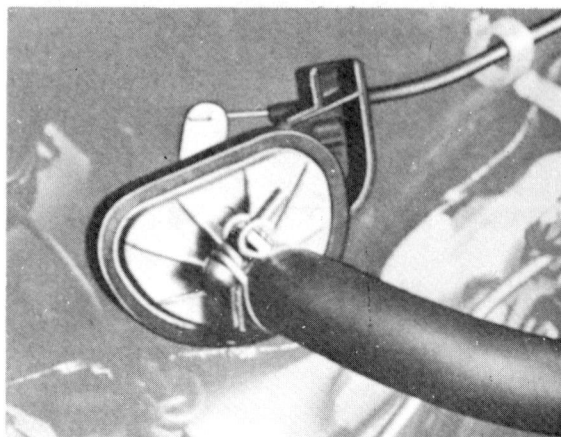

Fig. 12.49. Heater water valve and control cable (Sec. 27)

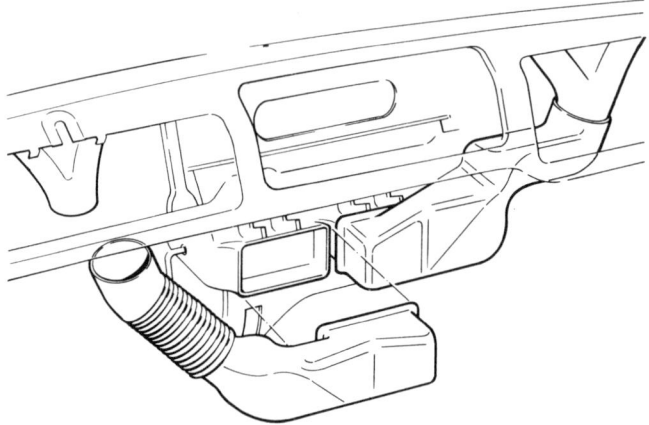

Fig. 12.51. Demister duct attachment to heater unit (Sec. 27)

Fig. 12.53. Extracting heater matrix (Sec. 27)

matrix to the car floor.

9   The radiator matrix should be renewed if it is leaking by levering it from the heater casing.

10 Installation is a reversal of removal, but apply sealant to all mating flanges to provide a good seal against the entry of water or dust.

11 When installation is complete, set the water valve cable by placing the heat control lever on the instrument panel to 'HOT' and then pushing the water valve lever fully towards the left-hand side of the car. Fit the outer cable clip to retain the cable in this position.

12 Now set the air control lever 0.24 in. (6.0 mm) up from the bottom of the escutcheon, push the flap operating lever fully forward and tighten the lockscrew.

13 Refill and bleed the cooling system as described in Chapter 2, Section 4.

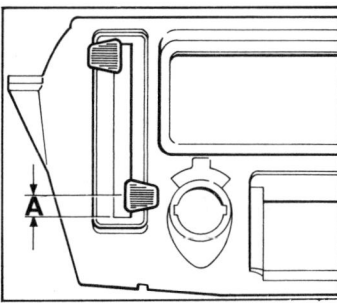

Fig. 12.54 Setting of heater control lever prior to connecting air distribution flap control rod (Sec. 27)

Chapter 13 Supplement :
Revisions and information on later models

Contents

1 Introduction

Since the introduction of the Chevette in mid-1975, there have been a number of modifications which are mainly of a minor nature. The major changes consist of a reduced engine compression ratio, sealed carburettor adjustments, Girling self-adjusting rear brakes, and the option of automatic transmission on L and GL models.

Subsequent to the printing of this manual the following additional models have been added to the Chevette range; servicing procedures, where different from those described in the main Chapters, are covered in this Supplement:

Chevette ES 3-door Hatchback, and 2-door Saloon

Chevette E 3-door Hatchback, 2- and 4-door Saloons, and 3-door Estate
Chevette Black Pearl limited edition 3-door Hatchback
Chevette L 3-door Hatchback, 2- and 4-door Saloons, and 3-door Estate
Chevette Special limited edition 2- and 4-door Saloons
Chevette L Sun Hatch limited edition 3-door Hatchback
Chevette GL 3-door Hatchback and 4-door Saloon
Chevette GLS 3-door Hatchback and 4-door Saloon
Bedford Chevanne (panel van)

In order to use the Supplement to the best advantage it is suggested that it is referred to before the main Chapters of the manual; this will ensure that any relevant information can be incorporated into the procedures given in Chapters 1 to 12. Time and cost will therefore be saved and the particular job will be completed correctly.

2 Specifications

The Specifications listed here are revisions of, or additional to, the main Specifications at the beginning of each Chapter

Engine (from number 1770434 on)

Compression ratio ... ...   8.7 : 1 (Chevanne 7.3 : 1)

Crankshaft marking for production undersize
White paint and letter 'M' on centre web ... ...   Main bearings 0.010in (0.254mm) undersize
Red paint and letter 'P' on centre web ... ...   Crankpins 0.010in (0.254mm) undersize

Minimum cylinder head depth ... ...   3.221in (81.81mm) after refacing

Cooling system

Thermostat opens ... ...   197°F (92°C)

Capacity (automatic transmission models) ... ...   10.7 Imp pint (6.1 litre)

Carburation

Carburettor identification (engine number 1817784 on)
Manual gearbox models 3696B, 3825B, 3871B, 3939B, 3946B, 3989
Automatic transmission models   3938

Metering needle
3696B, 3825B, 3871B, 3939B B1DV
3946B B1EU
3989 ... ...   B1FB
3938 ... ...   B1FA

Fast idle cam gap (3946B carburettor) ... ...   0.08 in (2.0 mm)

CO content (idling) ... ...   2.5% to 3.5%

Fuel tank capacity
Saloon models ... ...   9.9 Imp gal (45 litre)
Estate and Chevanne models ... ...   9.5 Imp gal (43 litre)

Fuel octane rating
7.3 to 1 engine   93
8.7 to 1 engine   97

Ignition system

Distributor (engine number 1639763 on)
Contact breaker points gap:
Delco-Remy ... ...   0.022 in (0.55 mm)
Bosch ... ...   0.016 in (0.40 mm)
Dwell angle:
Delco-Remy ... ...   49 to 51°
Bosch ... ...   47 to 53°

Spark plugs (except exhaust emission models)
Type ... ...   AC 43 5XLS

Clutch (chassis numbers KX150228 and LX100101 on)

Clutch pedal travel ... ...   4.0 in (101 mm)

Manual gearbox (chassis number FY127596 on)

Oil capacity ... ...   1.09 Imp pints (0.62 litres)

Automatic transmission
Torque converter stall speed ... ... 2200 to 2400 rpm

Fluid capacity
Total (including torque converter) ... ... 9.0 Imp pint (5.1 litre)
Service refill ... . 4.5 Imp pint (2.6 litre)

Torque wrench settings

	lbf ft	Nm
Brake band servo cover	17 to 19	23 to 26
Oil screen bolts	13 to 15	18 to 21
Oil pan bolts	7 to 9	10 to 13
Driveplate to crankshaft	25	34
Torque converter to driveplate	42	57
Speedometer cable bolt	2	3
Selector lever nut	8	11
Oil cooler hose unions	12	16

Suspension and steering
Steering toe-in (as from February 1978) ... ... 0.04 to 0.12 in (1.0 to 3.0 mm)

Wheels and tyres
Model

Model	Tyre size	Tyre Pressures			
		A		B	
		Front	Rear	Front	Rear
Hatchbacks and Saloons:					
ES and E models...	5.60 x 13	22 (1.55)	22 (1.55)	24 (1.69)	30 (2.11)
L and GL models	155SR x 13	21 (1.48)	25 (1.76)	22 (1.55)	29 (2.0)
GLS models	175/70SR x 13	21 (1.48)	25 (1.76)	22 (1.55)	29 (2.0)
Estates	155SR x 13	21 (1.48)	25 (1.76)	24 (1.69)	34 (2.39)
Chevanne	155SR x 13	21 (1.48)	25 (1.76)	24 (1.69)	34 (2.39)

A — *Up to 3 occupants or equivalent*
B — *Maximum load*
Tyre pressures given in lbf/in^2 (kgf/cm^2)
Note: *M + S (mud and snow) winter tyres may be fitted in which case the above tyre pressures should be increased by 3.0 lbf/in^2 (0.2 kgf/cm^2)*

---

3 Engine

Cylinder head gasket — installation
1 Contrary to the instructions given in Chapter 1, Section 34, it is now recommended that a 1 to 2 mm diameter bead of jointing compound (Hylomar PL 32/M) is applied to the upper left-hand face of the cylinder block along the outer push rod rail, and also along the outer edge of the cylinder head gasket upper face in the same vicinity.
2 Always tighten the head bolts in the sequence given in Chapter 1.

Engine compression ratio — changes
3 During April/May 1977 the cylinder head fitted to new cars was modified, resulting in the compression ratio being changed from 9.2 : 1, to 8.7 : 1; further details are given in the Specifications at the beginning of this Supplement.

Oil pump — refitting
4 As from engine number 1815809 (October/November 1977) the oil pump slot (Chapter 1, Section 33) is no longer offset, and a revised installation procedure is necessary.
5 Carry out the instructions given in Chapter 1, Section 33, Paragraph

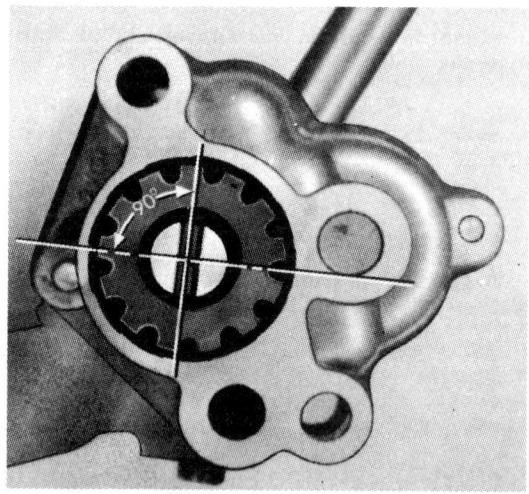

Fig. 13.2. Oil pump drive spindle position prior to installation (Sec 3)

1, then turn the oil pump drive gear until the drive spindle takes up the position shown in Fig. 13.2.
6 Fit the oil pump to the crankcase and check that, with the oil pump bolts inserted, the engagement to the camshaft has caused the spindle slot to turn to a position within the limits shown in Fig. 13.3 when viewed from above. If not, withdraw the oil pump and turn the spindle slightly so that the position will be correct when the oil pump is next inserted.

Crankcase ventilation system — changes
7 As from engine number 1817784 (October/November 1977) the crankcase ventilation system has been revised as shown in Fig. 13.4.
8 In addition to the maintenance procedure given in Chapter 1, Section 20, the combined air breather/oil filler cap should be periodically removed and cleaned out.

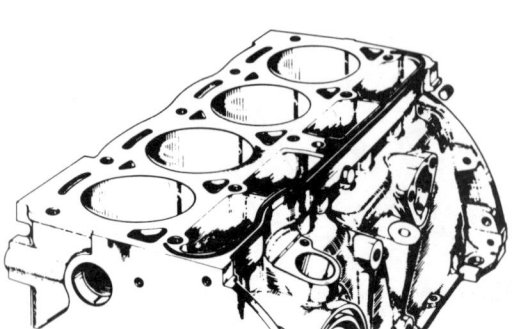

Fig. 13.1. Jointing compound location on engine cylinder block (Sec 3)

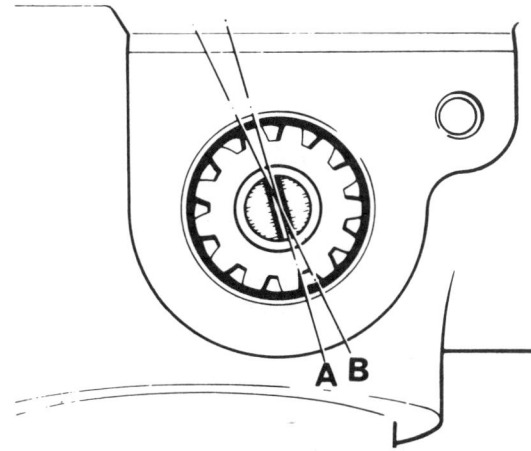

Fig. 13.3 Limits of oil pump spindle position (A to B) after installation (Sec 3)

Fig. 13.4. Modified crankcase ventilation system (Sec 3)

1   Manifold to rocker cover hose
2   Air cleaner to oil filler/breather cap
3   Oil filler cap

Engine rear mounting — general
9   Chevette models having a chassis number from FY 107261 onwards are fitted with extra spacers between the engine rear mounting cross-member and the underbody brackets. This effectively lowers the gearbox and allows oil to reach the rear cover bush; the spacers must always be fitted in their correct locations otherwise the life of the bush will be shortened.

Piston rings — changes
10   As from and including engine number 1739037, the ring fitted to the central groove of the piston has been modified and is now chamfered on its upper, inner edge. It is imperative that the ring is installed in the correct groove with the chamfer uppermost.

Crankshaft centre main bearing — changes
11   As from engine number 2111239 (December 1980) the crankshaft centre main bearing shells both incorporate flanged thrust washers whereas before only the upper shell incorporated the thrust washers. The new bearing shells can be fitted to earlier models if required.

Crankshaft rear main bearing cap — examination
12   The crankshaft rear main bearing cap incorporates an oil drain hole and if this becomes blocked, oil leakage may occur through the rear main oil seal. For this reason it is recommended that the oil drain hole is checked for obstruction whenever the sump is removed or the crankshaft rear oil seal renewed.

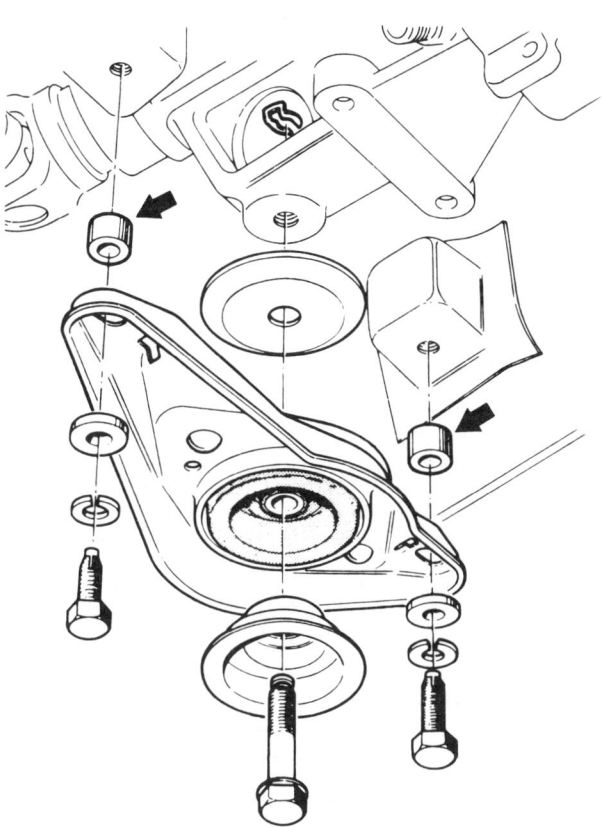

Fig. 13.5. Modified engine rear mounting showing the additional spacers (arrowed) (Sec 3)

Engine (automatic transmission models) — removal and refitting
13   Due to the weight consideration, the engine on automatic transmission models should be removed without the transmission.
14   The procedure is similar to that described in Chapter 1, Section 7 with the following exceptions:

   a) Remove the radiator with reference to Section 4 of this Supplement
   b) Unbolt the transmission front cover to expose the torque converter. Mark the driveplate and torque converter in relation to each other, then remove the driveplate-to-torque converter bolts. It will be necessary to turn the engine crankshaft with a spanner on the crankshaft pulley bolt in order to reach all of the bolts. On some models it will also be necessary to unbolt the engine-to-transmission brace
   c) Unscrew and remove the bolts securing the transmission to the engine then support the transmission with a trolley jack
   d) When separating the engine from the transmission, the torque converter must be kept firmly engaged with the transmission oil pump
   e) Refitting is a reversal of removal, but make sure that the torque converter keyway is fully engaged with the transmission oil pump drivegear tongues, and rotate the converter to check for free movement before fitting the engine

Driveplate (automatic transmission models) — description
15   On automatic transmission models a driveplate is fitted instead of the flywheel. Removal and refitting procedures are identical to those for the flywheel but it is not possible to renew the starter ring gear.

4 Cooling system

Viscous fan unit — description

1 Some models manufactured from 1981 on are equipped with a temperature-sensitive viscous fan unit. In order to remove this unit it is necessary to use Vauxhall tool No KM2024 or a similar cranked spanner.

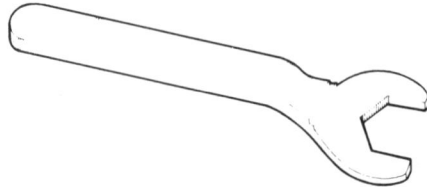

Fig. 13.6. Vauxhall tool number KM 2024 (Sec 4)

Radiator (automatic transmission models) — removal and refitting

2 On automatic transmission models a transmission oil cooler is incorporated into the bottom of the radiator.
3 Before removing the radiator, drain the fluid from the automatic transmission as described in Section 9, and unscrew the supply and return hoses. Take particular care to prevent foreign matter from entering the hoses and radiator otherwise serious damage may be caused to the automatic transmission.
4 After refitting the radiator fill the automatic transmission with the specified fluid as described in Section 9.

5 Carburation; fuel and exhaust systems

Air cleaner — description and testing

1 Models manufactured from 1980 on are equipped with a modified air cleaner incorporating additional internal air vanes and a new dual-acting temperature sensor valve.
2 The new sensor valve ensures that the intake air is temperature controlled even under heavy acceleration or at high speeds, whereas the previous sensor was not effective under these conditions.
3 The primary function test of the modified air cleaner is as given in Chapter 3 except that the closed temperature is 109°F (43°C), and the opening temperature between 109 and 135°F (43 and 57°C).
4 In order to carry out the secondary function test a vacuum pump is required. With the ambient temperature below 52°F (11°C) connect the vacuum pump to the brass outlet on the sensor. A vacuum of 20 in Hg should close the valve. Repeat the test with the ambient temperature above 95°F (35°C); the valve should remain open.
5 Make sure that the hose from the sensor plastic outlet is always connected to the inlet manifold, and the hose from the brass outlet is connected to the vacuum motor.

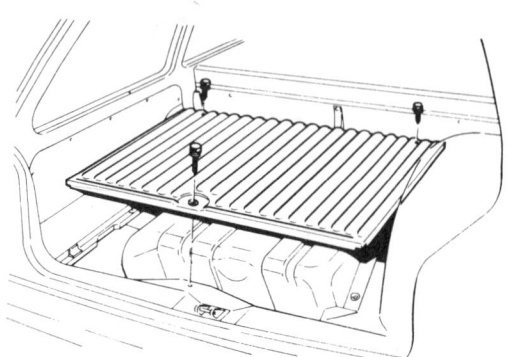

Fig. 13.8. Removing cargo floor on Estate and Chevanne models (Sec 5)

Fuel pump — modification

6 Chevette engines manufactured after February 1976 (engine number 1637850 on) are fitted with a modified fuel pump having a vertical outlet together with a flexible pipe and screw-type clips. An identical connection is fitted to the carburettor end of the fuel supply pipe.

Fuel tank (Chevette Estate and Chevanne) — removal, servicing and refitting

7 Lift the tailgate and remove the cargo floor by unscrewing the three self-tapping bolts.
8 Disconnect the fuel outlet pipe (no drain plug is fitted) and let the fuel drain from the tank into a suitable container.
9 Disconnect the fuel tank vent pipes from the top of the tank.
10 Removal of the fuel tank is now identical to the procedure given in paragraphs 6 to 9 inclusive of Chapter 3, Section 6.
11 Installation of the fuel tank is a reversal of removal.

Fuel tank (Saloon models) — removal, servicing and refitting

12 Open the boot lid then remove the tank trim board by turning the bottom retainers through 90°, and withdrawing the board from the upper clips.
13 Disconnect the fuel outlet pipe (no drain plug is fitted) and let the fuel drain from the tank into a suitable container.
14 Unclip and disconnect the vent pipe from the fuel tank.
15 Removal of the fuel tank is now identical to the procedure given in paragraphs 6 to 9 inclusive of Chapter 3, Section 6.
16 Refitting of the fuel tank is a reversal of removal.

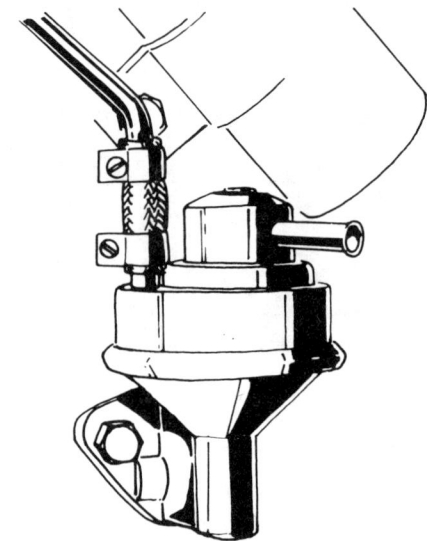

Fig. 13.7. Modified fuel pump (Sec 5)

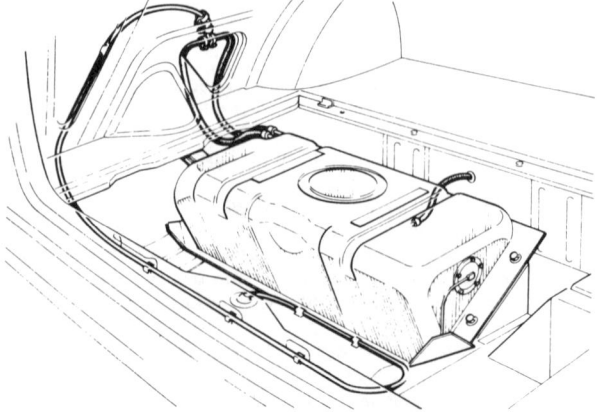

Fig. 13.9. Fuel tank, outlet pipe, and vent pipe on Estate and Chevanne models (Sec 5)

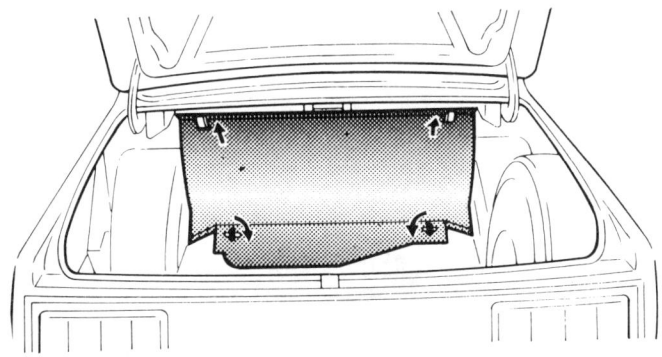

Fig. 13.10. Fuel tank trim board on Saloon models (Sec 5)

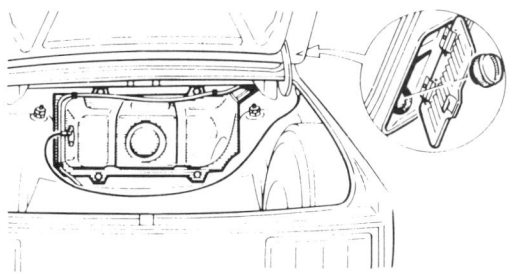

Fig. 13.11. Fuel tank location on Saloon models (Sec 5)

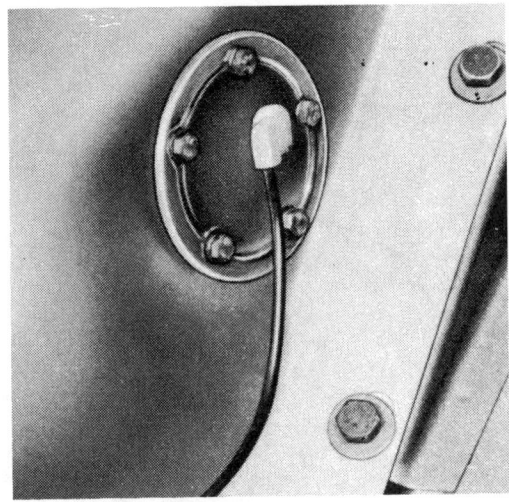

Fig. 13.12. Fuel tank transmitter unit location on Estate and Chevanne models (Sec 5)

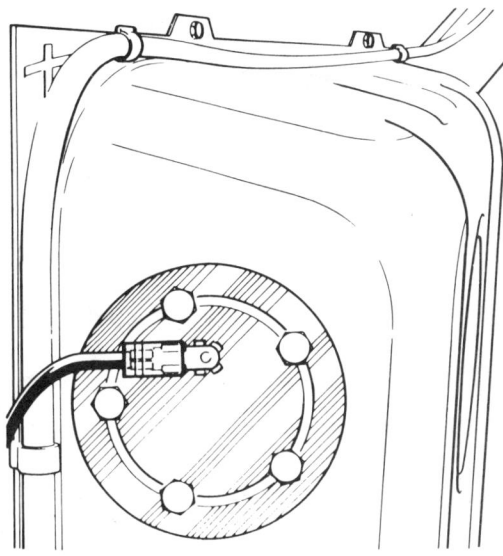

Fig. 13.13. Fuel tank transmitter unit location on Saloon models (Sec 5)

Fuel tank transmitter unit (Chevette Estate and Chevanne) — removal and refitting

17 The transmitter unit is located on the upper right-hand side of the fuel tank. First carry out the instructions in paragraphs 7 and 8 of this Section, then disconnect the transmitter unit lead.

18 The remaining procedure is as given in Chapter 3, Section 7 except that the transmitter terminal must be horizontal and pointing toward the rear of the vehicle.

Fuel tank transmitter unit (Saloon models) — removal and refitting

19 The transmitter unit is located on the left-hand side of the fuel tank. First carry out the instructions in paragraphs 12 and 13 of this Section, then disconnect the transmitter unit lead.

20 The remaining procedure is as given in Chapter 3, Section 7 except that the transmitter terminal must be horizontal and pointing toward the front of the vehicle.

Accelerator control — adjustment

21 On later right-hand drive models, the accelerator pedal position (not the cable adjustment) may be set after adjusting the cable by changing the length of the adjustable link shown in Fig. 13.14. The clamp bolt as described in Chapter 3 has been discontinued.

22 On later left-hand drive models, an adjustable stop is fitted to the top of the accelerator pedal. With the pedal fully released and in the idle position, the stop should be adjusted so that there is a small amount of slack in the cable.

Carburettor — modifications (general)

23 In accordance with EEC regulations, carburettors manufactured after October 1976 have the idle trimming screw sealed with a nylon sleeve and metal cap which are code numbered to indicate when adjustment has been made. Eventually it is envisaged that authorised garages only will be permitted to remove the seal and make adjustments, although currently there is no such legislation, and the owner may make an adjustment as described in Chapter 3.

24 In conjunction with the modifications given in the previous paragraph, the carburettor float chamber housing has been extended over the jet (mixture) adjuster, and in order to make any adjustment, a special castellated tool is required; the tool should be available at most accessory shops or motor factors.

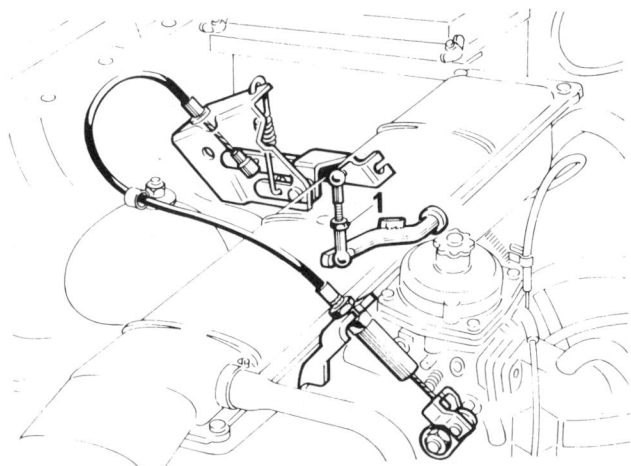

Fig. 13.14. Accelerator linkage adjustment (1) on late models. (Sec 5)

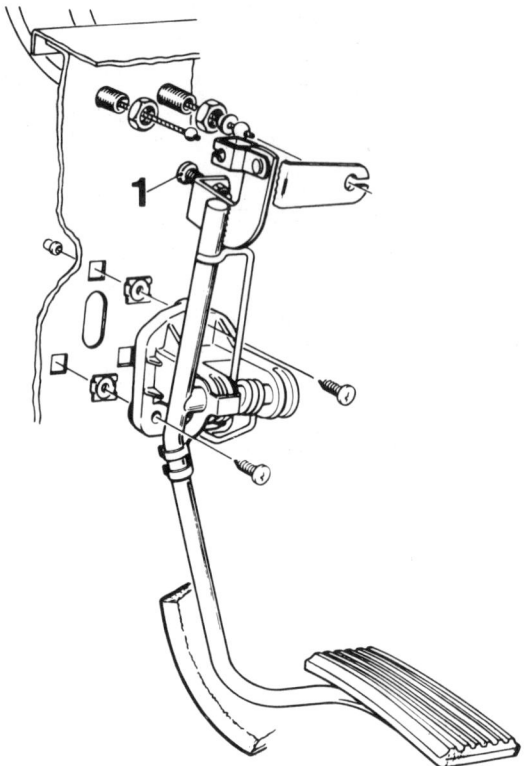

Fig. 13.15. Adjustable stop (1) fitted to accelerator pedal on late left-hand drive models (Sec 5)

Note that the automatic transmission detent cable is shown. As from 1981 models the accelerator pedal clevis is modified.

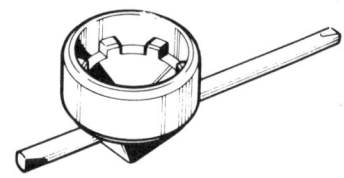

Fig. 13.17. Carburettor jet adjusting tool (Sec 5)

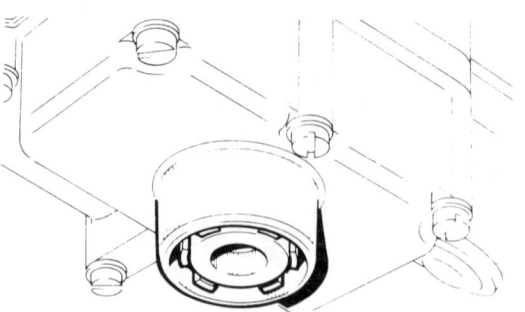

Fig. 13.16. The modified extended carburettor float chamber housing showing the slotted jet adjustment (Sec 5)

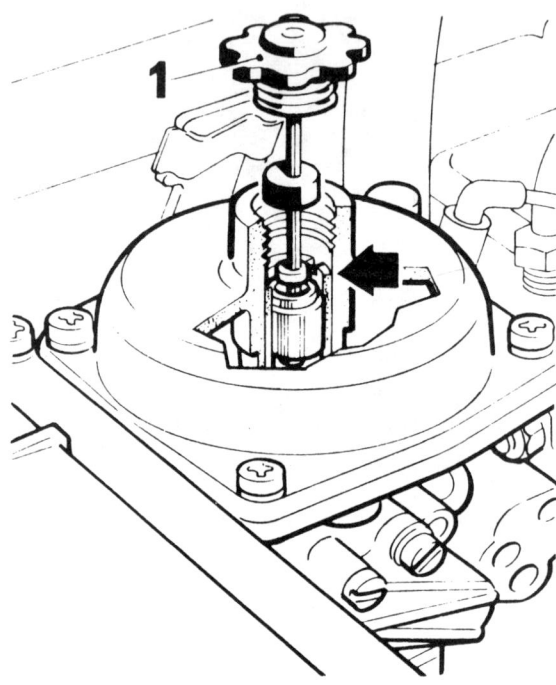

Fig. 13.18. Modified carburettor air valve (arrowed) and damper (Sec 5)

25 Chevette and Chevanne engines manufactured after October 1977 (engine number 1817784 on) are fitted with a carburettor having revised specifications as given in the Specifications at the beginning of this Chapter; a modified temperature compensator is also fitted.

26 As from 1980 models the two position adjustment on the cold start device has been discontinued, but in addition the air valve damper now incorporates a seal as shown in Fig. 13.18 to reduce oil loss from the damper.

27 As from chassis number KX 147323 (August 1981) a vent hose has been fitted to the carburettor in order to transfer any fuel over-spill away from the engine compartment. Besides the safety factor, the hose prevents the possibility of fuel fumes entering the passenger compartment.

Carburettor metering needle — modifications and adjustment
28 As from April 1977 an adjustable metering needle has been progressively fitted to Zenith/Stromberg carburettors, originally for the purpose of calibrating the fuel/air mixture during manufacture. Should it be found necessary to adjust the mixture on these early carburettors, the needle should be initially set so that the nylon washer is flush with the bottom face of the piston.

29 Where it is found that the idle trim screw (see Chapter 3, Section 11) requires turning more than four complete turns off of its seat, the metering needle should be positioned further into the piston in order

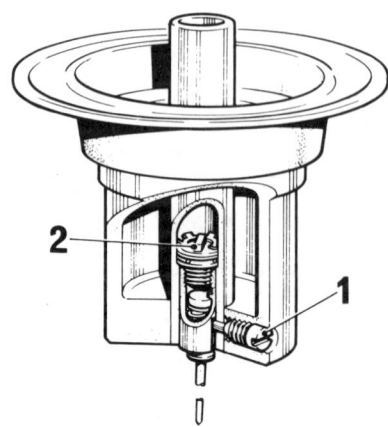

Fig. 13.19. Air valve with adjustable metering needle (Sec 5)

1 Grub screw   *2 Adjusting screw*

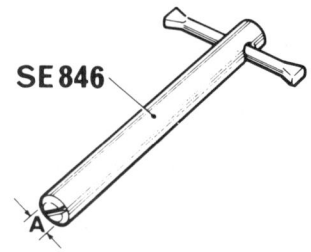

Fig. 13.20. Metering needle adjusting tool (Sec 5)

A = 0.24 in (6.0 mm)
Slot width = 0.08 in (2.0 mm)
Slot depth = 0.06 in (1.6 mm)

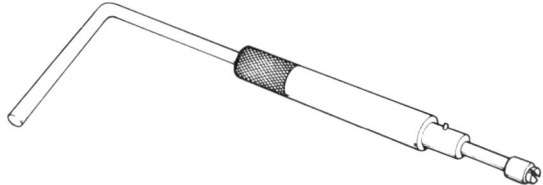

Fig. 13.21. Vauxhall tool number KM 2054 (sec 5)

to enrich the mixture. Similarly if it is found that the idle turn screw requires turning completely onto its seat, the needle should be moved out of the piston to weaken the mixture.

30 To adjust the metering needle, remove the air valve piston and loosen the needle retaining grub screw. Using tool number SE 846 (see Fig. 13.20) or a similar tool in the piston guide tube, turn the adjusting screw until the needle is set correctly then tighten the grub screw. Keep the adjusting screw pressed against the shoulder in the piston guide tube while turning it.

31 To remove the needle, first fully unscrew the locating grub screw, then turn the adjusting screw anti-clockwise until it is disengaged from the needle housing. On installation it should be remembered that the needle must be biased towards the air intake side of the carburettor.

32 Subsequent to tool number SE 846, tool number KM 2054 (see Fig. 13.21) has been developed in order to adjust the metering needle with the air valve in position in the carburettor. The needle retaining grub screw now incorporates a spring-loaded plunger which retains the needle housing in its correct position while allowing the needle to move up and down when the adjusting screw is turned.

33 To adjust the metering needle using tool number KM 2054, remove the hydraulic damper and insert the tool so that it engages the adjusting screw and the groove in the piston guide tube. Hold the knurled section stationary and turn the angled handle clockwise to enrich the mixture, or anti-clockwise to weaken it. It is essential to hold the knurled section stationary in order to prevent possible damage to the air valve diaphragm.

Single resonator exhaust system

34 From mid-1982 an exhaust system having one silencer and only one resonator is fitted as original equipment.

35 When removing or refitting the rear section of the exhaust system, it may be necessary to lower the back axle to provide sufficient clearance.

---

6 Ignition system

Distributor – modifications

1 Two modified distributors have been introduced to the 1256 cc engine fitted to Chevette and Chevanne models.

2 As from engine number 1639763 (December 1975) the new distributor has a different dwell angle and vacuum advance; details of the new dwell angle are given in the Specifications at the beginning of this Chapter. The distributor can be identified by the pear-shaped vacuum advance capsule as compared with the previous dome-shaped capsule. As from engine number 2163880 a Bosch distributor may be fitted as an alternative to the Delco-Remy type. Refer to the Specifications

Fig. 13.22. Correct fitted position of the distributor rotor (modified version) (Sec 6)

for the dwell angle and points gap.

3 To coincide with the oil pump modification described in Section 3 of this Chapter, the distributor drive shaft tongue is no longer offset; the distributor installation procedure is therefore different.

4 First turn the crankshaft until number 1 piston (nearest the radiator) is on its compression stroke with the crankshaft pulley pointer opposite the 9° BTDC mark.

5 Turn the rotor so that it points to the vacuum advance capsule, then install the distributor as described in Chapter 4 of this manual. The distributor and rotor should be positioned as shown in Fig. 13.22 when correctly fitted.

Contact breaker points -- general

6 It should be noted that all new contact breaker points are sprayed with a special anti-corrosive oil, and it is important to remove this coating with a fuel or methylated spirit moistened cloth prior to fitting the points to the distributor.

Spark plugs – changes

7 As from April 1978, the type of spark plugs fitted to all engines (with the exception of those equipped with an exhaust emission device) has been changed; further details are given in the Specifications at the beginning of this Supplement, and the spark plug gap remains as previously specified.

---

7 Clutch

Release bearing – modification

1 As from chassis numbers KX 150228 (RHD models) and LX 100101 (LHD models) a self-aligning clutch release bearing has been fitted. The new bearing is in constant contact with the clutch diaphragm spring and consequently the release fork return spring is no longer fitted. A torsion spring is now incorporated at the clutch pedal pivot to provide residual tension on the clutch cable.

2 The modified release bearing may be fitted to earlier models if required.

Clutch – adjustment

3 In conjunction with the modification described in paragraph 1, there is no longer any release fork free movement and the cable should be adjusted so that the clutch pedal travel is a total of 4 in (101 mm). This will normally bring the clutch pedal level with the brake pedal; as the clutch disc linings wear, the pedal will move upward thus increasing the pedal movement and it will then become necessary to adjust the cable.

---

8 Manual gearbox

Gearbox – removal and refitting

1 Some models are now equipped with a centre console which must be removed before removing the gearbox. The console is secured by three crosshead screws as shown in Fig. 13.23.

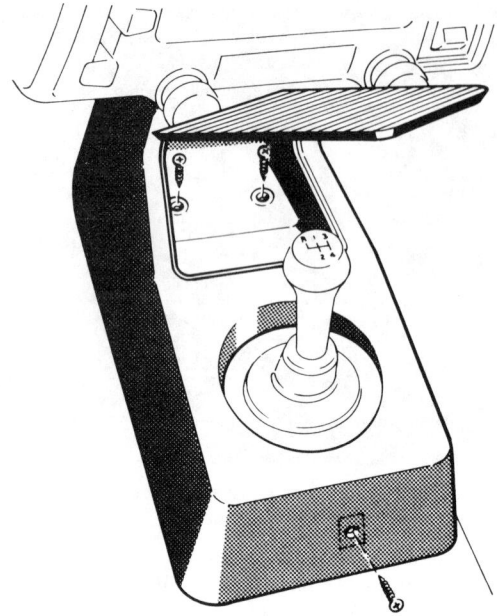

Fig. 13.23. Centre console screw locations (Sec 8)

4   A slightly weaker selector shaft detent spring is fitted.
5   The eccentric pin on the rear of the selector shaft is now part of the selector shaft and cannot therefore be removed or adjusted. The plastic insulator sleeve, which acts as a bearing surface for the gear lever, may be prised from the selector shaft with a screwdriver.
6   The gear lever ball is now retained by an upper and lower plastic seat, the upper seat being spring tensioned by the retainer. When fitting the gear lever, the seats and the insulator should be lubricated with a little grease.
7   A modified gear lever housing cover and reverse lamp switch have been fitted in conjunction with the modification described in paragraph 5.
8   As from late 1980 the gear lever has been modified as shown in Fig. 13.25. The rubber gaiter is now positioned further up the gear lever in order to eliminate any tension which might pull the lever out of gear.

9   Automatic transmission

Automatic transmission — general description

1   The GM three-speed automatic transmission is of the planetary gear set type, incorporating three multiple disc clutches and a single brake band to provide three forward speeds and reverse. Automatic gear selection is controlled by road speed, engine vacuum, and accelerator position. A three element torque converter transmits drive from the engine to the automatic transmission.
2   Due to the complex nature of the transmission, servicing should be

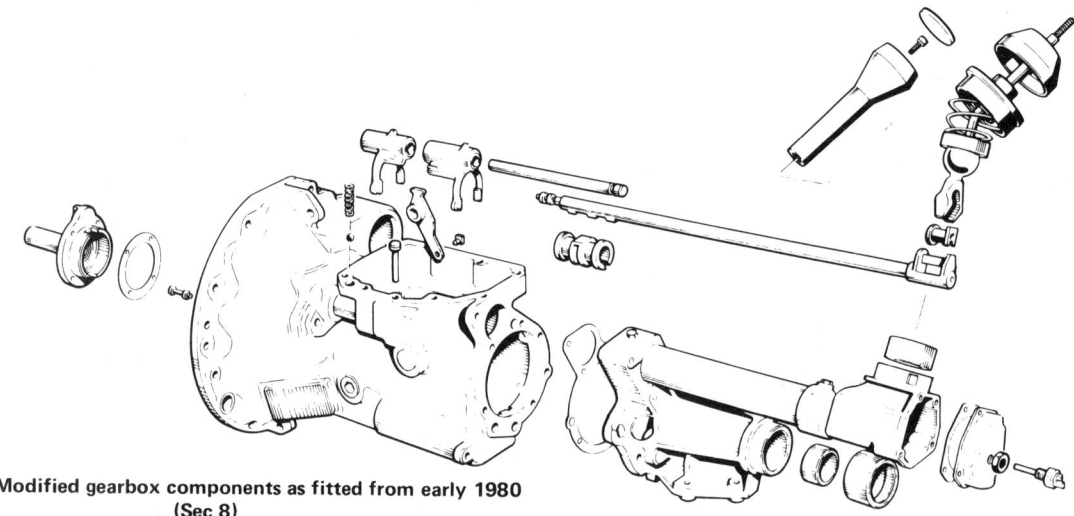

Fig. 13.24. Modified gearbox components as fitted from early 1980 (Sec 8)

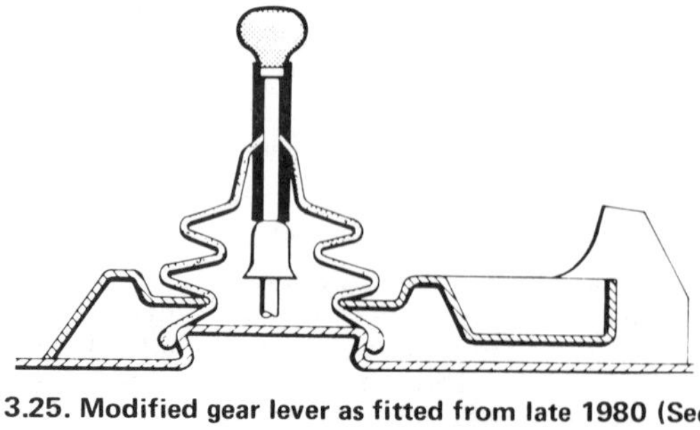

confined to the procedures described in the following paragraphs. If the unit develops a fault which cannot be rectified by the owner, it is essential that a suitably equipped garage or transmission specialist checks the transmission while it is still installed in the car.

Routine maintenance

3   The automatic transmission fluid level should be checked at each engine oil change. To do this, first make sure that the transmission is at normal operating temperature (driving the car for 10 to 15 miles is normally necessary).
4   With the car on level ground select 'P' or 'N' and allow the engine to idle. Remove the dipstick, wipe it clean, then reinsert it until the cap is seated. Remove the dipstick again and check that the fluid level is at or near the 'F' (full) or 'MAX' mark.
5   If necessary top up the fluid level with the specified fluid but note that the transmission should not be overfilled. The quantity of fluid necessary to raise the level from 'ADD' to 'F' or from 'MIN' to 'MAX' is 1 pint, and the fluid should be poured in through the dipstick tube.
6   On some models the dipstick incorporates cold level markings — checking the level must still be carried out as described in paragraphs 4 and 5 but use the lower temperature markings.

Fig. 13.25. Modified gear lever as fitted from late 1980 (Sec 8)

Gearbox — modifications

2   As from early 1980 several modifications have been made to the gearbox.
3   The eccentric adjusting pin for the reverse gear striking lever is not now adjustable, and the gearbox casing incorporates a blanking plug. The procedure given in Chapter 6. Section 8, paragraph 6 no longer applies.

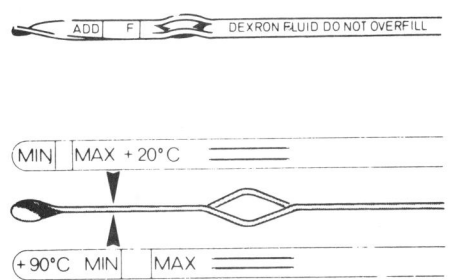

Fig. 13.26. Alternative automatic transmission dipsticks (Sec 9)

7 Occasionally check the security of all nuts and bolts on the transmission unit, and keep the exterior clean and free from mud or oil to prevent overheating.

8 Every 24 000 miles (40 000 km) or 2 years the transmission fluid should be renewed and the low band servo adjusted. Under heavy operating conditions this work should be carried out earlier.

9 Unscrew the drain plug and drain the fluid into a suitable container; take precautions to prevent scalding if the transmission is warm.

10 Unbolt the oil pan from the bottom of the transmission and remove the gasket.

11 Unbolt the oil pump suction screen and remove the gasket.

12 Unbolt the brake band servo cover and remove the gasket.

13 Loosen the locknut on the brake band servo piston then, using an

Allen key and torque wrench, tighten the adjusting bolt to 37 lbf in (4.2 Nm). Back off the bolt exactly five turns then tighten the locknut while holding the sleeve stationary.

14 Fit the brake band servo cover together with a new gasket.

15 Fit a new oil pump suction screen together with a new gasket. Do not attempt to clean the old screen.

16 Fit the oil pan together with a new gasket and check that the drain plug is tight.

17 Fill the transmission through the dipstick tube with the specified fluid, then check and top up the level if necessary as described in paragraphs 3 to 6.

Automatic transmission — removal and refitting

18 Position the car over a pit or on ramps. Alternatively jack up the car sufficiently high to allow the removal of the transmission, and support it with axle stands. Apply the handbrake.

19 Working under the car, unscrew the drain plug and drain the fluid into a suitable container; take precautions to prevent scalding if the transmission is warm.

20 Refit and tighten the drain plug, then unscrew the unions and disconnect the oil cooler hoses.

21 Remove the spring clip and clevis pin, and disconnect the selector lever linkage from the transmission selector arm.

22 Remove the propeller shaft as described in Chapter 7 and Section 10 of this Supplement.

23 Disconnect the speedometer cable from the transmission rear extension by unscrewing the collar.

24 Disconnnect the detent cable as follows. Unbolt and remove the retaining bracket, pull the ferrule from the transmission, and slide the cable stop from the detent valve.

25 Disconnect the vacuum hose from the modulator valve.

26 Unbolt the transmission front cover to expose the torque converter.

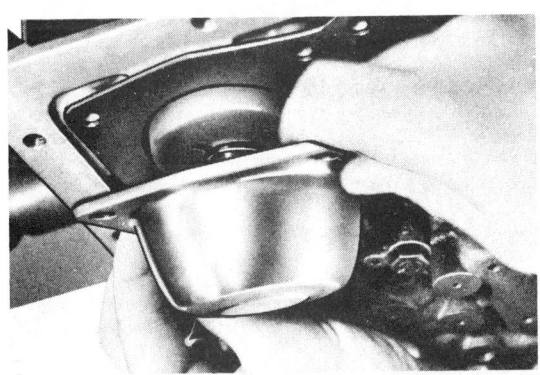

Fig. 13.27. Removing the automatic transmission brake band servo cover (Sec 9)

Fig. 13.28. Adjusting the automatic transmission brake band servo (Sec 9)

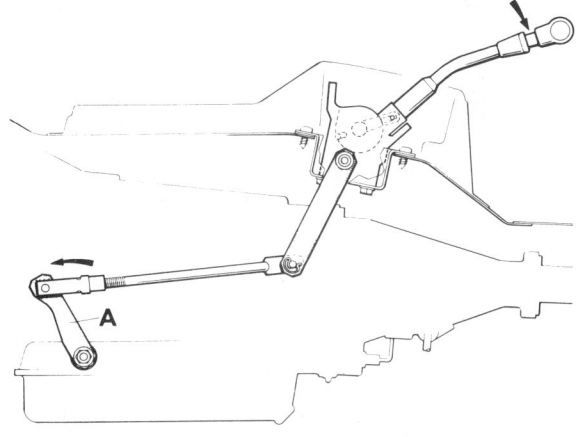

Fig. 13.29. Automatic transmission selector lever and linkage (Sec 9)

A *Transmission selector arm*

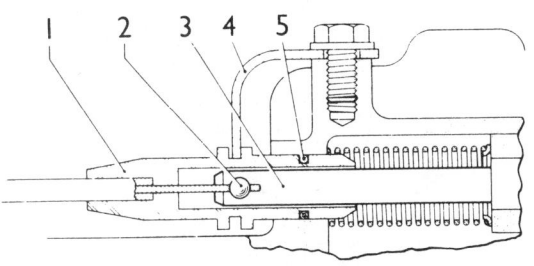

Fig. 13.30. Sectional view of the automatic transmission detent cable to transmission connection (Sec 9)

1 *Ferrule*	4 *Bracket*
2 *Cable stop*	5 *O-ring*
3 *Detent valve*	

Mark the driveplate and torque converter in relation to each other, then remove the driveplate to torque converter bolts. It will be necessary to turn the engine crankshaft with a spanner on the crankshaft pulley bolt in order to reach all of the bolts. On some models it will also be necessary to unbolt the engine to transmission brace.

27 Disconnect the exhaust downpipes from the manifold.

28 Unscrew and remove the bolts securing the transmission to the

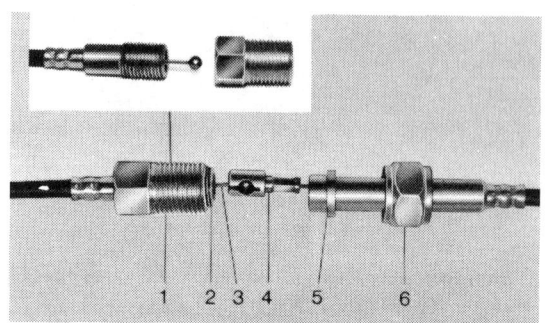

Fig. 13.31. Automatic transmission detent cable central connector (Sec 9)

1 Adjuster	4 Inner cable
2 Front cable	5 Flange
3 Inner cable	6 Locknut

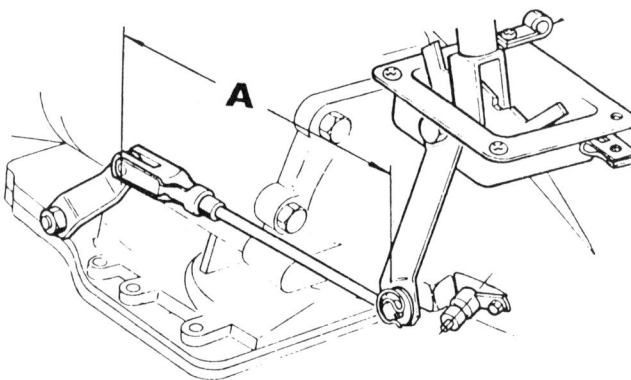

Fig. 13.32. Automatic transmission selector linkage adjustment

A   Adjustment dimension (see text)

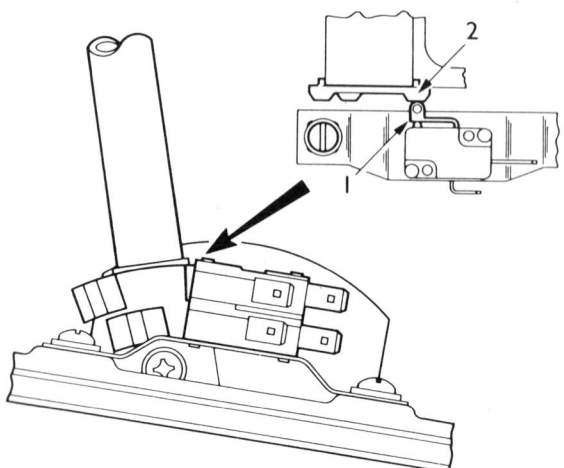

Fig. 13.33. Automatic transmission starter inhibitor switch roller (1) and lever rear cam (2) (Sec 9)

engine, then support the engine beneath the sump with a trolley jack and block of wood.

29 Due to the combined weight of the transmission and torque converter (approximately 110 lb/50 kg) it is recommended that a further trolley jack is positioned beneath the transmission to support it. An assistant will also be required.

30 Unbolt the transmission rear mounting from the body.

31 While keeping the torque converter firmly engaged with the transmission oil pump, carefully lower the jacks and withdraw the transmission from the engine. To prevent the ingress of foreign matter, plug the oil cooler hoses and the apertures in the transmission.

32 Refitting is a reversal of removal, but make sure that the torque converter keyway is fully engaged with the transmission oil pump drivegear tongues and rotate the converter to check for free movement. Make sure that the driveplate is correctly aligned with the torque converter. Adjust the detent cable and selector linkage as described in paragraphs 33 to 37 and 38 to 43, then fill the transmission with the specified fluid and top it up as described in paragraphs 3 to 6.

Automatic transmission detent cable — adjustment

33 The detent cable is in two parts and adjustment is made at the central connector (see Fig. 13.31).

34 Fully unscrew the adjuster locknut, then screw the adjuster onto the front cable until the inner threaded portion protrudes.

35 Make sure that the inner cables are connected together correctly then have an assistant fully depress the accelerator pedal and hold it down.

36 Pull the outer cables apart as far as possible and, while keeping them in this position, turn the adjuster until the inner threaded portion is in contact with the flange on the rear cable.

37 Back off the adjuster half a turn then tighten the locknut.

Automatic transmission selector linkage — adjustment

38 Jack up the front of the car and support it on axle stands. Apply the handbrake.

39 Move the selector lever to the 'P' (park) position.

40 If the selector linkage is disconnected from the transmission, move the transmission arm to the rearmost detent.

41 Adjust the linkage to obtain a dimension of 12.30 in (312.5 mm) as shown in Fig. 13.32.

42 Tighten the adjustment locknut (if fitted), then smear some multi-purpose grease on the clevis pin and slot, and reposition the rubber boot.

43 Lower the car to the ground.

Starter inhibitor switch — description and adjustment

44 The starter inhibitor switch is located in the selector lever assembly; its purpose is to confine starting of the engine to positions 'P' (park) and 'N' (neutral).

45 To adjust the switch first remove the console from the floor.

46 Move the selector lever to position 'P' (park), then adjust the switch position so that the upper roller is depressed by the rear cam on the lever.

47 Check that the starter will only operate in position 'P' (park) and 'N' (neutral).

48 Refit the console.

Automatic transmission extension housing oil seal — renewal

49 Remove the propeller shaft as described in Chapter 7 and Section 10 of this Supplement.

50 Extract the oil seal from the extension housing using a hooked tool or screwdriver.

51 Wipe clean the housing then drive the new seal in until flush using a metal tube or block of wood.

Automatic transmission — stall test

52 The stall test is primarily to test the torque converter. The engine and transmission must be at normal operating temperature before commencing the test.

53 Connect a tachometer to the engine and start the engine. With all brakes applied, select 'D' (drive) and fully depress the accelerator pedal. Note the maximum engine speed then release the pedal — the test must be completed in 10 seconds otherwise the transmission may overheat.

54 If the stall speed is considerably below that given in Specifications, then the engine may require tuning, the torque converter one-way

clutch may be slipping, or the stator support may be fractured.
55 If the stall speed is considerably more than that given in Specifications, then the torque converter oil supply may be faulty, the low band servo may need adjusting (see paragraphs 8 to 17), or the torque converter type is incorrect.

10 Propeller shaft

Tension spring (manual gearbox models) — modification

1 As from chassis number FY 131654 (August/September 1976), the tension spring is no longer located inside the sliding sleeve bore but is increased in diameter and locates against the sliding sleeve front face.
2 Should a new type propeller shaft be fitted to a vehicle bearing a chassis number prior to that given in paragraph 1, it is imperative to install the new larger diameter tension spring.

Propeller shaft (automatic transmission models) — general

3 The propeller shaft fitted to automatic transmission models, although similar to the manual gearbox version, does not incorporate a tension spring.
4 The removal and refitting procedure is similar to that described in Chapter 7, but instead of engaging a gear, the selector should be moved to position 'P' (park). Do not lubricate the output shaft splines with mineral gear oil — use only the specified automatic transmission fluid, and make sure that foreign matter does not enter the transmission.

11 Rear axle

Wheel studs — modification

1 During the latter part of 1976 modified wheel studs were introduced to Chevette and Chevanne models. Fig. 13.34 illustrates the previous and modified types.
2 The original wheel studs have 45 splines which locate with corresponding splines in the axle shafts, and the studs are peened to the axle shaft. The modified wheel studs have 31 splines and the axle shaft holes are plain; as the studs are pressed into the axle shaft, the splines are formed on the hole perimeter. The later type studs are not peened to the shaft.
3 Due to the design of each type of wheel stud, each must only be fitted to its corresponding axle shaft.
4 To facilitate fitting the new type wheel studs, a suitable length of tubing used as a spacer together with a wheel nut, can be used to draw the stud into the shaft.

Pinion extension housing mounting — modification

5 Chevette and Chevanne models manufactured from mid-1977 onwards are fitted with a modified single piece pinion extension housing rubber mounting incorporating an integral steel sleeve.
6 The procedure given in Chapter 8, Section 6 regarding the mounting removal applies only to the original arrangement incorporating the double mounting and two bump stops.
7 To remove the modified mounting rubber, first unscrew and remove the two mounting bolts and withdraw the crossmember. It is necessary to saw through the steel sleeve in order to release the mounting from the pinion extension housing.
8 Press the new mounting on to the extension housing with the groove between the rubber lugs in line with the housing upper rib, until the end of the steel sleeve is flush with the housing end face.

Pinion extension housing damper — description

9 A two kilogram damper is fitted to the rear axle pinion extension housing on late models in order to reduce vibration. It is secured by a U-bolt and should be positioned 1.2 to 1.6 in (35 to 40 mm) to the rear of the crossmember as shown in Fig. 13.37.

12 Braking system

Brake calipers and disc pads — general

1 Minor changes have been made to the brake calipers and disc pads on Chevette models manufactured after December 1975, and it is important that a combination of old and new units should not occur on any one vehicle. For this reason when servicing either of these components on pre-December 1975 models, both front caliper units or all four front disc pads should be renewed.

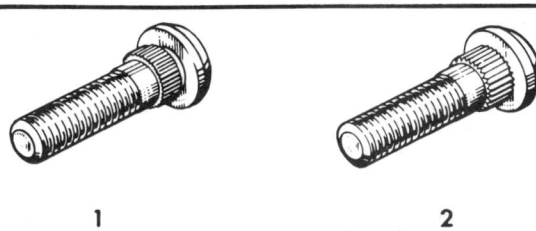

Fig. 13.34. Original (1) and modified (2) wheel studs (Sec 11)

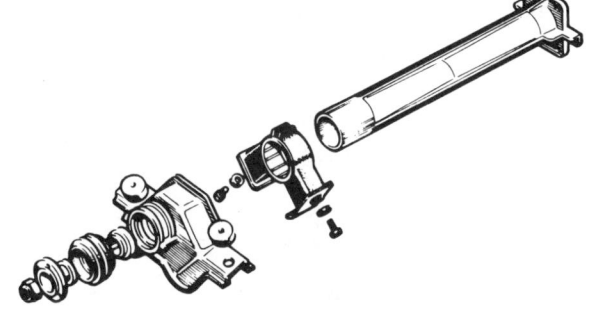

Fig. 13.35. The pinion extension housing mounting showing the modified rubber mounting with integral steel sleeve (Sec 11)

Fig. 13.36. Correct alignment of the pinion extension housing mounting rubber groove (arrowed) (Sec 11)

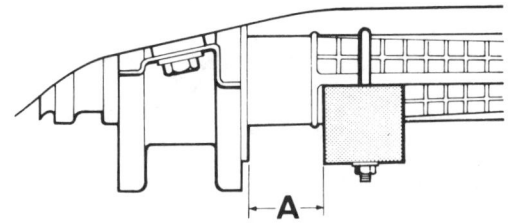

Fig. 13.37. Pinion extension housing damper (Sec 11)

A = 1.2 to 1.6 in (35 to 40 mm)

Disc brake pads — servicing

2   In order to assist the transfer of heat away from the disc pads, it is recommended that a small amount of Poly Butyl Cuprysil is smeared on to the pad backplate and shims during disc pad renewal. The compound should be available from most motor accessory shops.

Rear brakes — description

3   As from December 1975 the rear brakes are fitted with a modified self-adjusting mechanism. The friction type brake shoe adjusters are no longer fitted and therefore the references in Chapter 9 to the hexagon adjusters on the rear of the backplate do not apply.

4   The new mechanism comprises an adjustable strut fitted between the upper web of the forward shoe and the handbrake operating lever fitted to the rear shoe. When the footbrake is applied, any excessive slackness on the strut is automatically taken up by a ratchet mechanism mounted on the forward shoe which turns the adjustment nut and effectively lengthens the strut. This action continues on each application of the footbrake until the shoes are positioned correctly in relation to the drum. Note that the adjuster strut components are not interchangeable from side to side. The adjuster for the right-hand side of the car has a left-hand thread, and vice versa.

Rear brake shoes — removal and refitting

5   To remove the rear brake shoes, jack up the rear of the car and support it on axle stands. Chock the front wheels and remove the appropriate roadwheel(s).

6   Remove the retaining clips if fitted, and withdraw the brake drum after making sure that the handbrake is fully released. If difficulty is experienced, loosen the handbrake cable adjustment as described in Chapter 9; prise out the plug from the brake backplate and use a screwdriver to push the handbrake lever away from the shoe web.

7   Unhook the handbrake cable from the operating lever, then detach the adjustment operating lever and return spring from the forward shoe.

8   Release the front shoe from the backplate by depressing the steady spring cup and rotating it through 90°; remove the cup, spring and pin.

9   Lever the front shoe from the lower pedestal first, then from the wheel cylinder, and detach the return springs and adjustable strut.

10   Release the rear shoe from the backplate by depressing the steady spring cup and rotating it though 90° then removing the cup, spring and pin.

11   Lever the rear shoe from the lower pedestal and unhook both return springs.

12   Refitting the rear brake shoes is a reversal of the removal procedure, but the following additional points should be noted:

    a)   *Lightly smear the shoe contact points on the wheel cylinder, pedestal and backplate with approved brake grease*

    b)   *Make sure that the larger hooked end of the upper return spring is located in the rear brake shoe*

    c)   *If new shoes are being fitted it will be necessary to shorten the length of the upper strut before assembly to enable the brake drum to be fitted. To do this, simply turn the adjustment nut to reduce the number of visible threads*

    d)   *If the adjuster strut has been dismantled, make sure that the ratchet wheel has been refitted the right way round. This can be checked by making sure that the adjuster strut is lengthened by rising action of the adjustment operating lever*

    e)   *Before refitting the brake drum, check that the adjuster strut is located properly. On the leading shoe, the strut fork locates in a slot in the shoe web; on the trailing shoe, the fork locates around the handbrake operating lever, with the fork finger*

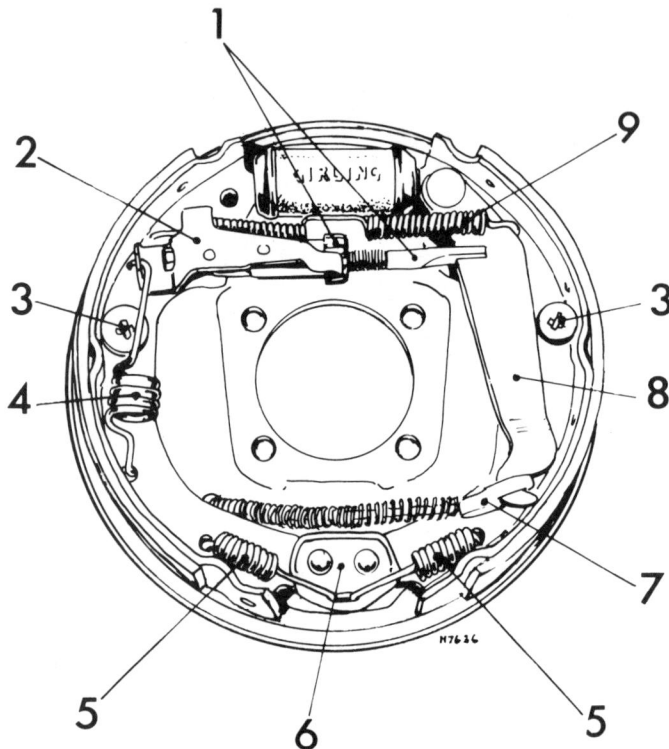

Fig. 13.38. Girling rear brake self-adjusting mechanism (Sec 12)

1 Self-adjusting strut	6 Lower shoe fixed pivot
2 Adjustment operating lever	7 Handbrake cable
3 Shoe support springs	8 Handbrake operating lever
4 Ratchet return springs	9 Upper shoe return spring
5 Lower shoe return springs	

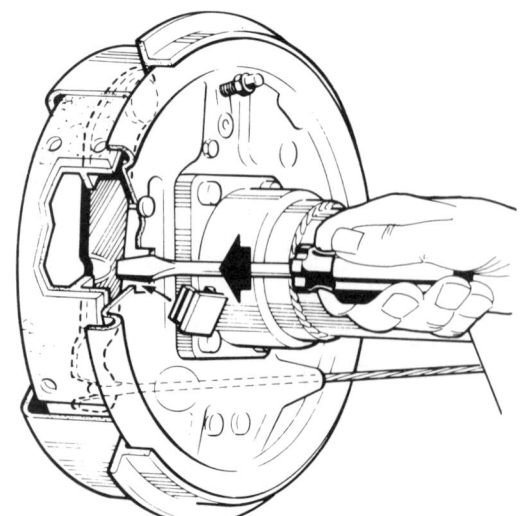

Fig. 13.39. Method of releasing the rear brake shoes (Sec 12)

Fig. 13.40. Removing the modified rear wheel cylinder (Sec 12)

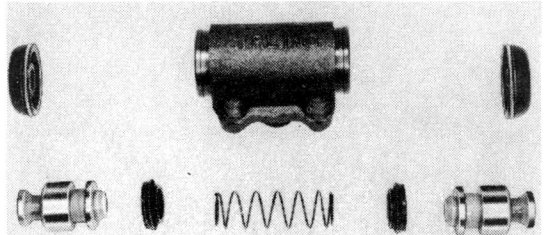

Fig. 13.41. Modified rear wheel cylinder components (Sec 12)

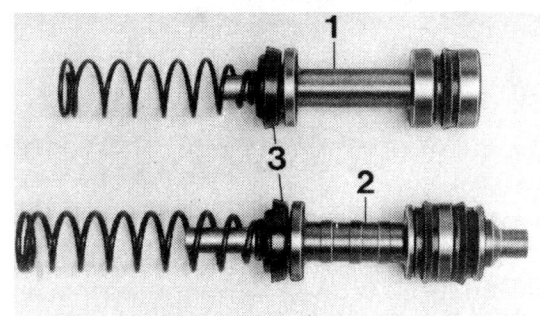

Fig. 13.43. Modified master cylinder pistons and seals (Sec 12)

1   Primary piston   2   Secondary piston   3   Front seals

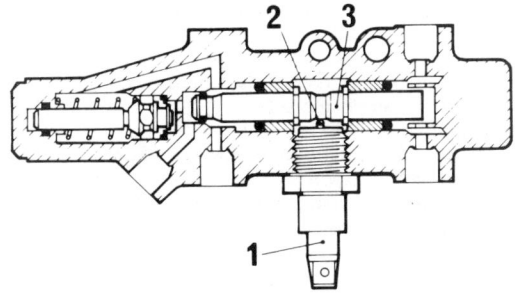

Fig. 13.45. Sectional view of the modified brake pressure regulating valve (Sec 12)

1   Warning switch   2   Plunger   3   Piston

which is hidden by the handbrake operating lever engaging in the slot in the rear shoe web. In order that the strut is not displaced when refitting the drum, it is advisable to extend the strut by rotating the ratchet wheel a few turns

f)   After refitting the brake drum and wheel as described in Chapter 9, depress the brake pedal a few times in order to adjust the brake shoes

g)   Adjust the handbrake as described in Chapter 9, Section 13

Rear wheel cylinder – description, removal, servicing and refitting

13   The modified wheel cylinders incorporated into the new self-adjusting rear brake system are similar to those described in Chapter 9 of this manual, the main difference being in the pistons.

14   To remove the wheel cylinder follow the instructions given in Chapter 9, Section 6 but, in order to release the brake shoes, place a screwdriver between the rear shoe web and the handbrake operating lever as shown in Fig. 13.40, or alternatively apply the handbrake a few notches.

15   Servicing the wheel cylinders is identical to the procedure given in Chapter 9 but ensure that the seals are assembled to the pistons with the smaller diameters facing inwards.

16   Refitting the wheel cylinders is a reversal of the removal procedure, with reference to Chapter 9, Section 6.

Fig. 13.42. Modified brake tandem master cylinder (Sec 12)

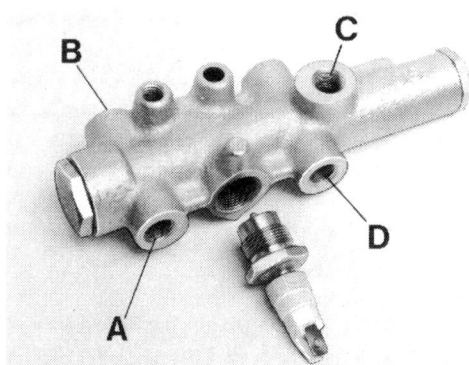

Fig. 13.44. Modified brake pressure regulating valve (Sec 12)

A   Fluid entry
B   Fluid exit to front brake calipers
C   Fluid exit to rear brakes
D   Fluid entry

Master cylinder – description, removal, servicing and refitting

17   As from December 1975 a modified tandem master cylinder is fitted to Chevette models which does not incorporate a brake pressure warning lamp actuator.

18   Removal of the master cylinder is similar to the procedure given in Chapter 9, Section 8, the main difference being the absence of the warning actuator leads.

19   To remove the fluid reservoir, extract the spring clips and retaining pins, then carefully prise out the two seals. The remaining servicing procedure is identical to that given in Chapter 9, although reference to Fig. 13.43 will reveal minor differences in the seals and pistons.

20   Refitting the master cylinder is a reversal of the removal procedure, with reference to Chapter 9, Section 8.

Pressure regulating valve – modification

21   As from December 1975 a modified pressure regulating valve is fitted to Chevette models. The new valve operates in a similar manner to the original unit described in Chapter 9, Section 9, but it now incorporates a brake pressure warning lamp actuator which warns the driver should either the front or rear independent brake circuit fail.

22   To remove the valve, disconnect the fluid lines and the warning actuator lead, then unscrew and remove the retaining bolt.

23   Refitting is a reversal of removal but the hydraulic system must be bled as described in Chapter 9, Section 12.

24   Should the warning actuator switch fail, it can be removed from the valve by unscrewing it without the need to disturb the hydraulic system.

Vacuum servo unit – modification

25   As from December 1975 a Girling type brake servo is fitted instead of the Delco-Moraine type shown in Chapter 9. In conjunction with the new servo the check valve is now fitted directly to the servo body.

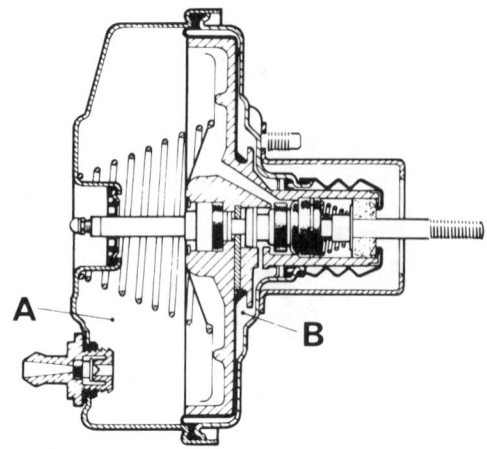

Fig. 13.46. Sectional view of the Girling brake servo (Sec 12)

  A   Inner chamber   B   Outer chamber

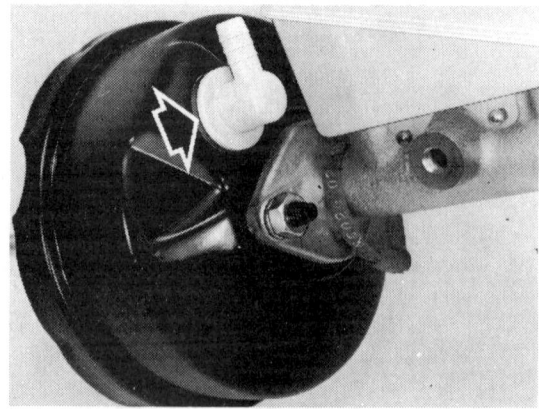

Fig. 13.47. Check valve location (arrowed) on the Girling brake servo (Sec 12)

13 Electrical system

Maintenance-free batteries — description

1   Some models manufactured from 1981 onward may be fitted with a Delco Freedom maintenance-free battery. This battery is sealed except for a small vent hole, and does not need to be topped up with distilled water.
2   The battery incorporates a test indicator on its top face. If a green dot is visible, the battery is in good condition. If the indicator is dark and no dot is visible, the battery requires charging as described in **Chapter 10.** However, extra care is necessary to prevent the electrolyte overheating or gassing excessively. If the indicator appears bright yellow the battery is faulty and should be renewed; in this condition do not charge the battery or connect jumper leads across it.

Alternator — dismantling, servicing, and reassembly

3   Alternators fitted to Chevette and Chevanne models manufactured between April 1976 and August 1977 were fitted with a modified regulator and an additional 40 ohm resistor between the diode trio and earth. The modifications were introduced at the date stamp F5 (shown on the alternator drive end shield) and concluded at the date stamp 7F.
4   The procedure for dismantling and servicing the alternator is identical to that given in Chapter 10, Section 8 except for the removal of the resistor, which is accomplished by unscrewing and removing the two retaining screws, washers and insulator.
5   When reassembling the alternator, ensure that the insulating sleeve

is positioned on the long retaining crosshead screw and that the washers are in the order shown in Fig. 13.49.
6   Vehicles fitted with the modified alternator may exhibit a tendency for the warning lamp to be slow in becoming extinguished when starting the engine from cold, but this is not an indication of a fault. Alternators on vehicles manufactured after August 1977 will allow the warning lamp to be extinguished at an engine speed of approximately 1500 rpm.
7   Alternators fitted to late models have a modified drive pulley as shown in Fig. 13.50. When assembling the pulley, make sure that the widest collar is located between the fan and the pulley, and when tightening the pulley nut use a socket key as shown in Fig. 13.51.

Pre-engaged starter solenoid — changes

8   On 1981 onward models a remote solenoid is fitted in the feed from the battery to the solenoid mounted on the starter (see Fig. 13.52). With this arrangement the ignition switch energises the remote solenoid, and the starter mounted solenoid operates separately since a link connects the solenoid battery terminal to the energising terminal.
9   The link must only be fitted where a remote solenoid is fitted.
10   A kit may be obtained from Vauxhall dealers in order to convert the single solenoid system to the double solenoid system.

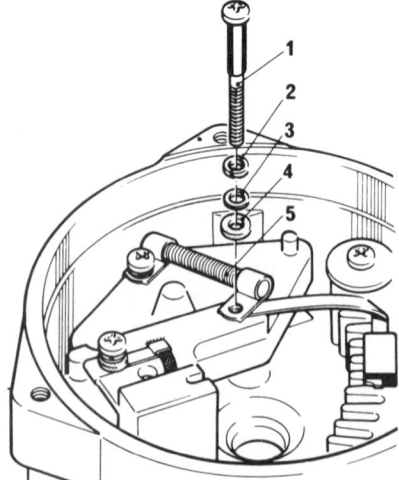

Fig. 13.49. Correct installation order of the alternator resistor retaining screw (Sec 13)

  1   Retaining screw
  2   Spring washer
  3   Plain washer
  4   Insulating washer
  5   Resistor

Fig. 13.48. Location (arrowed) of the alternator resistor (Sec 13)

Fig. 13.50. Modified alternator drive pulley components (Sec 13)

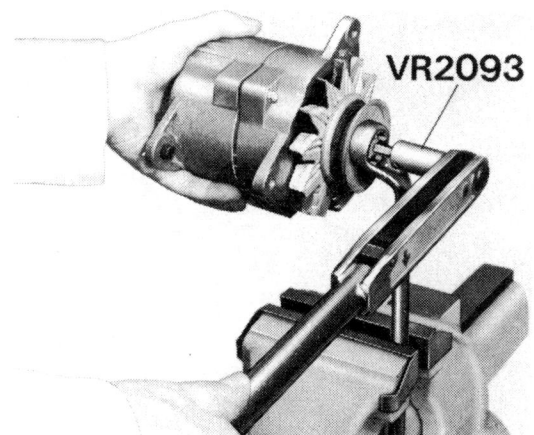

Fig. 13.51. Tightening the alternator pulley nut (Sec 13)

Fuses -- general

11 The 16 amp fuses described in Chapter 10, Section 15 are rated in accordance with the continental method which considers the normal load carried by the fuse. Under the UK rating, these fuses will blow at 32 amps.

12 Later Chevette and Chevanne models are fitted with 17.5 amp continental continuous rating (35 amp UK rating) fuses, and the following additional circuits are protected by the fuses (numbered as in Chapter 10).

   (3)   Luggage compartment light (saloon models)
   (6)   Tailgate wiper and washer

Instrument cluster — removal and refitting

13 It is recommended that the steering wheel is first removed as described in Chapter 11, Section 17, prior to removing the instrument cluster as described in Chapter 10, Section 25. This will provide more room for manoeuvring the cluster and therefore prevent unnecessary damage.

Heated rear window switch — bulb renewal

14 To remove the heated rear window switch illumination bulb, press the switch to the *on* position, then use a small screwdriver to carefully prise the switch cover from the base.

15 Unscrew the bulb from the switch base.

16 Refitting the new bulb is a reversal of the removal procedure and the cover is pressed into position on the switch base.

Heated rear window installation — precaution

17 Where a heated rear window is subsequently fitted to a Chevette E or ES model, it is essential to change the standard 28 amp alternator

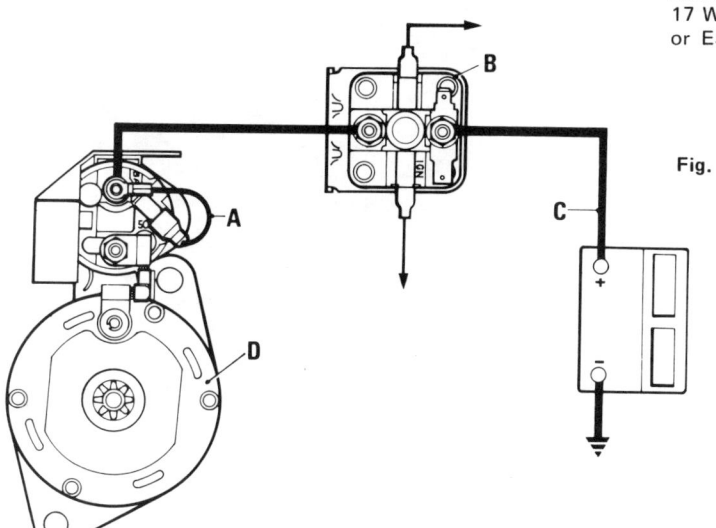

Fig. 13.52. Remote starter solenoid (B) fitted from 1981 models
(Sec 13)

A   Link
C   Cable
D   Starter

Fig. 13.53. Removing the heated rear window switch cover (Sec 13)

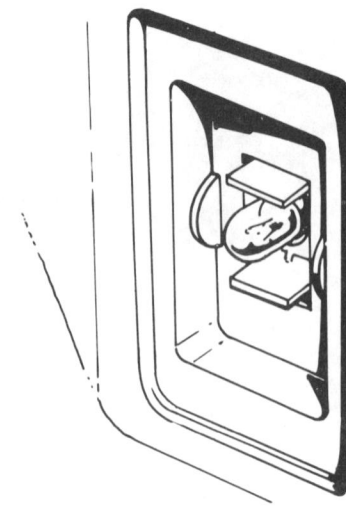

Fig. 13.54. Location of the heated rear window switch bulb (Sec 13)

Fig. 13.55. Rear lamp cluster lens on Estate and Chevanne models (Sec 13)

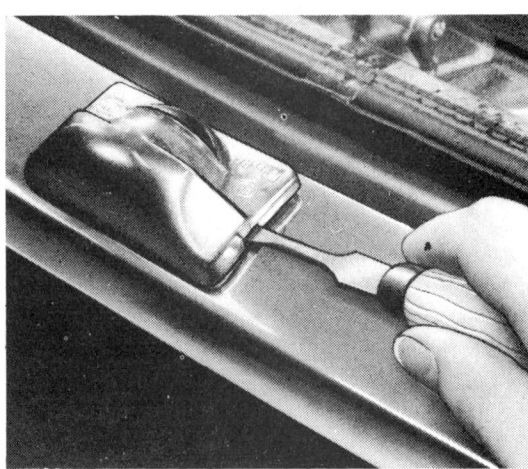

Fig. 13.56. Removing the rear number plate lamp on Estate and Chevanne models (Sec 13)

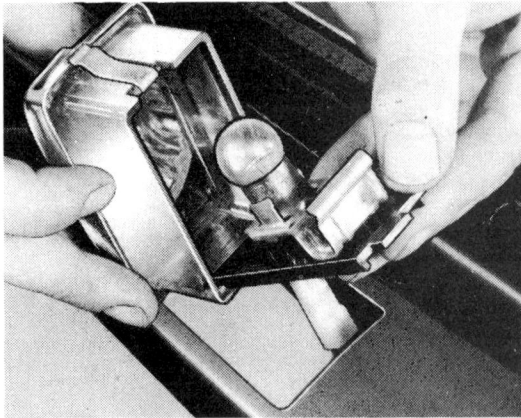

Fig. 13.57. Rear number plate lamp bulb location on Estate and Chevanne models (Sec 13)

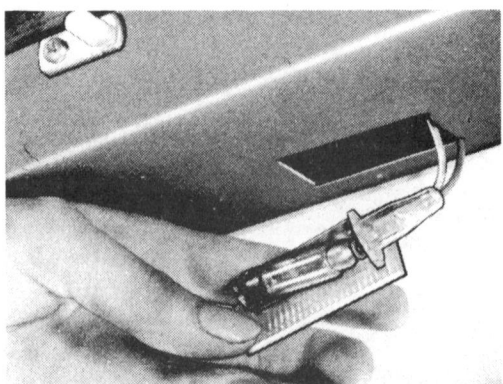

Fig. 13.58. Removing the rear interior lamp bulb on Estate and Chevanne models (Sec 13)

for the up-rated 45 amp version. Failure to do this could result in a discharged battery under certain operating conditons.

Lamp bulbs (Chevette Estate and Chevanne models) — renewal
18 Access to the rear lamp cluster bulbs is gained by unscrewing the four lens retaining screws and lifting the lens away from the lamp body.
19 Access to the rear number plate lamp bulb is gained by depressing the clip on one side of the lamp body with a screwdriver, at the same time easing the lamp from the rear bumper. Prise the base out of the lamp body to expose the bayonet type bulb.
20 Access to the rear interior lamp bulb on early models is gained by moving the lamp to the right on right-hand drive models or to the left

on left-hand drive models, then withdrawing it from its location to expose the festoon-type bulb. On later models simply prise it from its location.

Lamp bulbs (all models) — renewal
21 On all late models the passenger compartment interior light bulb or luggage compartment light bulb (saloon models) is renewed by prising the lamp from its location and withdrawing the bulb.
22 To renew the rear fog lamp bulb, remove the two screws and withdraw the lens, then twist the bayonet type bulb to remove it.

Ignition switch — modifications
23 If it is found that on early models the ignition key fouls the surround when it is operated, a plastic sleeve (part number 91053483) should be fitted, which will effectively centralise the switch in its surround.
24 On later models the four-position switch is marked 'B', 'O', 'I', and 'II'. The key can only be inserted or withdrawn when it is in position 'B'. To lock the steering, remove the key and turn the steering wheel until the lock engages; to unlock the steering, insert the key and turn it to position 'O'. With the key in position 'O' the steering is unlocked and the accessory circuits on. In position 'I' the ignition is switched on; position 'II' is for starting the engine.
25 To remove the ignition switch on later models, disconnect the battery negative lead, remove the lower steering column shroud, and remove the two retaining screws. To remove the lock barrel, turn the key to position 'I', then depress the retainer with a suitable tool (see Fig. 13.62) and withdraw the lock barrel. Note however that the lock barrel and switch must only be removed independently, otherwise the steering column lock may be damaged.

Windscreen washer — modification
26 The windscreen washer reservoir and pump assembly fitted to Chevette and Chevanne models manufactured after February 1977 may be of a different design to that shown in Chapter 10 of this manual; the alternative design is shown in Fig. 13.63.
27 The pump can be removed from the bottom of the reservoir by removing the filler cap, reaching into the reservoir, and unscrewing the nylon retaining nut.

Fig. 13.60. Modified ignition switch positions (Sec 13)

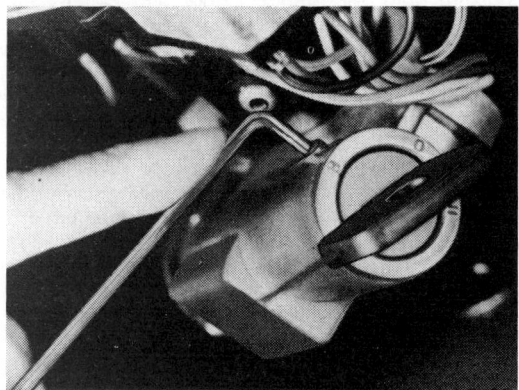

Fig. 13.62. Removing the modified ignition switch (Sec 13)

Tailgate wipe/wash system — general
28 Estate L models are equipped with a tailgate wipe/wash system; the reservoir and motor are located in the centre of the spare wheel in the luggage compartment.

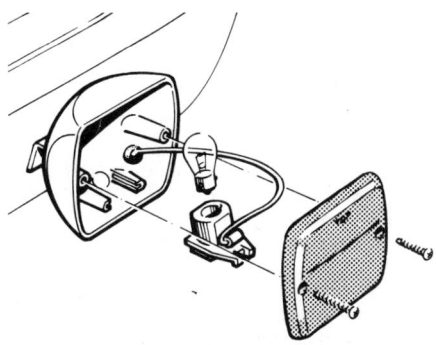

Fig. 13.59. Rear foglamp components (Sec 13)

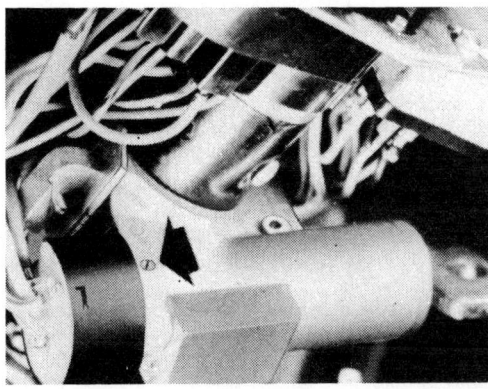

Fig. 13.61. Modified ignition switch retaining screw location (arrowed) (Sec 13)

Fig. 13.63. Alternative type of windscreen washer reservoir and pump (Sec 13)

29 Renewal of the tailgate wiper blade and arm is similar to that for the windscreen equivalent, and removal of the tailgate wiper motor is straightforward once the cover panel has been removed.

30 The switch is located on the steering column upper shroud and can be removed after removing the shroud and disconnecting the wires.

Radios and tape players — general

A radio or tape player is an expensive item to buy, and will only give its best performance if fitted properly. It is useless to expect concert hall performance from a unit that is suspended from the dashpanel by string with its speaker resting on the back seat or parcel shelf! If you do not wish to do the installation yourself there are many in-car entertainment specialists who can do the fitting for you.

Make sure the unit purchased is of the same polarity as the vehicle. Ensure that units with adjustable polarity are correctly set before commencing installation.

It is difficult to give specific information with regard to fitting, as final positioning of the radio/tape player, speakers and aerial is entirely a matter of personal preference. However, the following paragraphs give guidelines to follow, which are relevant to all installations.

Radios

Most radios are a standardised size of 7 inches wide, by 2 inches deep — this ensures that they will fit into the radio aperture provided in most cars. If your car does not have such an aperture, then the radio must be fitted in a suitable position either in, or beneath, the dashpanel. Alternatively, a special console can be purchased which will fit between the dashpanel and the floor, or on the transmission tunnel. These consoles can also be used for additional switches and instrumentation if required. Where no radio aperture is provided, the following points should be borne in mind before deciding exactly where to fit the unit:

a) *The unit must be within easy reach of the driver wearing a seatbelt*

b) *The unit must not be mounted in close proximity to a tachometer, the ignition switch and its wiring, or the flasher unit and associated wiring*

c) *The unit must be mounted within reach of the aerial lead, and in such a place that the aerial lead will not have to be routed near the components detailed in the preceding paragraph 'b'*

d) *The unit should not be positioned in a place where it might cause injury to the car occupants in an accident; for instance, under the dashpanel above the driver's or passenger's legs*

e) *The unit must be fitted really securely*

Some radios will have mounting brackets provided together with instructions: others will need to be fitted using drilled and slotted metal strips, bent to form mounting brackets — these strips are available from most accessory stores. The unit must be properly earthed, by fitting a separate earth lead between the casing of the radio and the vehicle frame.

Use the radio manufacturer's instructions when wiring the radio into the vehicle's electrical system. If no instructions are available, refer to the relevant wiring diagram to find the location of the radio 'feed' connection in the vehicle's wiring circuit. A 1-2 amp 'in-line' fuse must be fitted in the radio's 'feed' wire — a choke may also be necessary (see next Section).

The type of aerial used, and its fitted position is a matter of personal preference. In general the taller the aerial, the better the reception. It is best to fit a fully retractable aerial — especially, if a mechanical car-wash is used or if you live in an area where cars tend to be vandalised. In this respect electric aerials which are raised and lowered automatically when switching the radio on or off, are convenient, but are more likely to give trouble than the manual type.

When choosing a site for the aerial the following points should be considered:

a) *The aerial lead should be as short as possible; this means that the aerial should be mounted at the front of the vehicle*

b) *The aerial must be mounted as far away from the distributor and HT leads as possible*

c) *The part of the aerial which protrudes beneath the mounting point must not foul the roadwheels, or anything else*

d) *If possible the aerial should be positioned so that the coaxial lead does not have to be routed through the engine compartment*

e) *The plane of the panel on which the aerial is mounted should not be so steeply angled that the aerial cannot be mounted vertically (in relation to the 'end-on' aspect of the vehicle) most aerials have a small amount of adjustment available.*

Having decided on a mounting position, a relatively large hole will have to be made in the panel. The exact size of the hole will depend upon the specific aerial being fitted, although, generally, the hole required is of ¾ inch diameter. On metal bodied cars, a 'tank-cutter' of the relevant diameter is the best tool to be used for making the hole. This tool needs a small diameter pilot hole drilled through the panel, through which, the tool clamping bolt is inserted. On GRP bodied cars, a 'hole saw' is the best tool to use. Again, this tool will require the drilling of a small pilot hole. When the hole has been made the raw edges should be de-burred with a file and then painted, to prevent corrosion.

Fit the aerial according to the manufacturer's instructions. If the aerial is very tall, or if it protrudes beneath the mounting panel for a considerable distance it is a good idea to fit a stay between the aerial and the vehicle frame. This stay can be manufactured from the slotted and drilled metal strips previously mentioned. The stay should be securely screwed or bolted in place. For best reception it is advisable to fit an earth lead between the aerial body and the vehicle frame — this is essential on fibre glass bodied vehicles.

It will probably be necessary to drill one, or two holes through bodywork panels in order to feed the aerial lead into the interior of the car. Where this is the case ensure that the holes are fitted with rubber grommets to protect the cable, and to stop possible entry of water.

Positioning and fitting of the speaker depends mainly on its type. Generally, the speaker is designed to fit directly into the aperture already provided in the car (usually in the shelf behind the rear seats, or in the top of the dashpanel). Where this is the case, fitting the speaker is just a matter of removing the protective grille from the aperture and screwing or bolting the speaker in place. Take great care not to damage the speaker diaphragm whilst doing this. It is a good idea to fit a 'gasket' between the speaker frame and the mounting panel in order to prevent vibration — some speakers will already have such a gasket fitted.

If a 'pod' type speaker was supplied with the radio, the best acoustic results will normally be obtained by mounting it on the shelf behind the rear seat. The pod can be secured to the mounting panel with self-tapping screws.

When connecting a rear mounted speaker to the radio, the wires should be routed through the vehicle beneath the carpets or floor mats preferably through the middle, or along the side of the floorpan, where they will not be trodden on by passengers. Make the relevant connections as directed by the radio manufacturer.

By now you will have several yards of additional wiring in the car; use PVC tape to secure this wiring out of harm's way. Do not leave electrical leads dangling. Ensure that all new electrical connections are properly made (wires twisted together will not do) and completely secure.

The radio should now be working, but before you pack away your tools it will be necessary to 'trim' the radio to the aerial. Follow the radio manufacturer's instructions regarding this adjustment.

Tape players

Fitting instructions for both cartridge and cassette stereo tape players are the same and in general the same rules apply as when fitting a radio. Tape players are not usually prone to electrical interference like radio — although it can occur — so positioning is not so critical. If possible the player should be mounted on an 'even-keel'. Also, it must be possible for a driver wearing a seatbelt to reach the unit in order to change, or turn over, tapes.

For the best results from speakers designed to be recessed into a panel, mount them so that the back of the speaker protrudes into an enclosed chamber within the vehicle (eg. door interiors or the boot cavity).

To fit recessed type speakers in the front doors first check that there is sufficient room to mount the speaker in each door without it fouling the latch or window winding mechanism. Hold the speaker against the skin of the door, and draw a line, around the periphery of the speaker. With the speaker removed draw a second 'cutting' line, within the first, to allow enough room for the entry of the speaker back but at the same time providing a broad seat for the speaker flange. When you are sure that the 'cutting-line' is correct, drill a series of holes around its periphery. Pass a hacksaw blade through one of the holes and then cut through the metal between the holes until the centre section of the panel falls out.

De-burr the edges of the hole and then paint the raw metal to prevent corrosion. Cut a corresponding hole in the door trim panel — ensuring that it will be completely covered by the speaker grille. Now drill a hole in the door edge and a corresponding hole in the door surround. These holes are to feed the speaker leads through — so fit grommets. Pass the speaker leads through the door trim, door skin and out through the holes in the side of the door and door surround. Refit the door trim panel and then secure the speaker to the door using self-tapping screws. **Note:** *If the speaker is fitted with a shield to prevent water dripping on it, ensure that this shield is at the top.*

'Pod' type speakers can be fastened to the shelf behind the rear seat, or anywhere else offering a corresponding mounting point on each side of the car. If the 'pod' speakers are mounted on each side of the shelf behind the rear seat, it is a good idea to drill several large diameter holes through to the trunk cavity, beneath each speaker — this will improve the sound reproduction. 'Pod' speakers sometimes offer a better reproduction quality if they face the rear window — which then acts as a reflector — so it is worthwhile experimenting before finally fixing the speakers.

Radios and tape players — suppression of interference (general)

To eliminate buzzes, and other unwanted noises, costs very little and is not as difficult as sometimes thought. With a modicum of common sense and patience and following the instructions in the following paragraphs, interference can be virtually eliminated.

The first cause for concern is the alternator. The noise this makes over the radio is like an electric mixer and the noise speeds up when you rev up the engine (if you wish to prove this point, you can remove the fanbelt and try it). The remedy for this is simple; connect a 1.0 mf—3.0 mf capacitor between earth, probably the bolt that holds down

the generator base, and the *output* terminal on the alternator. This is most important, for if you connect it to the other terminal you will probably damage the generator permanently (see Fig. 13.64).

A second common cause of electrical interference is the ignition system. Here a 1.0 mf capacitor must be connected between earth and the SW or + terminal on the coil (see Fig. 13.65). This may stop the tick-tick sound that comes over the speaker. Next comes the spark itself.

There are several ways of curing interference from the ignition HT system. One is the use of carbon-cored HT leads as original equipment. Where copper cable is substituted then you must use resistive spark plug caps (see Fig. 13.66) of about 10 000 ohm to 15 000 ohm resistance. If, due to lack of room, these cannot be used, an alternative is to use 'in-line' suppressors; if the interference is not too bad, you may get away with only one suppressor in the coil to distributor line. If the interference does continue (a 'clacking' noise) then modify all HT leads.

At this stage it is advisable to check that the radio and aerial are well earthed, to see that the aerial plug is pushed well into the set and that the radio is properly trimmed (see preceding Section). In addition, check that the wire which supplies the power to the set is as short as possible and does not wander all over the car. At this stage it is a good idea to check that the fuse is of the correct rating. For most sets this will be about 1 to 2 amps.

At this point the more usual causes of interference have been suppressed. If the problem still exists, a look at the cause of interference may help to pinpoint the component generating the stray electrical discharges.

The radio picks up electromagnetic waves in the air; now some are made by regular broadcasters, and some, which we do not want, are made by the car itself. The home made signals are produced by stray electrical discharges floating around in the car. Common producers of these signals are electrical motors, ie, the windscreen wipers, electric screen washers, electric window winders, heater fan or an electric aerial if fitted. Other sources of interference are flashing turn signals

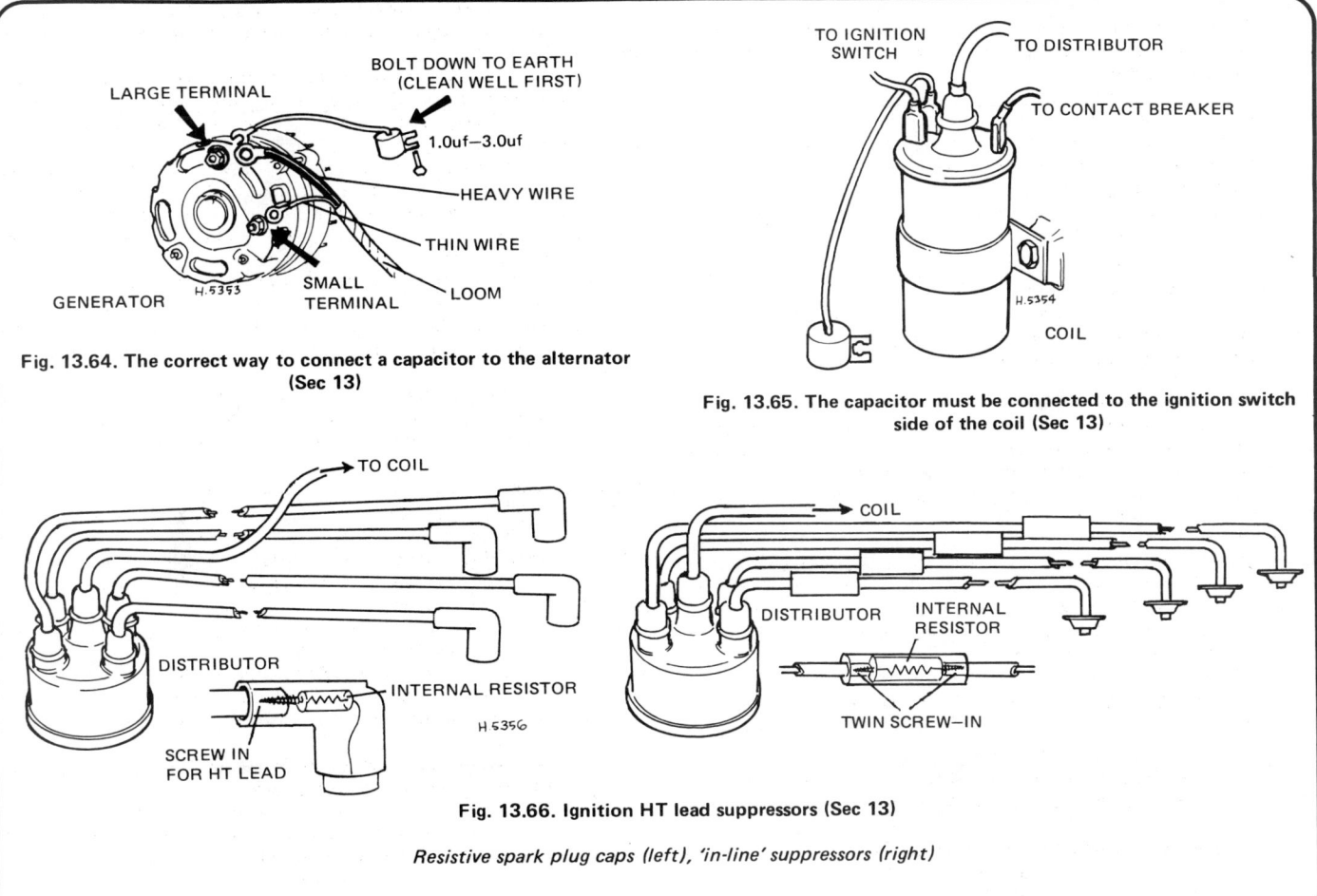

Fig. 13.64. The correct way to connect a capacitor to the alternator (Sec 13)

Fig. 13.65. The capacitor must be connected to the ignition switch side of the coil (Sec 13)

Fig. 13.66. Ignition HT lead suppressors (Sec 13)

Resistive spark plug caps (left), 'in-line' suppressors (right)

and instruments. The remedy for these cases is shown in Fig. 13.67 for an electric motor whose interference is not too bad and Fig. 13.68 for instrument suppression. Turn signals are not normally suppressed. In recent years radio manufacturers have included in the line (live) of the radio, in addition to the fuse, and 'in-line' choke. If your circuit lacks one of these, put one in as shown in Fig. 13.69.

All the foregoing components are available from radio stores or accessory stores. If you have an electric clock fitted this should be suppressed by connecting a 0.5 mf capacitor directly across it as shown for a motor in Fig. 13.67.

If after all this, you are still experiencing radio interference, first assess how bad it is, for the human ear can filter out unobtrusive unwanted noises quite easily. But if you are still adamant about eradicating the noise, then continue.

As a first step, a few 'experts' seem to favour a screen between the radio and the engine. This is OK as far as it goes — literally! — for the whole set is screened anyway and if interference can get past that then a small piece of aluminium is not going to stop it.

A more sensible way of screening is to discover if interference is coming down the wires. First, take the live lead; interference can get between the set and the choke (hence the reason for keeping the wires short). One remedy here is to screen the wire and this is done by buying screened wire and fitting that. The loudspeaker lead could be screened also to prevent 'pick-up' getting back to the radio although this is unlikely.

Without doubt, the worst source of radio interference comes from the ignition HT leads, even if they have been suppressed. The ideal way of suppressing these is to slide screening tubes over the leads themselves. As this is impractical, we can place an aluminium shield over the majority of the lead areas. In a vee- or twin-cam engine this is relatively easy but for a straight engine, the results are not particularly good.

Now for the really impossible cases, here are a few tips to try out. Where metal comes into contact with metal, an electrical disturbance is caused which is why good clean connections are essential. To remove interference due to overlapping or butting panels you must bridge the join with a wide braided earth strap (like that from the frame to the engine/transmission). The most common moving parts that could create noise and should be strapped are, in order of importance:

a) *Silencer to frame*
b) *Exhaust pipe to engine block and frame*
c) *Air cleaner to frame*
d) *Front and rear bumpers to frame*
e) *Steering column to frame*
f) *Bonnet and boot lids to frame*
g) *Hood frame to bodyframe on soft tops*

These faults are most pronounced when (1) the engine is idling, (2) labouring under load. Although the moving parts are already connected with nuts, bolts etc, these do tend to rust and corrode, thus creating a high resistance interference source.

If you have a 'ragged' sounding pulse when mobile, this could be wheel or tyre static. This can be cured by buying some anti-static powder and sprinkling inside the tyres.

If the interference takes the shape of a high pitched screeching noise that changes its note when the car is in motion and only comes now and then, this could be related to the aerial, especially if it is of the telescopic or whip type. This source can be cured quite simply by pushing a small rubber ball on top of the aerial as this breaks the electric field before it can form; but it would be much better to buy yourself a new aerial of a reputable brand. If, on the other hand, you are getting a loud rushing sound every time you brake, then this is brake static. This effect is most prominent on hot dry days and is cured only by fitting a special kit, which is quite expensive.

In conclusion, it is pointed out that it is relatively easy, and therefore, cheap, to eliminate 95 per cent of all noise, but to eliminate the final 5 per cent is time and money consuming. It is up to the individual to decide if it is worth it. Please remember also, that you cannot get a concert hall performance out of a cheap radio.

Finally, tape players are not usually affected by car noise but in a very bad case, the best remedies are the first three suggestions plus using a 3 — 5 amp choke in the 'live' line and in incurable cases screen the live and speaker wires.

Note: If your car is fitted with electronic ignition, then it is not recommended that either the spark plug resistors or the ignition coil capacitor be fitted as these may damage the system. Most electronic ignition units have built-in suppression and should, therefore, not cause interference.

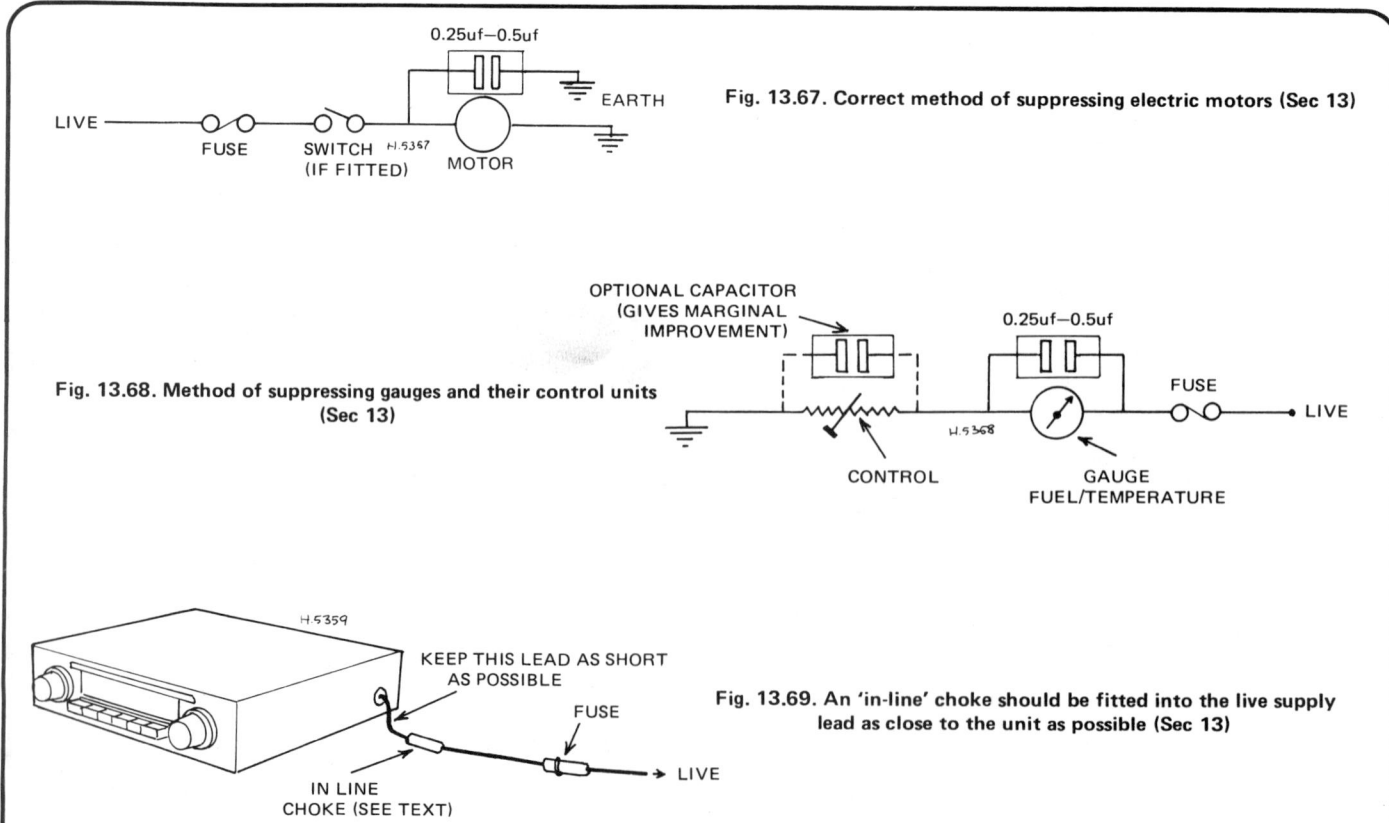

Fig. 13.67. Correct method of suppressing electric motors (Sec 13)

Fig. 13.68. Method of suppressing gauges and their control units (Sec 13)

Fig. 13.69. An 'in-line' choke should be fitted into the live supply lead as close to the unit as possible (Sec 13)

WIRING DIAGRAMS OVERLEAF

Note: *No wiring colour codes will be found on the option and accessory circuit diagrams; actual wiring colours may vary according to date and place of installation. Refer to main wiring diagram (Chapter 10) for colours of standard wiring.*

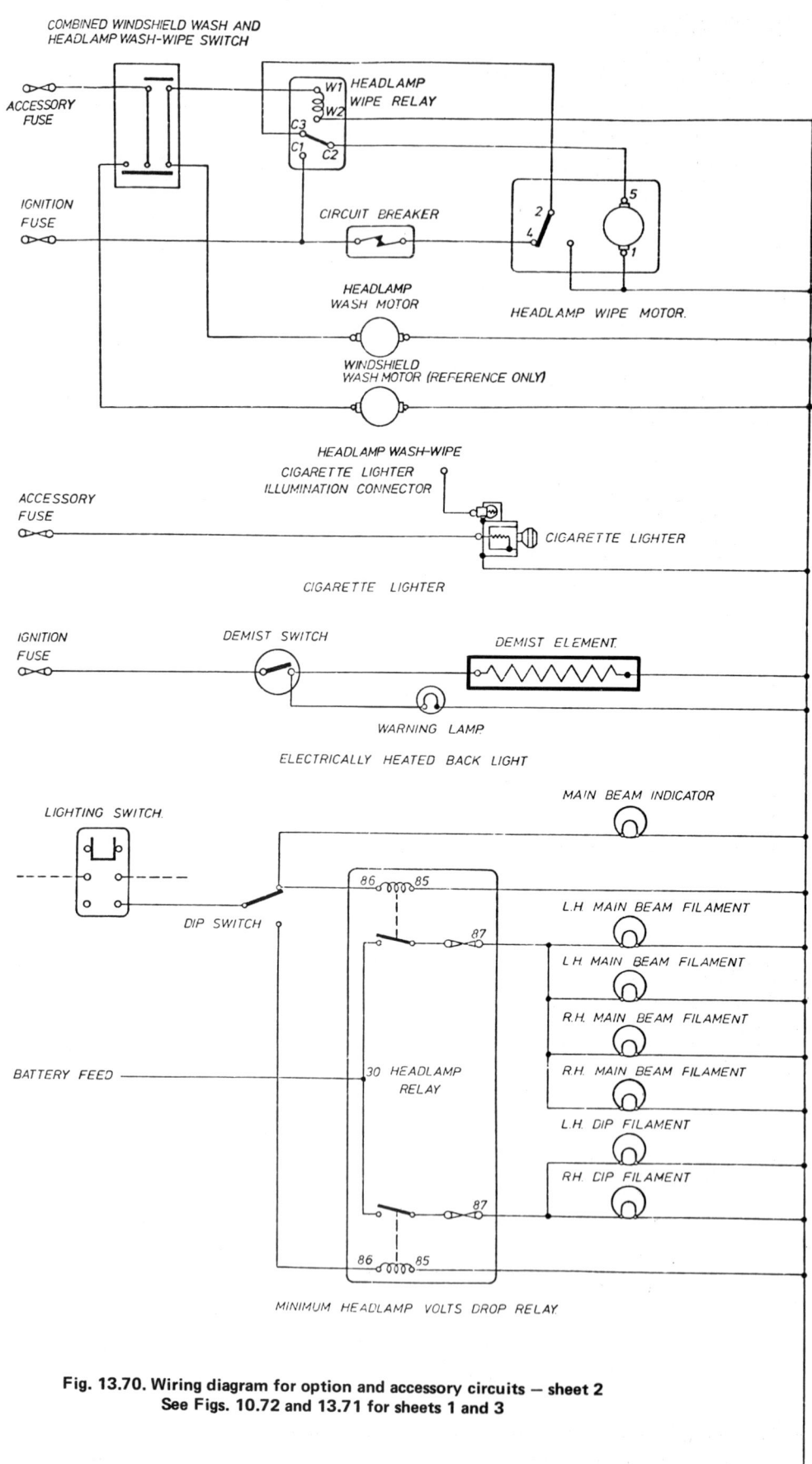

Fig. 13.70. Wiring diagram for option and accessory circuits — sheet 2
See Figs. 10.72 and 13.71 for sheets 1 and 3

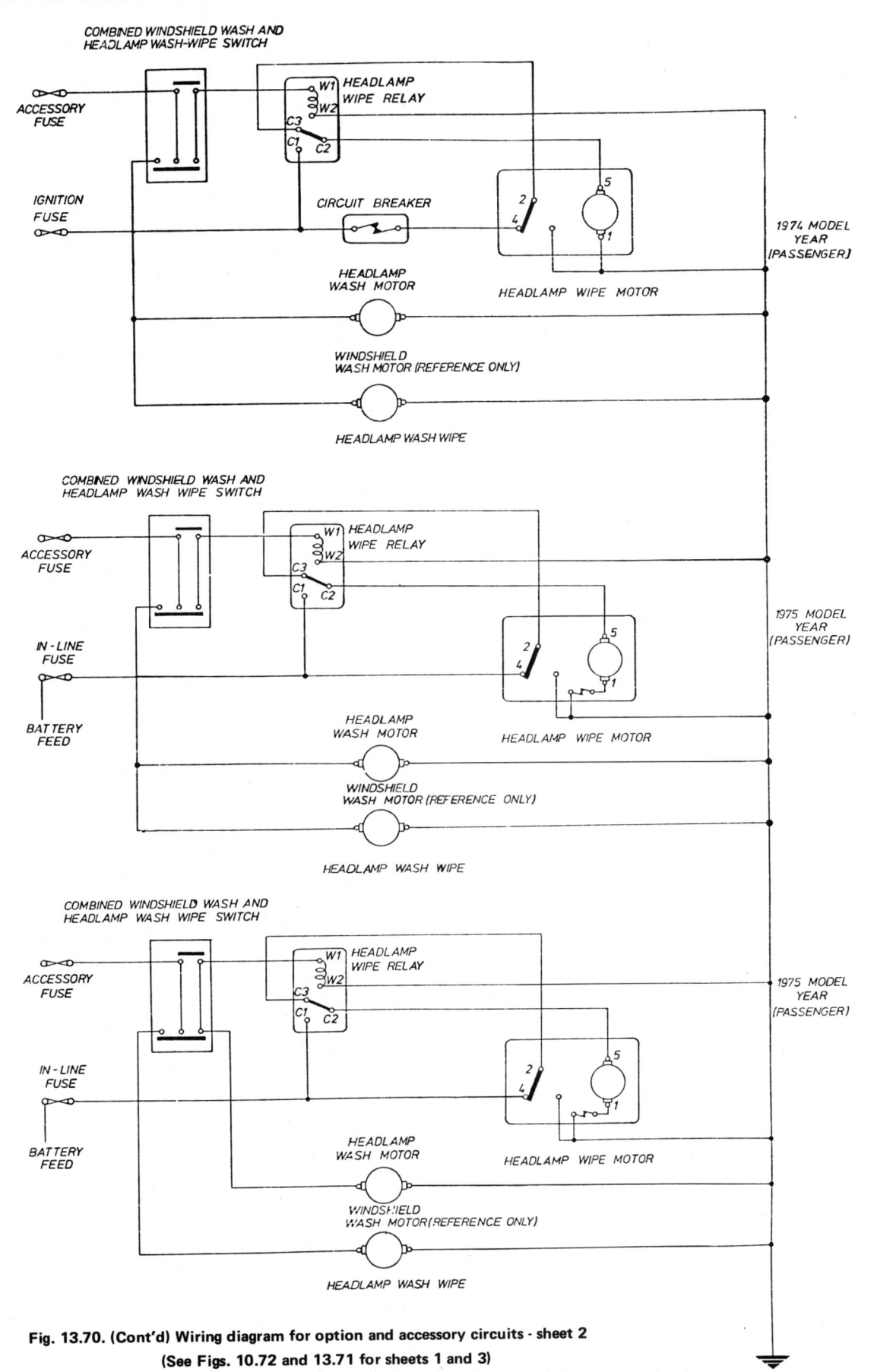

Fig. 13.70. (Cont'd) Wiring diagram for option and accessory circuits - sheet 2

(See Figs. 10.72 and 13.71 for sheets 1 and 3)

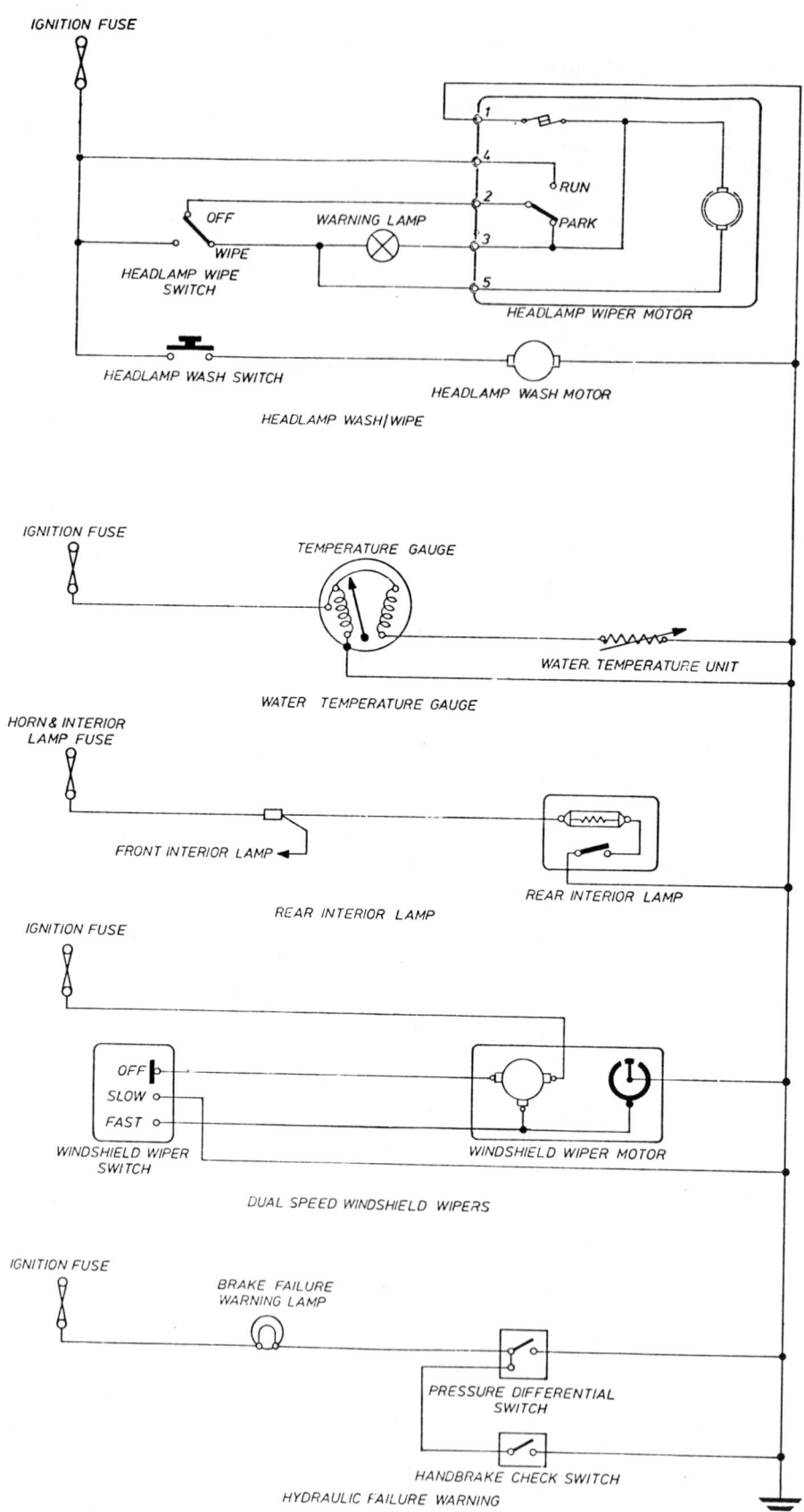

Fig. 13.71. Wiring diagram for option and accessory circuits — sheet 3
See Figs. 10.72 and 13.70 for sheets 1 and 2

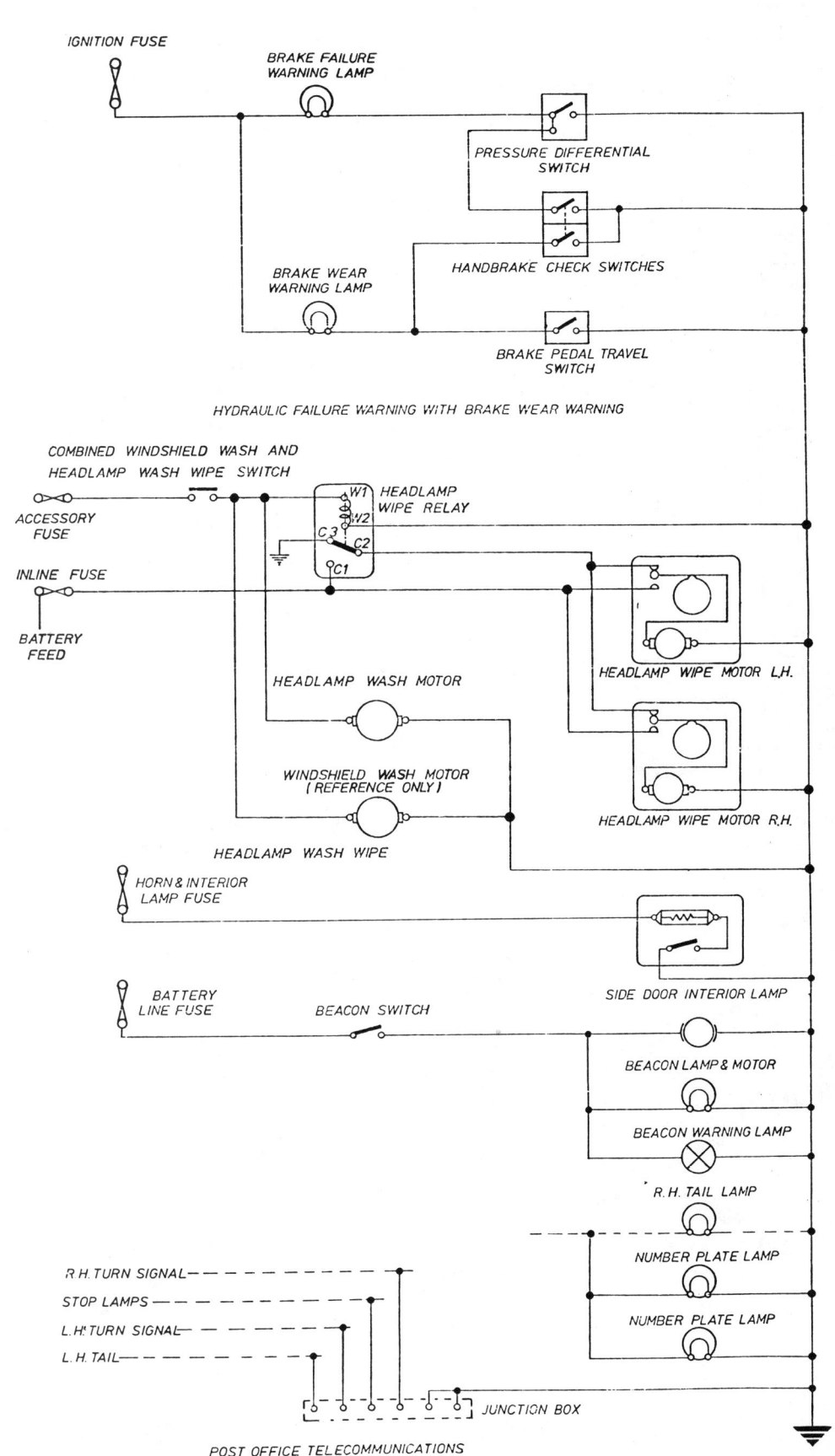

Fig. 13.71. (Cont'd) Wiring diagram for option and accessory circuits - sheet 3
(See Figs. 10.72 and 13.70 for sheets 1 and 2)

14 Suspension and steering

Rear shock absorber (Saloon models) - general

1   The rear shock absorber mountings on Saloon models are different from those on Hatchback, Estate and Chevanne models. The lower mountings are in brackets on the rear axle and the upper mountings are located in body mounting domes. Access to the upper mountings is gained by removing the fuel tank trim board. To do this turn the lower retainers through 90° and withdraw the trim board from the upper clips.

2   Apart from the information given in paragraphs 1 and 2, removal, testing, and refitting of the rear shock absorber is as given in Chapter 11.

Rear stabiliser bar deletion

3   From mid-1982, the rear stabiliser (anti-roll) bar is no longer fitted to Hatchback and Saloon models.

Steering knuckle — modification

4   As from chassis number FY 134033 for right-hand drive vehicles and FY 133467 for left-hand drive vehicles (June/July 1977) all Chevette

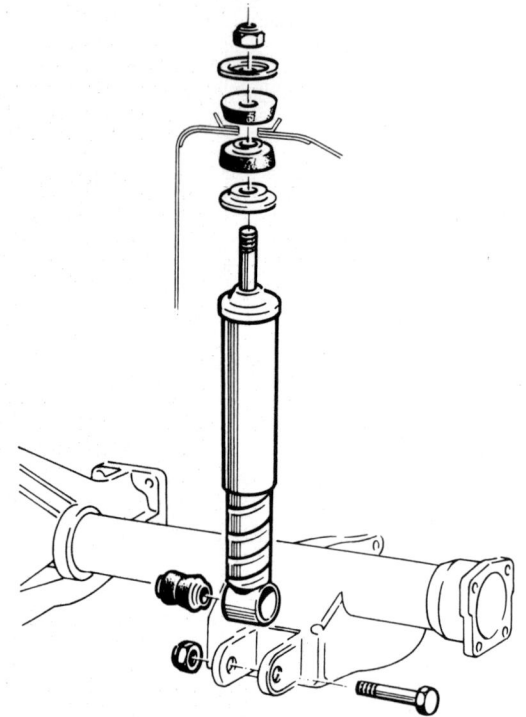

Fig. 13.72. Rear shock absorber components on Saloon models (Sec 14)

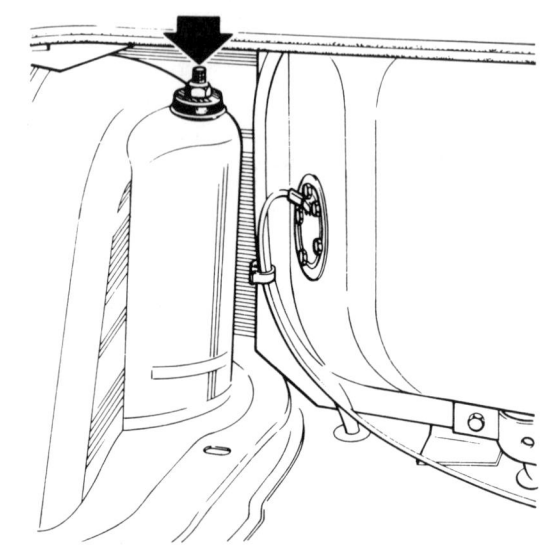

Fig. 13.73. Rear shock absorber upper mounting on Saloon models (Sec 14)

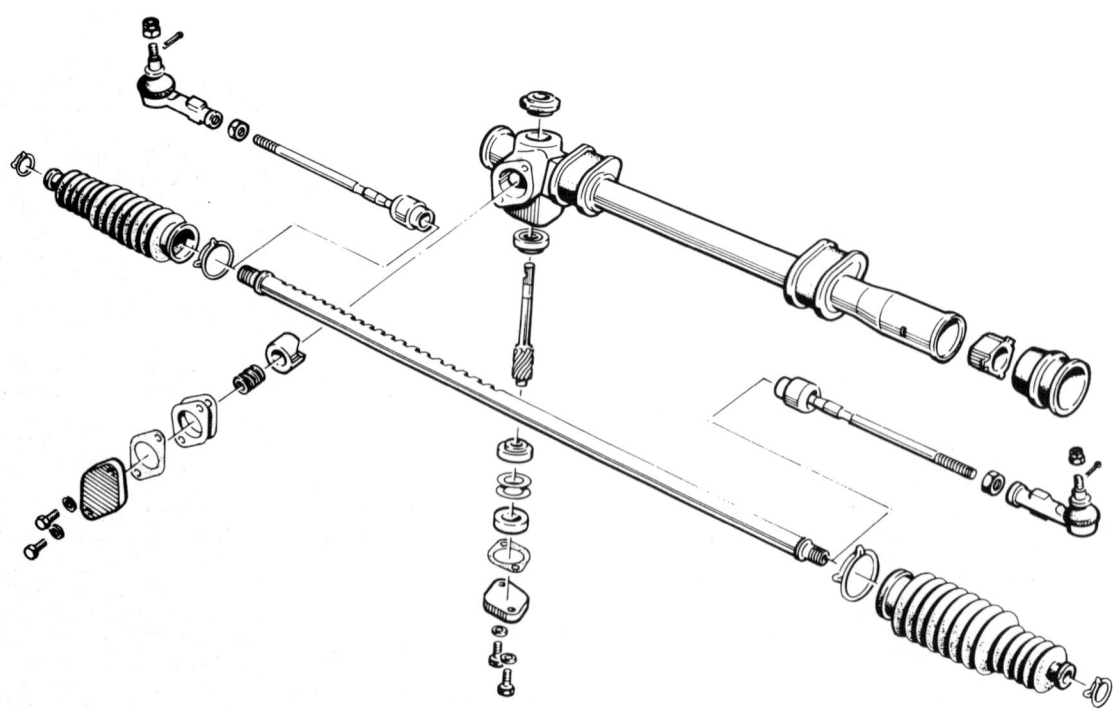

Fig. 13.74. Exploded view of the Cam Gears steering gear (Sec 14)

Saloon and Hatchback models are fitted with modified steering knuckles having larger stub axle diameters. The oil seals and inner wheel bearings for the modified knuckles also have different dimensions from those of the original components.

5 When renewing oil seals or bearings it is imperative to make sure that the original or modified versions are fitted only to the matching steering knuckle.

6 All Chevette Estate and Chevanne models are fitted with the modified steering knuckles.

Steering column — removal and refitting

7 On early models the steering column lower mounting bolt is of the shear head type and must be drilled out as described in Chapter 11. On later models, however, the bolt has a normal head and may be removed with a socket; it is not necessary to remove the clutch and brake pedal assemblies where this type of bolt is fitted.

Steering column shrouds (Estate L models) — removal and refitting

8 On Estate L models equipped with a tailgate wash/wipe system, the switch is located in the steering column upper shroud.

9 Removal of the shrouds is similar to that described in Chapter 11 but disconnect the battery negative lead before disconnecting the switch wiring. Refitting is a reversal of removal.

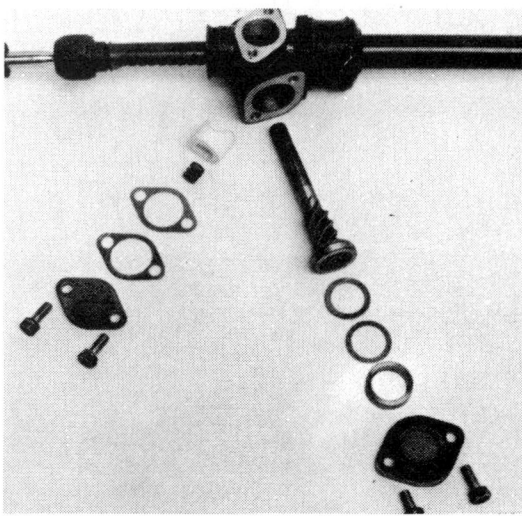

Fig. 13.75. Pinion and yoke components on the Cam Gears steering gear (Sec 14)

Steering gear (Cam Gears) — removal, overhaul, and refitting

10 Late 1980 models and onward are equipped with a Cam Gears type steering gear instead of the GM type described in Chapter 11.

11 Follow paragraphs 1 to 6 inclusive of Section 22 in Chapter 11.

12 Unbolt the yoke cover, and remove the shims, spring and yoke.

13 Unbolt the pinion cover, and remove the shims and pinion together with the outer bearing.

14 Prise the pinion oil seal from the housing.

15 Withdraw the rack from the pinion end of the housing, then extract the bush from the other end.

16 Using a soft metal drift, drive the pinion bearing from the housing.

17 Clean all the components in paraffin, wipe them dry, and examine them for wear and damage. Renew the components as necessary.

18 Commence reassembly by driving the pinion inner bearing into the housing using a metal tube on the outer race.

19 Insert the rack bush into the end of the housing, making sure that the three lugs are engaged correctly.

20 Insert the rack from the pinion end with the teeth facing the pinion position.

21 With the rack in a central position, lubricate the pinion gear and shaft with grease, then insert the pinion (with outer bearing) into the housing so that the pinch bolt flat faces the yoke cover when the pinion is fully entered.

22 Fit the pinion bearing shims followed by the spacer and a new gasket. Using a straight edge and feeler gauge, check that the spacer is between 0.001 and 0.005 in (0.025 and 0.127 mm) above the gasket face to give the correct pinion bearing preload when the cover is fitted. If necessary change the shims to obtain the correct preload.

23 Fit the pinion cover and tighten the bolts evenly.

24 Fit the yoke to the rack followed by the cover without the spring, shims, or gasket, and tighten the cover bolts finger tight. Using a feeler gauge, measure the clearance between the cover and the housing. The shim thickness must be this dimension plus between 0.0005 to 0.006 in (0.0127 to 0.1524 mm).

25 Remove the cover, then fit the spring, shims, new gasket, and cover. Tighten the bolts evenly.

26 Smear the pinion shaft and oil seal with grease, then press the oil seal into the housing.

27 Lubricate the rack with grease. Check that the torque required to turn the pinion is a maximum of 12 lbf in (1.4 Nm). A spring balance

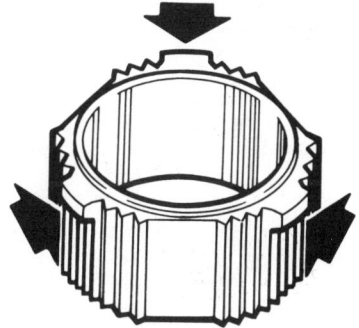

Fig. 13.76. Steering rack bush, showing locating lugs (arrowed) (Sec 14)

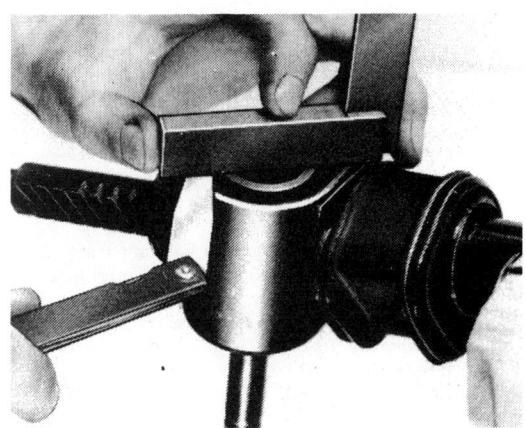

Fig. 13.77. Checking the pinion bearing preload (Sec 14)

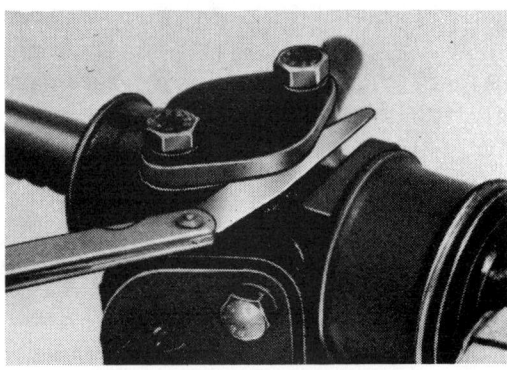

Fig. 13.78. Checking the yoke cover clearance (Sec 14)

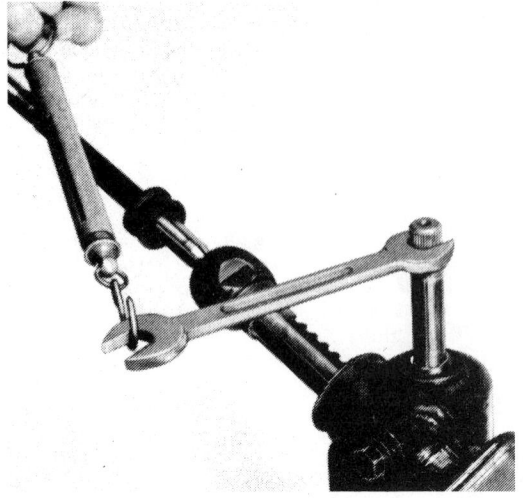

Fig. 13.79. Checking the pinion turning torque (Sec 14)

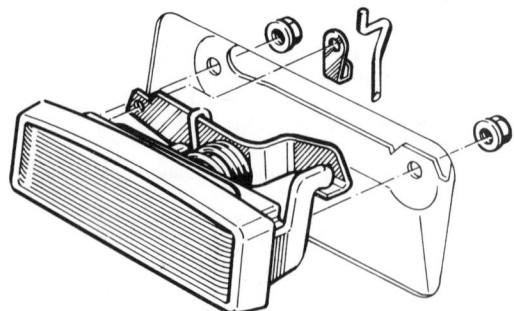

Fig. 13.81. Modified door exterior handle (Sec 15)

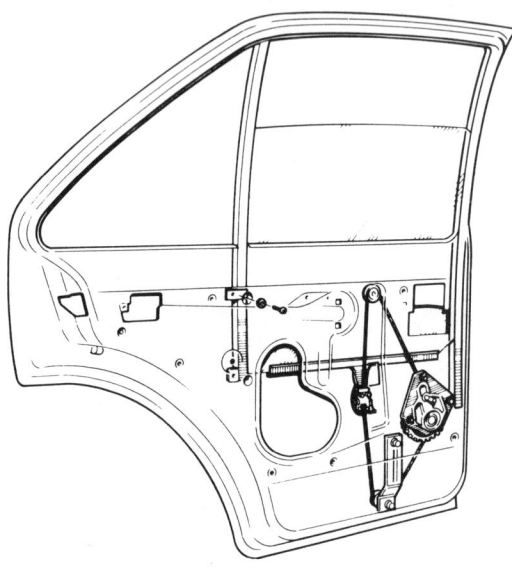

**Fig. 13.82. Rear door window components (4-door Saloon models)
(Sec 15)**

and spanner may be used as shown in Fig. 13.79. If the torque is more than the maximum amount, recheck the yoke and pinion shim thickness.
28 The remaining procedure is given in Chapter 11, paragraphs 18 to 24, but when staking the inner balljoints on original components the staking must be a minimum of 0.4 in (10.0 mm) away from the original staking.

15 Bodywork and fittings

Front wing — removal and refitting
1   As from 1980 the front wing has been modified and a weatherstrip has been fitted between the front of the wing and the main body.
2   The new wings can be fitted to earlier models provided that a mounting plate (available from Vauxhall dealers) is welded to the front of the new wing panel.

Front door trim panel — changes
3   On some later models the front door trim panel incorporates a plastic pocket. The pocket is secured to the trim panel by five screws.

Exterior door handle — modification
4   On later models the release rod has been modified as shown in Fig. 13.81. The rod has in effect been inverted, and adjustment is now made at its lower end.

Front door glass (Chevette 4-door Saloon models) — removal and refitting
5   The procedure is identical to that given in Chapter 12, Section 13, but in connection with paragraph 7 and Fig. 12.16 the dimension 'A' from the rear edge of the glass to the centre of the rear cable clamp is 6.6 in (168.3 mm).

Rear door glass (Chevette 4-door Saloon models) — removal and refitting
6   Remove the door interior trim panel as described in Chapter 12.
7   Temporarily refit the window regulator handle and wind down the glass until the cable-to-glass support clamp comes into view in the door aperture.
8   Whilst supporting the glass, unbolt the clamp to release the cable from the support channel; lower the glass.
9   Remove the door waist inner and outer weatherstrips.
10 Unscrew and remove the rear glass channel retaining screws, then extract the upper window frame channel insert.
11 With the glass raised, remove the rear glass channel.
12 Move the glass slightly to the rear then lift it carefully from the door frame.
13 If a new glass is being fitted, fit the support channel to its lower edge in accordance with Fig. 13.83.
14 Turn the window regulator handle until it can be rotated no further (anti-clockwise on right-hand door, clockwise on left-hand door). Now

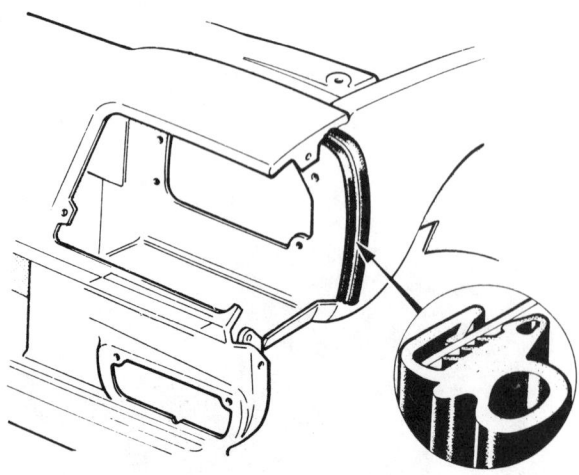

Fig. 13.80. Modified front wing weatherstrip location (Sec 15)

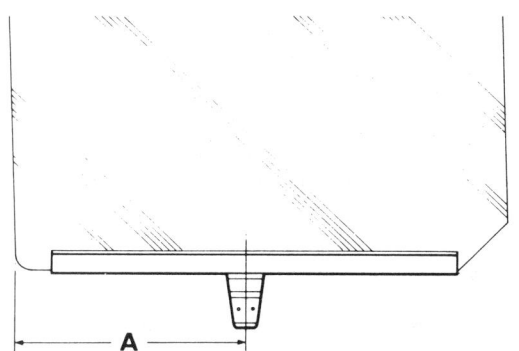

Fig. 13.83. Rear door glass lower support channel (4-door Saloon models (Sec 15)

A = 9.75 in (247.7 mm) from rear edge

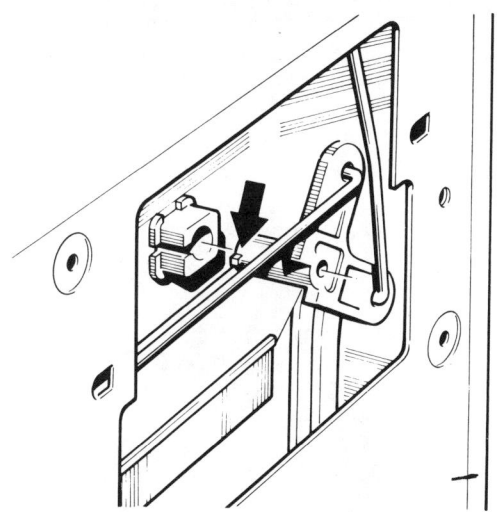

Fig. 13.84. Rear door lock remote control (4-door Saloon models) showing the locating peg arrowed (Sec 15)

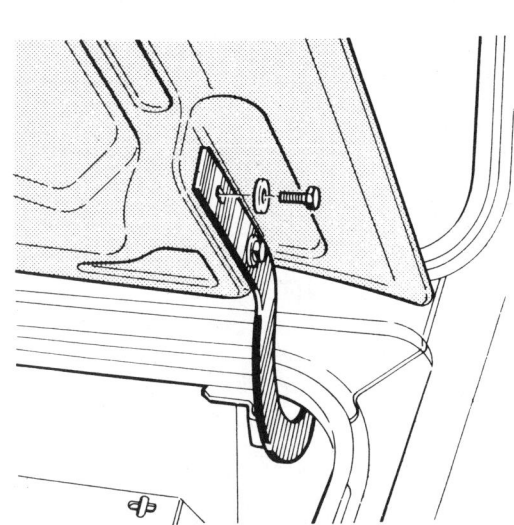

Fig. 13.85. Bootlid retaining bolts and hinge arm (Saloon models) (Sec 15)

turn the handle in the opposite direction until the notch on the cable drum appears in the door aperture. Continue turning until it appears for the second time. Do not move the regulator from this position.
15 Fit the glass squarely into the door frame channel and, with the glass raised, refit the rear glass channel and tighten the retaining screws.
16 Lower the glass and refit the upper window frame channel insert.
17 Refit the waist inner and outer weatherstrips.
18 Bolt the cable clamp to the support channel; any adjustment required can be made by loosening the clamp bolts and slightly moving the cable.

Rear door quarter window (Chevette 4-door Saloon model) — removal and refitting
19 Remove the rear door glass as described in paragraphs 2 to 14 inclusive.
20 Carefully pull the quarter window forwards to release it from the weatherseal.
21 Refitting is a reversal of removal.

Rear door lock remote control (Chevette 4-door Saloon model) — removal and refitting
22 Remove the door interior trim panel as described in Chapter 12.
23 To remove the crank connecting the lock button to the lock mechanism, first detach the lock mechanism from the door by unscrewing the two retaining screws.
24 Rotate the crank clockwise until the locating peg is aligned with the bracket slot, then withdraw the crank.
25 Refitting is a reversal of removal.

Boot lid (Chevette Saloon models) — removal and refitting
26 Open the boot lid and mark the hinge positions with a pencil.
27 Place cloth between the boot lid and the bodywork, then with the help of an assistant unscrew the mounting bolts and remove the boot lid.
28 Refitting is a reversal of removal, but check that the boot lid is aligned with the surrounding bodywork when closed; if not, loosen the mounting bolts and reposition the boot lid in the slotted holes as necessary.

Boot lid torque rod (Chevette Saloon models) — removal and refitting
29 It is not possible to remove the boot lid hinges as they are riveted to the main body; however the torque rods may be removed. First remove the boot lid as described in paragraphs 26 to 28.
30 Using an adjustable spanner and screwdriver, disconnect the torque rod from the centre of the rear shelf panel.

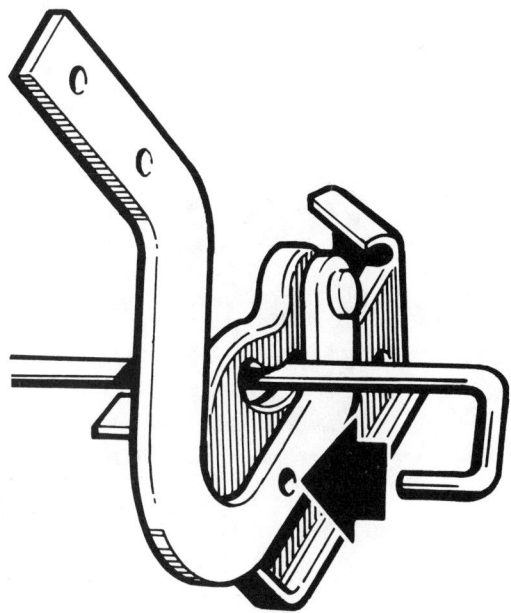

Fig. 13.86. Boot lid torque rod outer location (Saloon models) (Sec 15)

31 Unhook the outer end of the torque rod from the hinge arm and bracket.
32 Refitting is a reversal of removal but lubricate the friction surfaces with high melting point grease.

Boot lid latch (Chevette Saloon models) — removal and refitting

33 Open the boot lid, unscrew the two crosshead mounting screws, and withdraw the latch.
34 Refitting is a reversal of removal, but lubricate the friction surfaces with high melting point grease, and if necessary adjust the striker as described in paragraphs 39 and 40.

Boot lid lock (Chevette Saloon models) — removal and refitting

35 Remove the latch as described in paragraphs 33 and 34.
36 Turn the spring retainer through 90° and remove it. The lock can now be removed from the boot lid.
37 If necessary extract the circlip from the lock, insert the key, and withdraw the barrel.
38 Refitting is a reversal of removal, but lubricate the lock barrel with dry graphite; do not use ordinary oil. To facilitate fitting the lock spring retainer, place it on a piece of rubber or plastic tubing as shown in Fig. 13.90.

Boot lid striker (Chevette Saloon models) — removal, refitting and adjustment

39 Open the boot lid, remove the retaining bolt, and withdraw the striker.
40 When refitting the striker the hooked end must face forward. Adjust the position of the striker so that the boot lid shuts under firm hand pressure.

Rear quarter trim panels (Chevette Estate and Chevanne) — removal and refitting

41 The forward rear quarter trim panels are located in slots and are also retained by two screws, access to the lower retaining screw is gained by lifting the rear seat cushion vertical.
42 The rear quarter trim panels are retained by press-type fasteners, and a special tool is supplied by the manufacturers to lever out the fasteners (see Fig. 13.92). If it is not possible to obtain the special tool from the local Vauxhall/Bedford garage, careful use of a wide-bladed screwdriver will suffice.

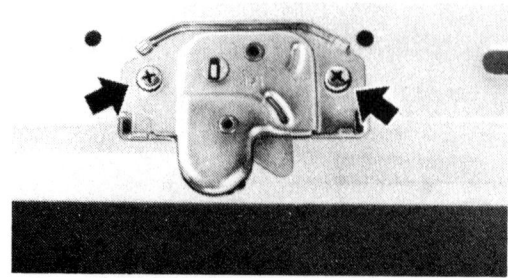

Fig. 13.87. Boot lid latch and locating screws (arrowed) (Saloon models) (Sec 15)

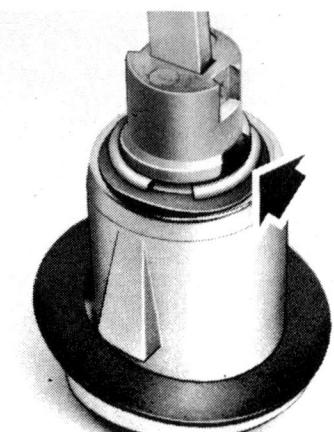

Fig. 13.89. Boot lid lock barrel retaining circlip (arrowed) (Saloon models) (Sec 15)

Fig. 13.88. Boot lid lock spring retainer location (arrowed) (Saloon models) (Sec 15)

Fig. 13.90. Using a rubber tube to refit the boot lid lock spring retainer (Saloon models) (Sec 15)

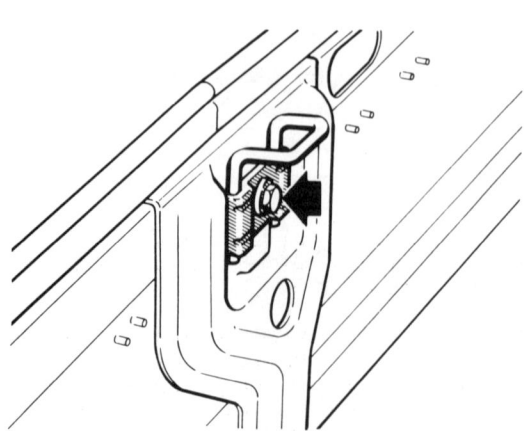

Fig. 13.91. Boot lid striker retaining bolt (arrowed) (Saloon models) (Sec 15)

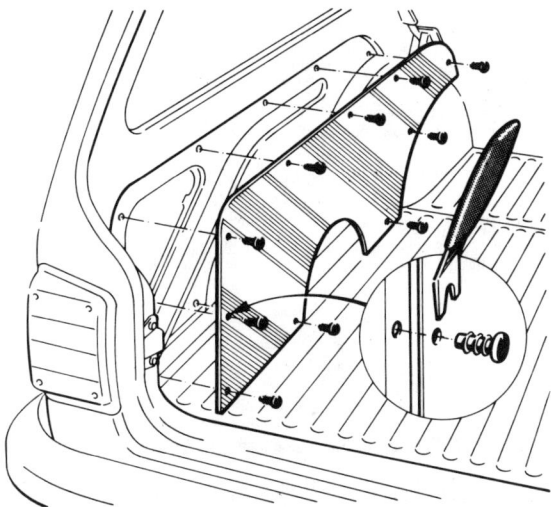

Fig. 13.92. Rear quarter trim panel on Estate and Chevanne models showing fastener removing tool (Sec 15)

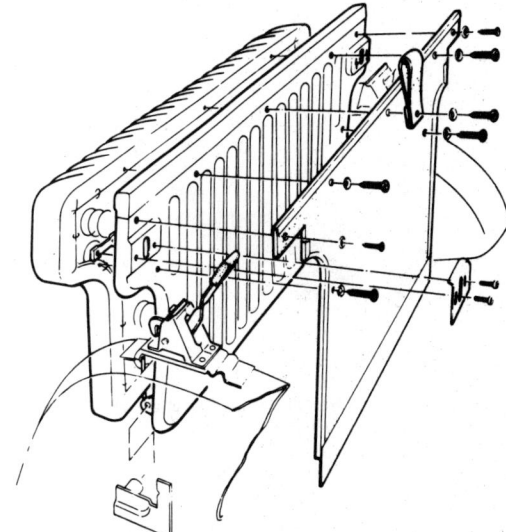

Fig. 13.93. Exploded view of the rear seat squab on Estate models (Sec 15)

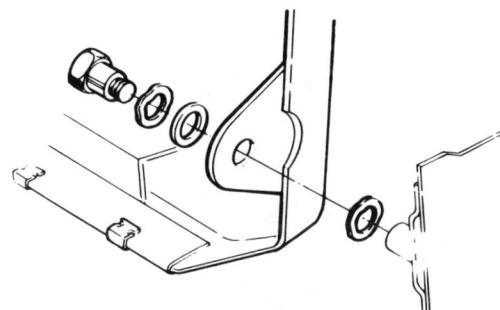

Fig. 13.94. Rear seat squab pivot bolt and washers on Estate models (Sec 15)

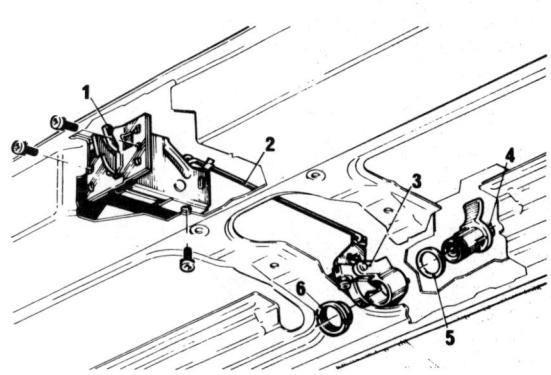

Fig. 13.95. Tailgate lock components on Estate and Chevanne models (Sec 15)

1	Latch	4	Push-button
2	Connecting rod	5	Washer
3	Remote control mechanism	6	Retaining ring

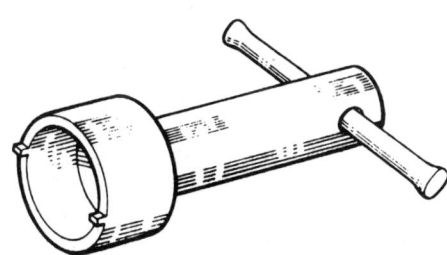

Fig. 13.96. Tailgate lock slotted spanner for Estate and Chevanne models (Sec 15)

Cargo floor (Chevette Estate and Chevanne) — removal and refitting

43 With the tailgate raised, unscrew and remove the three self-tapping bolts retaining the cargo floor, and lift the floor panel from the vehicle.
44 Refitting is a reversal of removal.

Rear seat squab (Chevette Estate) — removal and refitting

45 Pivot the rear seat cushion to its vertical position.
46 Unscrew and remove the five large self-tapping screws from the rear of the squab and lift the squab away.
47 The base panel pivot bolts will now be exposed, and they can be unscrewed and removed if it is necessary to remove the base panel.
48 Refitting is a reversal of removal but make sure that the pivot bolt washers are arranged as shown in Fig. 13.94.

Tailgate lock (Chevette Estate and Chevanne) — removal and refitting

49 Lift the tailgate and remove the interior trim panel as described in Chapter 12.
50 Working through the tailgate aperture, prise the connecting rod from the remote control lever and lower the rod.
51 To remove the push-button assembly a special slotted spanner will be required; if this cannot be borrowed from your local garage, a spanner can be made by using suitable diameter tubing (see Fig. 13.96). Insert the spanner through the tailgate aperture and unscrew the push-button assembly retaining ring; the remote mechanism and push-button assembly can then be withdrawn. Note the location of the washer.
52 Unscrew and remove the three tailgate lock crosshead retaining screws, and withdraw the lock and connecting rod through the aperture.
53 The push-button assembly lock barrel can be removed after extracting the retaining circlip, washer, and spring.
54 Refitting is a reversal of removal, but during refitting the lock must be in the locked position.

Tailgate hinges (Chevette Estate and Chevanne) — description

55 Two supporting hinges are bolted to the roof hinge rail by three bolts, and to the tailgate by two bolts. The roof rail section of the

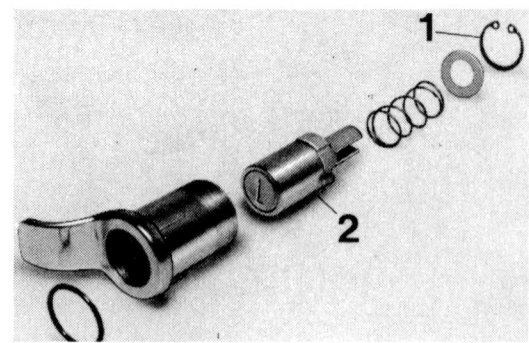

Fig. 13.97. Tailgate lock barrel components on Estate and Chevanne models (Sec 15)

1 Circlip
2 Barrel

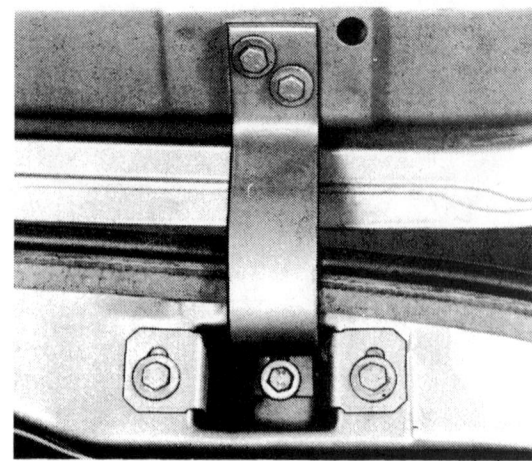

Fig. 13.98. Tailgate hinge location on Estate and Chevanne models (Sec 15)

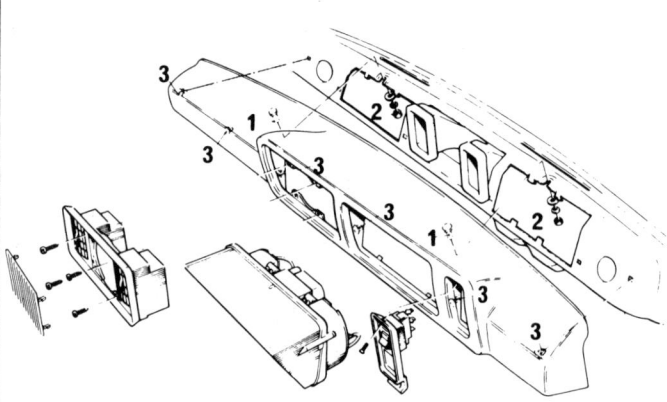

Fig. 13.99. Facia panel components on early models (Sec 15)

1 Studs
2 Nuts
3 Clips

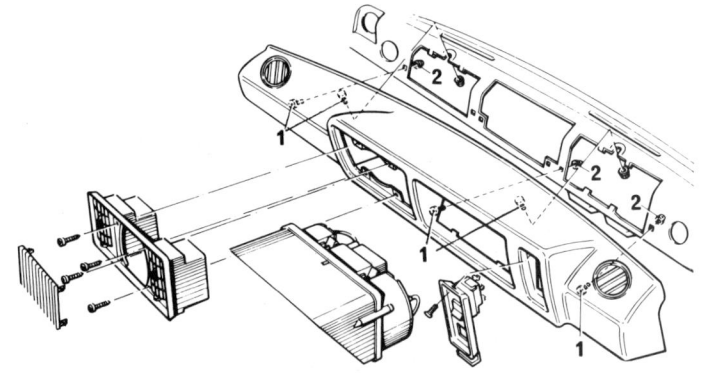

Fig. 13.100. Facia panel components on late models (Sec 15)

1 Studs
2 Nuts

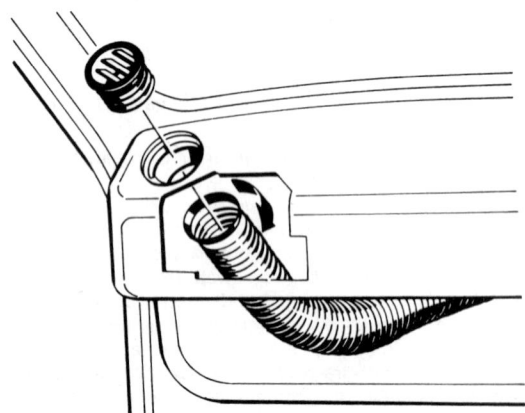

Fig. 13.101. Removing side vent tubes on late type facia (Sec 15)

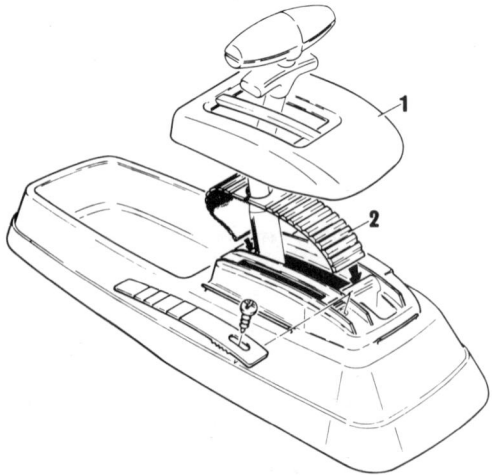

Fig. 13.102. Automatic transmission console components (Sec 15)

1 Top cover
2 Lever cover

hinge has elongated holes and is adjustable for position, therefore before removing the hinge its position should be marked by scribing a line around the hinge plate.

Facia panel — modifications

56 The facia panel is retained as shown in Figs. 13.99 and 13.100. On early models the facia is retained by two studs and six clips, whereas on later models it is retained by five studs.

57 When removing the later type facia, the side vent tubes must be unscrewed from the vent outlets. The outlets are prevented from turning by lugs which locate in a cut-out.

Centre console (automatic transmission models) — removal and refitting

58 Disconnect the battery negative lead.

59 Using a screwdriver, prise off the top cover then turn it through 90° and withdraw it over the gearshift lever.

60 Lift the lever cover then remove the three screws and withdraw the console.

61 Refitting is a reversal of removal.

Tools and working facilities

Introduction

A selection of good tools is a fundamental requirement for anyone contemplating the maintenance and repair of a motor vehicle. For the owner who does not possess any, their purchase will prove a considerable expense, offsetting some of the savings made by doing-it-yourself. However, provided that the tools purchased are of good quality, they will last for many years and prove an extremely worthwhile investment.

To help the average owner to decide which tools are needed to carry out the various tasks detailed in this manual, we have compiled three lists of tools under the following headings: *Maintenance and minor repair, Repair and overhaul,* and *Special.* The newcomer to practical mechanics should start off with the *Maintenance and minor repair* tool kit and confine himself to the simpler jobs around the vehicle. Then, as his confidence and experience grows, he can undertake more difficult tasks, buying extra tools as, and when, they are needed. In this way a *Maintenance and minor repair* tool kit can be built-up into a *Repair and overhaul* tool kit over a considerable period of time without any major cash outlays. The experienced do-it-yourselfer will have a tool kit good enough for most repair and overhaul procedures and will add tools from the *Special* category when he feels the expense is justified by the amount of use to which these tools will be put.

It is obviously not possible to cover the subject of tools fully here. For those who wish to learn more about tools and their use there is a book entitled *How to Choose and Use Car Tools* available from the publishers of this manual.

Maintenance and minor repair tool kit

The tools given in this list should be considered as a minimum requirement if routine maintenance, servicing and minor repair operations are to be undertaken. We recommend the purchase of combination spanners (ring one end, open-ended the other); although more expensive than open-ended ones, they do give the advantages of both types of spanner.

Combination spanners — 8, 9, 10, 11, 13, 15, 17, 19, 22, 24 and
32 mm
— 7/16, 1/2, 9/16, 5/8, 3/4, 13/16, 7/8 and
15/16 in AF
Adjustable spanner — 9 inch
Engine sump/gearbox/rear axle drain plug key
Spark plug spanner (with rubber insert)
Spark plug gap adjustment tool
Set of feeler gauges
Brake adjuster spanner
Brake bleed nipple spanner
Screwdriver — 4 in long x ¼ in dia (flat blade)
Screwdriver — 4 in long x ¼ in dia (cross blade)
Combination pliers — 6 inch
Hacksaw (junior)
Tyre pump
Tyre pressure gauge
Grease gun
Oil can
Fine emery cloth (1 sheet)
Wire brush (small)
Funnel (medium size)

Repair and overhaul tool kit

These tools are virtually essential for anyone undertaking any major repairs to a motor vehicle, and are additional to those given in the *Maintenance and minor repair* list. Included in this list is a com-

prehensive set of sockets. Although these are expensive they will be found invaluable as they are so versatile — particularly if various drives are included in the set. We recommend the ½ in square drive type, as this can be used with most proprietary torque wrenches. If you cannot afford a socket set, even bought piecemeal, then inexpensive tubular box spanners are a useful alternative.

The tools in this list will occasionally need to be supplemented by tools from the *Special* list.

Sockets (or box spanners) to cover range in previous list
Reversible ratchet drive (for use with sockets)
Extension piece, 10 inch (for use with sockets)
Universal joint (for use with sockets)
Torque wrench (for use with sockets)
'Mole' wrench — 8 inch
Ball pein hammer
Soft-faced hammer, plastic or rubber
Screwdriver — 6 in long x 5/16 in dia (flat blade)
Screwdriver — 2 in long x 5/16 in square (flat blade)
Screwdriver — 1½ in long x ¼ in dia (cross blade)
Screwdriver — 3 in long x 1/8 in dia (electricians)
Pliers — electricians side cutters
Pliers — needle nosed
Pliers — circlip (internal and external)
Cold chisel — ½ inch
Scriber
Scraper
Centre punch
Pin punch
Hacksaw
Valve grinding tool
Steel rule/straight-edge
Allen keys
Selection of files
Wire brush (large)
Axle-stands
Jack (strong scissor or hydraulic type)

Special tools

The tools in this list are those which are not used regularly, are expensive to buy, or which need to be used in accordance with their manufacturers' instructions. Unless relatively difficult mechanical jobs are undertaken frequently, it will not be economical to buy many of these tools. Where this is the case, you could consider clubbing together with friends (or joining a motorists' club) to make a joint purchase, or borrowing the tools against a deposit from a local garage or tool hire specialist.

The following list contains only those tools and instruments freely available to the public, and not those special tools produced by the vehicle manufacturer specifically for its dealer network. You will find occasional references to these manufacturers' special tools in the text of this manual. Generally, an alternative method of doing the job without the vehicle manufacturer's special tool is given. However, sometimes, there is no alternative to using them. Where this is the case and the relevant tool cannot be bought or borrowed, you will have to entrust the work to a franchised garage.

Valve spring compressor
Piston ring compressor
Balljoint separator
Universal hub/bearing puller

Impact screwdriver
Micrometer and/or vernier gauge
Dial gauge
Stroboscopic timing light
Dwell angle meter/tachometer
Universal electrical multi-meter
Cylinder compression gauge
Lifting tackle (photo)
Trolley jack
Light with extension lead

Buying tools

For practically all tools, a tool factor is the best source since he will have a very comprehensive range compared with the average garage or accessory shop. Having said that, accessory shops often offer excellent quality tools at discount prices, so it pays to shop around.

Remember, you don't have to buy the most expensive items on the shelf, but it is always advisable to steer clear of the very cheap tools. There are plenty of good tools around at reasonable prices, so ask the proprietor or manager of the shop for advice before making a purchase.

Care and maintenance of tools

Having purchased a reasonable tool kit, it is necessary to keep the tools in a clean serviceable condition. After use, always wipe off any dirt, grease and metal particles using a clean, dry cloth, before putting the tools away. Never leave them lying around after they have been used. A simple tool rack on the garage or workshop wall, for items such as screwdrivers and pliers is a good idea. Store all normal spanners and sockets in a metal box. Any measuring instruments, gauges, meters, etc, must be carefully stored where they cannot be damaged or become rusty.

Take a little care when tools are used. Hammer heads inevitably become marked and screwdrivers lose the keen edge on their blades from time to time. A little timely attention with emery cloth or a file will soon restore items like this to a good serviceable finish.

Working facilities

Not to be forgotten when discussing tools, is the workshop itself. If anything more than routine maintenance is to be carried out, some form of suitable working area becomes essential.

It is appreciated that many an owner mechanic is forced by circumstances to remove an engine or similar item, without the benefit of a garage or workshop. Having done this, any repairs should always be done under the cover of a roof.

Wherever possible, any dismantling should be done on a clean, flat workbench or table at a suitable working height.

Any workbench needs a vice: one with a jaw opening of 4 in (100 mm) is suitable for most jobs. As mentioned previously, some clean dry storage space is also required for tools, as well as for lubricants, cleaning fluids, touch-up paints and so on which become necessary.

Another item which may be required, and which has a much more general usage, is an electric drill with a chuck capacity of at least 5/16 in (8 mm). This, together with a good range of twist drills, is virtually essential for fitting accessories such as mirrors and reversing lights.

Last, but not least, always keep a supply of old newspapers and clean, lint-free rags available, and try to keep any working area as clean as possible.

Jaw gap (in)	Spanner size
0.250	¼ in AF
0.276	7 mm
0.313	5/16 in AF
0.315	8 mm
0.344	11/32 in AF; 1/8 in Whitworth
0.354	9 mm
0.375	3/8 in AF
0.394	10 mm
0.433	11 mm
0.438	7/16 in AF
0.445	3/16 in Whitworth; ¼ in BSF
0.472	12 mm
0.500	½ in AF
0.512	13 mm
0.525	¼ in Whitworth; 5/16 in BSF

Jaw gap (in)	Spanner size
0.551	14 mm
0.562	9/16 in AF
0.591	15 mm
0.600	5/16 in Whitworth; 3/8 in BSF
0.625	5/8 in AF
0.630	16 mm
0.669	17 mm
0.686	11/16 in AF
0.709	18 mm
0.710	3/8 in Whitworth; 7/16 in BSF
0.748	19 mm
0.750	¾ in AF
0.813	13/16 in AF
0.820	7/16 in Whitworth; ½ in BSF
0.866	22 mm
0.875	7/8 in AF
0.920	½ in Whitworth; 9/16 in BSF
0.937	15/16 in AF
0.945	24 mm
1.000	1 in AF
1.010	9/16 in Whitworth; 5/8 in BSF
1.024	26 mm
1.063	1.1/16 in AF; 27 mm
1.100	5/8 in Whitworth; 11/16 in BSF
1.125	1.1/8 in AF
1.181	30 mm
1.200	11/16 in Whitworth; ¾ in BSF
1.250	1¼ in AF
1.260	32 mm
1.300	¾ in Whitworth; 7/8 in BSF
1.313	1.5/16 in AF
1.390	13/16 in Whitworth; 15/16 in BSF
1.417	36 mm
1.438	1.7/16 in AF
1.480	7/8 in Whitworth; 1 in BSF
1.500	1½ in AF
1.575	40 mm; 15/16 in Whitworth
1.614	41 mm
1.625	1.5/8 in AF
1.670	1 in Whitworth; 1.1/8 in BSF
1.688	1.11/16 in AF
1.811	46 mm
1.813	13/16 in AF
1.860	1.1/8 in Whitworth; 1¼ in BSF
1.875	1.7/8 in AF
1.969	50 mm
2.000	2 in AF
2.050	1¼ in Whitworth; 1.3/8 in BSF
2.165	55 mm
2.362	60 mm

A Haltrac hoist and gantry in use during a typical engine removal sequence

Safety First!

Professional motor mechanics are trained in safe working procedures. However enthusiastic you may be about getting on with the job in hand, do take the time to ensure that your safety is not put at risk. A moment's lack of attention can result in an accident, as can failure to observe certain elementary precautions.

There will always be new ways of having accidents, and the following points do not pretend to be a comprehensive list of all dangers; they are intended rather to make you aware of the risks and to encourage a safety-conscious approach to all work you carry out on your vehicle.

Essential DOs and DON'Ts

DON'T rely on a single jack when working underneath the vehicle. Always use reliable additional means of support, such as axle stands, securely placed under a part of the vehicle that you know will not give way.

DON'T attempt to loosen or tighten high-torque nuts (e.g. wheel hub nuts) while the vehicle is on a jack; it may be pulled off.

DON'T start the engine without first ascertaining that the transmission is in neutral (or 'Park' where applicable) and the parking brake applied.

DON'T suddenly remove the filler cap from a hot cooling system — cover it with a cloth and release the pressure gradually first, or you may get scalded by escaping coolant.

DON'T attempt to drain oil until you are sure it has cooled sufficiently to avoid scalding you.

DON'T grasp any part of the engine, exhaust or catalytic converter without first ascertaining that it is sufficiently cool to avoid burning you.

DON'T syphon toxic liquids such as fuel, brake fluid or antifreeze by mouth, or allow them to remain on your skin.

DON'T inhale brake lining dust — it is injurious to health.

DON'T allow any spilt oil or grease to remain on the floor — wipe it up straight away, before someone slips on it.

DON'T use ill-fitting spanners or other tools which may slip and cause injury.

DON'T attempt to lift a heavy component which may be beyond your capability — get assistance.

DON'T rush to finish a job, or take unverified short cuts.

DON'T allow children or animals in or around an unattended vehicle.

DO wear eye protection when using power tools such as drill, sander, bench grinder etc, and when working under the vehicle.

DO use a barrier cream on your hands prior to undertaking dirty jobs — it will protect your skin from infection as well as making the dirt easier to remove afterwards; but make sure your hands aren't left slippery.

DO keep loose clothing (cuffs, tie etc) and long hair well out of the way of moving mechanical parts.

DO remove rings, wristwatch etc, before working on the vehicle — especially the electrical system.

DO ensure that any lifting tackle used has a safe working load rating adequate for the job.

DO keep your work area tidy — it is only too easy to fall over articles left lying around.

DO get someone to check periodically that all is well, when working alone on the vehicle.

DO carry out work in a logical sequence and check that everything is correctly assembled and tightened afterwards.

DO remember that your vehicle's safety affects that of yourself and others. If in doubt on any point, get specialist advice.

IF, in spite of following these precautions, you are unfortunate enough to injure yourself, seek medical attention as soon as possible.

Fire

Remember at all times that petrol (gasoline) is highly flammable. Never smoke, or have any kind of naked flame around, when working on the vehicle. But the risk does not end there — a spark caused by an electrical short-circuit, by two metal surfaces contacting each other, or even by static electricity built up in your body under certain conditions, can ignite petrol vapour, which in a confined space is highly explosive.

Always disconnect the battery earth (ground) terminal before working on any part of the fuel system, and never risk spilling fuel on to a hot engine or exhaust.

It is recommended that a fire extinguisher of a type suitable for fuel and electrical fires is kept handy in the garage or workplace at all times. Never try to extinguish a fuel or electrical fire with water.

Fumes

Certain fumes are highly toxic and can quickly cause unconsciousness and even death if inhaled to any extent. Petrol (gasoline) vapour comes into this category, as do the vapours from certain solvents such as trichloroethylene. Any draining or pouring of such volatile fluids should be done in a well ventilated area.

When using cleaning fluids and solvents, read the instructions carefully. Never use materials from unmarked containers — they may give off poisonous vapours.

Never run the engine of a motor vehicle in an enclosed space such as a garage. Exhaust fumes contain carbon monoxide which is extremely poisonous; if you need to run the engine, always do so in the open air or at least have the rear of the vehicle outside the workplace.

If you are fortunate enough to have the use of an inspection pit, never drain or pour petrol, and never run the engine, while the vehicle is standing over it; the fumes, being heavier than air, will concentrate in the pit with possibly lethal results.

The battery

Never cause a spark, or allow a naked light, near the vehicle's battery. It will normally be giving off a certain amount of hydrogen gas, which is highly explosive.

Always disconnect the battery earth (ground) terminal before working on the fuel or electrical systems.

If possible, loosen the filler plugs or cover when charging the battery from an external source. Do not charge at an excessive rate or the battery may burst.

Take care when topping up and when carrying the battery. The acid electrolyte, even when diluted, is very corrosive and should not be allowed to contact the eyes or skin.

If you ever need to prepare electrolyte yourself, always add the acid slowly to the water, and never the other way round. Protect against splashes by wearing rubber gloves and goggles.

Mains electricity

When using an electric power tool, inspection light etc which works from the mains, always ensure that the appliance is correctly connected to its plug and that, where necessary, it is properly earthed (grounded). Do not use such appliances in damp conditions and, again, beware of creating a spark or applying excessive heat in the vicinity of fuel or fuel vapour.

Ignition HT voltage

A severe electric shock can result from touching certain parts of the ignition system, such as the HT leads, when the engine is running or being cranked, particularly if components are damp or the insulation is defective. Where an electronic ignition system is fitted, the HT voltage is much higher and could prove fatal.

Fault diagnosis

Introduction

The car owner who does his or her own maintenance according to the recommended schedules should not have to use this section of the manual very often. Modern component reliability is such that, provided those items subject to wear or deterioration are inspected or renewed at the specified intervals, sudden failure is comparatively rare. Faults do not usually just happen as a result of sudden failure, but develop over a period of time. Major mechanical failures in particular are usually preceded by characteristic symptoms over hundreds or even thousands of miles. Those components which do occasionally fail without warning are often small and easily carried in the car.

With any fault finding, the first step is to decide where to begin investigations. Sometimes this is obvious, but on other occasions a little detective work will be necessary. The owner who makes half a dozen haphazard adjustments or replacements may be successful in curing a fault (or its symptoms), but he will be none the wiser if the fault recurs and he may well have spent more time and money than was necessary. A calm and logical approach will be found to be more satisfactory in the long run. Always take into account any warning signs or abnormalities that may have been noticed in the period preceding the fault — power loss, high or low gauge readings, unusual noises or smells, etc — and remember that failure of components such as fuses or spark plugs may only be pointers to some underlying fault.

The pages which follow here are intended to help in cases of failure to start or breakdown on the road. There is also a Fault Diagnosis Section at the end of each Chapter which should be consulted if the preliminary checks prove unfruitful. Whatever the fault, certain basic principles apply. These are as follows:

Verify the fault. This is simply a matter of being sure that you know what the symptoms are before starting work. This is particularly important if you are investigating a fault for someone else who may not have described it very accurately.

Don't overlook the obvious. For example, if the car won't start, is there petrol in the tank? (Don't take enyone else's word on this particular point, and don't trust the fuel gauge either!) If an electrical fault is indicated, look for loose or broken wires before digging out the test gear.

Cure the disease, not the symptom. Substituting a flat battery with a fully charged one will get you off the hard shoulder, but if the underlying cause is not attended to, the new battery will go the same way. Similarly, changing oil-fouled spark plugs for a new set will get you moving again, but remember that the reason for the fouling (if it wasn't simply an incorrect grade of plug) will have to be established and corrected.

Don't take anything for granted. Particularly, don't forget that a 'new' component may itself be defective (especially if it's been rattling round in the boot for months), and don't leave components out of a fault diagnosis sequence just because they are new or recently fitted. When you do finally diagnose a difficult fault, you'll probably realise that all the evidence was there from the start.

Electrical faults

Electrical faults can be more puzzling than straightforward mechanical failures, but they are no less susceptible to logical analysis if the basic principles of operation are understood. Car electrical wiring exists in extremely unfavourable conditions — heat, vibration and chemical attack — and the first things to look for are loose or corroded connections, and broken or chafed wires, especially where the wires pass through holes in the bodywork or are subject to vibration.

All metal-bodied cars in current production have one pole of the battery 'earthed', ie connected to the car bodywork, and in nearly all modern cars it is the negative (—) terminal. The various electrical components — motors, bulb holders etc — are also connected to earth,

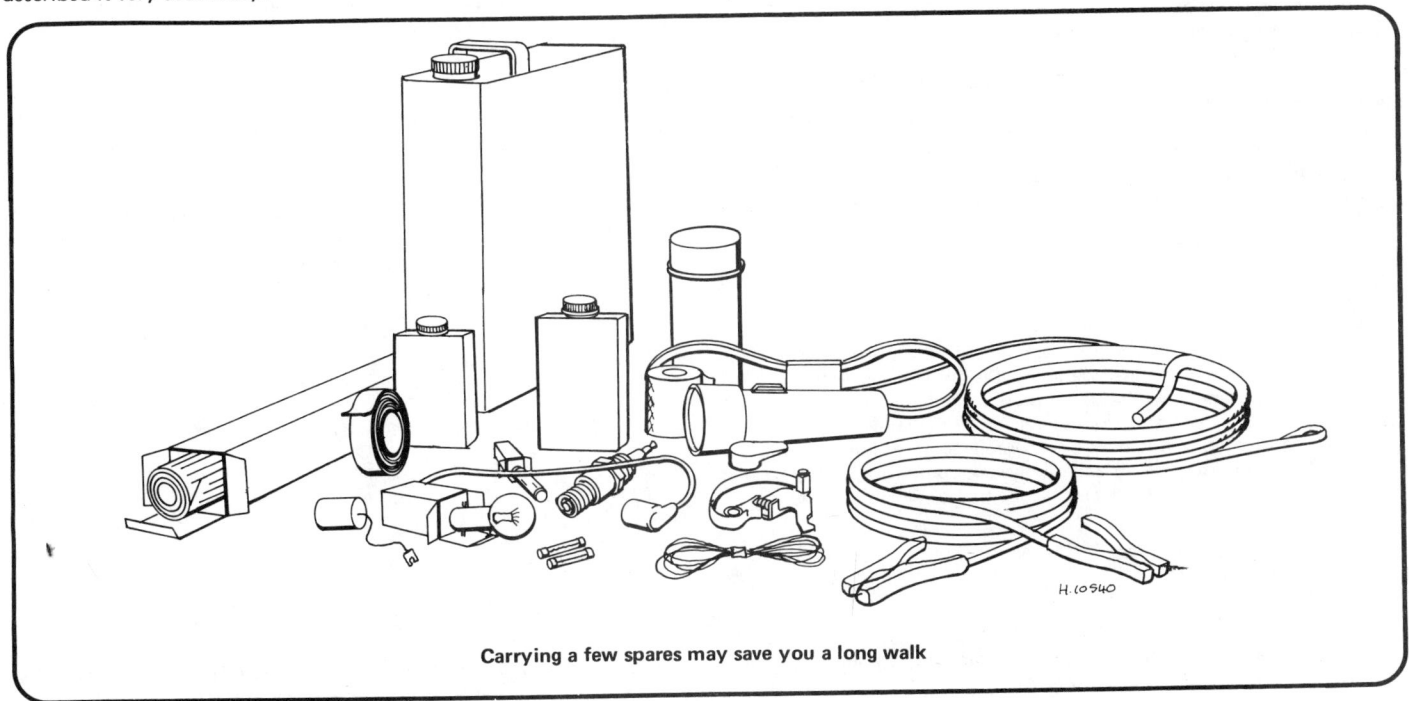

Carrying a few spares may save you a long walk

either by means of a lead or directly by their mountings. Electric current flows through the component and then back to the battery via the car bodywork. If the component mounting is loose or corroded, or if a good path back to the battery is not available, the circuit will be incomplete and malfunction will result. The engine and/or gearbox are also earthed by means of flexible metal straps to the body or subframe; if these straps are loose or missing, starter motor, generator and ignition trouble may result.

Assuming the earth return to be satisfactory, electrical faults will be due either to component malfunction or to defects in the current supply. Individual components are dealt with in Chapter 10. If supply wires are broken or cracked internally this results in an open-circuit, and the easiest way to check for this is to bypass the suspect wire temporarily with a length of wire having a crocodile clip or suitable connector at each end. Alternatively, a 12V test lamp can be used to verify the presence of supply voltage at various points along the wire and the break can be thus isolated.

If a bare portion of a live wire touches the car bodywork or other earthed metal part the electricity will take the low-resistance path thus formed back to the battery: this is known as a short-circuit. Hopefully a short-circuit will blow a fuse, but otherwise it may cause burning of the insulation (and possibly further short-circuits) or even a fire. This is why it is inadvisable to bypass persistently blowing fuses with silver foil or wire.

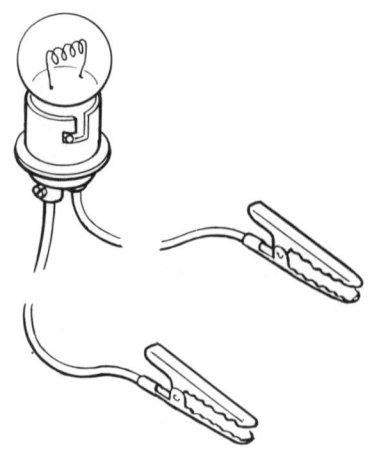

A simple test lamp is useful for investigating electrical faults

Spares and tool kit

Most cars are only supplied with sufficient tools for wheel changing; the *Maintenance and minor repair* tool kit detailed in *Tools and working facilities,* with the addition of a hammer, is probably sufficient for those repairs that most motorists would consider attempting at the roadside. In addition a few items which can be fitted without too much trouble in the event of breakdown should be carried. Experience and available space will modify the list below, but the following may save having to call on professional assistance:

> *Spark plugs, clean and correctly gapped*
> *HT lead and plug cap — long enough to reach the plug furthest from the distributor*
> *Distributor rotor, condenser and contact breaker points*
> *Drivebelt(s) — emergency type may suffice*
> *Spare fuses*
> *Set of principal light bulbs*
> *Tin of radiator sealer and hose bandage*
> *Exhaust bandage*
> *Roll of insulating tape*
> *Length of soft iron wire*
> *Length of electrical flex*
> *Torch or inspection lamp (can double as test lamp)*
> *Battery jump leads*
> *Tow-rope*
> *Ignition waterproofing aerosol*
> *Litre of engine oil*
> *Sealed can of hydraulic fluid*
> *Emergency windscreen*
> *Worm drive hose clips*
> *Tube of filler paste*
> *Tyre valve core*

If spare fuel is carried, a can designed for the purpose should be used to minimise risks of leakage and collision damage. A first aid kit and a warning triangle, whilst not at present compulsory in the UK, are obviously sensible items to carry in addition to the above.

When touring abroad it may be advisable to carry additional spares which, even if you cannot fit them yourself, could save having to wait while parts are obtained. The items below may be worth considering:

> *Clutch and throttle cables*
> *Cylinder head gasket*
> *Alternator brushes*

One of the motoring organisations will be able to advise on availability of fuel etc in foreign countries.

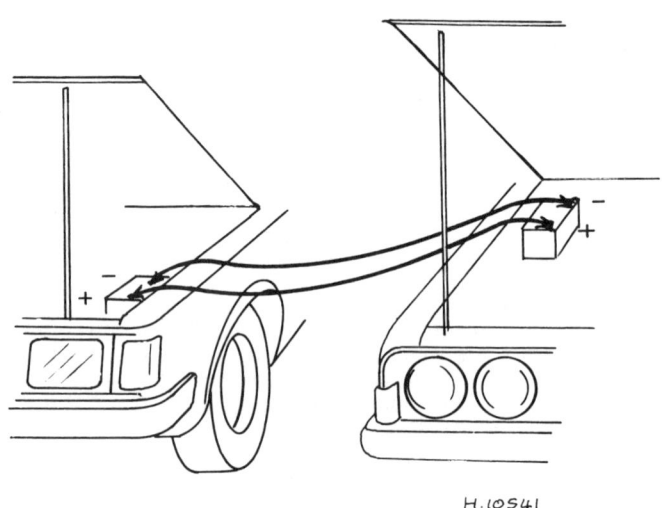

H.10541

Correct way to connect jump leads. Do not allow car bodies to touch!

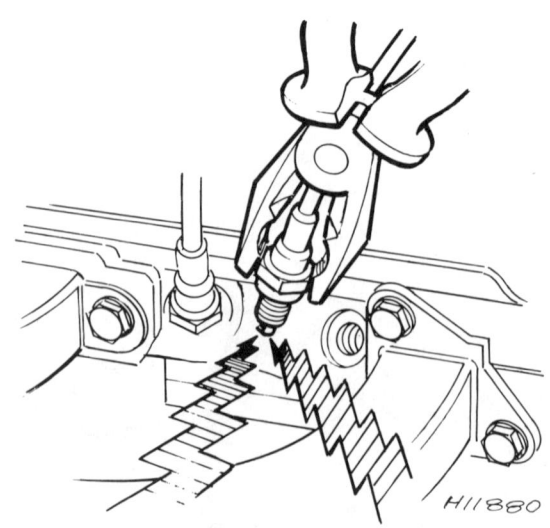

H11880

Crank engine and check for spark. Note use of insulated pliers — dry cloth or a rubber glove will suffice

Engine will not start

Engine fails to turn when starter operated
Flat battery (recharge, use jump leads or push start on manual gearbox models)
Battery terminals loose or corroded
Battery earth to body defective
Engine earth strap loose or broken
Starter motor (or solenoid) wiring loose or broken
Automatic transmission selector in wrong position, or inhibitor switch faulty
Ignition/starter switch faulty
Major mechanical failure (seizure) or long disuse (piston rings rusted to bores)
Starter or solenoid internal fault (see Chapter 10)

Starter motor turns engine slowly
Partially discharged battery (recharge, use jump leads, or push start on manual gearbox models)
Battery terminals loose or corroded
Battery earth to body defective
Engine earth strap loose
Starter motor (or solenoid) wiring loose
Starter motor internal fault (see Chapter 10)

Starter motor spins without turning engine (inertia type only)
Flat battery
Starter motor pinion sticking on sleeve
Flywheel gear teeth damaged or worn
Starter motor mounting bolts loose

Engine turns normally but fails to start
Damp or dirty HT leads and distributor cap (crank engine and check for spark)
Dirty or incorrectly gapped CB points
No fuel in tank (check for delivery at carburettor)
Excessive choke (hot engine) or insufficient choke (cold engine)
Fouled or incorrectly gapped spark plugs (remove, clean and regap)
Other ignition system fault (see Chapter 4)
Other fuel system fault (see Chapter 3)
Poor compression (see Chapter 1)
Major mechanical failure (eg camshaft drive)

Engine fires but will not run
Insufficient choke (cold engine)
Air leaks at carburettor or inlet manifold
Fuel starvation (see Chapter 3)
Ballast resistor defective, or other ignition fault (see Chapter 4)

Engine cuts out and will not restart

Engine cuts out suddenly — ignition fault
Loose or disconnected LT wires
Wet HT leads or distributor cap (after traversing water splash)
Coil or condenser failure (check for spark)
Other ignition fault (see Chapter 4)

Engine misfires before cutting out — fuel fault
Fuel tank empty
Fuel pump defective or filter blocked (check for delivery)
Fuel tank filler vent blocked (suction will be evident on releasing cap)
Carburettor needle valve sticking
Carburettor jets blocked (fuel contaminated)
Other fuel system fault (see Chapter 3)

Engine cuts out — other causes
Serious overheating
Major mechanical failure (eg camshaft drive)

Engine overheats (water-cooled)

Ignition (no-charge) warning light illuminated
Slack or broken drivebelt — retension or renew (Chapter 2)

Ignition warning light not illuminated
Coolant loss due to internal or external leakage (see Chapter 2)
Thermostat defective
Low oil level
Brakes binding
Radiator clogged externally or internally
Engine waterways clogged
Ignition timing incorrect or automatic advance malfunctioning
Mixture too weak

Note: *Do not add cold water to an overheated engine or damage may result*

Low engine oil pressure

Gauge reads low or warning light illuminated with engine running
Oil level low or incorrect grade
Defective gauge or sender unit

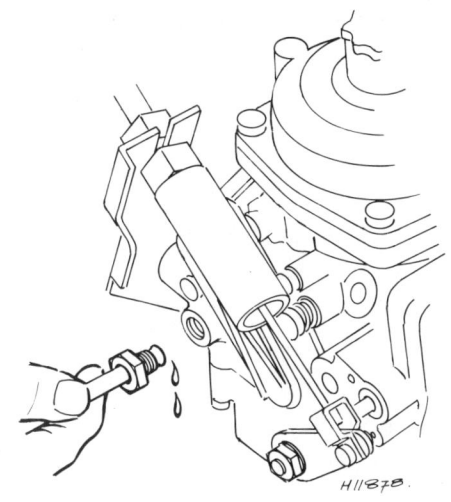

Remove fuel pipe from carburettor and check that fuel is being delivered

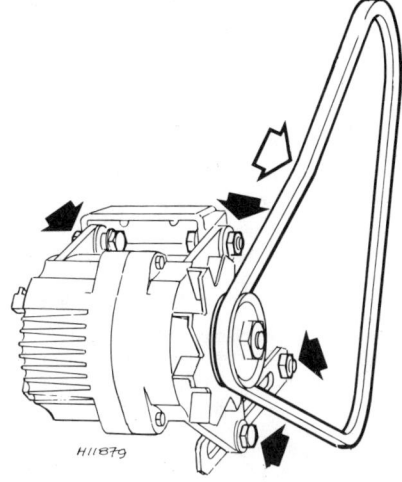

A slack drivebelt may cause overheating and battery charging problems. Slacken bolts (arrowed) to adjust

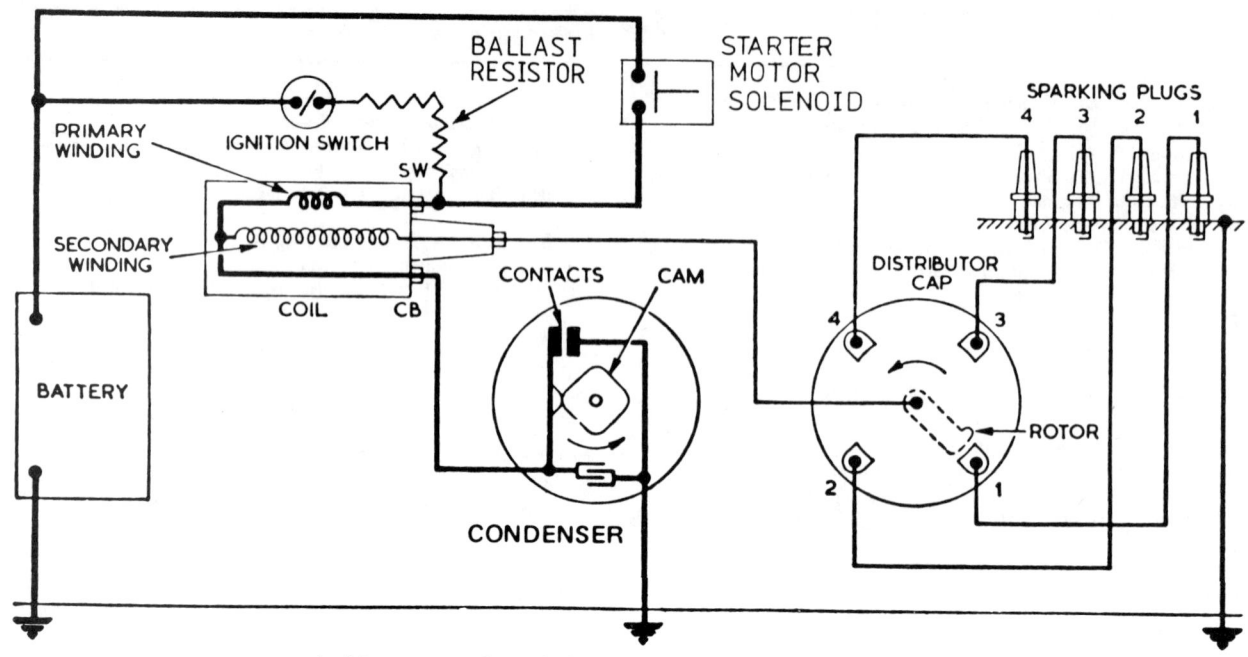

Ignition system schematic diagram. Ballast resistor is bypassed when
starter motor operates

Wire to sender unit earthed
Engine overheating
Oil filter clogged or bypass valve defective
Oil pressure relief valve defective
Oil pick-up strainer clogged
Oil pump worn or mountings loose
Worn main or big-end bearings

Note: *Low oil pressure in a high-mileage engine at tickover is not necessarily a cause for concern. Sudden pressure loss at speed is far more significant. In any event, check the gauge or warning light sender before condemning the engine!*

Engine noises

Pre-ignition (pinking) on acceleration

Incorrect grade of fuel
Ignition timing incorrect
Distributor faulty or worn
Worn or maladjusted carburettor
Excessive carbon build-up in engine

Whistling or wheezing noises

Leaking vacuum hose
Leaking carburettor or manifold gasket
Blowing head gasket

Tapping or rattling

Incorrect valve clearances
Worn valve gear
Worn timing chain
Broken piston ring (ticking noise)

Knocking or thumping

Unintentional mechanical contact (eg fan blades)
Worn fanbelt
Peripheral component fault (alternator, water pump, etc)
Worn big-end bearings (regular heavy knocking, perhaps less under load)
Worn main bearings (rumbling and knocking, perhaps worsening under load)
Piston slap (most noticeable when cold)

Conversion factors

Length (distance)
Inches (in)	X	25.4	= Millimetres (mm)	X 0.039	= Inches (in)
Feet (ft)	X	0.305	= Metres (m)	X 3.281	= Feet (ft)
Miles	X	1.609	= Kilometres (km)	X 0.621	= Miles

Volume (capacity)
Cubic inches (cu in; in^3)	X	16.387	= Cubic centimetres (cc; cm^3)	X 0.061	= Cubic inches (cu in; in^3)
Imperial pints (Imp pt)	X	0.568	= Litres (l)	X 1.76	= Imperial pints (Imp pt)
Imperial quarts (Imp qt)	X	1.137	= Litres (l)	X 0.88	= Imperial quarts (Imp qt)
Imperial quarts (Imp qt)	X	1.201	= US quarts (US qt)	X 0.833	= Imperial quarts (Imp qt)
US quarts (US qt)	X	0.946	= Litres (l)	X 1.057	= US quarts (US qt)
Imperial gallons (Imp gal)	X	4.546	= Litres (l)	X 0.22	= Imperial gallons (Imp gal)
Imperial gallons (Imp gal)	X	1.201	= US gallons (US gal)	X 0.833	= Imperial gallons (Imp gal)
US gallons (US gal)	X	3.785	= Litres (l)	X 0.264	= US gallons (US gal)

Mass (weight)
Ounces (oz)	X	28.35	= Grams (g)	X 0.035	= Ounces (oz)
Pounds (lb)	X	0.454	= Kilograms (kg)	X 2.205	= Pounds (lb)

Force
Ounces-force (ozf; oz)	X	0.278	= Newtons (N)	X 3.6	= Ounces-force (ozf; oz)
Pounds-force (lbf; lb)	X	4.448	= Newtons (N)	X 0.225	= Pounds-force (lbf; lb)
Newtons (N)	X	0.1	= Kilograms-force (kgf; kg)	X 9.81	= Newtons (N)

Pressure
Pounds-force per square inch (psi; lbf/in^2; lb/in^2)	X	0.070	= Kilograms-force per square centimetre (kgf/cm^2; kg/cm^2)	X 14.223	= Pounds-force per square inch (psi; lbf/in^2; lb/in^2)
Pounds-force per square inch (psi; lbf/in^2; lb/in^2)	X	0.068	= Atmospheres (atm)	X 14.696	= Pounds-force per square inch (psi; lbf/in^2; lb/in^2)
Pounds-force per square inch (psi; lbf/in^2; lb/in^2)	X	0.069	= Bars	X 14.5	= Pounds-force per square inch (psi; lbf/in^2; lb/in^2)
Pounds-force per square inch (psi; lbf/in^2; lb/in^2)	X	6.895	= Kilopascals (kPa)	X 0.145	= Pounds-force per square inch (psi; lbf/in^2; lb/in^2)
Kilopascals (kPa)	X	0.01	= Kilograms-force per square centimetre (kgf/cm^2; kg/cm^2)	X 98.1	= Kilopascals (kPa)

Torque (moment of force)
Pounds-force inches (lbf in; lb in)	X	1.152	= Kilograms-force centimetre (kgf cm; kg cm)	X 0.868	= Pounds-force inches (lbf in; lb in)
Pounds-force inches (lbf in; lb in)	X	0.113	= Newton metres (Nm)	X 8.85	= Pounds-force inches (lbf in; lb in)
Pounds-force inches (lbf in; lb in)	X	0.083	= Pounds-force feet (lbf ft; lb ft)	X 12	= Pounds-force inches (lbf in; lb in)
Pounds-force feet (lbf ft; lb ft)	X	0.138	= Kilograms-force metres (kgf m; kg m)	X 7.233	= Pounds-force feet (lbf ft; lb ft)
Pounds-force feet (lbf ft; lb ft)	X	1.356	= Newton metres (Nm)	X 0.738	= Pounds-force feet (lbf ft; lb ft)
Newton metres (Nm)	X	0.102	= Kilograms-force metres (kgf m; kg m)	X 9.804	= Newton metres (Nm)

Power
Horsepower (hp)	X	745.7	= Watts (W)	X 0.0013	= Horsepower (hp)

Velocity (speed)
Miles per hour (miles/hr; mph)	X	1.609	= Kilometres per hour (km/hr; kph)	X 0.621	= Miles per hour (miles/hr; mph)

Fuel consumption*
Miles per gallon, Imperial (mpg)	X	0.354	= Kilometres per litre (km/l)	X 2.825	= Miles per gallon, Imperial (mpg)
Miles per gallon, US (mpg)	X	0.425	= Kilometres per litre (km/l)	X 2.352	= Miles per gallon, US (mpg)

Temperature

Degrees Fahrenheit (°F) $= (°C \times \frac{9}{5}) + 32$

Degrees Celsius (Degrees Centigrade; °C) $= (°F - 32) \times \frac{5}{9}$

It is common practice to convert from miles per gallon (mpg) to litres/100 kilometres (l/100km), where mpg (Imperial) x l/100 km = 282 and mpg (US) x l/100 km = 235

Index

Printed by
Haynes Publishing Group
Sparkford Yeovil Somerset
England